Sadlier

We Are the Church

Parish Edition Catechist Guide
Grade Three

Sadlier

A Division of William H. Sadlier, Inc.

Nihil Obstat
Reverend John G. Stillmank, S.T.L.
Censor Librorum

Imprimatur
✠ Most Reverend William H. Bullock
Bishop of Madison
June 11, 2003

The *Nihil Obstat* and *Imprimatur* are official declarations that a book or pamphlet is free of doctrinal or moral error. No implication is contained therein that those who have granted the *Nihil Obstat* and *Imprimatur* agree with the contents, opinions, or statements expressed.

The Ad Hoc Committee to Oversee the Use of the Catechism, United States Conference of Catholic Bishops, has found the doctrinal content of this teacher manual, copyright 2004, to be in conformity with the *Catechism of the Catholic Church*.

William H. Sadlier, Inc.
9 Pine Street
New York, NY 10005-1002

ISBN: 0-8215-5513-8
123456789/07 06 05 04 03

Sadlier

WE BELIEVE Drawn from the wisdom of the community, this program was developed by nationally recognized experts in catechesis, curriculum, and child development. These teachers of the faith and practitioners helped to frame these age-appropriate and appealing lessons. In addition, a team including respected catechetical, liturgical, pastoral, and theological experts shared their insights and inspired the development of the program.

Contributors to the inspiration and development of the program are:

Gerard F. Baumbach, Ed.D.
Executive Vice President and Publisher

Carole M. Eipers, D.Min.
Director of Catechetics

Catechetical and Liturgical Consultants

Reverend Monsignor John F. Barry
Pastor, American Martyrs Parish
Manhattan Beach, CA

Sister Linda Gaupin, CDP, Ph.D.
Director of Religious Education
Diocese of Orlando

Sister Maureen Shaughnessy, SC
Assistant Secretary for Catechesis
and Leadership Formation,
USCCB, Department of Education

Mary Jo Tully
Chancellor, Archdiocese of Portland

Reverend Monsignor John M. Unger
Assoc. Superintendent for Religious Education
Archdiocese of St. Louis

Curriculum and Child Development Consultants

Brother Robert R. Bimonte, FSC
Former Superintendent of Catholic Education
Diocese of Buffalo

Gini Shimabukuro, Ed.D.
Associate Director/Associate Professor
Institute for Catholic Educational Leadership
School of Education, University of San Francisco

Catholic Social Teaching Consultants

John Carr
Secretary, Department of Social Development
and World Peace, USCCB

Joan Rosenhauer
Coordinator, Special Projects
Department of Social Development and
World Peace, USCCB

Inculturation Consultants

Reverend Allan Figueroa Deck, SJ, Ph.D.
Executive Director, Loyola Institute for
Spirituality, Orange, CA

Kirk Gaddy
Principal, St. Katharine School
Baltimore, MD

Reverend Nguyễn Việt Hưng
Vietnamese Catechetical Committee

Dulce M. Jiménez-Abreu
Director of Spanish Programs
William H. Sadlier, Inc.

Scriptural Consultant

Reverend Donald Senior, CP, Ph.D., S.T.D.
Member, Pontifical Biblical Commission
President, The Catholic Theological Union
Chicago, IL

Theological Consultants

Most Reverend Edward K. Braxton, Ph.D., S.T.D.
Official Theological Consultant
Bishop of Lake Charles

Norman F. Josaitis, S.T.D.
Staff Theologian, William H. Sadlier, Inc.

Reverend Joseph A. Komonchak, Ph.D.
Professor, School of Religious Studies
The Catholic University of America

Most Reverend Richard J. Malone, Th.D.
Auxiliary Bishop, Archdiocese of Boston

Sister Maureen Sullivan, OP, Ph.D.
Assistant Professor of Theology
St. Anselm College, Manchester, NH

Mariology Consultant

Sister M. Jean Frisk, ISSM, S.T.L.
International Marian Research Institute
Dayton, OH

Media/Technology Consultants

Sister Caroline Cerveny, SSJ, D.Min.
Director of Educational Learning Technology
William H. Sadlier, Inc.

Sister Judith Dieterle, SSL
Past President, National Association of
Catechetical Media Professionals

Sister Jane Keegan, RDC
Editor in Chief, CyberFaith.com
William H. Sadlier, Inc.

Educational Advisors

Grade K	Noelle Deinken, Thousand Oaks, CA Bernadette Miller, Wantagh, NY
Grade 1	Gerry Mayes, Vero Beach, FL Nancy McGuirk, Staten Island, NY
Grade 2	Joan Fraher, Altamonte Springs, FL Dr. Jeannette Holmes, Stockton, CA
Grade 3	Robin Keough, Boston, MA Mary Olson, Buffalo Grove, IL
Grade 4	Michaele Durant, San Diego, CA Sarah Pollard, Covington, KY
Grade 5	Rose Heinrichs, Grosse Pointe, MI Anne Kreitsch, Howard Beach, NY
Grade 6	Barbara Connors, Seekonk, MA Sue MacPherson, Ballwin, MO

Contents

UNIT 1 Jesus Gives Us the Church 17

1 God Sends Us His Own Son

• God the Son became one of us. • Jesus grew up in Nazareth. • Jesus begins his work. • Jesus shows us how to live as his followers.

Luke 1:26–35; 2:41–51; 4:14–15; Matthew 3:2, 17; 13:55; 1 Corinthians 12:3
As Catholics . . . The Title *Lord*
Our Catholic Life: Holy Childhood Association
Sharing Faith with My Family

2 Jesus Teaches Us About God's Love

• Jesus tells us how much God loves us. • Jesus teaches about the Kingdom of God. • Jesus teaches about the gift of faith. • Jesus dies and rises to save us.

Romans 10:13; Psalm 118:1; Matthew 6:26–33; Luke 1:38; 17:5–6; 23:33–34; 24:1–12 Mark 4:35–41; 10:45
As Catholics . . . Mary, An Example of Faith
Our Catholic Life: The Bible in Our Lives
Sharing Faith with My Family

3 Christ Will Come Again

• Jesus has power over life and death. • Jesus will come again. • When Jesus Christ comes again, he will judge all people. • Jesus teaches us to love others.

Matthew 24:42; 25:31–43; John 11:1–3; 17–44; 16:22; Mark 12:28–32
As Catholics . . . Miracles of Jesus
Our Catholic Life: Care for All People
Sharing Faith with My Family

4 The Church Begins

• Jesus promises to send the Holy Spirit. • The Holy Spirit comes to the disciples. • The Church begins on Pentecost. • The early Church grows.

Matthew 28:16–20; Acts of the Apostles 2:1–4, 32, 36, 38, 41, 42; 9:3–5
As Catholics . . . Evangelization
Our Catholic Life: Good News for All
Sharing Faith with My Family

5 We Learn About the Early Church

• The apostles led the Church. • The disciples of Jesus share the good news. • The followers of Jesus stood up for their faith. • Many of our ancestors in faith are examples of holiness.

Matthew 28:19; Acts of the Apostles 2:42, 45; John 15:12
As Catholics . . . An Early Christian Symbol
Our Catholic Life: All Saints
Sharing Faith with My Family

6 The Church Year

• The Church Year celebrates Jesus.

Mark 11:9; Matthew 28:20
Sharing Faith with My Family

7 Ordinary Time

• In Ordinary Time, we celebrate the life and teachings of Jesus Christ.

2 Corinthians 13:13
Sharing Faith with My Family

GRADE 2
Scope & Sequence

	Unit 1 Jesus Christ is With Us Always	Unit 2 Jesus Calls Us to Penance and Reconciliation
FAITH STATEMENTS FOR EACH CHAPTER	**1** God the Father sent his Son, Jesus, to be with us. • Jesus is human like us. • Jesus did things only God can do. • Jesus, the Son of God, taught us about God the Father and God the Holy Spirit. **2** Jesus gathered many followers to be his disciples. • Jesus died and rose to new life. • Jesus promised to send the Holy Spirit. • The Holy Spirit helps the Church to grow. **3** We belong to the Catholic Church. • Catholics celebrate God's love by praying and worshiping. • Our Church celebrates with seven special signs called sacraments. • Jesus is present with us in the sacraments. **4** At Baptism we become children of God and members of the Church. • At Baptism we receive grace, a share in God's life. • We celebrate the sacrament of Baptism with special words and actions. • We can show that we are children of God by what we say and do. **5** We celebrate the gift of the Holy Spirit in the sacrament of Confirmation. • Confirmation seals us with the Gift of the Holy Spirit and strengthens us. • We celebrate the sacrament of Confirmation with special words and actions. • The Holy Spirit helps baptized Catholics and confirmed Catholics. **6** The Church year helps us to follow Jesus. **7** In Ordinary Time, we celebrate Jesus Christ and learn to follow him.	**8** The Bible is the book of God's word. • The Old Testament is the first part of the Bible. • The New Testament is the second part of the Bible. • Jesus wants us to listen to his teachings. **9** Jesus taught us the Great Commandment. • The Ten Commandments help us to live as God's children. • God wants us to show him our love and respect. • God wants us to show that we love others as we love ourselves. **10** Jesus wants us to follow the commandments. • God gives each person free will. • Friendship with God is hurt by sin. • Jesus taught us about God's forgiveness. **11** Jesus invites us to celebrate God's forgiveness. • Jesus shares God's forgiveness and peace in the sacrament of Penance and Reconciliation. • We examine our conscience. • We tell God we are sorry for our sins. **12** We ask for God's forgiveness in the sacrament of Reconciliation. • We celebrate God's forgiveness in the sacrament of Reconciliation. • We celebrate the sacrament of Reconciliation with our parish community. • Jesus wants us to forgive others. **13** Advent is a season of waiting and preparing. **14** Christmas is a season to give glory to God.
CATECHISM OF THE CATHOLIC CHURCH	Paragraphs: 422, 470, 548, 243–244, 787, 638, 729, 737, 1267–69, 1119, 1123, 1127, 1213, 1267, 1250, 1234–1243, 1265–66, 1285, 1295–96, 1299–1300, 1303, 1168, 1173	Paragraphs: 104, 121, 124, 127, 2055, 2059, 2067, 2069, 2074, 1730, 1850, 981, 1441, 1446, 1454, 1451, 1455, 1468, 1469, 1425, 524, 526
SCRIPTURE AND THE RITES OF THE CHURCH	Matthew 8:14–15; 4:18–22; 28:1–5; 6:9; 19:14 Luke 8:22–25 Acts of the Apostles 2:1–4, 38–41 Psalms 100:1–5; 145:2 Mark 11:1, 8–10; 2:14 Rite of Baptism; Rite of Confirmation John 10:14	Isaiah 48:17; 9:1 Samuel 7:22 Luke 4:42–43; 15:4–6, 11–24; 2:1–20 Matthew 7:24–27; 22:35–39; 18:21–23 Psalms 113:3; 119:64 Rite of Penance John 15:9–10
SAINTS AND CATHOLIC PROFILES; FEASTS AND DEVOTIONS	Our Lady of the Rosary / The Holy Family — Feast of Pentecost / Chrism—Blessed Oil / The Church Year / Ordinary Time / The Rosary	Saint Francis of Assisi / Saint Philip Neri — Aspirations / The Bible / An Act of Contrition / Advent and the Advent Wreath / Christmas

T8

15 Jesus brings us life. • Jesus celebrated a special meal with his disciples. • In the Eucharist we remember and celebrate what Jesus did at the Last Supper. • The Mass is a meal and a sacrifice.

16 We are united with Jesus Christ and to one another. • The Church celebrates the Mass. • The parish gathers for the celebration of Mass. • When Mass begins, we praise God and ask for his forgiveness.

17 We listen to God's word during the Liturgy of the Word. • We listen and respond to readings from the Old Testament and the New Testament. • We listen as the gospel is proclaimed. • Together we pray the creed and the general intercessions.

18 We bring forward the gifts of bread and wine. • The eucharistic prayer is the great prayer of thanks and praise. • We pray the Our Father and ask God for forgiveness and peace. • We receive Jesus Christ in Holy Communion.

19 We are sent to share God's love with others. • Jesus is present in the Blessed Sacrament. • Jesus is with the Church as we share God's love. • Jesus is with us as we share his peace with others.

20 Lent is a season of preparing.

21 The Three Days celebrate the death and Resurrection of Jesus.

22 We are called by God. • Married people and single people are called by God. • Priests are called by God. • Religious sisters and brothers are called by God.

23 Catholics belong to parish communities. • Bishops lead and serve the Church. • The pope is the leader of the Church. • The Church is in every part of the world.

24 Prayer keeps us close to God. • Jesus prayed to God his Father. • Jesus teaches us to pray. • We pray as Jesus did.

25 The Church honors the saints. • The Church honors Mary. • We honor Mary with special prayers. • We honor Mary on special days.

26 We live in God's love. • Jesus taught us to love others. • We love and respect others. • We respect God's creation.

27 Easter is a season to celebrate the Resurrection of Jesus.

Paragraphs: 1406, 1339, 1341, 1382, 1348, 1368, 1389, 2643, 1349, 197, 1350, 1353, 1355, 1386, 1332, 1418, 1397, 1416, 628, 540

Paragraphs: 30, 1604, 1658, 1578, 1618, 2179, 886, 882, 831, 2560, 2599, 2759, 2767, 957, 963, 2676, 971, 1694, 1823, 1825, 307, 641

John 6:2–14,51; 15:5; 14:27; 13:34–35
Mark 14: 22–24
Luke 22:19; 8:1; 15:8–10
Matthew 18:20
The Roman Missal
Galatians 3:26–28

Isaiah 43:1
Philippians 4:4–5
Luke 11:1; 1:28–30,38–42; 24:1–9; 22:19
1 Corinthians 13:4,8,13
John 13:34–35; 15:12
Colossians 3:13

Saint Frances of Rome
Saint Paul

The Blessed Sacrament
Grace Before Meals
Celebration of the Mass
Holy Days of Obligation
Lent
Ash Wednesday
The Three Days

Saint Elizabeth Ann Seton
Saints Peter and Paul
Saint Brigid
Saint Catherine of Siena
Saint Rose of Lima
Saint Martin de Porres
Saint John Bosco
Saint Frances Cabrini
Mary, Mother of God

Morning Prayer
Evening Prayer
Processions
The Rosary
The Hail Mary
Feast Days of the Blessed
    Mother

Sadlier We Believe Scope and Sequence

FAITH STATEMENTS FOR EACH CHAPTER

Unit 1

❶ God the Son became one of us. • Jesus grew up in Nazareth. • Jesus begins his work. • Jesus shows us how to live as his followers.

❷ Jesus tells us how much God loves us. • Jesus teaches about the Kingdom of God. • Jesus teaches about the gift of faith. • Jesus dies and rises to save us.

❸ Jesus has power over life and death. • Jesus will come again. • When Jesus Christ comes again, he will judge all people. • Jesus teaches us to love others.

❹ Jesus promises to send the Holy Spirit. • The Holy Spirit comes to the disciples. • The Church begins on Pentecost. • The early Church grows.

❺ The apostles led the Church. • The disciples of Jesus share the good news. • The followers of Jesus stood up for their faith. • Many of our ancestors in faith are examples of holiness.

❻ The Church Year celebrates Jesus.

❼ In Ordinary Time, we celebrate the life and teachings of Jesus Christ.

Unit 2

❽ Jesus chose the apostles to lead the Church. • The pope and bishops are the successors of the apostles. • The Church is one and holy. • The Church is catholic and apostolic.

❾ The Church is the Body of Christ and the people of God. • We profess our faith through the Apostles' Creed. • The Holy Spirit guides the Church. • The Church continues to teach the true message of Jesus.

❿ Jesus teaches his followers how to pray. • We can pray with others or by ourselves. • There are different kinds of prayer. • The Church prays at all times.

⓫ We belong to a parish. • Many people serve our parish. • Our parish worships together. • Our parish cares for others.

⓬ God calls each of us. • God calls everyone to be holy. • God calls some men to be priests. • God calls some people to religious life.

⓭ The season of Advent helps us prepare for the coming of the Son of God.

⓮ The Christmas season is a special time to celebrate that God is with us.

CATECHISM OF THE CATHOLIC CHURCH

Unit 1

Paragraphs: 460, 533, 517, 561, 104–108, 541, 153, 638, 547–549, 671, 678, 1970, 729, 731, 732, 849, 551, 763–765, 769, 2030, 1168, 1163

Unit 2

Paragraphs: 765, 880, 811, 823, 830, 857, 782, 789, 194, 798, 771, 2759, 2655, 2626–2643, 2691, 2697, 2179, 1348, 2182, 2186, 1213, 825, 1719, 1565, 915, 524, 526

SCRIPTURE AND THE RITES OF THE CHURCH

Unit 1

Luke 1:26–35; 2:41–51; 4:14–15; 1:38; 17:5–6; 23:33–34; 24:1–12
Matthew 3:2,17; 13:55; 6:26–33; 24:42; 25:31–43; 28:16–20; 28:19; 28:20
1 Corinthians 12:3
Romans 10:13
Psalm 118:1
Mark 4:35–41; 10:45; 12:28–32; 11:9
John 11:1–3, 17–44; 16:22; 15:12
Acts of the Apostles 2:1–4, 32, 36, 38, 41, 42; 9:3–5; 2:42, 45
2 Corinthians 13:13

Unit 2

John 6:35; 8:12; 11:25; 14:26; 15:15; 13:34
1 John 4:11,12
Matthew 16:18; 18:20; 25:40
1 Corinthians 12:14–21
1 Peter 2:10
Psalms 113:3; 141:2a
Luke 11:1, 9; 3:4; 2:1–12
1 Samuel 3:10
Isaiah 43:1
Philippians 4:4–5

SAINTS AND CATHOLIC PROFILES; FEASTS AND DEVOTIONS

Unit 1

Saint Peter Claver
Mary, An Example of Faith
Saint Paul
Saint Perpetua
Saint Felicity
Saint Augustine

The Bible
The Feast of All Saints
The Feast of the Holy Cross
The Church Year
Ordinary Time

Unit 2

Saint Teresa of Avila
Saint Martin de Porres
Blessed Pope John XXIII
Saint Francis of Assisi
Saint Clare of Assisi
Saint Nicholas
Saint Lucy
Saint Stephen
Saint John
Holy Innocents

The Apostles' Creed
The Lord's Prayer
Prayer Posture
Forms of Prayer
The Liturgy of the Hours
Pilgrimages
Advent
Christmas

15 The Church celebrates the sacraments. • Baptism, Confirmation, and Eucharist are the sacraments of Christian initiation. • Reconciliation and Anointing of the Sick are sacraments of healing. • Holy Orders and Matrimony are sacraments of service to others.

16 Jesus celebrated Passover and the Last Supper. • The Mass is a sacrifice and a meal. • We take part in the Mass. • We celebrate Mass each week.

17 We gather to praise God. • We listen to God's word. • We receive Jesus Christ. • We go out to love and serve the Lord.

18 We make the choice to love God. • God is our forgiving Father. • The sacrament of Reconciliation has several parts. • The Church celebrates the sacrament of Reconciliation.

19 Jesus cared for and healed the sick. • The Church heals us in Jesus' name. • We believe in eternal life with God. • The Church celebrates eternal life with God.

20 The season of Lent is a time of preparation for Easter.

21 The Three Days celebrate that Jesus passed from death to new life.

22 Jesus brings God's life and love to all people. • Jesus shares his mission with his disciples. • The Church works for justice and peace. • We live out the good news of Jesus Christ.

23 People around the world have different beliefs about God. • The Jewish faith is important to Christians. • Christ calls his followers to be united. • The Church works for Christian unity.

24 The Catholic Church is all over the world. • Catholics share the same faith. • Catholics celebrate their faith in different ways. • We are the light of the world.

25 We belong to the communion of saints. • Mary is the greatest of all the saints. • The Church remembers and honors Mary. • God calls us to be saints.

26 Jesus used parables to teach about the Kingdom of God. • Jesus taught that the Kingdom of God will grow. • Jesus' miracles were signs of the Kingdom of God. • The Kingdom of God grows.

27 In the Easter season, we celebrate the Resurrection of Jesus.

Paragraphs: 1113, 1212, 1421, 1534, 1340, 1323, 1348, 1343, 1359, 1349, 1355, 1694, 1428, 1439, 1450–1460, 1469, 1503, 1511, 1681, 1684, 540, 647

Paragraphs: 543, 551, 2419, 2449, 843, 839, 838, 855, 835, 1203, 1204, 2105, 957, 972, 971, 2013, 546, 541, 548, 2818, 644

John 3:16–17
Luke 5:17–25; 22:19; 15:11–32
Psalms 106:1; 118:28
Matthew 26:26–28; 28:1; 14:35,36
The Roman Missal
Rite of Penance
Rite of Anointing of the Sick
Isaiah 55:3
Rite of Baptism
Mark 10:46–52

John 20:19,21; 17:20–21; 20:19–29
Luke 4:16–19; 4:42–43; 1:38; 11:1; 13:18–19; 2:10
Deuteronomy 6:4
Matthew 5:14,16; 13:3–8, 18–23; 14:22–33
Psalm 86:10–13
Romans 8:14

Saint Katharine Drexel	Blessed Sacrament
Our Lady of Guadalupe	Sacramentals
Pope John Paul II	Ash Wednesday
Martyrs of El Salvador:	Holy Days of Obligation
Srs. I. Ford, M. Clarke,	Celebration of the Mass
and D. Kazel;	Mass Cards
Jean Donovan	Lent
Saint Isaac Jogues	The Three Days
Saint Joan of Arc	

Saint John the Baptist	All Souls' Day
Mary, greatest of all	The Mysteries of the Rosary
the saints	Hail Mary
Saint Elizabeth of Hungary	Litany
Saint Louise de Marillac	The Easter Season
Saint Charles Lwanga	
Saint Joan of Arc	
Saint Andrew Nam-Thuong	
Saint Dominic Savio	
Being canonized a saint	

Sadlier We Believe **Scope and Sequence**

T11

Unit 1 Growing in Jesus Christ

Unit 2 The Commandments Help Us to Love God

FAITH STATEMENTS FOR EACH CHAPTER

Unit 1

1. God sent his only Son to us. • Jesus shows us how to live. • Jesus Christ is our Savior. • The disciples spread the good news of Jesus Christ.

2. Jesus trusted God his Father. • Jesus taught the Beatitudes. • Jesus taught about the Kingdom of God. • Jesus' disciples share his mission.

3. God gives us the freedom to choose. • Sin leads us away from God. • Sin can be things people do or fail to do. • We are called to value and respect all people.

4. God calls us to be close to him • God gives us the gift of conscience. • We form our conscience. • We examine our conscience.

5. Jesus tells us about God's forgiveness and love. • We receive God's forgiveness in the sacrament of Reconciliation. • We celebrate the sacrament of Reconciliation. • Reconciliation brings peace and unity.

6. Throughout the liturgical year we remember and celebrate Jesus Christ.

7. During the season of Ordinary Time, we celebrate the life and teachings of Jesus Christ.

Unit 2

8. God calls his people. • The Ten Commandments are God's laws for his people. • Jesus teaches us about God's law. • Jesus teaches us to love one another.

9. We believe in the one true God. • We honor the one true God. • We love God above all things. • We place our hope and trust in God.

10. God's name is holy. • We respect God's name. • We call upon God's name. • We respect and honor sacred places.

11. God gave us a special day to rest and to worship him. • We keep the Lord's Day holy by participating in Sunday Mass. • The Lord's Day is a day for rest and relaxation. • We keep the Lord's Day holy by caring for the needs of others.

12. The Introductory Rites unite us and prepare us for worship. • During the Liturgy of the Word, we hear the word of God. • During the Liturgy of the Eucharist, we offer gifts of bread and wine and receive the Body and Blood of Jesus Christ. • In the Concluding Rite we are sent to live as disciples of Jesus.

13. In Advent we prepare for the coming of the Lord.

14. During the Christmas season we celebrate the Son of God coming into the world.

CATECHISM OF THE CATHOLIC CHURCH

Unit 1

Paragraphs: 422, 544, 430, 767, 609, 1716, 543, 764, 387, 1850, 1853, 1878, 1776, 1777, 1785, 1454, 1423–1424, 1441, 1448, 1468–1469, 1168, 1163

Unit 2

Paragraphs: 2057, 2060, 2052–2053, 2055, 2085, 2096, 2093, 2098, 2143, 2144, 2153, 1186, 2172, 2177, 2185, 2186, 1348, 1349, 1355, 1397, 524, 528

SCRIPTURE AND THE RITES OF THE CHURCH

Unit 1

John 1:29; 6:35; 8:12; 10:11; 11:25; 14:6–7; 11:41–42; 20:21–23; 15:12
Matthew 4:10; 5:1–10, 12; 9:12; 7:12
Luke 17:20–21; 22:42; 10:30–34; 15:11–12, 14, 17–20; 15:4–7; 6:36
Galatians 3:26–28; 6:14, 16, 18
Psalms 139:1–3; 51:3, 4, 8, 12; 113:3; 25:4
1 Timothy 1:5
2 Corinthians 13:11
Rite of Penance
Revelation 22:20
The Roman Missal
Mark 6:50

Unit 2

Psalms 119:33–35; 86:10–12; 105:3; 113:3
Exodus 3:6–10; 13:21–22; 20:2–5; 3:14; 20:8
Isaiah 9:5; 60:1–4
Matthew 22:36–37, 39; 5:8; 6:21, 25–26; 21:12, 13; 5:7; 18:20; 2:1–12
John 13:34–35
Deuteronomy 6:4–5
Luke 1:30, 38; 4:1–8; 11:2; 22:19; 1:46–49
1 Corinthians 3:21–23; 11:23–26
Acts of the Apostles 2:42; 9:4
The Roman Missal
Revelation 21:4

SAINTS AND CATHOLIC PROFILES; FEASTS AND DEVOTIONS

Unit 1

Saint Rose Philippine Duchesne
Saints Matthew, apostle and evangelist
Saint Mark, evangelist
Saint Luke, evangelist
Saint John, apostle and evangelist
Saint Francis of Assisi
Saint John Vianney
Saint Thomas More
Dorothy Day
Oscar Romero

Feast of the Immaculate Conception
Act of Contrition
The Liturgical Year
Ordinary Time

Unit 2

Saint Paul
Saint Brigid
Our Lady of Guadalupe
Saint Juan Diego
The prophet Isaiah

Adoration of the Blessed Sacrament
The Jesus Prayer
Veneration of the Saints
Feast of Our Lady of Guadalupe

Holy Days of Obligation
Corporal Works of Mercy
Spiritual Works of Mercy
The Mass:
   Liturgy of the Word
   Liturgy of the Eucharist
Advent
Christmas
The Feast of the Epiphany

15 God wants us to love and respect others. • In our families we learn to love God and others. • In our families we have the responsibility to love and respect one another. • Citizens and leaders work together for peace.

16 Human life is sacred. • The right to life is the most basic human right. • We respect the gift of life. • Promoting peace is a way to respect life.

17 God creates each person with the ability to show and share love. • We are called to chastity. • Friendships are one way we grow in love. • The love between a husband and wife is very special.

18 We are called to act with justice. • We respect the property of others. • God's creation is meant for all people. • We are called to help all people meet their basic needs.

19 God teaches us what it means to be true. • We are called to witness to the truth of our faith. • We have a responsibility to tell the truth. • We have a responsibility to respect the truth.

20 Lent is the season of preparation for Easter.

21 The Easter Triduum celebrates the joy of the cross.

22 Feelings are a gift from God. • God created us to share love. • God calls us to be pure of heart. • The virtue of modesty helps us to be pure of heart.

23 We are called to have generous hearts. • Jesus taught us to trust in God above all things. • Depending upon God brings happiness. • Jesus teaches us that God's law is love.

24 Jesus is our model of holiness. • We open our hearts and minds in prayer. • The sacraments draw us closer to God. • The Holy Spirit shares special gifts with us.

25 The Church is a worldwide community. • We have responsibilities as members of the Church. • We celebrate the sacraments. • We have an active role in the Church community.

26 The virtues of faith, hope, and love bring us closer to God. • Mary is our model for virtue and discipleship. • The cardinal virtues guide us. • We are called to live a life of love.

27 During the season of Easter, we celebrate the Resurrection of Jesus.

Paragraphs: 2199, 2207, 2206, 2238, 2258, 2270, 2288, 2304, 2331, 2348, 2347, 2361, 2401, 2412, 2415, 2446, 2465, 2472, 2483, 2469, 540, 617

Paragraphs: 2516, 2520, 2519, 2524, 2538, 2544, 2547, 1970, 1698, 2766, 1123, 1831, 814, 2041, 2042, 2043, 1813, 967, 1805, 1825, 645

Luke 2:46–52; 3:11; 19:8
Matthew 8:4; 22:37, 39; 5:4, 21–22, 43–45; 6:11; 5:6; 5:10, 37; 7:12; 19:30; 1:18–21, 24
Exodus 20:12; 20:13; 20:14; 20:15; 20:16
Jeremiah 1:5
Psalms 139:14; 33:4; 119:89, 90, 142, 145
Deuteronomy 5:17
Genesis 1:27–28; 30–31
Isaiah 58:5–7; 43:20; 53:1, 10
James 2:15–17
John 18:37; 13:4–5
Acts of the Apostles 1:8
Sirach 19:6
The Roman Missal

Ezekiel 36:26–28
Matthew 3:16; 5:8; 9:25; 5:3, 17; 11:25; 18:20; 5:9, 16; 10:32–33; 22:39
Mark 11:15
Luke 1:38; 12:15, 22–24; 22:42; 23:34; 10:16; 2:51
John 11:35; 11:41–42; 14:26; 16:13; 13:6–17; 21:1–14
Exodus 20:17
Romans 13:10; 5:5
Acts of the Apostles 20:33–35; 1:3–12; 2:1–4
Galatians 5:22–23
1 Corinthians 11:24; 13:13
Psalms 103:1–5; 119:33
1 Thessalonians 5:18

Saint Edith Stein
Saint Vincent de Paul
Saint Louise de Marillac
Saint Charles Lwanaga and the Uganda Martyrs
Saint Joseph
Saint John the Baptist
Frederic Ozanam

Feast of the Holy Family
Saint Joseph's Day practices
Respect Life Sunday
National Prayer Vigil for Life
Prayer of Saint Francis
Lent
The Easter Triduum
The Veneration of the Cross

Saint Katharine Drexel
Saint Thérèse of Lisieux
Blessed Pope John XXIII
Saint Teresa de los Andes
Saint Josephine Bakhita
Saints Isidore and Maria
Saint Monica
Saint Augustine
Mary, our model
Pope John Paul II
Saint Francis of Assisi

Sacramentals
Liturgy of the Hours
The Feast of the Ascension
The Feast of Pentecost

Sadlier **We Believe** Scope and Sequence

Welcome !

Across the ages, Jesus calls to each child we teach: *"Follow me"* (Luke 9:23). Each child looks to the Church for help in answering "yes" to Jesus.

Your vocation to teach young people about Jesus is an awesome one. The *We Believe* program is designed for you.

We Believe consistently integrates:

Content that is faithful to the teachings of the Catholic Church and that holistically embraces the four pillars of the *Catechism of the Catholic Church*: Creed, Liturgy and Sacraments, Moral Life, Prayer

Activities and reflections that involve the children and their families in catechesis, prayer, and living their faith

Reliance on Scripture, Catholic social teaching, vocation awareness, and mission

Review and assessment that reinforce the essential content of the lesson

Music and prayer that echo and anticipate liturgical celebrations

Methodologies that engage the experience of the child, modeled on Jesus' "pedagogy of faith" (cf. *General Directory for Catechesis*, 137, 140)

Media and technology used in service to faith and in the context of family

Reflection and activities that integrate catechesis, liturgy and life

Jesus sent the apostles to "Go . . . make disciples of all nations" (Matthew 28:19).

The Church in every age has embraced this mission of evangelization and proclaimed the gospel of Jesus through its catechetical ministry.

As you carry on Jesus' mission, you can rely on *We Believe* because it is:

- **Rooted in Scripture**

- **Faithful to the Tradition of the Catholic Church**

- **Spirited by the *General Directory for Catechesis***

☩ **Christocentric**, centering on the Person of Jesus Christ

☩ **Trinitarian**, inviting relationship with God the Father, God the Son, and God the Holy Spirit

☩ **Ecclesial**, supporting faith that is lived in the domestic church and the universal Church.

The Child's Pages

Together in the footsteps of Jesus

To help you, the catechist, to nurture each child's relationship with Jesus and to facilitate each child's faith response, this program employs an easy-to-use catechetical process for each lesson: *We Gather, We Believe, We Respond.* This three-part process echoes the "pedagogy of the faith" which Jesus himself modeled.

WE GATHER

Children gather in prayer at the beginning of every chapter. They gather to pray and focus on their life. They respond to God's call and his grace through prayer and reflection on their experience. They pray, sing, and explore the ways the faith speaks to their lives.

WE BELIEVE

Each chapter presents the truths of the Catholic faith found in Sacred Scripture and Tradition, and in accordance with the Magisterium of the Church. The main faith statements of each chapter are highlighted. The content of faith is presented in ways that are age-appropriate, culturally sensitive, and varied.

WE BELIEVE

Jesus has power over life and death.

Jesus loved his friends. Among his best friends were Martha, Mary, and their brother Lazarus. This family lived in a town called Bethany.

📖 John 11:1–3, 17–44

One day Lazarus became very sick. His sisters sent a message to Jesus telling him about Lazarus. When Jesus reached Bethany, Lazarus had already died and been buried.

Martha cried to Jesus that, if he had been there, he could have cured Lazarus. Jesus said, "I am the resurrection and the life; whoever believes in me, even if he dies, will live." Martha told Jesus, "I have come to believe that you are the Messiah, the Son of God." (John 11:25, 27)

Mary, Lazarus's other sister, came to greet Jesus. She was also crying. The sisters showed Jesus where Lazarus was buried, and Jesus began to cry.

A huge rock lay across the entrance to the place where Lazarus was buried. Jesus ordered that it be taken away. Then Jesus cried out in a loud voice, "Lazarus, come out!" (John 11:43) With that, Lazarus came out.

Jesus had raised Lazarus from the dead and more people began to believe that Jesus was the Messiah, the Son of God.

✋ Jesus is the Resurrection and the life. If he asked you, "Do you believe this?" what would you say?

36

Jesus will come again.

One day the disciples wanted Jesus to tell them when the world would end. But Jesus said, "Stay awake! For you do not know on which day your Lord will come." (Matthew 24:42)

Jesus did not mean that our bodies should never go to sleep. He meant that we should always be preparing for his coming. We do this through prayer and the things we say and do.

Jesus was born in Bethlehem. That was his first coming. Jesus will come again at the end of time, and we will see him for ourselves. Jesus' coming at the end of time will be a joyful event. It is called his second coming.

When Christ comes again, we will be filled with joy and happiness. We will know Jesus because we will see him. Our life with the risen Christ will go on in joy forever.

✋ We can "stay awake" for the second coming of Jesus Christ by living each day the way he taught us. Write one way you will "stay awake" in faith this week.

_____

_____

Key Word
second coming (p. 253)

As Catholics...

Jesus' raising Lazarus from the dead was a miracle. Jesus' miracles—walking on water, calming the seas, healing the sick—went beyond human power. Each miracle was a call to believe that Jesus was sent by God to save his people. Jesus' miracles were special signs that helped people to trust and believe in God. They showed people that God's Kingdom was present in their lives.

37

WE RESPOND

Throughout each chapter children are encouraged to respond in prayer, faith, and life. They are invited to respond to the message of the lesson. Through prayer, song, and actions that express their beliefs, children are called to live out their discipleship among their peers, their families, and their school and parish communities.

Plus . . .

The chapter concludes with a *Review* page that offers standard and alternative assessments. These provide opportunities for children to demonstrate learning and express faith. In addition, the *We Respond in Faith* page invites the children to take time to reflect and pray. They remember the four main doctrinal statements and Key Words as well as gain inspiration from a true story of Catholics living out their faith in the world.

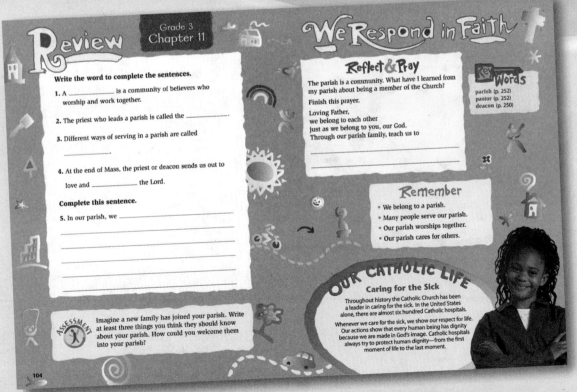

We love and serve the Lord and others by:
* studying and learning more about our Catholic faith
* sharing the good news
* sharing what we have—our money, our time, and our talents—with one another
* caring for those in need—the sick, the poor, and the hungry
* making peace with others, even those who hurt us
* working for justice by treating all people fairly and with respect
* protecting the rights of people who cannot stand up for themselves.

All these actions are not just nice things to do. They are ways to show that we are true followers of Jesus Christ and members of his Body, the Church.

WE RESPOND
What kinds of things take place in your parish? List some of these things using the letters below.

P
A
R
I
S
H

St. Joseph the Worker Clean-up Come Join Us!

As Catholics...
Some parishes do not have priests to serve them. So the bishop of the diocese selects a *pastoral administrator* to serve the parish. This administrator leads parish activities. He or she guides the parish in religious education and prayer. However, the bishop always assigns a priest to celebrate Mass and the other sacraments at these parishes.

Do you know of any parishes with a pastoral administrator?

103

Review
Grade 3 Chapter 11

Write the word to complete the sentences.

1. A _____ is a community of believers who worship and work together.

2. The priest who leads a parish is called the _____.

3. Different ways of serving in a parish are called _____.

4. At the end of Mass, the priest or deacon sends us out to love and _____ the Lord.

Complete this sentence.

5. In our parish, we _____

ASSESSMENT Imagine a new family has joined your parish. Write at least three things you think they should know about your parish. How could you welcome them into your parish?

We Respond in Faith

Reflect & Pray

The parish is a community. What have I learned from my parish about being a member of the Church?

Finish this prayer.

Loving Father,
we belong to each other
just as we belong to you, our God.
Through our parish family, teach us to _____

Key Words
parish (p. 252)
pastor (p. 252)
deacon (p. 250)

Remember
* We belong to a parish.
* Many people serve our parish.
* Our parish worships together.
* Our parish cares for others.

OUR CATHOLIC LIFE

Caring for the Sick

Throughout history the Catholic Church has been a leader in caring for the sick. In the United States alone, there are almost six hundred Catholic hospitals.

Whenever we care for the sick, we show our respect for life. Our actions show that every human being has dignity because we are made in God's image. Catholic hospitals always try to protect human dignity—from the first moment of life to the last moment.

104

The Child's Pages

The Seasonal Chapters and the Web site for We Believe

Not Just Added On...But Completely Integrated Within the Text.

Sadlier *We Believe* integrates liturgy and catechesis through culturally-rich and diverse prayer experiences, ritual celebrations, and special lessons on the liturgical year and seasons. *We Believe* Music CDs also incorporate liturgical music to foster the children's participation in parish worship and devotional practices.

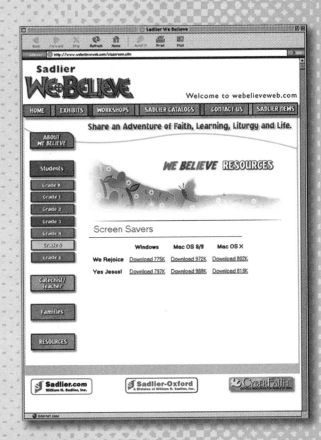

Colorful photos and illustrations set the tone for successful learning experiences.

www.WeBelieveweb.com

connects you, the catechist, as well as the children and their families to a Web-based support system.

Log on and explore a rich array of educational activities to complement your lessons, plus great resources for prayer, liturgy, retreats, and religion projects. Enjoy a safe learning environment with family-based faith activities that are motivating and fun for children and their families.

The Family Pages

No other catechetical program has so much for the family.

Three special family components are integrated into the pupil text and, when utilized together throughout the program, complete the circle of catechesis.

Sharing Faith as a Family

These four unit openers provide an overview of the doctrine, additional resources, and faith formation for parents, and applications to family life. The activities and discussion on these pages are directed by a family member.

Sharing Faith with My Family

These 27 family pages invite participation in each chapter through prayer, activities, information, and review. Activities and discussions on these pages are child-initiated, inviting the child to be the evangelizer.

Sharing Faith in Class and at Home

This unique chapter in each book integrates the grade level material and utilizes a combination of stories, discussion questions, and activities that further the connections among catechists, children, and families. Suggested ways to utilize this chapter can be found in the Chapter 28 Planning Guide.

Don't Forget...

Families will also have access to the program Web site, finding safe web activities for their children and family-based faith activities to share.

www.WeBelieveweb.com

The Catechist's Pages

Sadlier We Believe Program Overview

Your Guide—Clear, Concise, Complete!

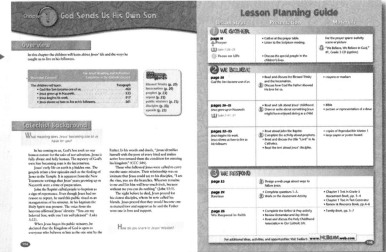

First, Use the Overview and Planning Pages.

Background and Lesson preparation Planning Guide provide enrichment and structure for the catechist.

Then, Use the Additional Resource Pages.

Connections, Catechist Development, and Reproducible Master pages are all in your Guide.

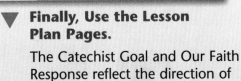

Finally, Use the Lesson Plan Pages.

The Catechist Goal and Our Faith Response reflect the direction of each lesson.

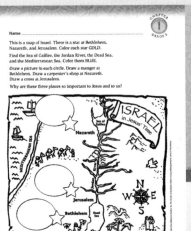

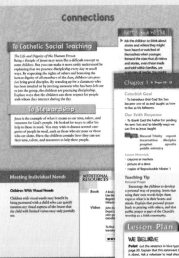

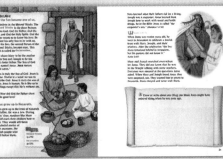

All you need to get started is

1. your grade level Sadlier *We Believe* text for each child in your class

2. your grade level *We Believe* guide

3. your grade level *We Believe* Music CD.

Catechist Development

Sadlier is committed to supporting you, the catechist, in your faith and in your ministry. The Sadlier *We Believe* program includes twenty-one Catechist Development articles. Each article provides you with on-going development and helps you to become more aware of the elements of effective catechesis. The opening article precedes the Introductory Chapter and the other articles are found in the final section of your guide.

Each article addresses a specific topic and is written by a nationally recognized expert in that field. The *Resources* section follows each article and offers print and video suggestions to enable you to delve further into the topic. The *Ways to Implement* offers some practical ideas to bring the topic to life in your class. Finally, the *Catechist Corner* features an idea from a catechist and the successful implementation of that idea.

Here are the twenty-one topics, their authors, and the pages on which you can find the articles in your Sadlier *We Believe* Catechist Guide:

Topics and Authors

For additional ideas, activities, and opportunities: Visit Sadlier's **www.WeBelieveweb.com**

Understanding the Child

by Gini Shimabukuro, Ed.D.

Dr. Gini Shimabukuro is a Professor and Associate Director of the Institute for Catholic Educational Leadership at the University of San Francisco. She is rooted in Catholic education, with teaching experience at the elementary level.

Essential to the building of a gospel-based learning community is the sincere, ongoing effort to understand each child. This understanding permits the educator to fulfill the Christian call to formation and transformation of learners.

Since the Second Vatican Council in the 1960s, Church documentation related to education offers insight into this concept through the "integral formation" of the child. "Integral formation" refers to teaching that fosters the unification of the many aspects of the child—spiritual, moral, religious, intellectual, developmental, social, emotional, physical—and to learning that enables the child to make necessary connections among these interior dimensions.

Effective formation, then, precludes an awareness of these many human dimensions as active in the learning process and of their relationship to each other: emotional with religious, intellectual with physical, moral with developmental, and so on.

In order to achieve this holistic goal of learning that is integrated and formative, it is necessary to understand that teaching is more than mere transmission of knowledge. We need to design content-based processes that will empower the child to interiorize his or her learning.

Resources

Groome, Thomas. *Educating for Life*. Allen, Texas: Thomas More Publishing Co. 1998.

The Congregation for Catholic Education, The Religious Dimension of Education in a Catholic School, Boston: Daughters of St. Paul, 1988.

Ways to Implement Understanding the Child

- Explore the preferred learning style of each child in your class or group. Discuss the different ways that people learn, sharing your own preferred style. Design lessons that embrace a variety of learning styles.

- When building a classroom or group community, introduce activities that encourage all members to know each other better, such as, exercises that prompt students to share their ethnic backgrounds, childhood experiences, feelings, hopes for the future, and so on. Appropriate sharing in these areas provides the "glue" for a tightly knit learning community.

- Investigate the emerging research on the brain and learning in order to incorporate the best classroom practices in the design and delivery of instruction.

- Be available to the children by modeling active listening skills. Encourage their social, moral and emotional development.

For additional ideas, activities, and opportunities, visit Sadlier's

www.WE BELIEVE web.com

Catechist Corner

With thanks to:
Catherine Foley
Grade 3 Catechist
St. Anthony of Padua Church
Red Bank, New Jersey

Catherine designs a bulletin board that contains a church on one side and types of homes on the other. A footbridge connects the two sides of the display. On the "church side," Catherine displays pictures of people and events from the parish. She asks the children to contribute pictures of themselves with their families and pictures of themselves during a church celebration (Baptism, first Eucharist, a wedding). The pictures of the children and their families are placed on the "home side" of the display. The pictures of the children celebrating special church events are placed on the footbridge. The bulletin board is a great conversation piece that helps Catherine get to know the children and their families.

Notes

We Believe

The *We Believe* program will help us to

learn *celebrate* **share** and **live our Catholic faith.**

Throughout the year we will hear about many saints and holy people.

Saint Andrew Nam-Thuong

Saint Augustine

Saint Charles Lwanga

Saint Clare of Assisi

Saint Dominic Savio

Saint Elizabeth of Hungary

Saint Felicity

Saint Francis of Assisi

Saint Joan of Arc

Saint John the Apostle

Blessed Pope John XXIII

Pope John Paul II

Saint Katharine Drexel

Saint Louise de Marillac

Saint Lucy

Saint Martin de Porres

Martyrs of El Salvador—
Sisters Ita Ford, Maura Clarke,
and Dorothy Kazel; Jean
Donovan

Saint Nicholas

Our Lady of Guadalupe

Saint Paul

Saint Perpetua

Saint Peter Claver

Saint Stephen

Together, let us grow as a community of faith.

Welcome!

WE GATHER

✞ **Leader:** Welcome, everyone, to Grade 3
We Believe. As we begin each chapter,
we gather in prayer. We pray to God together.

Let us sing the
We Believe song!

♫ We Believe, We Believe in God

We believe in God;
We believe, we believe in Jesus;
We believe in the Spirit who gives us life.
We believe, we believe in God.

We believe in the Holy Spirit,
Who renews the face of the earth.
We believe we are part of a living Church,
And forever we will live with God.

We believe in God;
We believe, we believe in Jesus;
We believe in the Spirit who gives us life.
We believe, we believe in God.

means it's time to

think about

talk about

write about

draw about

act out

Life

at home

in our neighborhood

at school

in our parish

in our world

> When we see **We Gather** we also come together as a class.

Talk about your life right now. What groups do you belong to?

What does belonging to these groups tell other people about you?

Each day we learn more about God.

WE BELIEVE

We learn about

- the Blessed Trinity: God the Father, God the Son, and God the Holy Spirit
- Jesus, the Son of God who became one of us
- the Church and its history and teachings
- the Mass and the sacraments
- our call to discipleship.

We find out about the different ways Catholics live their faith and celebrate God's love.

> When we see **We Believe** we learn more about our Catholic faith.

Whenever we see ✝ we make the sign of the cross. We pray and begin our day's lesson.

Each of these signs points out something special that we are going to do.

📖 is an open Bible. When we see it or something like this (John 17:20–21), we hear the word of God. We hear about God and his people. We hear about Jesus and the Holy Spirit.

 means we have an activity. We might

talk   **write**   **act**
draw
sing
work together   **imagine**

There are all kinds of activities! We might see in any part of our day's lesson. Be on the lookout!

🎵 means it is time to sing or listen to music! We sing songs we know, make up our own songs, and sing along with those in our *We Believe* music program.

Key Words means it is time to review the important words we have learned in the day's lesson.

As Catholics...

Each week, we discover something special about our faith in the **As Catholics** box. Don't forget to read it!

WE RESPOND

We can respond by

- thinking about ways our faith affects the things we say and do

- sharing our thoughts and feelings

- praying to God.

Then in our homes, neighborhood, school, parish, and world, we can say and do the things that show love for God and others.

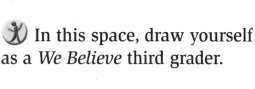 In this space, draw yourself as a *We Believe* third grader.

When we see **We Respond** we think about and act on what we have learned about God and our Catholic faith.

We are so happy you are with us!

Review

Here we answer questions about what we have learned in this chapter.

Reflect & Pray

We take a few moments to think about our faith and to pray.

We review each of the Key Words.

Review

Grade 3
Chapter 1

Circle the letter beside the correct answer.

1. The _____ is the three Persons in one God.
   a. Incarnation   b. Bible   c. Blessed Trinity

2. The _____ is the truth that the Son of God became man.
   a. Incarnation   b. Bible   c. Blessed Trinity

3. The name Jesus means "_____."
   a. God gives   b. God loves   c. God saves

4. "One who is sent" is _____.
   a. an apostle   b. a disciple   c. a follower

Complete this sentence.

5. When Jesus was growing up in his family,

_____

_____

_____

_____

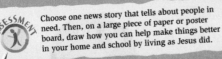

ASSESSMENT Choose one news story that tells about people in need. Then, on a large piece of paper or poster board, draw how you can help make things better in your home and school by living as Jesus did.

24

We Respond in Faith

Reflect & Pray

Jesus is divine and human. He teaches us about God's love and mercy. He shows us how to live as his faithful followers. Complete the prayer in your own words.

Jesus, I want to follow your example. Jesus, help me to

_____

_____

Key Words

Blessed Trinity (p. 250)
Incarnation (p. 251)
prophet (p. 253)
repent (p. 253)
public ministry (p. 253)
disciples (p. 251)
apostle (p. 250)

Remember

- God the Son became one of us.
- Jesus grew up in Nazareth.
- Jesus begins his work.
- Jesus shows us how to live as his followers.

OUR CATHOLIC LIFE

Holy Childhood Association

The Holy Childhood Association invites children to help one another. One way that children can help one another is by collecting money for needy families all over the world. Adult members of the Holy Childhood Association tell children how families in other countries live. They show children how their money helps other children's families all over the world.

Remember

We recall the four main faith statements of the chapter.

ASSESSMENT We do a chapter activity that will show that we have discovered more about our Catholic faith.

OUR CATHOLIC LIFE

Here we read an interesting story about the ways people make the world better by living out their Catholic faith.

SHARING FAITH
with My Family

At the end of each chapter you'll bring a page like this home to share with your family.

Sharing What I Learned

Talk about
WE GATHER
WE BELIEVE   WE RESPOND
with your family.

WE BELIEVE
Family Contract

As a **We Believe** family, this year we promise to

_____

_____

Names

_____

_____

_____

WE ARE THE CHURCH

A Family Prayer
(Lead your family in prayer.)

People who love us make love grow. Thank you, God, for our family.

People who love us make love grow. Thank you, God, for all the friends of our family.

Most of all, thank you, God, for loving us!

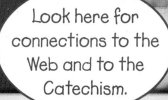

Look here for connections to the Web and to the Catechism.

Visit Sadlier's
www.WeBelieveweb.com

Connect to the Catechism
References are given here to connect to the *Catechism of the Catholic Church.*

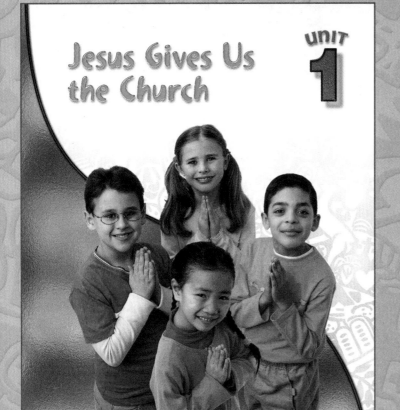

Jesus Gives Us the Church

UNIT 1

CLASS CONNECTION

Point out the unit title to the children. Ask them what they think they will be learning more about in this unit. Have a class discussion preparing the children for this unit.

HOME CONNECTION

Sharing Faith as a Family

Sadlier *We Believe* calls on families to become involved in:

• learning the faith

• prayer and worship

• living their faith.

Highlighting of these unit family pages and the opportunities they offer will strengthen the partnership of the Church and the home.

For additional information and activities, encourage families to visit Sadlier's

www.WeBelieveweb.com

UNIT 1 SHARING FAITH as a Family

Belonging to a Family of Faith

What happens when a new person joins a family? A newborn baby, an adopted child, the spouse of a son or daughter—each one is *initiated* in some way. This entails sharing the family's story, including a "Who's Who" and how each person is related to the other. New members also enter the family by participating in its celebrations and learning its rules. In the best-case scenario, this process is one of *welcoming* and establishes a sense of belonging.

This is not unlike what happens in the sacrament of Baptism. Rather than expecting a newly baptized infant or adult to instantly know everything about the Catholic community, he or she is initiated through taking part in its rituals, understanding its symbols, and learning its story.

Your child will be learning more this year about what it means to follow Jesus and to belong to the Church. Just as you teach your child what it means to be part of your family, so you can help her or him take an active part in the Church. Participate in the life of the parish, talk to your child about your faith, and tell stories about Jesus. All of these things will guide your child towards taking his or her place as a precious part of the Body of Christ.

A Meditation on Holiness

As your child learns about the early Church in this unit, he or she will realize that we are all called to holiness by our membership in the Church. Try to schedule a few moments to be by yourself. We know this might not be easy to do. Close the door. Put on some soothing music.

Breathe very deeply, in and out, three times as you think to yourself: **Re** (inhale) **lax** (exhale). Feel your head drop as you count backwards from ten to zero. Now stay there for a moment of relaxation.

From the Catechism

"'The Christian family ... can and should be called a *domestic church*.' It is a community of faith, hope, and charity."
(*Catechism of the Catholic Church*, 2204)

What Your Child Will Learn in Unit 1

One of the major emphases of Unit 1 concerns the ways that Jesus teaches us about God's love. The children will see how Jesus teaches about the Kingdom of God and shows us a God of mercy. The children will be introduced to the meaning of life everlasting. This is followed by a examination of the Church's beginnings. The children will see the early followers of Jesus share the good news with people throughout the world. They will become aware of followers who stood up for their faith under the most trying of circumstances. Lastly, the children will learn that we are all called to holiness—each in our own way.

Plan & Preview

▶ You might create a stage backdrop for all the figures collected in this unit. Help your child to look at pictures of the Holy Land. Obtain a shoebox lid or comparable stiff cardboard that the family can use to draw a scene. The figures can then be placed in front of the "stage" setting. Props such as rocks and bushes can be made from sponges and paper maché. Your creativity is needed!

Quietly, in your mind, say the words,

Holy, holy, holy Lord,

(pause)

God of power and might,

(pause)

heaven and earth are full of your glory.

(pause)

Hosanna in the highest.

At each pause reflect on what the words are saying to you right now. What images do you see? How do you see yourself as a person of holiness today? Visualize this as you count from one to five, lifting your head up and opening your eyes.

18

Chapter 1 God Sends Us His Own Son

Overview

In this chapter the children will learn about Jesus' life and the ways he taught us to live as his followers.

Doctrinal Content	For Adult Reading and Reflection *Catechism of the Catholic Church*
The children will learn:	Paragraph
• God the Son became one of us.	460
• Jesus grew up in Nazareth.	533
• Jesus begins his work.	517
• Jesus shows us how to live as his followers.	561

Key Words

Blessed Trinity (p. 20)
Incarnation (p. 20)
prophet (p. 23)
repent (p. 23)
public ministry (p. 23)
disciples (p. 23)
apostle (p. 23)

Catechist Background

What meaning does Jesus' becoming one of us have for you?

In his coming to us, God's Son took on our human nature for the sake of our salvation. Jesus is fully divine and fully human. The mystery of God's own Son becoming man is the Incarnation.

Jesus' early life on earth is a hidden one. The gospels relate a few episodes such as the finding of Jesus in the Temple. It is apparent from the New Testament writings that Jesus' years growing up in Nazareth were a time of preparation.

John the Baptist called people to baptism as a sign of repentance. Even though Jesus had no reason to repent, he used this public ritual as an inauguration of his mission. At his baptism the Holy Spirit was present. The voice from the heavens affirmed Jesus' identity: "You are my beloved Son; with you I am well pleased" (Luke 3:22).

When Jesus began his public ministry, he declared that the Kingdom of God is open to everyone who believes in him as the one sent by the Father. In his words and deeds, "Jesus identifies himself with the poor of every kind and makes active love toward them the condition for entering his kingdom" (CCC 544).

Those who followed Jesus were called to carry out the same mission. Their relationship was so intimate that Jesus could say to his disciples, "I am the vine, you are the branches. Whoever remains in me and I in him will bear much fruit, because without me you can do nothing" (John 15:5).

The night before he died, Jesus prayed for his closest disciples, whom he now called his friends. Jesus prayed that they would become one in mutual love and support as he and the Father were one in love and support.

How do you share in Jesus' mission?

Lesson Planning Guide

Lesson Steps	Presentation	Materials
① WE GATHER		
page 19 ✝ **Prayer**  *Luke 1:26–35* ☀ **Focus on Life**	• Gather at the prayer table. • Listen to the Scripture reading. • Discuss the special people in the children's lives.	For the prayer space: nativity scene or picture "We Believe, We Believe in God," #1, Grade 3 CD (option)
② WE BELIEVE		
page 20 *God the Son became one of us.*	• Read and discuss the Blessed Trinity and the Incarnation. 🕴 Discuss how God the Father showed his love for us.	• crayons or markers
pages 20–21 *Jesus grew up in Nazareth.*  *Luke 2:41–51*	• Read and talk about Jesus' childhood. 🕴 Draw or write about something Jesus might have enjoyed doing as a child.	• Bible • picture or representation of a dove
pages 22–23 *Jesus begins his work.* *Jesus shows us how to live as his followers.*	• Read about John the Baptist. 🕴 Complete the activity about prophets. • Read and discuss the title "Lord" in As Catholics. • Read the text about Jesus' disciples.	• copies of Reproducible Master 1 • large paper or poster board
③ WE RESPOND		
page 23	🕴 Design a web page about ways to follow Jesus.	
page 24 **Review**	• Complete questions 1–5. 🕴 Work on the *Assessment Activity*.	• Chapter 1 Test in Grade 3 Assessment Book, pp. 3–4 • Chapter 1 Test in Test Generator • Review & Resource Book, pp.4–6
page 25 **We Respond in Faith**	• Complete the *Reflect & Pray* activity. • Review *Remember* and *Key Words*. • Read and discuss the Holy Childhood Association in *Our Catholic Life*. • Discuss **Sharing Faith with My Family**.	• Family Book, pp. 5–7

For additional ideas, activities, and opportunities: Visit Sadlier's www.WeBelieveweb.com

Name _____

This is a map of Israel. There is a star at Bethlehem, Nazareth, and Jerusalem. Color each star GOLD.

Find the Sea of Galilee, the Jordan River, the Dead Sea, and the Mediterranean Sea. Color them BLUE.

Draw a picture in each circle. Draw a manger at Bethlehem. Draw a carpenter's shop at Nazareth. Draw a cross at Jerusalem.

Why are these three places so important to Jesus and to us?

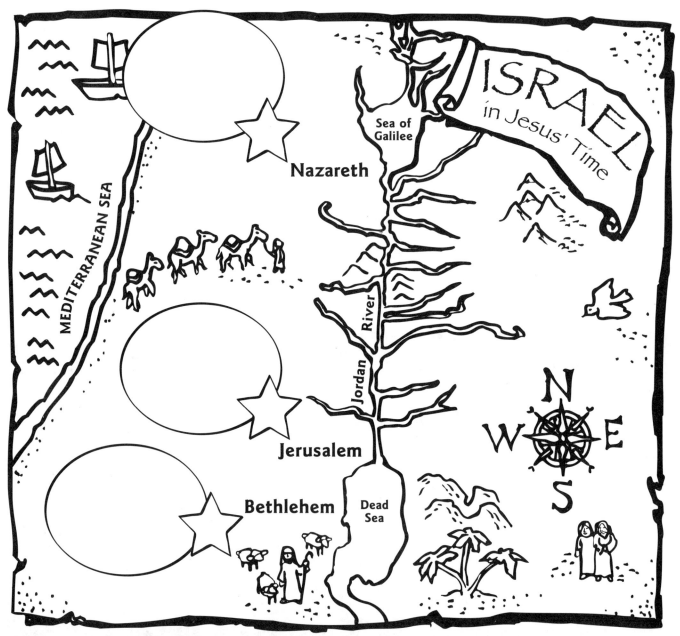

Connections

To Catholic Social Teaching

The Life and Dignity of the Human Person
Being a disciple of Jesus may seem like a difficult concept to some children. But you can make it more easily understood by explaining that we practice discipleship every day in small ways. By respecting the rights of others and honoring the human dignity of all members of the class, children can practice being good disciples. By standing up for a classmate who has been insulted or by inviting someone who has been left out to join the group, the children are practicing discipleship. Explore ways that the children can show respect for people with whom they interact during the day.

To Stewardship

Jesus is the example of what it means to use time, talent, and resources for God's people. He looked for ways to offer his help to those in need. You may wish to discuss several categories of people in need, such as those who are poor or those who are alone. Have the children consider how they can use their time, talent, and resources to help these people.

FAITH and MEDIA

▶ Ask the children to think about stories and videos they might have heard or watched of themselves when younger. Remind the class that all videos and stories, even those made and told within families, are examples of media. You might also mention some other examples of media such as the Internet, television and movies, and messages sent by mail, telephone, and e-mail.

▶ As part of your discussion of what Jesus might have liked to do as a child (page 21), remind the children that what they are doing is similar to what people who work in media—people such as writers and filmmakers—do when they make television programs and write books and articles about the lives of real people.

Meeting Individual Needs

Children With Visual Needs

Children with visual needs may benefit by being partnered with a child who can quietly mention any visual aspects of the lesson that the child with limited vision may only partially see.

ADDITIONAL RESOURCES

Book *A Book About Jesus,* American Bible Society, 1991. Use the first two sections of the book, "The Beginning," pages 7–22, and "Jesus Works Miracles," pages 23–40.

Video *John the Baptist,* Nest Entertainment, 1990. Depicts the life of one of God's greatest prophets who gave all to prepare for Jesus and finally beholds the Lamb of God. (30 minutes)

To find more ideas for books, videos, and other learning material, visit Sadlier's

www.WE BELIEVE web.com

Chapter Story

Sarah was angry. The special box she kept under her bed had been pulled out, and everything she had saved in it was scattered all over the floor. She knew immediately who was to blame. "Mom!" yelled Sarah. "Mom, come and look at what Jenny did!"

"Oh, dear," said Mom when she saw the mess. "I'm sorry, Sarah. That must have happened while I was on the phone for a minute. We'll have to find another hiding place for your special box."

"Well . . . okay," said Sarah. "But why does Jenny have to be so mean?"

"Oh, Sarah," said Mom. "Jenny's not being mean! She's just curious. She's acting just like a normal three-year-old. You did things like that too, you know, when you were Jenny's age."

"I did?" asked Sarah. "Like what?"

Mom smiled. "Well, you know the junk drawer in the kitchen, where we keep the tape and string? You used to pull a chair up to the counter, climb up, and take everything out of the drawer! We had to put a lock on it!"

Sarah laughed. "I did that? I wish I could put a lock on my special box!"

"That's a good idea, Sarah!" said Mom. "Some day you'll be able to share lots of things with Jenny, but right now she is too little to realize how important your treasure box is to you. This weekend we'll look for a box with a lock!"

▶ *What were you like when you were Jenny's age? How are you different now?*

God Sends Us His Own Son

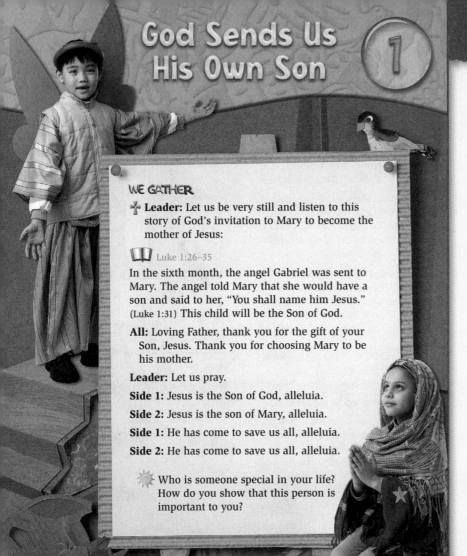

WE GATHER

✝ **Leader:** Let us be very still and listen to this story of God's invitation to Mary to become the mother of Jesus:

📖 Luke 1:26–35

In the sixth month, the angel Gabriel was sent to Mary. The angel told Mary that she would have a son and said to her, "You shall name him Jesus." (Luke 1:31) This child will be the Son of God.

All: Loving Father, thank you for the gift of your Son, Jesus. Thank you for choosing Mary to be his mother.

Leader: Let us pray.

Side 1: Jesus is the Son of God, alleluia.

Side 2: Jesus is the son of Mary, alleluia.

Side 1: He has come to save us all, alleluia.

Side 2: He has come to save us all, alleluia.

☀ Who is someone special in your life? How do you show that this person is important to you?

19

PREPARING TO PRAY

The children will listen to words of the angel Gabriel to Mary at the Annunciation. They will respond in prayer.

• Ask a volunteer to be the prayer leader and another to read the scripture. Allow the children to practice their parts.

• Divide the class into two groups to say the two parts of the prayer. Have the children read through the prayer on page 19 silently, concentrating especially on the part they will say. Explain how they will recite the prayer with one child reading the part for the leader; Side 1 and Side 2 reading their parts; and everyone reading the part for All.

The Prayer Space

• Display a nativity scene or pictures of a nativity scene. Invite the children to place these items in the prayer space.

📖 **This Week's Liturgy**
Visit **www.webelieveweb.com** for this week's liturgical readings and other seasonal material.

Lesson Plan

WE GATHER   ___ minutes

✝ Pray

• Invite the children to gather together and to place the selected pictures or figures in the prayer space.

• Have them open their books to the prayer on page 19. Signal the child leader to begin the prayer.

• Signal the reader to read the Scripture passage.

• As needed, prompt each group to take their parts.

• You may want to conclude by playing "We Believe, We Believe in God," #1, from the Grade 3 CD (option).

 Focus on Life

• Have the children discuss special people in their lives. Then tell the children that in this lesson they will learn about Jesus' childhood and about the special people in his life.

• Share the *Chapter Story* on guide page 19E.

Home Connection Update

Invite the children to talk with a partner. Ask the partners to share a story that showed how they helped their families this summer.

Catechist Goal

• To introduce that God the Son became one of us and taught us how to live as his followers

Our Faith Response

• To thank God the Father for sending his own Son and to identify ways we can live as Jesus taught

 Blessed Trinity   repent Incarnation   disciples prophet   apostle public ministry

Lesson Materials

• crayons or markers
• picture of a dove
• copies of Reproducible Master 1

Teaching Tip

Personal Prayer

Encourage the children to develop a personal way of praying. Stress that using their own words helps them express what is in their hearts and minds. Explain that personal prayer leads to praying with others, and that public prayer is part of the Church's worship as a faith community.

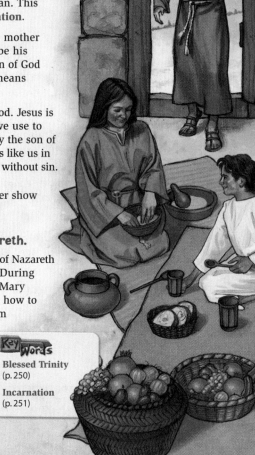

WE BELIEVE

God the Son became one of us.

We believe in the Blessed Trinity. The **Blessed Trinity** is the three Persons in one God: God the Father, God the Son, and God the Holy Spirit. God the Father wants us to know his love. So he sent his only Son to be with us. God the Son, the second Person of the Blessed Trinity, became man. This truth is called the **Incarnation**.

God chose Mary to be the mother of his Son and Joseph to be his Son's foster father. The Son of God was named Jesus. *Jesus* means "God saves."

Jesus is truly the Son of God. Jesus is divine. *Divine* is a word we use to describe God. Jesus is truly the son of Mary. Jesus is human. He is like us in all things except this: He is without sin.

How did God the Father show us his great love?

Jesus grew up in Nazareth.

Jesus grew up in the town of Nazareth in Galilee. He was a Jew. During Jesus' time, mothers like Mary would teach their children how to pray. They would tell them wonderful stories of their ancestors, the Jewish people who lived before them.

Key Words

Blessed Trinity (p. 250)

Incarnation (p. 251)

20

Lesson Plan

WE BELIEVE   ___ minutes

Point out the sentence in blue type at the top of page 20. Explain that this statement tells what the page is about. Ask a volunteer to read aloud this statement.

Write on the board the words *Blessed Trinity* and *Incarnation*.

Ask children to underline or highlight the definitions of these words in their text as you read the first paragraph.

Read aloud the next two paragraphs.

Discuss ways that God the Father showed his great love for us.

Ask the children to read aloud the second statement. Encourage the children to think about what life might have been like for Jesus as he grew up in Nazareth.

Invite volunteers to read the next remaining paragraphs and Scripture story about Jesus' life in Nazareth.

Sons learned what their fathers did for a living. Joseph was a carpenter. Jesus learned from Joseph how to work with wood and build things. So in the Bible Jesus is called "the carpenter's son." (Matthew 13:55)

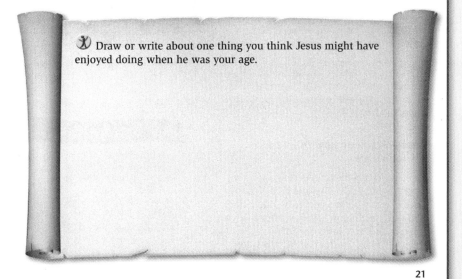

📖 Luke 2:41–51

When Jesus was twelve years old, he went to Jerusalem to celebrate a Jewish feast with Mary, Joseph, and their relatives. After the celebration "the boy Jesus remained behind in Jerusalem, but his parents did not know it." (Luke 2:43)

Mary and Joseph searched everywhere for Jesus. They did not know that he was in the Temple talking with some teachers. Everyone was amazed at the questions Jesus asked. When Mary and Joseph found Jesus, they were surprised, too. They wanted him to return to Nazareth. Jesus obeyed and went with them.

🖐 Draw or write about one thing you think Jesus might have enjoyed doing when he was your age.

21

ACTIVITY BANK

Parish
Signs of Jesus' Presence

If possible, take the children to the church and let them explore the many signs of Jesus' presence. Form the class into groups as ask each group to find and list as many different signs of Jesus as they can. Invite the groups to share their lists. Were there any surprises? Did the groups find the same signs? How did the signs help them to remember that Jesus is always with us?

Curriculum Connection
Art

Activity Materials: cardboard, tape, glue, scissors, poster paint

Use reference books or other materials to show what the town of Nazareth and the Temple might have looked like. Form groups. Distribute cardboard, tape, glue, and scissors. Have one group make a model of the Temple. Ask the other groups to make a model of "streets" or sets of buildings that might have been in the town of Nazareth. Distribute poster paint to paint the models. Display them for the school or parish to see.

Ask: *How would you feel if you became separated from your parents?* (Allow children to respond.) *How do you think Mary and Joseph might have reacted to the situation?* (They may have been upset with Jesus or worried that something had happened to Jesus; they may have asked people to help them search for Jesus.)

🖐 **Invite** a volunteer to read the directions for the activity on page 21.

Give the children an opportunity to draw their pictures and share what they drew with the class.

Quick Check
✔ *Who are the three Persons of the Blessed Trinity?* (God the Father, God the Son, God the Holy Spirit)

✔ *What did children in Jesus' time learn from their parents?* (knowledge of prayer and heritage and skills to make a living)

As Catholics...

The Title Lord

After you have presented the lesson, read the *As Catholics* text aloud to the children. Ask them what word people used to show they believed that Jesus was divine. (Lord) Have them recall the meaning of the word *divine*. (*Divine* is a word used to describe God.)

Jesus begins his work.

Jesus had a cousin named John. John was a prophet. A **prophet** is someone called by God to speak to the people.

John prepared the people for Jesus. He told them, "Repent, for the kingdom of heaven is at hand."(Matthew 3:2). **Repent** means to turn away from sin and to ask God for help to live a good life.

Many people were baptized by John. This washing with water was a sign of their turning away from sin and their turning to God.

Even though Jesus was without sin, he went to John to be baptized. As Jesus came out of the water, God the Holy Spirit came upon him like a dove. A voice was heard saying, "This is my beloved Son, with whom I am well pleased." (Matthew 3:17)

Soon after this Jesus began his own work among the people. This was called his **public ministry**.

Prophets remind us that God loves us and cares for us. What are some ways you can remind people that God loves them?

Jesus shows us how to live as his followers.

Jesus called people to believe in God. He taught about God's love and healed many people. Jesus invited people to follow him and learn from him. Many women and men said yes to Jesus' invitation. Those who followed Jesus were called his **disciples**.

22

As Catholics...

When the first followers of Jesus used the title *Lord*, they were saying they believed Jesus was divine. By calling Jesus *Lord* people showed their respect for and trust in Jesus' divine power.

What are some other titles we have for Jesus?

Lesson Plan

WE BELIEVE (continued)

Ask a volunteer to read aloud the statement at the top of page 22.

Read aloud the text.

Assign children the roles of God the Father, someone to hold up a dove to symbolize the presence of the Holy Spirit, John the Baptist, people to be baptized, and Jesus. Ask these children to act out the story as you read it again.

Talk about what prophets do. Ask: *How can we be like prophets, reminding people about God?*

Read aloud the second statement on page 22.

Ask the children to read silently the next two paragraphs and list the things Jesus did in his ministry. (He taught about God's love; healed people; he called in people to believe in God; he invited them to be his disciples; he reached out to those ignored by others; he fed the hungry; he comforted the lonely and poor.)

Read aloud the last two paragraphs. Draw attention to the art of Jesus at prayer. Remind the children that Jesus prayed often. Ask: *How did Jesus show his love for his Father?*

Ask volunteers to explain what *disciples* and *apostles* were. (Possible responses: Disciples followed Jesus; apostles were sent by Jesus to share in his work in a special way)

In his ministry, Jesus tried to reach out to those who were ignored by others. He healed the sick and fed the hungry. He spent time with the poor and lonely. Jesus showed us how to be his disciples by the way he lived.

Jesus showed his love for God his Father by praying often. Once Jesus went by himself to a mountain to pray. He spent the whole night there in prayer. The next day he called his disciples together and chose twelve men to be his apostles. The word **apostle** means "one who is sent."

Jesus' apostles shared in his life and his work in a special way. They traveled with Jesus and became his close friends. They helped him teach and spread the message of God's love.

WE RESPOND

 Use the computer screen below to design a Web page. Use words and drawings to show people from all over the world some ways to follow Jesus.

Key Word

prophet (p. 253)
repent (p. 253)
public ministry (p. 253)
disciples (p. 251)
apostle (p. 250)

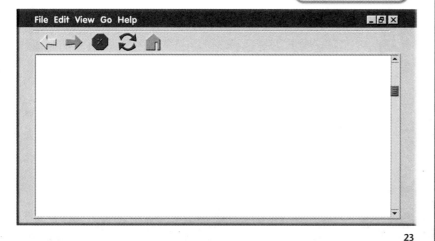

File Edit View Go Help

23

ACTIVITY BANK

Multiple Intelligences
Musical-Rhythmic
Activity Materials: percussion instruments

Have the children work in small groups. Ask each group to write a short song or special beat that encourages people to become followers of Jesus. Have the children integrate clapping, or use percussion instruments to supply a steady beat. Remind the groups that the goal of their songs is to convince others to become disciples of Jesus. Have the groups present their songs at different times.

WE RESPOND   ___ minutes

Connect to Life Talk about ways people can be Jesus' disciples.

 Invite the children to complete the activity showing ways to follow Jesus.

Distribute Reproducible Master 1 on guide page 19C and read aloud the directions. As a group or home activity, encourage the children to make symbols that will help them to identify the important places on the map.

Review

CHAPTER TEST

Chapter 1 Test is provided in the Grade 3 Assessment Book.

Sadlier
We Believe
Assessment Book
Reproducible Masters   Grade 3

Circle the letter beside the correct answer.

1. The _____ is the three Persons in one God.

   a. Incarnation   **b.** Bible   **c.** Blessed Trinity

2. The _____ is the truth that the Son of God became man.

   a. Incarnation   **b.** Bible   **c.** Blessed Trinity

3. The name Jesus means "_____."

   a. God gives   **b.** God loves   **c.** God saves

4. "One who is sent" is _____.

   a. an apostle   **b.** a disciple   **c.** a follower

Complete this sentence.

5. When Jesus was growing up in his family, _____

   _____See pages 20–21._____

   _____

   _____

   _____

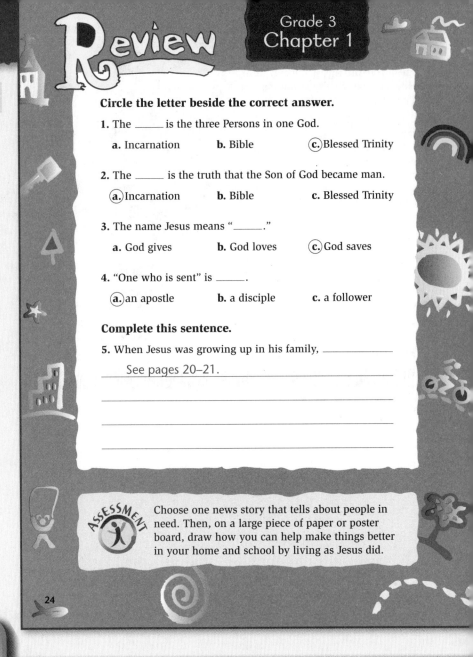

ASSESSMENT Choose one news story that tells about people in need. Then, on a large piece of paper or poster board, draw how you can help make things better in your home and school by living as Jesus did.

24

Lesson Plan

Review _____ minutes

Chapter Review Ask children to look through their books and pose questions to the class based on the *Key Words* and the ideas in the chapter. Have the children complete questions 1–4. Ask volunteers to say which answers are correct and why they think so. For question 5 give children the opportunity to brainstorm ideas. Then ask them to complete the sentence and share their answers.

Assessment Activity Read aloud the directions for the activity and answer any questions the children may have. Give the children the option of writing rather than drawing, or combining written text with drawings. Help the children generate ideas for the assign-

ment. Ask children to discuss what they know about real people who have needs that are not met, such as not having enough food. Ask: *What can we do to help these people?* You may wish to have the children work on the *Assessment Activity* over the weekend with their families.

 _____ minutes

Reflect & Pray Explain to children that they will both pray and reflect, or think about the prayer. Invite a volunteer to read the text. Then encourage children to write prayerfully and respectfully to Jesus. Provide quiet time for this activity and encourage reflection.

Reflect & Pray

Jesus is divine and human. He teaches us about God's love and mercy. He shows us how to live as his faithful followers. Complete the prayer in your own words.

Jesus, I want to follow your example. Jesus, help me to

_____

_____

_____

Key Words

Blessed Trinity (p. 250)
Incarnation (p. 251)
prophet (p. 253)
repent (p. 253)
public ministry (p. 253)
disciples (p. 251)
apostle (p. 250)

Remember

- God the Son became one of us.
- Jesus grew up in Nazareth.
- Jesus begins his work.
- Jesus shows us how to live as his followers.

Our Catholic Life

Holy Childhood Association

The Holy Childhood Association invites children to help one another. One way that children can help one another is by collecting money for needy families all over the world. Adult members of the Holy Childhood Association tell children how families in other countries live. They show children how their money helps other children's families all over the world.

HOME CONNECTION

Sharing Faith with My Family

Make sure to send home the family page (text page 26).

Encourage the children to enjoy leading their families in prayer, as suggested on the page.

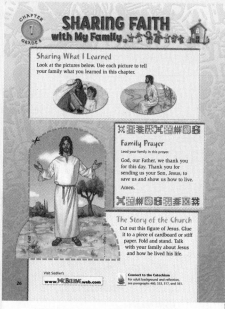

PUPIL PAGE 26

For additional information and activities, encourage families to visit Sadlier's

www.WEBELIEVE.web.com

🔑 Key Words To review the *Key Words,* have the children write clues for each one. Ask volunteers to read a clue and call on a child to name the correct word for it.

Remember Have a volunteer read aloud the four statements. Invite the children to consider the ways these beliefs make a difference in their lives. Gather the children in the prayer space. Ask them to point out the objects that relate to key ideas learned in the chapter.

Our Catholic Life Read the text about the Holy Childhood Association. Visit the Web site for the Association. It is linked through www.webelieveweb.com. You might consider a class project to help the Holy Childhood Association, such as collecting money during Advent or Lent to be sent to the Association for its work.

Plan Ahead for Chapter 2

Prayer Space: Bible, crucifix, cut-out paper crosses

Lesson Materials: small seeds, copies of Reproducible Master 2, Grade 3 CD

Chapter 2 — Jesus Teaches Us About God's Love

Overview

In Chapter 1 the children learned about the ministry of Jesus and that we can live our lives as followers of Jesus. In this chapter the children will be introduced to Jesus' teaching about God's love and the Kingdom of God.

Doctrinal Content	For Adult Reading and Reflection *Catechism of the Catholic Church*
The children will learn:	Paragraph
• Jesus tells us how much God loves us.	104–108
• Jesus teaches about the Kingdom of God.	541
• Jesus teaches about the gift of faith.	153
• Jesus dies and rises to save us.	638

Key Words

Bible (p. 29)
Kingdom of God (p. 29)
faith (p. 31)
crucified (p. 31)
Resurrection (p. 31)

Catechist Background

When am I conscious of God's love for me?

A country-western singer laments that we have looked for love in all the wrong places. Thousands of poets have ransacked metaphors and similes to compare love to everything under the sun. The authors of the Bible, especially the psalmist in the Old Testament and Saint John in the New Testament, have penned some of the most beautiful lines about love. With great simplicity Saint John states, "God is love" (1 John 4:8).

The Bible is the story of God's love for his people. We see the love of God the Father in sending us his only Son. The love of Jesus is for us in his teachings, his compassion, his service to others, and most especially his death and Resurrection. Today God's love is active in the world through the building up of the Kingdom of God.

The love of God was so evident in Jesus of Nazareth that people were drawn to him. He assured his listeners that faith in God would enable them to trust God's love and care for them. "The Lord asks us to love as he does, even our *enemies*, to make ourselves the neighbor of those furthest away, and to love children and the poor as Christ himself" (CCC 1825).

Followers of Jesus show their love for others by respecting them, by helping those in need, and by promoting peace and justice. In these ways Christians continue to build up the Kingdom of God.

How do my words and actions show that I trust in God's love for me?

Lesson Planning Guide

Lesson Steps	Presentation	Materials

① WE GATHER

page 27 ✝ **Prayer** ☀ **Focus on Life**	• Gather at the prayer table. ♪ Respond in song. • Have children share their answers to the questions.	For the prayer space: crucifix, paper crosses ♪ "Lift High the Cross," #2, Grade 3 CD

② WE BELIEVE

pages 28–29 *Jesus tells us how much God loves us.* *Jesus teaches us about the Kingdom of God.*	• Discuss the text about the Bible and the guidance of the Holy Spirit. 🏃 Talk about favorite Bible stories. • Read and discuss the text about the Kingdom of God. 🏃 Write or draw about the Kingdom of God.	• pencils or markers
pages 30–31 *Jesus teaches about the gift of faith.* 📖 *Luke 17:5–6* *Jesus dies and rises to save us.* 📖 *Luke 23:33–24:12*	• Read and discuss the text and Scripture about the gift of faith. 🏃 Complete the activity about sharing faith. • Read and discuss the text and Scripture about Jesus' death and Resurrection.	• small seeds • large paper or poster board

③ WE RESPOND

page 31	🏃 Complete activity about how the women felt when they found the empty tomb.	
page 32 **Review**	• Complete questions 1–5. 🏃 Work on the *Assessment Activity.*	• Chapter 2 Test in Grade 3 Assessment Book, pp. 5–6 • Chapter 2 Test in Test Generator • Review & Resource Book, pp.13–15
page 33 **We Respond in Faith**	• Complete the *Reflect & Pray* activity. • Review *Remember* and *Key Words.* • Read and discuss *Our Catholic Life* about The Bible in Our Lives. • Discuss **Sharing Faith with My Family.**	• Family Book, pp. 14–16

For additional ideas, activities, and opportunities: Visit Sadlier's **www.WE BELIEVE.web.com**

27B

Name —————————————————————————————————

This is the story of the death and Resurrection of Jesus.

Put the events in the correct order by numbering them from 1 to 5.

The first event is numbered for you.

Then color the picture of the empty tomb.

_____ Jesus' body was laid in a tomb.
A great stone was rolled in front of it.

_____ Early on Sunday morning, the women went to the tomb. But the body of Jesus was not there!

_____ Jesus was crucified. He said, "Father, forgive them." (Luke 23:34)

1 Powerful people hated Jesus because of what he said and did.

_____ The women told Peter and the disciples. Peter ran to the tomb. He was amazed. Jesus had truly risen from the dead!

Connections

To Parish

The parish church building is like a home to parishioners. Help the children realize that the parish church is not only a building to gather for Mass. Everything in the church that has significance for parishioners—from the holy water fonts to the altar. Tell the children that they can always go to the parish church to pray and celebrate with other parish members. These people will always be there to help them.

To Scripture

Jesus taught about God's love for people through his interactions with people. The following gospel passages depict some of the ways in which Jesus' actions demonstrated God's love for people.

Luke 5:17–26   Jesus heals a paralyzed man.
Mark 10:13–16   Jesus blesses the little children.
Luke 19:1–10   Jesus visits with Zacchaeus.
John 13:12–15   Jesus washes his disciples' feet.

Encourage the children to learn one of the ways Jesus showed God's love and care during his public ministry.

FAITH and MEDIA

▶ Remind the children that the Bible, like all books, is an example of media. But that because the Holy Spirit guided the authors of the Bible, it is unlike any other book every written. The Bible is the greatest medium of mass communication in the history of the world.

▶ As a footnote to the **Teaching Tip**, tell the children that photographs and artwork are media, too. We should judge the work of artists and photographers with the same "eye for truth" that we bring to our evaluation of the work of writers, reporters, and filmmakers.

Meeting Individual Needs

English Language Learners

When possible, pair children who do not speak English as a first language with partners who can reread text or clarify and summarize discussion points. The attitude of the person helping out here is as important as their skill in the English language. Assign helpers who are sensitive to the language difficulties of the child and who are able to patiently help with instruction.

ADDITIONAL RESOURCES

Book *The Winds Obey Him,* Rochelle Nielson Barsuhn, The Dandelion House, 1983. Use the Bible stories on pages 12 –22 to help the child grow in faith.

Video *Jesus Dies on the Cross,* CCC of America, 1997. From *A Kingdom Without Frontiers* series, Jesus carries His heavy cross to Calvary where He dies a painful death. (30 minutes)

To find more ideas for books, videos, and other learning material, visit Sadlier's

www.WeBelieve.web.com

Focus on Life

Chapter Story

Jason's father happily placed a large slice of meatloaf on his plate, then looked at his wife and smiled. "This is a great meal, Dolores." He turned to his two children at the table and said, "Kids, do you see how much mom loves us? Look what she made for us." Jason looked up from his plate with an amused expression. "Mom doesn't cook because she loves us," he said. "That's just her job."

"Oh really?" his mother responded. "Well, Jason, maybe you don't realize I could've just placed some bread and butter on the table and called it dinner."

"But I thought mom did things for us because she had to," Jason said. His little sister looked at him in disbelief.

"Look, Jason," his father explained. "Mom and I both do a lot of things around here. The point is that we could do things differently than we do, but . . ."

"But you love us!" Jason said, ending his father's words.

Jason smiled. It made sense now. Mom cooked the meal and did a thousand other things because she loved her family.

"Nice going, Jason," his father chimed in. Then with a sly grin on his face, his father continued, "Of course you know it's your night to do the dishes."

Everyone broke into laughter and began to eat.

▶ *What lesson did Jason learn from the conversation before eating dinner?*

Jesus Teaches Us About God's Love

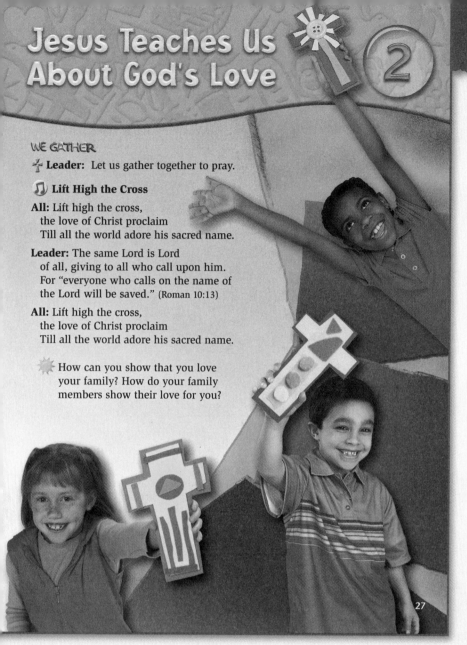

WE GATHER

✛ **Leader:** Let us gather together to pray.

♫ **Lift High the Cross**

All: Lift high the cross,
the love of Christ proclaim
Till all the world adore his sacred name.

Leader: The same Lord is Lord
of all, giving to all who call upon him.
For "everyone who calls on the name of
the Lord will be saved." (Roman 10:13)

All: Lift high the cross,
the love of Christ proclaim
Till all the world adore his sacred name.

How can you show that you love
your family? How do your family
members show their love for you?

PREPARING TO PRAY

The children will sing a song in praise
of the cross of Christ. They will listen
to Scripture and pray together.

• Invite one of the children to lead
the prayer. Allow preparation time.

• Practice singing or saying the
refrain from "Lift High the Cross,"
#2 on the Grade 3 CD.

♫ For words and music to all
the songs on the Grade 3 CD,
see Sadlier's *We Believe*
Program Songbook.

The Prayer Space
• Along with a crucifix, place cut-out
paper crosses on the table in the
prayer space, so that each child has
one to hold during the prayer time.

📖 **This Week's Liturgy**
Visit **www.webelieveweb.com** for
this week's liturgical readings and
other seasonal material.

Lesson Plan

WE GATHER ___ minutes

✛ **Pray**

• Have the prayer leader begin the opening prayer.

• Sing the song, "Lift High the Cross," #2 on the
Grade 3 CD. Encourage them to lift their paper crosses
up during each recitation or singing of the words
Lift high the cross.

• If time allows, you may invite children to decorate
their crosses. Have scraps of felt or construction paper
available, as well as scissors and glue. Use stiff paper or
cardboard for backing.

Focus on Life
• Share the *Chapter Story* on guide page 27E.

• Have the children think about how they can show
that they love their families. Share answers. Tell the
children that in this lesson they will learn about God's
love for them.

Home Connection Update

Invite the children to share experiences of
using the Chapter 1 family page. Ask: *Did
you have an opportunity to lead your family
in prayer?*

Catechist Goal

• To emphasize Jesus' teaching about God's love for us, about the Kingdom of God, and about the gift of faith

Our Faith Response

• To rejoice in Jesus' Resurrection

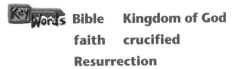 **Bible   Kingdom of God   faith   crucified   Resurrection**

Lesson Materials

• Bible
• small seeds
• copies of Reproducible Master 2

Teaching Tip

Seeing What Is Not There

Throughout the pupils' text are photos and artwork that complement the written word. Often, the children are asked to look at the artwork and describe what is happening in the scene. Sometimes you could ask the children what might be missing from a picture or artwork. This technique might also help them read between the lines and lead to more critical thinking.

28

WE BELIEVE

Jesus tells us how much God loves us.

Jesus taught that God loves each one of us. There are many examples of God's great love. We can read about them in the Bible. The **Bible** is a collection of books about God's love for us and about our call to live as God's people. It is also called *Scripture.*

The Bible has two parts, called *testaments.* The Old Testament is about the people of God before the time of Jesus. The New Testament is about the life of Jesus Christ and the beginning of the Church.

The human authors of the Bible were guided by God the Holy Spirit, the third Person of the Blessed Trinity. They wrote about things that God wanted to share with us. Yet the human authors did choose the words for the stories they wrote.

Talk about your favorite story about Jesus from the Bible.

Jesus teaches about the Kingdom of God.

Jesus must have been a wonderful teacher. We learn from the Bible that crowds followed him to hear what he had to say. Jesus often taught about the **Kingdom of God**, which is the power of God's love active in the world. Jesus wanted everyone to change their lives and turn to God.

Lesson Plan

WE BELIEVE   ___ minutes

Ask a volunteer to read aloud the first statement.

Invite the children to read silently the first three paragraphs.

Talk together about the Bible, a book about God's love for us.

Emphasize the following points:

• In the books of the Bible, we read about God's love for us and his call to live as his people.

• The Old and New Testaments are the two parts of the Bible or Scripture.

• Guided by the Holy Spirit, the authors of the Bible wrote in their own words about the things God wanted to share with us.

Encourage the children to share stories from the Bible that they remember. Ask about their favorite stories.

Invite a volunteer to read aloud the second statement. Then have a volunteer read aloud the next paragraph.

Ask: *What did Jesus want the people to do?* (He wanted everyone to change their lives and turn to God.)

Read aloud the definition of *Kingdom of God.* Ask the children to give examples of God's love in the world.

28

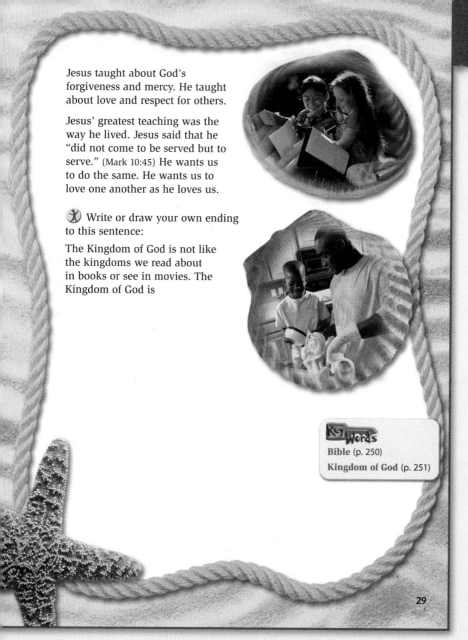

Jesus taught about God's forgiveness and mercy. He taught about love and respect for others.

Jesus' greatest teaching was the way he lived. Jesus said that he "did not come to be served but to serve." (Mark 10:45) He wants us to do the same. He wants us to love one another as he loves us.

✖ Write or draw your own ending to this sentence:

The Kingdom of God is not like the kingdoms we read about in books or see in movies. The Kingdom of God is

Key Words

Bible (p. 250)
Kingdom of God (p. 251)

29

ACTIVITY BANK

Liturgy
The Readings
Activity Materials: Bibles for children
Invite the children to work in pairs or small groups. Explain that the readings we hear at Sunday Mass are taken from the Bible. Explain that the first reading usually comes from the Old Testament. Help the children find this. Explain that the second reading comes from the New Testament. Then help the children find the gospel in books of Matthew, Mark, Luke, and John. Explain that the gospel is always the third reading at Sunday Mass. Everyone stands to hear the gospel proclaimed by the priest or deacon.

Multiple Intelligences
Naturalist
Activity Materials: flower seeds, soil pots or cut milk cartons, watering cans
Provide the children with an experience of helping something to grow. Assign individuals or groups to plant and care for the plants. Remind the children that God wants his Kingdom to grow and flourish even more than we want our plants to grow!

Read the two paragraphs on the top of page 29.

Discuss any confusion the children might have about equating the Kingdom of God with kingdoms in fairy tales or kingdoms on earth ruled by kings and queens. Note that Jesus came to serve and to show us God's love.

✖ **Invite** the children to write or draw their own endings to the paragraph about the Kingdom of God.

Ask the children to share their work and to tell how they showed the power of God's love at work.

Quick Check
✔ *What do we call the collection of books about God's love for us?* (the Bible)

✔ *How does a disciple of Jesus live in the Kingdom of God?* (through loving and respecting others)

Jesus teaches about the gift of faith.

Faith is a gift from God. This means that God helps us to believe and trust in him. Jesus teaches us about faith in God by his stories and his actions.

📖 Luke 17:5–6

One day Jesus was teaching. His apostles asked him to give them more faith. Jesus replied, "If you have faith the size of a mustard seed, you would say to [this] mulberry tree, 'Be uprooted and planted in the sea,' and it would obey you." (Luke 17:6)

A mustard seed is very tiny. It is about the size of the tip of a pencil. A mulberry tree is very strong. Imagine being able to make this tree lift itself into the sea!

Jesus was telling his apostles that faith is very powerful. Faith allows us to believe what we cannot see or feel or touch.

🧍 Write one way other people share their faith with you.

_____

_____

30

The Mulberry Tree by Vincent van Gogh

Jesus dies and rises to save us.

Jesus lived his life in such a way that people knew he loved God. Some powerful people hated Jesus because of what he did and said.

📖 Luke 23: 33–24:10

Jesus was arrested and put to death. Like a criminal, Jesus was **crucified**, nailed to a cross. Yet even as he was dying, Jesus prayed, "Father, forgive them, they know not what they do." (Luke 23:34)

Lesson Plan

WE BELIEVE (continued)

Ask a volunteer to read aloud the first statement and paragraph on page 30.

Stress that the gift of faith enables us to trust in God's words and in his promise to love us.

📖 **Hold** up some small seeds. Then read aloud Luke 17:5–6.

Ask: *In this story, what does the tiny seed represent?* (faith)

🧍 **Encourage** the children to think about ways other people share their faith. Then have them complete the writing activity.

Invite volunteers to read the second statement and the following paragraph on page 30.

📖 **Read** aloud Luke 23:33–24:10. Ask: *Why did the other disciples run away?* (out of fear that they, too might be arrested and crucified as Jesus was)

Mary, the mother of Jesus, and other women disciples stayed by Jesus' cross with John the apostle. The other disciples hid because they were afraid. After Jesus died, his body was laid in a tomb.

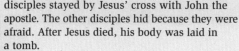 Luke 24: 1–12

Early Sunday morning some women returned to the tomb. They were carrying oils and spices to anoint the body of Jesus. When they reached the tomb, they saw that it was empty. The body of Jesus was not there!

Two men in dazzling garments told the women, "He is not here, but he has been raised." (Luke 24:6) The women went and told the apostles the news.

We call Jesus' being raised from the dead the **Resurrection**. Jesus died and rose so that all people could be saved and live with God forever.

Key Words

faith (p. 251)
crucified (p. 250)
Resurrection (p. 253)

WE RESPOND

Pretend you were with the women who went to the tomb. How would you have felt? What would you have done and said? Act it out.

31

ACTIVITY BANK

Teaching Note
Children Who Are Grieving

When a family member dies, children often feel the loss deeply. There is no one way to handle this painful episode in a child's life. Yet our faith in the Resurrection can uphold us. When appropriate, assure the grieving child, "Your grandma (or other relative) is with God. She still loves you very much and Jesus is taking care of her."

Ask a volunteer to read aloud the Scriptural account in Luke's gospel of the women and their finding the empty tomb. Point out that the women were expecting to find the body of Jesus in the tomb. They were *not* expecting to be told that Jesus was risen.

WE RESPOND

____ minutes

Connect to Life Invite children to think about how they would have felt if they were the women who went to the tomb.

Ask volunteers to act out their responses.

Pray Conclude the lesson by praying:

Christ has died,
Christ is risen,
Christ will come again.
Amen.

Distribute copies of Reproducible Master 2 on guide page 31G. Ask the children to list the events of Jesus' death and Resurrection in the correct order.

CHAPTER TEST

Chapter 2 Test is provided in the Grade 3 Assessment Book.

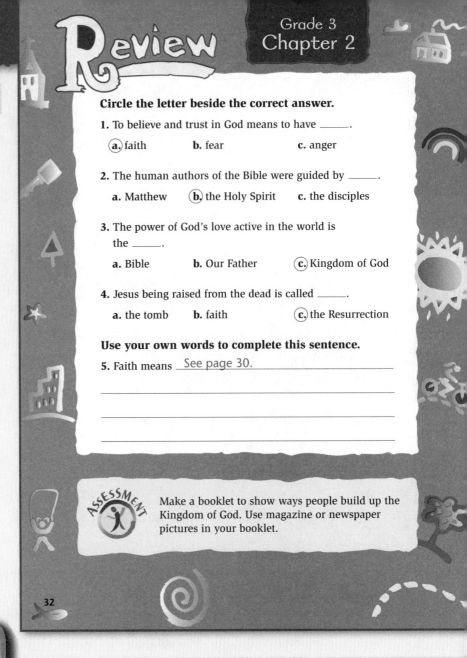

Review

Circle the letter beside the correct answer.

1. To believe and trust in God means to have _____.

   a. faith   **b.** fear   **c.** anger

2. The human authors of the Bible were guided by _____.

   a. Matthew   **b.** the Holy Spirit   **c.** the disciples

3. The power of God's love active in the world is the _____.

   a. Bible   **b.** Our Father   **c.** Kingdom of God

4. Jesus being raised from the dead is called _____.

   a. the tomb   **b.** faith   **c.** the Resurrection

Use your own words to complete this sentence.

5. Faith means ___See page 30.___

_____

_____

_____

ASSESSMENT Make a booklet to show ways people build up the Kingdom of God. Use magazine or newspaper pictures in your booklet.

32

Lesson Plan

 ___ minutes

Chapter Review Tell the children that they are going to check their understanding of what they have learned during the chapter. Have the children complete questions 1–4. Have volunteers offer their answers. Clear up any misconceptions that arise. Have the children read and answer question 5. You may want to direct them to the pages in the text before they write their answers. Then invite the children to share their answers.

Assessment Activity Read aloud the activity directions. When the booklet is complete, have each child explain the images he or she selected.

 ___ minutes

Reflect & Pray Read aloud the first sentence. Ask the children to close their eyes and think about an ending for the next sentence after you read the beginning of it. Allow them sufficient quiet time to reflect. Then have them write their own ending to the prayer. You may want to give examples.

Key Words Have the children work with a partner. Ask them to quiz each other on the definitions. Have one partner say each word while the other gives the definition or have one give a definition to be matched with a *Key Word*. Then have the partners switch roles.

Reflect & Pray

All the disciples except John and the women ran away in fear when Jesus was crucified. Jesus, keep me close to you, especially when

_____

_____

_____

_____

_____

Key Words

Bible (p. 250)
Kingdom of God (p. 251)
faith (p. 251)
crucified (p. 250)
Resurrection (p. 253)

Remember

- Jesus tells us how much God loves us.
- Jesus teaches about the Kingdom of God.
- Jesus teaches about the gift of faith.
- Jesus dies and rises to save us.

OUR CATHOLIC LIFE

The Bible in Our Lives

The Bible is an important book in the lives of all Catholics. When we celebrate the sacraments, we listen to readings from this special book. As we gather with our parish community at these celebrations, we hear about God's never-ending love and kindness for his people. We learn how God wants us to live. For Catholics the Bible, the Word of God, is an important part of our faith. Each day the Word of God can come alive in our lives if we are listening to what God has to say to us.

HOME CONNECTION

Sharing Faith with My Family

Make sure to send home the family page (text page 34).

Encourage them to share the Kingdom Cards with their family members.

PUPIL PAGE 34

For additional information and activities, encourage families to visit Sadlier's

www.WeBelieve.web.com

Remember Have the children number the doctrinal statements, 1–4. Ask four volunteers to read aloud the statements.

Our Catholic Life Read aloud the text. Ask: *What have you learned about the Bible this week?* You may want to set aside time each day to read a few verses of the Scripture with the children. Then play quiet music for a few minutes and ask them to spend time thinking about what they heard. The gospels, the Book of Psalms, and the letters of Saint Paul and Saint John are good sources for easy-to-understand verses.

Plan Ahead for Chapter 3

Prayer Space: strips of cloth, a balance scale, a coat or blanket

Lesson Materials: Grade 3 CD, Bible, copies of Reproducible Master 3

Chapter 3   Christ Will Come Again

Overview

In Chapter 2 the children learned about the Kingdom of God and the gift of faith. In this chapter the children will learn about the last judgment and that Jesus taught us to love others.

Doctrinal Content	For Adult Reading and Reflection *Catechism of the Catholic Church*
The children will learn:	Paragraph
• Jesus has power over life and death.	547–549
• Jesus will come again.	671
• When Jesus Christ comes again, he will judge all people.	678
• Jesus teaches us to love others.	1970

Key Words

second coming (p. 37)
last judgment (p. 38)
heaven (p. 38)

Catechist Background

When you hear the words "Christ will come again," what images come to mind?

In the poetic prologue to Saint John's Gospel, we read that those who believed in Jesus saw his glory. That glory was revealed to them even before the Resurrection. They had seen the Son of God perform mighty works and messianic signs. He had healed the sick, cleansed the lepers, given sight to the blind. More than that, he had raised the dead. Jesus made it clear that when it came to his own death, he would lay down his life of his own accord. "I have power to lay it down, and power to take it up again. This command I have received from my Father" (John 10:18).

At the Last Supper Jesus promised his friends that he would come again and take them to himself. (See John 14:3.) This second coming will follow a period of terrible trial in which many believers' faith will be tested.

In his parable of the sheep and the goats, Jesus prepares us for the last judgment. Those who will inherit the Kingdom are the believers who followed his example of mercy. "For I was hungry and you gave me food, I was thirsty and you gave me drink, a stranger and you welcomed me" (Matthew 25:35). The works of mercy are the criteria upon which we will be judged. Heaven or eternal life with God belongs to the merciful.

The followers of Jesus in every age will always be distinguished by their love for others. Jesus' words echo in their hearts: "I give you a new commandment: love one another. As I have loved you, so you also should love one another. This is how all will know that you are my disciples, if you have love for one another" (John 13:34–35).

How does the second coming of Christ give you hope?

Lesson Planning Guide

Lesson Steps	Presentation	Materials

 WE GATHER

page 35 **Prayer** 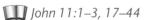 **Focus on Life**	• Gather in the prayer space. • Listen to Scripture. • Respond in song. • Discuss the questions about people with special power.	For the Prayer Space: strips of cloth, a balance scale, a coat or blanket "Whatsoever You Do," #3, Grade 3 CD

 **WE BELIEVE**

page 36 *Jesus has power over life and death.* *John 11:1–3, 17–44*	• Read and discuss the story of Lazarus. Answer the question about belief in the Resurrection. • Read and discuss the miracles of Jesus in *As Catholics*.	• Bible
page 37 *Jesus will come again.*	• Read and discuss the text about the second coming of Christ. • Complete the activity about "staying awake" in faith.	"Stay Awake," #4, Grade 3 CD
page 38 *When Jesus comes again, he will judge all people.* *Matthew 25:31–43*	• Read the scriptural story of the last judgment. • Complete the activity about ways your parish can care for others.	• balance scale and objects to weigh
page 39 *Jesus teaches us to love others.* *Mark 12:31–43*	• Read and discuss the text about the greatest commandment. • Act out situations showing ways to be a good neighbor.	• copies of Reproducible Master 3

 **WE RESPOND**

page 39	• Talk about the importance of love.	
page 40 **Review**	• Complete questions 1–5. • Work on the *Assessment Activity*.	• Chapter 3 Test in Grade 3 Assessment Book, pp. 7–8 • Chapter 3 Test in Test Generator • Review & Resource Book, pp. 10–12
page 41 **We Respond in Faith**	• Complete the *Reflect & Pray* activity. • Review *Remember* and *Key Words*. • Read and discuss *Our Catholic Life*. • Discuss **Sharing Faith with My Family**.	• Family Book, pp.11–13

For additional ideas, activities, and opportunities: Visit Sadlier's **www.WeBelieveweb.com**

Name _____

How do people follow Jesus in their actions?
Cut out and give a "Good Deeds Certificate" to people
you see who are choosing to follow Jesus.
You can write the good deed you saw on the back.

_____ ,
(Name)
I saw you choosing to follow Jesus!
_____
(Your Name)

_____ ,
(Name)
I saw you choosing to follow Jesus!
_____
(Your Name)

_____ ,
(Name)
I saw you choosing to follow Jesus!
_____
(Your Name)

_____ ,
(Name)
I saw you choosing to follow Jesus!
_____
(Your Name)

_____ ,
(Name)
I saw you choosing to follow Jesus!
_____
(Your Name)

_____ ,
(Name)
I saw you choosing to follow Jesus!
_____
(Your Name)

Connections

To Catholic Social Teaching

Solidarity of the Human Family
A significant part of Jesus' teaching to love as he loves is to grow in our understanding and acceptance of all people through awareness of other cultures. To help the children do this, have them research the celebration of feasts of saints in other cultures. The children can share their findings through written reports or visual presentations. Help the children to see that we celebrate our common beliefs in many diverse ways.

To Stewardship

Explain that the gift of time is part of stewardship. Our time is one of the most valuable gifts we can offer to others. Give examples of ways the children can be good stewards of time—reading a story with an elderly relative; playing with a younger sibling or a neighbor's child and thus freeing up a parent to attend to work around the home. Ask for other suggestions.

FAITH and MEDIA

▶ If the children do the optional "Newspaper Story" activity in the Activity Bank, remind them that when we write a news story or any sort of report, we must make a clear distinction in our story between what is fact and what is opinion. We must also make sure that when we leave some details out of the story we are not changing or distorting the meaning of the story. And, of course, we must research and double check all the facts in our story to make sure everything we say is really true.

Meeting Individual Needs

Children With Medical Challenges

If you have not already done so, check your registration files to note children's allergies and medical challenges (asthma, and so). Keep these on a list, perhaps on a large index card, in a place of easy reference—taped to your desk or to the wall. Include parents' phone numbers and other emergency numbers on this list. Be aware of children who may at times need special help or consideration. Be especially aware of food allergies when planning group celebrations.

ADDITIONAL RESOURCES

Book *The Winds Obey Him,* Rochelle Nielson Barsuhn. The Dandelion House, 1983. The Bible stories on pages 24–31 emphasize Jesus' victory over death.

Video *Jesus Raises Lazarus,* CCC of America, 1997. From A Kingdom Without Frontiers series, Jesus raises Lazarus from the dead then dines with Mary and Martha. (30 minutes)

To find more ideas for books, videos, and other learning material, visit Sadlier's

www.WeBelieveweb.com

Focus on Life

Chapter Story

Richard lived on Maple Street, where after school each day he liked to play with his friends. Three blocks away, in between Maple Street and Becker Road, lived several boys Richard's age. These boys were often mean to other children at school. Most people referred to them as "bullies."

One day, Richard heard his mother talking about needing butter to cook a special dish for dinner, but she didn't have time to run to the store on Becker Road. Richard decided to surprise her by going to the store himself. In order to get there he'd have to ride past the street where the bullies lived, but he thought he'd take his chances. As he rode his bike down Becker Road, Richard was nervous, and hoped the boys wouldn't see him.

Richard arrived at the store, bought the butter, and began to ride back home. Just as he was riding past the bullies' street, however, his pant leg got caught in his bike chain, and his bike quickly stopped. He knew how to get his pant leg out, but on this day, it just wouldn't come free. Richard began to panic. Then he saw one of the bullies come out of his house and walk down the street toward him. Richard was scared, and worked even harder to try to free his leg. Just then, from the other direction, a boy who Richard knew came walking past. "Hi, Richard," he said. "Hi, Dan," Richard answered. He was glad to see a friend. Dan looked down and saw the problem, and quickly helped Richard get his pant leg out of the bike chain.

"Thanks, Dan!" Richard said. He was so happy that his friend had helped him. Richard quickly rode home, relieved that nothing bad had happened. His mother was surprised and happy he had bought the butter.

Richard said, "Mom, you may be happy, but I'm even happier. A friend of mine really helped me out today. And you know what, Mom? I'll never forget it."

▶ *What could Dan have done instead of helping Richard?*

Christ Will Come Again ③

WE GATHER

Leader: Let us listen to the words of Jesus in Saint Matthew's Gospel:

Reader: "For I was hungry and you gave me food, I was thirsty and you gave me drink, a stranger and you welcomed me, naked and you clothed me, ill and you cared for me, in prison and you visited me." (Matthew 25: 35–36)

The Gospel of the Lord.

All: Praise to you, Lord Jesus Christ.

🎵 **Whatsoever You Do**

Chorus
  Whatsoever you do
    to the least of my people,
  that you do unto me.

  When I was hungry,
      you gave me to eat;
  When I was thirsty,
      you gave me to drink.
  Now enter into the home
      of my Father. (Chorus)

Have you ever heard about someone who has special power? Describe what that person could do.

PREPARING TO PRAY

The children will listen to the words of the last judgment from Matthew's gospel. They will respond in song.

• Ask a volunteer to be the prayer leader and another child to read the passage from Scripture. Allow these children time to practice their parts.

• Practice singing "Whatsoever You Do," #3 on the Grade 3 CD. Invite the children to think of motions to accompany the words. They can also use simple props.

The Prayer Space
• Gather strips of cloth, a balance scale, and a coat or blanket. The strips of cloth relate to the story of Lazarus, the balance scale represents judging and Judgment Day, and the coat or blanket symbolizes the comfort and assistance that Catholics offer to those in need.

📖 **This Week's Liturgy**
Visit www.webelieveweb.com for this week's liturgical readings and other seasonal material.

Lesson Plan

WE GATHER
___ minutes

✝ Pray
• Invite the children to the prayer space and open their books to the gathering prayer.
• Tell the children about the prayer space items.
• Remind the children that the word *I* in the Scripture and in the song refers to Jesus.
• Have the prayer leader begin the opening prayer.
• Have the reader proclaim the Scripture.
• Sing the song together.

Focus on Life
• Share the *Chapter Story* on guide page 35E.
• Talk about "special powers." Invite children to share their responses to the question on the bottom of page 35.

Home Connection Update
Invite the children to talk about the Chapter 2 family page. *What activity card did you receive? How much time did you plan to complete the activity?*

Catechist Goal

• To introduce the concept that Jesus has power over life and death, and that he will come again at the end of time

Our Faith Response

• To see Jesus in those in need and to identify ways to love God and to care for all people

 **second coming**

last judgment

heaven

Lesson Materials

• Grade 3 CD

• Bible

• copies of Reproducible Master 3

As Catholics...

Miracles of Jesus

After you have presented the lesson, read aloud the text. Tell the children that Jesus worked miracles not only to help others but also to call the people to believe that he was sent by God to be our Savior.

WE BELIEVE

Jesus has power over life and death.

Jesus loved his friends. Among his best friends were Martha, Mary, and their brother Lazarus. This family lived in a town called Bethany.

📖 John 11:1–3, 17–44

One day Lazarus became very sick. His sisters sent a message to Jesus telling him about Lazarus. When Jesus reached Bethany, Lazarus had already died and been buried.

Martha cried to Jesus that, if he had been there, he could have cured Lazarus. Jesus said, "I am the resurrection and the life; whoever believes in me, even if he dies, will live." Martha told Jesus, "I have come to believe that you are the Messiah, the Son of God." (John 11:25, 27)

Mary, Lazarus's other sister, came to greet Jesus. She was also crying. The sisters showed Jesus where Lazarus was buried, and Jesus began to cry.

A huge rock lay across the entrance to the place where Lazarus was buried. Jesus ordered that it be taken away. Then Jesus cried out in a loud voice, "Lazarus, come out!" (John 11:43) With that, Lazarus came out.

Jesus had raised Lazarus from the dead and more people began to believe that Jesus was the Messiah, the Son of God.

✘ Jesus is the Resurrection and the life. If he asked you, "Do you believe this?" what would you say?

36

Lesson Plan

WE BELIEVE ___ minutes

Invite a volunteer to read aloud the statement on page 36.

Read aloud the first paragraph to set the stage for the story of the raising of Lazarus.

📖 **Ask** the children to read the Scripture passage on page 36. If time permits, read the entire passage from the Bible (John 11:1–3, 17–44) , and ask the children to act out the story.

Explain that there is a major difference between Lazarus rising from the dead and Jesus' own Resurrection. Say: *Lazarus returned to his earthly life, living much*

in the same way as he did before his death. Jesus, however, did not return to his earthly life. Instead, he rose to new life with God the Father. That new life is the life we will share with Jesus forever.

✘ **Talk** about Jesus as the Resurrection and the life. Be sure that the children understand that if we believe in him, Jesus brings each of us life with God forever.

Ask a volunteer to read the statement on page 37. Then have volunteers read the paragraphs that follow.

Remind the children that we prepare for and recall Jesus' first coming during the season of Advent and in the celebration of his birth at Christmas.

Jesus will come again.

One day the disciples wanted Jesus to tell them when the world would end. But Jesus said, "Stay awake! For you do not know on which day your Lord will come." (Matthew 24:42)

Jesus did not mean that our bodies should never go to sleep. He meant that we should always be preparing for his coming. We do this through prayer and the things we say and do.

Jesus was born in Bethlehem. That was his first coming. Jesus will come again at the end of time, and we will see him for ourselves. Jesus' coming at the end of time will be a joyful event. It is called his **second coming**.

When Christ comes again, we will be filled with joy and happiness. We will know Jesus because we will see him. Our life with the risen Christ will go on in joy forever.

We can "stay awake" for the second coming of Jesus Christ by living each day the way he taught us. Write one way you will "stay awake" in faith this week.

_____

_____

Key Word

second coming (p. 253)

37

As Catholics...

Jesus' raising Lazarus from the dead was a miracle. Jesus' miracles—walking on water, calming the seas, healing the sick—went beyond human power. Each miracle was a call to believe that Jesus was sent by God to save his people. Jesus' miracles were special signs that helped people to trust and believe in God. They showed people that God's Kingdom was present in their lives.

ACTIVITY BANK

Faith and Media

Newspaper Story

Activity Materials: newspapers, pencils

Help the children to write a newspaper article that tells the story of Lazarus. Begin by reading through some newspaper articles as a group. List characteristics of newspaper articles on the board, such as headline, dateline, and lead. Explain that the lead summarizes the most important information in the story, and is always the first paragraph. Then have the children write their articles, incorporating the elements mentioned above. When the first draft is completed, ask the children to edit on another's work for spelling and grammar errors. Final articles can be word processed and published on the computer.

Explain that we need to "stay awake", be prepared and ready for Christ's second coming. It will be a joyful event at the end of time. This is also a good time to sing or listen to the song "Stay Awake," #4 on the Grade 3 CD.

Ask: *Name some ways you can "stay awake" for the second coming.* (by keeping your eyes open for opportunities to serve God and others in works of mercy; by being aware of your words and actions; and by participating in the sacraments, especially the Eucharist and Reconciliation; by listening to God's word in the Bible and in prayer).

Ask the children to personally choose some ways to "stay awake" in faith this week. Encourage them to share their responses.

Quick Check

✔ *After Lazarus was raised from the dead, what did some people believe about Jesus?* (Some people believe that Jesus was the Son of God, and that this power had been given to him by God the Father.)

✔ *What will happen when Christ comes again?* (We will be filled with joy and happiness. We will see Christ and will be with him forever.)

ACTIVITY BANK

Multiple Intelligences
Verbal-Linguistic

Have the children write narratives about the second coming of Jesus. Ask them to write the stories in first person ("*I . . .*") that tell about the joy and happiness most humans will share when Jesus comes. Encourage them to imagine what the second coming might be like. Have them describe the authors' (i.e. their) feelings ("*I was thrilled! Jesus was so kind to me.*") You may wish to have the children read these aloud to the group, or rewrite them on decorative paper in their best penmanship. Display the finished stories in the room or send them home.

Teaching Tip
Using Praise

Praise is an immensely valuable tool that we may often forget to use. Yet, all children respond to praise. As you teach, offer praise whenever you can to motivate your group and individuals within the group.

When Jesus Christ comes again, he will judge all people.

People can choose to be with God or to turn away from God. These choices will determine whether people can be with God in heaven or not. **Heaven** is life with God forever.

 Matthew 25:31–43

Jesus told his followers that at the end of time he will come in glory with all the angels. He will separate all the people into two groups, one to his right and one to his left.

Then he will tell the people on his right that they are blessed by his Father. He will say, "For I was hungry and you gave me food, I was thirsty and you gave me drink, a stranger and you welcomed me, naked and you clothed me, ill and you cared for me, in prison and you visited me." Then the people on his right will ask when they saw him like this. And he will say, "Amen, I say to you, whatever you did for one of these least brothers of mine, you did for me." (Matthew 25:35–36, 40)

Jesus will then tell those on his left to go away from him forever because they did not care for him when he was hungry, thirsty, a stranger, ill, unclothed, or in prison.

When we choose to love and care for other people, especially those who are poor or weak, we love and care for Jesus. At the last judgment we will be judged by the way we treated others. The **last judgment** is Jesus Christ coming at the end of time to judge all people.

Name one way your parish can care for Jesus by caring for others.

_____

_____

38

Key Words
heaven (p. 251)
last judgment (p. 251)

Lesson Plan

WE BELIEVE (continued)

Invite a volunteer to read the statement on page 38. Read aloud the first paragraph.

Explain that the choices made now affect our friendship with God. Point out that Jesus calls us to make choices that show love for God and others. Jesus wants us to make the choices that lead us to be with him forever in heaven.

Ask volunteers to read the first two Scripture paragraphs. Then read the final paragraphs. Ask: *When we help someone in need, whom are we helping?* (Jesus himself) *What will happen to those who choose not to care for others?* (They will not be with Jesus forever in heaven.)

Work with the children to find ways that their parishes show care for others. Gather at the prayer space. Draw attention to the scale. Explain that a scale can be used to show that the choices people make can be weighed or judged. Their good choices go on one side, while their wrong ones go on the other. (Drop paper clips on each side of the scale to show this.) Each choice makes a difference. Stress that Jesus will *always* weigh or judge our choices not only with justice but also with love and mercy. Christ is a forgiving, loving friend who judges us according to God's way, not solely by human standards.

Jesus teaches us to love others.

Jesus lived his life in perfect love of God the Father and in service to others. He is our example of holiness.

 Mark 12:28–32

One day, a man asked Jesus which commandment was the greatest. Jesus replied, "'You shall love the Lord your God with all your heart, with all your soul, with all your mind, and with all your strength.' The second is this: 'You shall love your neighbor as yourself.' There is no other commandment greater than these." (Mark 12:30–31)

If we love God with all of our heart and we love others as we love ourselves, we are choosing to follow Jesus. Jesus can help us make the right choices. He can give us the courage to treat others as we would like to be treated.

✖ We all have chances to be good neighbors. Act out how you can be a good neighbor in the situation shown on this page.

WE RESPOND

In a group talk about why you think Jesus told us that love is the most important thing of all.

LOVE GOD! LOVE YOUR NEIGHBOR AS YOURSELF

39

ACTIVITY BANK

Community

Interviews

Activity Materials: writing journal or tape recorder; drawing materials

Have the children interview a family member, preferably a parent, adult family friend or neighbor, or older member of their parish. The interview questions might include: *When did he or she come to the aid of someone in need? What were the needy person's circumstances? What did he or she do to help the person?* Have the children write a brief paragraph that explains and describes this information. Then have them illustrate the scene.

Catholic Social Teaching

The Rights and Responsibilities of the Human Person

Brainstorm with the group about things that governments, local or national, can do to help those in need. Decide on one or two things they would like to see accomplished. Then list some ways that they can help to make these things happen.

Ask a volunteer to read the statement and first paragraph on page 39.

📖 **Choose** a volunteer to read aloud Jesus' words from the Gospel of Mark. Explain that Jesus' answer was based on God's commands written in the Old Testament. Jesus was calling the people to live by the Ten Commandments. Jesus' Great Commandment sums up the commandments.

✖ **Have** children act out ways to be a good neighbor and follow Jesus' commandment in the situation on the page.

WE RESPOND ___ minutes

Connect to Life Ask a volunteer to read aloud the *We Respond* sentence. Encourage the children to discuss why they believe that "love is the most important thing of all."

Distribute copies of Reproducible Master 3 on guide page 35C. Have the children brainstorm a list of good deeds they can do.

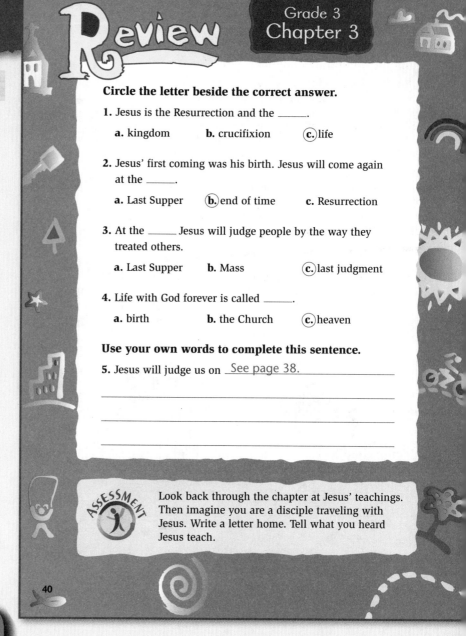

Review

CHAPTER TEST

Chapter 3 Test is provided in the Grade 3 Assessment Book.

Sadlier
We Believe
Assessment Book
Reproducible Masters   Grade 3

Circle the letter beside the correct answer.

1. Jesus is the Resurrection and the _____.
   a. kingdom   b. crucifixion   (c.) life

2. Jesus' first coming was his birth. Jesus will come again at the _____.
   a. Last Supper   (b.) end of time   c. Resurrection

3. At the _____ Jesus will judge people by the way they treated others.
   a. Last Supper   b. Mass   (c.) last judgment

4. Life with God forever is called _____.
   a. birth   b. the Church   (c.) heaven

Use your own words to complete this sentence.

5. Jesus will judge us on _See page 38._
   _____
   _____
   _____

ASSESSMENT

Look back through the chapter at Jesus' teachings. Then imagine you are a disciple traveling with Jesus. Write a letter home. Tell what you heard Jesus teach.

40

Lesson Plan

Review   ___ minutes

Chapter Review Read the first four questions aloud, including the answer choices. Have the children read question 5. Remind them that they may look back in the chapter pages to find information with which to complete the sentence. Ask them to share their answers.

Assessment Activity Help the children to understand that we find Jesus' teachings in the Scriptures. Help them to find the Scripture references in the chapter and to write down the teachings of Jesus. With this list, they can imagine themselves as disciples and write their "letters home."

We Respond in Faith   ___ minutes

Reflect & Pray Allow a moment of silence for them to reflect on the meaning of the prayer words. Ask the children to finish the prayer. Say: *The prayer can be completed in a variety of ways. Think of times you need help. Do you need help in being kind to others? Do you need help to remember that God loves you?*

🔑 **Key Words** Review the meanings of the *Key Words*. Invite the children to make up riddles about them.

We Respond in Faith

Reflect & Pray

Think about the choices you make. How do they help you to follow Jesus?

Complete this prayer.

Jesus, help me

_____

_____

_____

Key Words

second coming (p. 253)
heaven (p. 251)
last judgment (p. 251)

Remember

- Jesus has power over life and death.
- Jesus will come again.
- When Jesus Christ comes again, he will judge all people.
- Jesus teaches us to love others.

OUR CATHOLIC LIFE

Care for All People

Catholics in every country reach out to those in need because we see all people as created and loved by God. The Catholic Church defends the rights of the poor and needy, the sick and the dying. We are reminded in many of the writings of Pope John Paul II to do what we can to feed the hungry, to provide homes for the homeless, and to work for peace and justice.

HOME CONNECTION

Sharing Faith with My Family

Make sure to send home the family page (text page 42).

Encourage the children to ask family members to help them cut out and glue the picture of Mary, Martha, and Lazarus.

PUPIL PAGE 42

For additional information and activities, encourage families to visit Sadlier's

www.WeBelieve.web.com

Remember Have the children write the doctrinal statements on a sheet of paper with things that they have learned underneath each of the doctrinal statements. Ask them to compare their answers with a partner.

Our Catholic Life Read aloud "Care for All People." Have the children speak about people that they know who have offered help to people in need. You may wish to read the following quote from Pope John Paul II in his speech to Catholic relief organizations in 1995: "With courage and compassion, Christians must be ever attentive to the cry of the poor, serving the Lord who is present in their suffering."

Plan Ahead for Chapter 4

Prayer Space: red tablecloth, picture of a dove, bowl of holy water

Lesson Materials: copies of Reproducible Master 4

Chapter 4 The Church Begins

Overview

In Chapter 3 the children learned about Jesus' second coming. In this chapter the children will learn about the Holy Spirit coming at Pentecost and about the growth of the early Church.

Doctrinal Content	For Adult Reading and Reflection *Catechism of the Catholic Church*
The children will learn:	Paragraph
• Jesus promises to send the Holy Spirit.	787
• The Holy Spirit comes to the disciples.	638
• The Church begins on Pentecost.	729
• The early Church grows.	737

Key Words

mission (p. 45)
Ascension (p. 45)
Pentecost (p. 45)
Church (p. 46)
Christians (p. 46)

Catechist Background

How have you faced the absence of a loved one? How did your life change? How did you cope?

Throughout his farewell discourse at the Last Supper, Jesus sensed that his apostles would be at a loss without him. His arrest and crucifixion would shatter their confidence in him and in themselves. That is why Jesus told them, "I have much more to tell you, but you cannot bear it now. But when he comes, the Spirit of truth, he will guide you to all truth" (John 16:12–13).

At Pentecost the disciples experienced the transforming power of the Holy Spirit. They were strengthened to proclaim the good news of Jesus. The Church was born and grew as more and more people believed in Jesus. Those baptized in his name and confirmed by the Spirit were eventually called Christians.

The Holy Spirit sets in motion the mission of the Church to proclaim Christ by word and action to all people. Truly, "we live in the Church at a privileged moment of the Spirit" (*On Evangelization in the Modern World,* 75). Through the Spirit, the Church begun on Pentecost is alive and well in the Church of today.

How does the Holy Spirit help you to share your faith?

Lesson Planning Guide

Lesson Steps	Presentation	Materials

1 WE GATHER

page 43 ✝ **Prayer** ☀ **Focus on Life**	• Have the children take the various parts and pray together. • Talk about ways to overcome fears, and about people who help us.	For the prayer space: red table-cloth, picture of dove, bowl of holy water

2 WE BELIEVE

page 44 *Jesus promises to send the Holy Spirit.* 📖 *Matthew 28:16–20*	• Read and discuss the text about Jesus' Ascension and the apostles' mission. 🏃 Describe disciples' feelings as they waited for the Holy Spirit to come.	
page 45 *The Holy Spirit comes to the disciples.* 📖 *Acts of the Apostles 2:1–41*	• Read and discuss the text and Scripture about coming of the Holy Spirit at Pentecost. 🏃 Write description of how the disciples changed when the Holy Spirit came to them	• copies of Reproducible Master 4 • paper and colored pencils
page 46 *The Church begins on Pentecost.*	• Read and discuss the text about the early Church. 🏃 Complete the activity about giving a speech about following Jesus.	
page 47 *The early Church grows.* 📖 *Acts of the Apostles 9:3–5*	• Read and discuss the text about the growth of the early Church and Paul's conversion. • Read and discuss evangelization in *As Catholics*.	

3 WE RESPOND

page 47	• Discuss the question about the ways to show people we are followers of Jesus Christ.	
page 48 **Review**	• Complete questions 1–5 🏃 Work on *Assessment Activity*.	• Chapter 4 Test in Assessment Book, pp. 9–10 • Chapter 4 Test in Test Generator • Review & Resource Book, pp.13–15
page 49 **We Respond in Faith**	• Complete the *Reflect & Pray* activity. • Review the *Remember* and *Key Words*. • Read and discuss *Our Catholic Life* about Good News for All. • Discuss **Sharing Faith with My Family**.	• Family Book, pp.14–16

For additional ideas, activities, and opportunities: Visit Sadlier's **www.WeBelieveweb.com**

In the frame, draw a picture of something Jesus said or did. Below write about the good news of Jesus to someone you care about. Cut out, fold, paste together and mail the postcard with a postcard stamp.

———— Fold ————

Dear _____ ,

I'm writing to you to tell you the good news of Jesus!

_____

_____

To:

_____

_____

_____

Connections

To Catholic Social Teaching

Option for the Poor and Vulnerable
The first Christians spread the good news of Jesus in many ways. They spoke of Jesus, and they also tended to people who were sick and helped people who were needy. Serving people in need is an important dimension of Catholic social teaching, and an important part of what it means to be a Christian. Like Jesus, Christians do the works of love, justice, and peace. As children read about the disciples, ask: *How can you follow the example set by the early Christians?*

To Stewardship

As members of the Body of Christ, the Church, the children share in the responsibility to be good stewards of their time, talents, and treasure. Sharing their treasure may seem difficult for children at this age. Ask: *What are your treasures?* (Possible answers may include toys, CD's, videos, books.) Help the children recognize that if they share their treasure with others, they are doing the work of Jesus and the Church.

FAITH and MEDIA

▶ Remind the children that the Church today uses the most up-to-date media to share the good news of Jesus. The first disciples had to travel far and wide to deliver the good news in person, or they had to hand write letters to be delivered by messengers who traveled long distances on foot, on horseback, or on ships.

▶ Also remind them that when acting out the Scripture stories the choices they make in their preparation and acting of the story—as scenario writers, directors, and actors—will affect the way viewers understand the story.

Meeting Individual Needs

Children with Attention Deficit Disorder (ADD)

Children who have Attention Deficit Disorder frequently have a difficult time staying on task and organized. It is often helpful to provide them with succinct lists of things to accomplish. This can be a list of things to be done during the lesson, such as *ask one question, answer one question, pay attention to each speaker*, and so on. Be sure to affirm their efforts to follow their lists.

ADDITIONAL RESOURCES

Videos *Pentecost Passage,* Twenty-Third Publications, 1991. From *Following Jesus through the Church Year.* Krispin learns the story of Pentecost and is at Stephen's martyrdom. (10 minutes)

Christian Corner, Twenty-Third Publications, 1991. From *Following Jesus through the Church Year,* Krispin is present as St. Paul tells the story of his conversion. (10 minutes)

To find more ideas for books, videos, and other learning material, visit Sadlier's

www.WeBelieve.web.com

Focus on Life

Chapter Story

It was mid-August and Carla and her mother were shopping for new clothes for Carla for school. "Do you like *these* shoes, Carla?" her mother asked as she held up a pair of penny loafers.

"Not really, Mom," she replied.

Carla shrugged her shoulders and put a sad look on her face. Her mom knew something was wrong. "What is it, Carla? You normally love to pick out new clothes for school. Let's talk," her mom said. They walked to a nearby food stand and bought lunch.

After taking a few bites of her hot dog, Carla began to tell her mom what was bothering her. "I'm nervous about going to the new school, Mom," she said. "My friends aren't going there and I'm not going to know anybody—not even the teachers or the principal."

Carla's mom had suspected that Carla was worried about moving to the new school, but she knew things about Carla that could help her. "Carla, remember when you started kindergarten, how scared you were? And what happened after just a few weeks? And when you were in second grade, you were sad that you were in Mrs. Smith's class and all your friends were in Ms. Gibson's? What happened then?"

"I made lots of new friends," Carla replied.

"Honey, you have *always* made new friends! You have *always* gotten along with others. You have done it before, and you can do it again," her mom said.

"You're right, Mom. I *can* do it! No matter what, I can make friends." She quickly felt better. Moving to a new school wasn't so scary now. "Hey, Mom, let's look at those shoes again. I think I saw a pair I liked."

▶ *How can Carla make friends in her new school?*

The Church Begins

WE GATHER

✝ **Mary:** Come, my children, let us pray.
There will come to us this day
The Helper who will show the way.

All: Let us wait and let us pray.

Peter: Listen, listen, do you hear
A wind that is blowing strong and clear?

Andrew: A wind that seems to stir in me
No longer fear, but bravery.

James: Look, look, above each the same,
A burning fire, a glowing flame.

John: And we are filled with great desire
To spread his word like a mighty fire.

All: Spirit of Jesus, fill us all
With life and love to heed your call.
Make us brave, strong, and true.
Disciples all, we will follow you.

Alleluia. Amen.

☀ Think back to a time
when you were afraid of
something. Who or
what gave you the
courage to overcome
your fear?

PREPARING TO PRAY

The children will pray with Mary and the apostles at the coming of the Holy Spirit at Pentecost. They will ask the Holy Spirit to make them brave disciples, too.

• Invite volunteers to place the selected items on the table as part of the gathering prayer.

• Choose five children to play the parts of Mary, Peter, Andrew, James, and John. Invite the other children to join in playing the parts of the other disciples and to read the sections marked "All."

The Prayer Space

• Place a red tablecloth over the prayer table, since red is the liturgical symbol of Pentecost. Include on the table a picture or some other depiction of a dove to represent the Holy Spirit. Place a bowl of holy water on the table to represent Baptism into the Church.

📖 **This Week's Liturgy**
Visit **www.webelieveweb.com** for this week's liturgical readings and other seasonal material.

Lesson Plan

WE GATHER ___ minutes

✝ Pray

• Invite the children to gather together in the prayer space and come forward to bless themselves with holy water.

• Encourage the children to imagine that they are the early disciples of Jesus gathered together after the Ascension of Jesus.

• Have the children speak their parts, and encourage them to use gestures to accompany their lines.

☀ Focus on Life

• Have the children think about overcoming a fear. Encourage them to share their answers to the question.

• Share the *Chapter Story* on guide page 43E.

Home Connection Update

Invite the children to talk about the Chapter 3 family page. *Did you and your family enjoy doing the Church story activity together?*

Catechist Goal

• To highlight that Jesus promised to send the Holy Spirit and that this promise was fulfilled at Pentecost, the day the Church began.

Our Faith Response

• To name the ways the Holy Spirit helps us to be disciples of Jesus today

Key Words   mission   Ascension
                 Pentecost   Church
                 Christians

Lesson Materials

• copies of Reproducible Master 4

Teaching Tip

Naming Feelings

Children may lack the vocabulary to name what they are feeling. To help them name their feelings provide words to describe feelings such as angry, anxious, proud, brave, disappointed, or hurt. Naming our feelings can be a first step toward dealing with them and recognizing those feelings in others.

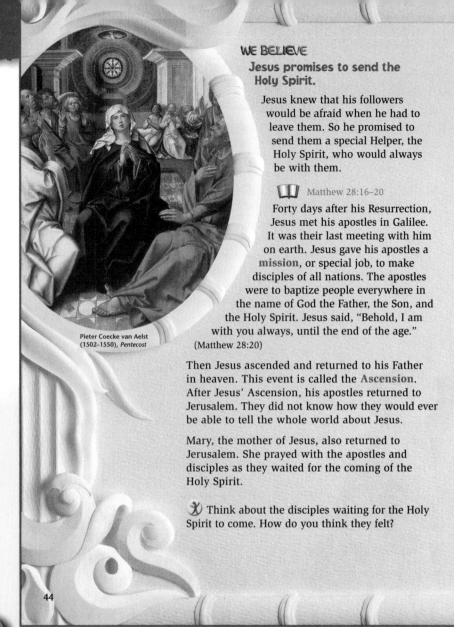

Pieter Coecke van Aelst
(1502–1550), *Pentecost*

WE BELIEVE

Jesus promises to send the Holy Spirit.

Jesus knew that his followers would be afraid when he had to leave them. So he promised to send them a special Helper, the Holy Spirit, who would always be with them.

📖 Matthew 28:16–20

Forty days after his Resurrection, Jesus met his apostles in Galilee. It was their last meeting with him on earth. Jesus gave his apostles a **mission**, or special job, to make disciples of all nations. The apostles were to baptize people everywhere in the name of God the Father, the Son, and the Holy Spirit. Jesus said, "Behold, I am with you always, until the end of the age." (Matthew 28:20)

Then Jesus ascended and returned to his Father in heaven. This event is called the **Ascension**. After Jesus' Ascension, his apostles returned to Jerusalem. They did not know how they would ever be able to tell the whole world about Jesus.

Mary, the mother of Jesus, also returned to Jerusalem. She prayed with the apostles and disciples as they waited for the coming of the Holy Spirit.

✖ Think about the disciples waiting for the Holy Spirit to come. How do you think they felt?

44

Lesson Plan

WE BELIEVE   ___ minutes

Ask a volunteer to read the statement and the first paragraph.

📖 **Read** the Scripture story of the Ascension.

Emphasize the following points:

• Jesus knew that his followers would be afraid without him so he promised to send the Holy Spirit.

• Jesus gave his apostles a mission to make all nations disciples.

• In his Ascension, Jesus returned to his Father. The disciples and Mary waited in Jerusalem for the coming of the Holy Spirit.

✖ **Read** aloud the statement on page 56 again. Ask the children to think about how the disciples waiting for the Holy Spirit might have felt. Encourage the children to share their answers and discuss as a group.

Ask a volunteer to read the statement on page 45. Remind the children that Jesus had promised to send the Holy Spirit.

📖 **Invite** volunteers to read aloud the Scripture story in the following paragraphs.

The Holy Spirit comes to the disciples.

Acts of the Apostles 2:1–41

Inside a room where they had gathered, the disciples heard a noise that sounded like a great wind. They saw what seemed to be flames of fire that spread out and touched each one of them. Suddenly, the disciples were filled with the Holy Spirit. They were changed in a wonderful way.

A large crowd was outside. The disciples came out of the room and began to speak about Jesus with great courage. Then Peter, the leader of all of the disciples, spoke to the people. He told them that God had raised Jesus from the dead. Peter told them that this Jesus who had been crucified and rose is truly the Lord, Jesus Christ.

When Peter spoke to the crowd, the people understood him in their different languages. They asked him what they should do. Peter replied, "Repent and be baptized, every one of you, in the name of Jesus Christ for the forgiveness of your sins; and you will receive the gift of the holy Spirit." (Acts of the Apostles 2:38) Many people accepted this message, and about three thousand people were baptized that day. The day on which the Holy Spirit came to the disciples is called **Pentecost**. The Holy Spirit comes to us, too. The Holy Spirit helps us to be brave followers of Jesus.

In the flame, write words that describe how the disciples were changed when the Holy Spirit came to them.

Key Words

mission (p. 252)
Ascension (p. 250)
Pentecost (p. 252)

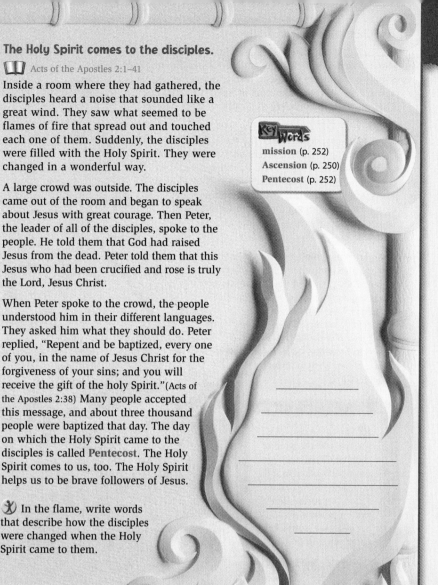

45

ACTIVITY BANK

ACTIVITY BANK

Multicultural Connections
Languages

Ask the children who speak languages besides English to say a message of faith in that language. Messages may include the following: *Jesus is risen*, *We believe*, and *Come, Spirit, come.*

Curriculum Connections
Language Arts
(Public Speaking)

The Holy Spirit gave the apostles the courage to speak about Jesus. Invite the children. Take a moment now to ask the Holy Spirit to help you write a paragraph about Jesus for the first Pentecost. What would you like to say? Give them time to write, and allow them to ask you or their classmates for help. Have them practice reading aloud their paragraphs to one another. Then ask volunteers to take turns reading their paragraphs to the group.

Stress that the Holy Spirit filled the disciples with strength and courage and they began to spread the good news of Jesus. The disciples went out to speak about Jesus to many people who heard their message in their own language and understood the good news.

Have the children complete the activity on page 45. Tell them that the disciples were made more courageous and stronger by the power and presence of the Holy Spirit. The disciples used this new strength to spread the good news of Jesus and to help others believe in him. Explain that we should try to do the same.

Quick Check

✔ *What was the mission that Jesus gave to his disciples?* (To make disciples of all the nations and to baptize people everywhere in the name of the Father, the Son, and the Holy Spirit.)

✔ *What happened to the disciples after they received the Holy Spirit?* (They were changed; they had the courage to speak about Jesus, and people heard and understood the disciples in their own languages.)

The Church begins on Pentecost.

On Pentecost, the disciples shared their good news about Jesus with the people gathered around them. Soon, many people were baptized and received the Holy Spirit. This was the beginning of Jesus' Church. The **Church** is the community of people who are baptized and follow Jesus Christ.

The new believers listened to the teaching of the apostles. They came together for prayer and for "the breaking of the bread" as Jesus and the apostles did at the Last Supper. (Acts of the Apostles 2:42) They shared everything they owned with one another. They cared for those among them who were poor or in need. They treated everyone with love and respect.

Soon after the coming of the Holy Spirit, the apostles and other disciples began to travel. They preached the good news of Jesus to people in other cities and countries. Communities of new believers grew everywhere. Those people who were baptized began to be called **Christians**, because they were followers of Jesus Christ.

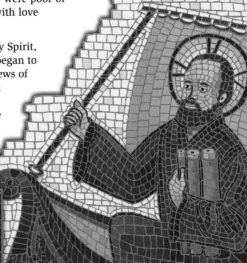

Key Words

Church (p. 250)
Christians (p. 250)

Imagine that you are back in the time of the first Christians. You have been asked to talk to a large crowd about following Jesus. Work with a partner on a speech that would tell them what to do.

46

As Catholics...

Evangelization (Telling the Good News)

Ask the children whether anyone has ever asked them about their Catholic faith. Has anyone ever asked them about Jesus, or what Mass is like? If someone did, what would they say? Stress that when they talk about their Catholic faith, they are sharing the good news!

Lesson Plan

WE BELIEVE (continued)

Invite a volunteer to read the statement.

Ask volunteers to read aloud the paragraphs. Emphasize the following points:

• The Church is the community of people who are baptized and follow Jesus.

• The early believers came together to listen to the teaching of the apostles, to pray, and to break bread. They shared everything.

• After receiving the Holy Spirit, the disciples began to spread the good news of Jesus. They showed care and concern for the people they met, especially those most in need.

Have the children act out a scene from the early days of the Church. Form two groups. One group will be the disciples; the other will be a crowd of townspeople. Have the groups make their own scenarios and use their own words to dramatize the preaching of the good news, baptizing of new believers, sharing of food, and so on.

Invite a volunteer to read the statement on page 47.

Point out that the Holy Spirit gave the disciples courage to preach the good news. Because of their preaching, many people came to believe and be baptized. Explain to the children that many of the people and their religious leaders did not approve of this new community of believers. Stress that the enemies of the Church tried to stop the disciples.

The early Church grows.

As the Church grew, people in power began to worry that too many people were becoming Christians. At that time the disciple Stephen preached about Jesus. Because of Stephen, many people became Christians. The enemies of the Church were very angry, and they had Stephen put to death.

 Acts of the Apostles 9:3–5

Saul of Tarsus was one of the men determined to stop those who believed in Jesus. One day Saul was traveling along a road and a bright light from the sky suddenly flashed around him. He fell to the ground and heard a voice saying to him, "Saul, Saul, why are you persecuting me?" Saul wanted to know who was speaking to him. Then he heard, "I am Jesus, whom you are persecuting." (Acts of the Apostles 9:4, 5)

Saul's life changed forever. Three days later he was baptized. Saul, also known as Paul, became one of the greatest followers of Jesus Christ in history.

Paul made many trips to build up Christian communities throughout the world. His preaching and example encouraged many people to believe in Christ. His work and the work of many others helped the Church to grow. People of all races, languages, and nationalities came to believe in Jesus Christ.

As Catholics...

The apostles and the first disciples told the good news of Jesus Christ to everyone. This is called *evangelization*. We are called to go out and evangelize, too. Our pope and bishops want each of us to be a part of the "new evangelization." This means that the good news of Jesus makes as much of a difference today as it did in the time of the first disciples.

WE RESPOND

We are too young to go all over the world telling people about Jesus Christ. But we can show the people in our neighborhood and parish family that we are followers of Jesus Christ. How can we do this?

_____

_____

_____

47

ACTIVITY BANK

Parish
Sharing Opportunities

Ask the children: *What does the local parish do for those who are needy? How can children and their families contribute to these activities?* Then, ask them to think of other areas of need that are not being met. What can they do to care for this need? Record the children's responses.

Catholic Social Teaching
Call to Family, Community and Participation
Activity Materials: art supplies for brochure

Encourage the children to support missionaries. Contact the local Catholic Charities office in your diocese. Ask about ways your group can help people who are needy. Ask them to provide you with a list of items that are needed. Have your group make fliers or brochures to post so that others can be aware of ways to help.

Ask volunteers to read aloud the text and Scripture story which includes the story of Paul.

WE RESPOND ___ minutes

Connect to Life Invite the children to think about telling others about Jesus Christ.

Have children answer the *We Resond* question. Encourage volunteers to share their answers. Explain that we can help one another as we work to become good followers of Jesus.

Distribute copies of Reproducible Master 4 on guide page 43C. Ask the children to write a postcard that tells the good news of Jesus and send it to someone they love.

CHAPTER TEST

Chapter 4 Test is provided in the
Grade 3 Assessment Book.

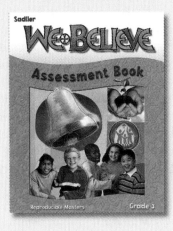

Circle the letter beside the correct answer.

1. Jesus promised to send the _____.
   - (a.) Holy Spirit
   - b. Messiah
   - c. Father

2. Jesus told the apostles to go and _____.
   - a. hide
   - (b.) baptize
   - c. be afraid

3. The Holy Spirit came upon the disciples on _____.
   - a. the Ascension
   - b. Easter
   - (c.) Pentecost

4. All those who are baptized and follow Christ are called _____.
   - a. teachers
   - b. enemies
   - (c.) Christians

Use your own words to complete the sentence.

5. The Holy Spirit is always __See page 44.__

_____

_____

_____

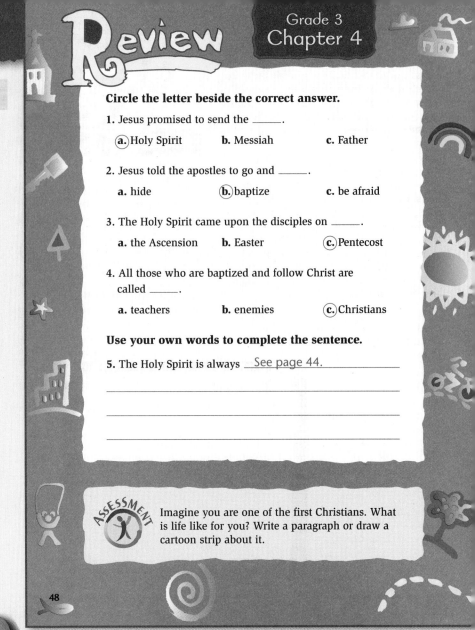

ASSESSMENT Imagine you are one of the first Christians. What is life like for you? Write a paragraph or draw a cartoon strip about it.

48

Lesson Plan

 ___ minutes

Chapter Review Tell the children that they are now going to check their understanding of what they have learned. Then have the children complete questions 1–4. Clear up any misconceptions. Have the children to read and answer question 5.

Assessment Activity Encourage the children to use their imagination and creativity to explain what life was like for the first Christians. Emphasize that the purpose of the activity is to show their understanding of what was learned in the chapter. The paragraph or comic strip must be accurate, based on what was read and learned in the chapter.

 ___ minutes

Reflect & Pray Read the introduction to the reflective activity aloud. Explain what they can do to complete the prayer. Allow time for the children to write their prayer. Encourage each to go to the prayer space, to use the holy water to sign themselves with the sign of the cross, and to say their prayer.

Key Words Write the *Key Words* from this chapter on the board. Ask the children to write a sentence using each of the words. Invite them to draw a picture that helps explain the meaning of each word.

Reflect & Pray

We can carry out Jesus' work in the world by sharing the good news, praying, and helping others.

Think about what you can do this week at home and in school to continue Jesus' work.

Jesus, help me to carry on your work in the world. Help me to

_____

_____

Key Words

mission (p. 252)
Ascension (p. 250)
Pentecost (p. 252)
Church (p. 250)
Christians (p. 250)

Remember

- Jesus promises to send the Holy Spirit.
- The Holy Spirit comes to the disciples.
- The Church begins on Pentecost.
- The early Church grows.

OUR CATHOLIC LIFE

Good News for All

Today, the Church proclaims the good news of Jesus everywhere on earth and in every language. For example, if we travel to South America, we would hear Jesus' message in Spanish or Portuguese. In Africa, we might hear it in Swahili. Here in our own country, Mass and the other sacraments are celebrated in Mandarin, German, Polish, Spanish, and many other languages, as well as English. No matter the language, the message of Jesus' love will always be the same.

HOME CONNECTION

Sharing Faith with My Family

Make sure to send home the family page (text page 50).

Encourage the children to design a stained-glass window with their family members.

PUPIL PAGE 50

For additional information and activities, encourage families to visit Sadlier's

www.WeBelieveweb.com

Remember Have the children silently read the four doctrinal statements. Ask them to write as many things as they can remember about the doctrinal statements in a notebook. Have the children share their responses. Refer to the water and the red tablecloth on the prayer table. Ask volunteers to recall what these objects represent.

Our Catholic Life Read aloud the text. Ask the children to think of times that they have gone to church when they were away from their home parish. What was the same? What was different? Discuss these points.

Plan Ahead for Chapter 5

Prayer Space: early Christian symbol of a fish, stones or rocks, a newspaper

Lesson Materials: copies of Reproducible Master 5, paper strips, stapler and glue

We Learn About the Early Church

Overview

In Chapter 4 the children learned about the beginning of the Church. In this chapter they will learn about the apostles who led the Church and about those who remained true followers of Jesus despite the risk of losing their lives.

Doctrinal Content	For Adult Reading and Reflection *Catechism of the Catholic Church*
The children will learn:	Paragraph
• The apostles led the Church.	551
• The disciples of Jesus share the good news.	763–765
• The followers of Jesus stood up for their faith.	769
• Many of our ancestors in faith are examples of holiness.	2030

Key Words

Acts of the Apostles (p. 53)

gospel (p. 53)

martyrs (p. 54)

Catechist Background

What is your favorite memory of the Church?

What has kept the Church moving forward is its recalling that we are a pilgrim Church. During this journey we realize that "The Church is in history, but at the same time she transcends it. It is only 'with the eyes of faith' that one can see her in her visible reality and at the same time in her spiritual reality as bearer of divine life" (CCC 770).

After the apostles came bursting out of the upper room on Pentecost, it wasn't long before opposition to the followers of the crucified Jesus of Nazareth intensified. Some Jewish leaders banned the use of his name. Greeks and Romans declared the Christians to be atheists because they would not honor the gods who protected their cities. Although the Church grew at a brisk pace, the early Christians paid a high price for their faith. From Stephen's stoning in Jerusalem to the martyrs of the Roman coliseum, those who professed belief in Jesus as Lord were considered traitors.

Pray for the grace to stand up for your faith.

Lesson Planning Guide

Lesson Steps	Presentation	Materials

1 WE GATHER

page 51 **Prayer** **Focus on Life**	• Pray the Jesus prayer. • Talk about what leaders do. Ask children if they would like to be leaders. Why or Why not?	For the prayer space: early Christian symbol of a fish; stones or rocks; a newspaper

2 WE BELIEVE

page 52 *The apostles led the Church.*	• Read and discuss the text about the apostles and the early Christians. 🏃 Write reasons why the apostles were good leaders	
page 53 *The disciples of Jesus share the good news.*	• Read and discuss the text about the gospel, the good news of Jesus Christ, Son of God and Savior. 🏃 Make a gospel chain with a partner.	• strips of construction paper • stapler and glue
pages 54–55 *The followers of Jesus stood up for their faith.* *Many of our ancestors in faith are examples of holiness.*	• Read and discuss the text about the Romans' persecution of Christians. 🏃 Complete the activity. • Read about an early Christian symbol in *As Catholics*.	• copies of Reproducible Master 5
	• Read and discuss the text about our ancestors in faith. • Discuss children's favorite saints.	

3 WE RESPOND

page 55	🏃 Circle the words in the puzzle to complete the sentences in the activity.	
page 56 **Review**	• Complete questions 1–5. 🏃 Work on the *Assessment Activity*.	• Chapter 5 Test in Grade 3 Assessment Book, pp.11–12 • Chapter 5 Test in Test Generator • Review & Resource Book, pp.16–18
page 57 **We Respond in Faith**	🏃 Complete the *Reflect & Pray* activity. • Review the *Remember* and *Key Words*. • Read and discuss *Our Catholic Life*. • Discuss **Sharing Faith with My Family**.	• Family Book, pp.17–19

For additional ideas, activities, and opportunities: Visit Sadlier's **www.WeBelieveweb.com**

Name _____

The fish symbol was used by the early Christians. The letters ICHTHUS (fish) also stood for the name and good news of Jesus Christ.

Color the fish and the letters. Cut it out and put a string or ribbon through the hole. Hang this sign of Jesus in a special place.

ICHTHUS

Jesus Christ, Son of God, Savior

Connections

To Parish

Just as the early Church could not have been so successful without the apostles and disciples, so, too, today's Church relies upon the hard work and dedication of volunteers, parishioners, and Church leaders. Consider having your children make a list of all the people in the parish who contribute to the life of the parish. Decide on a way to thank them for their service.

To Saints

As the children read about saints and martyrs, stress the heroic efforts these men and women made to spread the good news of Jesus. Some even died for the faith. You might want to mention some saints who served in our own country, for example, Saint Isaac Jogues, Blessed Kateri Tekakwitha, Saint Elizabeth Seton, and Saint Katharine Drexel.

FAITH and MEDIA

▶ Explain to the children that murals and mosaics that tell a story are forms of media. Such murals have been placed in churches over the centuries not only as decoration, but also as ways to teach people the story of our salvation and the lives of the saints. You might also bring in art books or visit the Internet with the children to show them some examples, such as Giotto's murals of the life of Christ in the Arena Chapel in Padua, or the murals of the life of Saint Peter by the artists Masaccio, Masolino, and Filippino Lippi in the Brancacci Chapel in Florence.

Meeting Individual Needs

Children Using Wheelchairs

In role-playing exercises or dramatizations, make sure children who use wheelchairs can fully participate. Look for ways to include these children in all activities. Carefully plan so that any classroom experience is one in which the entire class can participate.

ADDITIONAL RESOURCES

Book *Saints of the Americas,* Anne Joan Flanagan, FSP, Pauline Books and Media, 2000. This coloring book tells the stories of various saints who lived in the Americas.

Video *Saints for Kids, Vol. 2, St. Stephen,* Pauline Books and Media, 1998. This animated story tells of how Stephen was the first saint to give his life for Jesus. (5 minutes of 14-minute tape)

To find more ideas for books, videos, and other learning material, visit Sadlier's

www.WeBelieveweb.com

Focus on Life

Chapter Story

There once was a young man who was loyal and brave. His name was Tarcisius. He lived a few hundred years after Christ. In those days, the Christians had to hide their faith because they faced terrible persecution. Anyone known to be a Christian was put to death, simply for being a member of the Church.

Young Tarcisius had proven himself trustworthy so the leaders of the Church gave him an important mission. He was to secretly carry the Blessed Sacrament—Holy Communion—to the Christians who were in hiding or in prison. The priests could not do so because they were easily recognized. But the Christian children like Tarcisius were not noticed as easily.

One day as Tarcisius was carrying the sacrament of the Eucharist, he was stopped by a group of non-believers or pagans. They asked him what it was he was carrying. Tarcisius would not show what he had with him because he did not want the people to do anything terrible to the Blessed Sacrament. Again and again, the people demanded that Tarcisius give in to them. But Tarcisius was strong in his faith and would not give in. The nonbelievers became so angry that they hit him over and over again. They used stones and sticks until he fell and died.

When the people who had killed Tarcisius turned his body over they searched his clothes to find what he had been hiding. They found nothing. Miraculously, there was no trace of the Blessed Sacrament on his hands or in his clothing. The Blessed Sacrament did not fall into the hands of evildoers. This is an old story that we remember to this day about brave and faithful Saint Tarcisius.

Today, Saint Tarcisius is the patron saint of altar servers. His feast day is August 15.

▶ *What do you most admire about Saint Tarcisius?*

We Learn About the Early Church

(5)

WE GATHER

✝ **Leader:** Let us gather in a prayer circle. Sit in a comfortable position.

Become still . . . still . . . still.

Close your eyes. Now, as you breathe out, whisper the name

Jesus

Jesus

Jesus.

Have you ever wanted to be a leader of a group or team? What does a leader do?

51

The children will pray in a meditative way, using the name of Jesus.

• Choose volunteers to place the items in the prayer space at the appointed time.

The Prayer Space

• Gather the following items: an image or likeness of a fish to represent the sign of the early Christians; stones or rocks to represent the strength of the Church; and a newspaper to represent the spreading of the good news of Jesus.

 This Week's Liturgy

Visit **www.webelieveweb.com** for this week's liturgical readings and other seasonal material.

Lesson Plan

WE GATHER

_____ minutes

✝ Pray

• Invite the children to the prayer space by saying, *We gather in prayer.* Give the children a few moments to get settled into their prayer circle.

• Encourage the children to relax and sit comfortably. Once they have settled into a quiet state, invite them to whisper the name *Jesus* reverently three times. Provide an additional moment of silence after this.

• Remind the children that Jesus asked us to use his name in prayer. He is with us when we honor his name. (see Matthew 18:20) We can say his name quietly at prayer, at any time!

Focus on Life

• Have the children share responses to the questions. Tell the children that in this lesson they will learn that the apostles were the first leaders of the Church.

Home Connection Update

Invite the children to talk about the Chapter 4 family page. *Did the family enjoy doing the stained-glass activity, or any of the other activities?*

Catechist Goal

• To explain how the apostles led the early Church and how followers of Jesus stood up for their faith

Our Faith Response

• To follow the saints as models of holiness and disciples who stood up for their faith

Key Words Acts of the Apostles

gospel   martyrs

Lesson Materials

• copies of Reproducible Master 5

• strips of construction paper

• tape

Teaching Tip

Focus on the Good News

This chapter emphasizes the good news of our faith. Often our society encourages negativity. To help the children be witnesses to the good news, model a positive attitude toward them and the Church. Highlight the good news of our faith and the ways in which the children do good in their lives.

WE BELIEVE
The apostles led the Church.

The apostles lived with Jesus for three years. They knew how kind and caring he was. They ate and drank with him. They heard his words every day. They saw him heal the sick and raise the dead.

Wherever they went, the apostles began to tell everyone about Jesus Christ. They baptized all those who believed in Jesus. In each place that they visited, the apostles gathered these new Christians together. This is how they formed the Church. The apostles had to move on to continue the work of Jesus so they chose leaders in each place.

There is a wonderful book in the New Testament that tells the story of the work of the apostles in the early Church. It is called the **Acts of the Apostles**. In that book, we read that the early Christians listened to the teachings of the apostles and looked after one another "according to each one's need." (Acts of the Apostles 2:45) The Church grew because Christians loved and served one another.

Name one way the apostles were good leaders of the Church.

_____

_____

PHILIPPI

CORINTH

52

Lesson Plan

WE BELIEVE ___ minutes

Ask a volunteer to read the statement on page 52.

Invite volunteers to read the paragraphs that follow.

Emphasize the following points:

• The apostles were with Jesus from the beginning of his public ministry.

• The apostles chose Church leaders in each place they preached the good news.

Describe the apostles and the early Christians. Ask: *What were some of the things the apostles did in the early Church?* (The apostles told everyone about Jesus, baptized, and gathered Christians together.) *Why did the Church grow?* (The Church grew because Christians loved and served one another.)

Ask the children to complete the activity. Then ask volunteers to share their answers with the group.

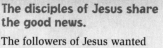

The disciples of Jesus share the good news.

The followers of Jesus wanted everyone they met to know the good news of Jesus Christ:

- Jesus is the Son of God. He came into the world to become one of us and show us, in person, the love of God.

- Jesus is the Savior of the whole world. All of us have been saved by the life, death, and Resurrection of Jesus Christ.

Those who believed and accepted the good news were baptized and became members of the Church. They listened to what the apostles told them about Jesus and his teachings. They gathered together to share the Eucharist and "devoted themselves to the teaching of the apostles." (Acts of the Apostles 2:42)

Another word for "good news" is *gospel*. The **gospel** is the good news that we are saved by Jesus Christ, the Son of God. Like the first disciples, we are called to share the gospel.

Work with a partner. On a strip of paper, write some good news about Jesus that you wish to share with someone. Gather in a circle and share your good news. Then make a gospel chain.

EPHESUS

Key Words

Acts of the Apostles (p. 250)

gospel (p. 251)

53

ACTIVITY BANK

Multicultural Connection
Roots of Faith

Jesus sent the apostles out to "make disciples of all nations." Most of us come from rich faith traditions in this country or another country. Share with the group the various ways that you and people you know express your faith.

Liturgy
Listening to the Gospel Reading

Provide the children with the reference to the gospel for the upcoming Sunday. Have them read it at home. Emphasize that they should listen attentively while the gospel is being read at Mass. After hearing it read at Mass, ask them to go home and write what the gospel meant to them. Have the children share their work the next time the group meets.

Read aloud the statement on page 53. Have the children read silently the paragraphs that follow.

Stress that the Holy Spirit gave the apostles the desire to share the good news about Jesus. They baptized people who accepted the good news of Jesus. Point out that we hear the good news or the gospel at Mass. We stand out of respect when the gospel is proclaimed.

Form small groups or pairs. Ask the children to complete the activity to make a gospel chain.

Quick Check

✔ *Why did the apostles choose new leaders for each place they visited?* (because they had to move on to a new place and wanted the new community to continue)

✔ *What does* gospel *mean?* (good news)

As Catholics...

An Early Christian Symbol

After you have presented the lesson, read aloud the text. Ask the children to discuss how the fish sign was used by the early Christians. Use Reproducible Master 5 (page 51C) during the lesson. Have children think of places in their world where they could display the fish sign to show their faith.

As Catholics...

In Greek the word *fish, ichthus,* is made up of the first letters of "Jesus Christ," "Son of God," and "Savior." The fish was an important sign for the early Christians. They put this sign on the walls of places where they gathered to celebrate their faith. They also used it to mark the places where Christians were buried. Because it was a sign that the Romans did not use, Christians felt safe in using it. This simple sign stood for both the name and good news of Jesus Christ.

The followers of Jesus stood up for their faith.

The Church began at a time when many countries were part of the Roman Empire. The Romans wanted everyone to worship their false gods. But the Christians would worship only the one, true God. Many Romans thought the Christians were a threat to the emperor's power. Soon the Christians were forced to worship Roman gods or face death.

The Roman leaders tried to make the Christians give up their faith in Jesus Christ. Many Christians were put in prison because they would not. Some Christians even died for their faith. We call people who die for their faith **martyrs**.

Name someone you know who stands up for his or her faith. Pray for that person.

Many of our ancestors in faith are examples of holiness.

Millions of Christians have lived before us. They are our ancestors in faith. Because of their holy lives the Church calls some of them saints.

Saints Perpetua and Felicity are two examples of holiness. Both of them were preparing to become Christians in the early years of the Church. Because of this they were arrested and treated terribly by the guards. Yet they both refused to worship Roman gods. They continued to believe in Jesus even when they were put to death.

Key Word
martyrs (p.252)

54

Lesson Plan

WE BELIEVE (continued)

Invite a volunteer to read aloud the first statement on page 54.

Ask volunteers to read aloud the two paragraphs that follow. Emphasize the following points:

• The Romans thought the Christians were a threat to them.

• When people were discovered to be Christian, they continued to believe, even if it meant being thrown into prison or put to death. The Holy Spirit gave the early Christians strength and courage.

Do the activity together, and pray for people of faith.

Ask a volunteer to read the next statement on page 54. Invite the children to read silently the text that follows.

Stress that the saints are examples to us and show us different ways to live holy lives. Point out that although they may have lived long ago, the saints heard the same call to be holy that we do.

Share the *Chapter Story* on guide page 51E about Saint Tarcisius.

Saint Augustine lived in North Africa. He was very popular when he was young. He was so busy enjoying himself that he never had time to think about God. As he grew older, he began to feel that his life had no meaning.

Augustine realized that God could give his life meaning. Augustine began to change. His love and need for God continued to grow. Augustine became a bishop and one of the Church's great writers.

These saints may have lived years ago, but their call to be holy is the same as ours is today.

Benozzo Gozzoli (1420–1497), *Saint Augustine*

ACTIVITY BANK

Curriculum Connection
Dramatic Role-Playing

Encourage the children to talk about the difficult life early Christians endured. Set up a role-play situation in which an early Christian shares his or her faith with another person who is not a Christian. Then ask other children to role-play the same situation.

Multiple Intelligences
Bodily-Kinesthetic

Have small groups or partners think about some of the main things they learned in the chapter. Then, invite the children to make up a brief skit based on one of the four faith statements in this lesson. You may have two or more groups working on one faith statement. Give the children time to practice before asking them to share their skits with the group.

WE RESPOND

How can you follow the saints who are our models of holiness? Circle the words in the letter box that will complete the sentences. Write the words on the lines provided.

F	A	I	R	J	U	S	T
H	E	L	P	E	X	O	H
A	W	O	R	S	H	I	P
I	T	S	A	U	M	N	D
R	G	O	Y	S	R	U	O

We can tell others about _____JESUS_____.

We can _____PRAY_____ and _____WORSHIP_____ together, especially at Mass.

We can try to _____HELP_____ others, especially those most in need.

We can be _____FAIR_____ and _____JUST_____ to all people.

55

WE RESPOND   ___ minutes

Connect to Life Discuss with the children ways they can follow the example of the saints.

Have the children complete the word search activity on page 55. Tell the children they may find words in the puzzle by reading either across or down. Have them work on the puzzle with a partner.

CHAPTER TEST

Chapter 5 Test is provided in the Grade 3 Assessment Book.

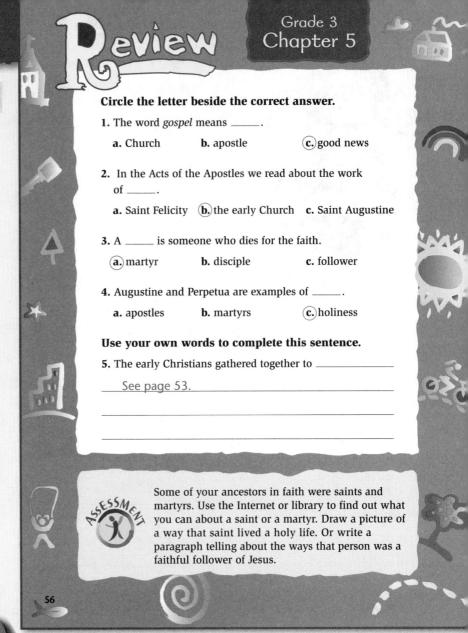

Review

Circle the letter beside the correct answer.

1. The word *gospel* means _____.
   a. Church   b. apostle   c. good news

2. In the Acts of the Apostles we read about the work of _____.
   a. Saint Felicity   b. the early Church   c. Saint Augustine

3. A _____ is someone who dies for the faith.
   a. martyr   b. disciple   c. follower

4. Augustine and Perpetua are examples of _____.
   a. apostles   b. martyrs   c. holiness

Use your own words to complete this sentence.

5. The early Christians gathered together to _____
   See page 53. _____

   _____

   _____

ASSESSMENT

Some of your ancestors in faith were saints and martyrs. Use the Internet or library to find out what you can about a saint or a martyr. Draw a picture of a way that saint lived a holy life. Or write a paragraph telling about the ways that person was a faithful follower of Jesus.

56

Lesson Plan

Review   ___ minutes

Chapter Review Explain to the children that they are now going to review what they have learned. Have them complete questions 1–4. Ask the children to say aloud each of the correct answers. Clear up any misconceptions. Have them complete question 5.

Assessment Activity Invite a volunteer to read aloud directions. Allow the children to consult resource books such as children's books of the Bible, biblical dictionaries, and other sources of information. Assist them in their search. Invite the children to share their stories.

Sharing Faith in Class and at Home At this time you may want to work on pages 233–234 of

Chapter 28. Refer to the *Lesson Planning Guide* on page 233B before you present these pages.

We Respond in Faith   ___ minutes

Reflect & Pray Help the children decide on a saint to whom they will write a letter. Explain that the letter is a way to call upon a saint to pray for them. Ask the children to think about the type of assistance they need from the saint.

 **Key Words** Write the *Key Words* on the board. Invite the children to suggest synonyms or other words that describe each word. Write these on the board. Ask volunteers to find and read the correct definition. Ask the children to decide how well their synonyms described each word.

Reflect & Pray

I want to share the good news of Jesus Christ. This week, I especially want to share the part of the good news that tells us that

_____

I will need help to do this. I will ask one of my ancestors in faith (a saint I have learned about from my parents or in school) to help me.

Dear

_____

Key Words

Acts of the Apostles (p. 250)
gospel (p. 251)
martyrs (p. 252)

Remember

- The apostles led the Church.
- The disciples of Jesus share the good news.
- The followers of Jesus stood up for their faith.
- Many of our ancestors in faith are examples of holiness.

OUR CATHOLIC LIFE

All Saints

By our Baptism we have all been called to become holy, or to become saints. We must decide on how we can be holy, how we can love, and how we can serve God. We can look at the lives of the saints, the holy women and men who have gone before us. The saints come from every country, race, and culture. Their lives were filled with love for God. On November 1, All Saints' Day, the Church remembers all of the saints who are already celebrating God's life and love in heaven.

HOME CONNECTION

Sharing Faith with My Family

Make sure to send home the family page (text page 58).

Encourage the children to lead their family members in the good news prayer.

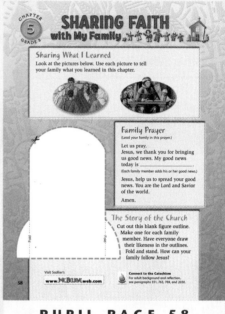

PUPIL PAGE 58

For additional information and activities, encourage families to visit Sadlier's

www.WEBELIEVEweb.com

Remember Review the important ideas of the chapter by discussing the four doctrinal statements. Have the children find each statement in the chapter and ask them to write one idea about it on a separate slip of paper. Collect the slips. Have the children take turns drawing a slip and read aloud the statement to which it relates. Show items from the prayer space and ask them to identify the objects that relate to ideas they have learned in this chapter.

Our Catholic Life Read aloud the text. Discuss All Saints' Day and other days on which the Church helps us to remember our saints. Invite children to share their ideas about ways to celebrate the saints.

Plan Ahead for Chapter 8

Prayer Space: candle, holy water, a globe, picture of the pope and bishops

Lesson Materials: medium-sized rock, cardboard ring, scissors, glue, and construction paper, copies of Reproducible Master 8

The Church Year

By means of the yearly cycle the Church celebrates the whole mystery of Christ, from his incarnation until the day of Pentecost and the expectation of his coming again.

(Norms Governing Liturgical Calendars, 17)

Overview

In this chapter the children will learn that the Church year celebrates Jesus.

For Adult Reading and Reflection
You may want to refer to paragraphs 1163 and 1168 of the *Catechism of the Catholic Church*.

Catechist Background

In what ways does your spirit respond to the annual passing of the seasons?

Throughout the course of each year, the Church celebrates the saving work of Jesus Christ in a cycle of feasts and seasons. "Within the cycle of a year, moreover, she unfolds the whole mystery of Christ, not only from His incarnation and birth until His ascension, but also as reflected in the day of Pentecost, and the expectation of a blessed, hoped-for return of the Lord" (*Documents of Vatican II*, Constitution on the Sacred Liturgy, 102).

During the Advent and Christmas seasons, the Church recalls and celebrates the mystery of the Incarnation, from the Annunciation to Epiphany. These feasts commemorate the beginning of our salvation story. They also communicate to the faith community the "first fruits of the Paschal mystery" (CCC 1171).

During the seasons of Lent, the Triduum, and Easter, the Church recalls and celebrates the passion, death, Resurrection, and Ascension of the Lord. The people of God are thus enriched by Christ's powers and merits, which are once again made present to them.

Within the context of the liturgical year, the Church commemorates the saving actions of our God, gives thanks, perpetuates the remembrance of those actions, and teaches the next generation to enter into them.

How will you open yourself more fully to the riches of the liturgical year?

Lesson Planning Guide

Lesson Steps	Presentation	Materials
① WE GATHER		
page 59 **Introduce the Season**	• Read the *Chapter Story*. • Introduce the Church year. • Proclaim the words on the banner. • Proclaim the Scripture story.	• colored chalk • Bible
page 60	• Recall a celebration memory.	
② WE BELIEVE		
pages 60–61 *The Church year celebrates Jesus.*	• Read and discuss the seasons of the Church's year. • Make Church year booklets. • Present the time line of the Church's year.	• construction paper, writing paper, markers, and scissors • paper punch • heavy yarn or ribbons
③ WE RESPOND		
page 62	🏃 Complete the activity. • Brainstorm ways of celebrating that Jesus is with us.	• yardstick
page 63 **We Respond in Prayer**	• Listen to Scripture. 🎵 Sing the song.	• prayer space items: wreaths of flowers, straw, or branches; framed picture of Jesus; a white candle; a bright table covering. 🎵 "Jesus Is with Us," Owen Alstott, #5, Grade 3 CD • rhythm instruments
Guide pages 64A–64B **We Respond in Faith**	• Explain the individual Church year project. • Explain the Church year group project. • Discuss the Sharing Faith with My Family page.	• Reproducible Master 6 • construction paper, writing paper, colored pens and pencils • Family Book, pp. 20–21

For additional ideas, activities, and opportunities: Visit Sadlier's **www.WeBelieve.web.com**

Focus on Life

Chapter Story

Summer vacation was only half over when it happened. Sally Trumble was eating breakfast and wondering what to do with herself today.

"Morning, Sally. Did you sleep well?" Her father's voice was cheerful. He had the day off and was going to celebrate by playing golf.

"I guess so," Sally mumbled. "I just wish I had something to do today, Dad. I am so bored!"

Just then Sally's mom came into the kitchen. "You do have something to do today, my girl," she said. "We are going to get out the calendar and go to work."

"Work?" asked Sally. She hoped her mother wasn't going to give her more chores to do. Mrs. Trumble laughed and said, "I mean working out our plans for celebrating the seasons."

"What seasons?"

"All of them, Sally. We'll start with summer and go through the whole year, deciding what's special about each time of the year and how our family will celebrate it."

As he was leaving for the day, Mr. Trumble reminded Sally to include a football game and a tailgate picnic in her plans for October.

Mrs. Trumble placed a large calendar, a set of markers, and some paper on the table. Then she and Sally began marking all the holidays of every kind from Christmas to Ground Hog Day, from Uncle Max's birthday to the Trumble's tenth anniversary. They even made a few new ones like Ice Cream Appreciation Day in July and Downhill Sledding Day in January.

"This is fun, Mom. I never realized there were so many things to celebrate in one year."

"Every year and every season is God's gift to us, Sally. This calendar will help our whole family to be grateful for all we have to celebrate."

It was already lunchtime by the time Sally realized that she wasn't bored anymore.

▶ *Think about a special time of the year. How do you celebrate it?*

The Church Year

6

| Advent | Christmas | Ordinary Time | Lent | Three Days | Easter | Ordinary Time |

HOSANNA

"Hosanna!
Blessed is he who comes in
the name of the Lord!"
Mark 11:9

59

Catechist Goal

• To celebrate Jesus as we focus on the Church year

Our Faith Response

• To decide how to pray in harmony with the season

ADDITIONAL RESOURCES

Book   *Celebrating the Liturgical Year: Special Seasons, Special Feasts,* Hi-Time Pflaum, 2000. These reproducible handouts offer activities for each liturgical season.

Video   *The Angel's Church Year Lesson,* Twenty-Third Publications, 2001. Three angels take children on a journey through the Church year to show how Jesus is with us always. (11 minutes)

To find more ideas for books, videos, and other learning material, visit Sadlier's

www.WEBELIEVEweb.com

Lesson Plan

Introduce the Season ___ minutes

• **Gather** in the prayer space. Let children know that we are about to praise and welcome Jesus as we begin to look at the Church year. Remind them that *Hosanna* is a Hebrew word used to praise God. It was often shouted or sung with enthusiasm. Invite all to offer together the opening prayer on page 59.

• **Read** or tell the story of Sally Trumble and her summer vacation on guide page 59C. At the end of the story, call on volunteers to share their thoughts on the importance of celebrating special days. How do such celebrations help us to appreciate and be grateful for the seasons God gives us? What celebrations would they like to add to Sally's list?

• **Using** colored chalk, sketch a large circle on the board. Draw a sun symbol in the center. Divide the circle into four segments for summer, autumn, winter, and spring. Then invite volunteers to turn this circle of the seasons into the circle of the Church year. Have them decide who should be in the center (Jesus) and draw him over the sun. Ask them to print the names of any Church seasons they already know in the proper seasonal segment.

• **Hold** the large Bible and tell the story of Jesus' entry into Jerusalem from which the opening prayer is taken (Mark 11:1–12). Simplify the story and end with *"They praised and welcomed him by shouting 'Hosanna!' Let's pray that now: Hosanna!"*

59

Lesson Materials

- construction paper, writing paper, markers, scissors
- paper punch
- heavy yarn or ribbon
- yardstick
- Grade 3 CD
- rhythm instruments
- Reproducible Master 6
- colored pens and pencils

Teaching Note

Spiritual Formation

Communicating to your children a deep love for and appreciation of the liturgical year is a primary way of contributing to their spiritual formation. Through your own prayer and spiritual reading, reflect on ways the liturgical seasons have helped to form you as an adult Catholic. Share with the class in as many ways as possible how celebrating the seasons nurtures our growth as followers of Jesus and members of the Church.

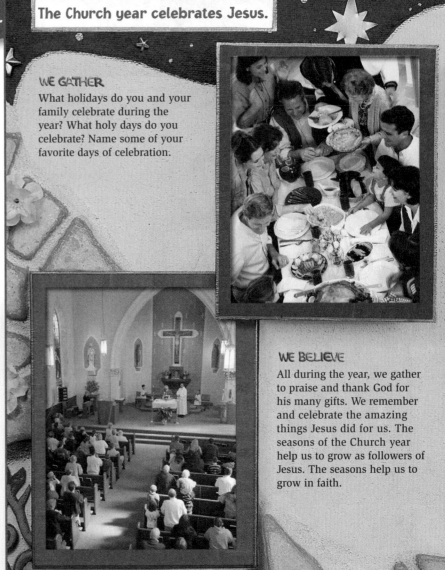

The Church year celebrates Jesus.

WE GATHER

What holidays do you and your family celebrate during the year? What holy days do you celebrate? Name some of your favorite days of celebration.

WE BELIEVE

All during the year, we gather to praise and thank God for his many gifts. We remember and celebrate the amazing things Jesus did for us. The seasons of the Church year help us to grow as followers of Jesus. The seasons help us to grow in faith.

60

Lesson Plan

WE GATHER ___ minutes

Focus on Life Before the children consider the *We Gather* questions, let them know that you want to share with them an important holiday memory from your childhood. Conclude your story by telling how you celebrate that same holiday today. Then have children read and respond to the questions. List their favorite days of celebration on the board.

Remind the children that we celebrate with our families in many ways. What occasion do you think the family in the photo on page 60 is celebrating? We celebrate with our Church family too. What do we celebrate? (Jesus and all he does for us) How? (in the Mass and sacraments) What is being celebrated in the photo on page 60? (the Mass, most likely on Saturday night or Sunday)

WE BELIEVE ___ minutes

• **Have** a volunteer read aloud the *We Believe* statement. Find out how the children think celebrating the Church year might help us. Then have them silently read the first paragraph to check their responses (to grow as followers of Jesus, to grow in faith). Invite volunteers to read each of the next six seasonal paragraphs aloud. After each reading, ask: *What do we celebrate in this season of the Church year?*

• **Divide** the group into six sections. Assign each group a season of the Church year to read silently. Then read aloud sentences from the chart at random. When a group hears a fact about "its season," the members are to raise their hands or stand up together as they name the season.

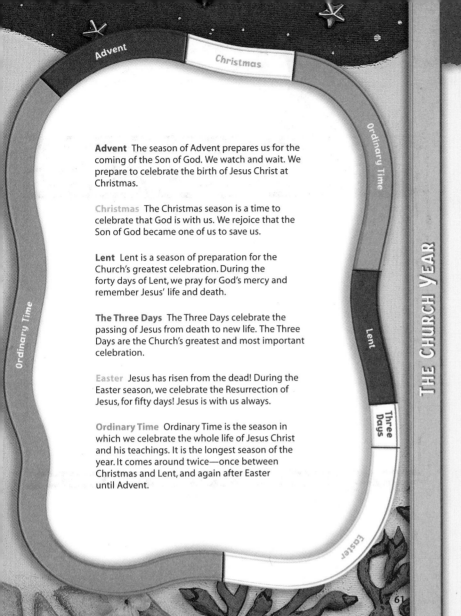

Advent The season of Advent prepares us for the coming of the Son of God. We watch and wait. We prepare to celebrate the birth of Jesus Christ at Christmas.

Christmas The Christmas season is a time to celebrate that God is with us. We rejoice that the Son of God became one of us to save us.

Lent Lent is a season of preparation for the Church's greatest celebration. During the forty days of Lent, we pray for God's mercy and remember Jesus' life and death.

The Three Days The Three Days celebrate the passing of Jesus from death to new life. The Three Days are the Church's greatest and most important celebration.

Easter Jesus has risen from the dead! During the Easter season, we celebrate the Resurrection of Jesus, for fifty days! Jesus is with us always.

Ordinary Time Ordinary Time is the season in which we celebrate the whole life of Jesus Christ and his teachings. It is the longest season of the year. It comes around twice—once between Christmas and Lent, and again after Easter until Advent.

61

ACTIVITY BANK

Faith and Media
Seasonal Videos
Activity materials: Catholic video catalogues

Invite children to look through Catholic video catalogues to find movies that match any of the seasons of the Church year. Have them make a large oval chart on poster board with six seasons and three videos for families to enjoy in those seasons.

• **Distribute** one sheet of construction paper and three sheets of white paper to each child. Provide markers and scissors. Invite the children to make booklets in which each of the six seasons of the liturgical year has its own page. Each page should name the season and tell what we celebrate at that time. As time allows, have the children design booklet covers with symbols of their favorite holy days.

Quick Check

✔ *What do we celebrate during the Church year?* (the amazing things Jesus did for us)

✔ *What are the six seasons of the Church year?* (Advent, Christmas, Lent, the Three Days, Easter, and Ordinary Time)

CONNECTION

To Mary

Remind the children that Mary, the Mother of God, is honored on many feasts during the Church year. We honor Mary because she is closely involved with the saving work of her Son. Find the Marian feasts of this present season. Invite children to suggest original ways of expressing our love for Mary on those days. Encourage them to pray daily for Mary's guidance in following Jesus.

To Catholic Social Teaching

Option for the Poor and Vulnerable

Remind the children that one of the primary ways of following Jesus during the Church year is to show his love for poor and needy people. List various parish efforts to do this. Discuss ways to participate. Draw up an action plan together.

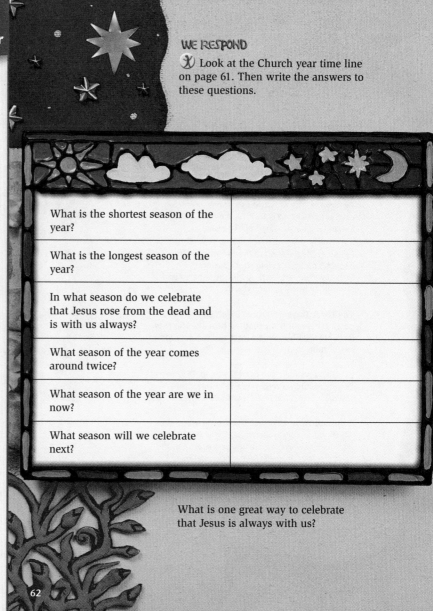

WE RESPOND

Look at the Church year time line on page 61. Then write the answers to these questions.

What is the shortest season of the year?	
What is the longest season of the year?	
In what season do we celebrate that Jesus rose from the dead and is with us always?	
What season of the year comes around twice?	
What season of the year are we in now?	
What season will we celebrate next?	

What is one great way to celebrate that Jesus is always with us?

62

Lesson Plan

WE RESPOND ___ minutes

Connect to Life Supply a yardstick and have two volunteers measure each other's height. Ask how much they think they have grown since last year at this time. Observe that we can measure our physical growth in various ways. Ask: *How do we measure how much we are growing from year to year as followers of Jesus?* (Accept all reasonable responses.) Emphasize that how we celebrate the Church year is one good "yardstick" of how much we are growing in our faith.

Have the children turn to *We Respond* on page 62 and look at the chart. Then ask them to write their answers to the six questions. Ask them to compare answers. Then clarify any misconceptions.

• **Brainstorm** responses to the final *We Respond* question. List on the board ways of celebrating that Jesus is always with us. Ideas include: beginning each day with a prayer of gratitude to Jesus for being our constant companion; going to Mass during the week whenever possible; making a Jesus shrine in our homes. Have the children each choose one idea to put into practice.

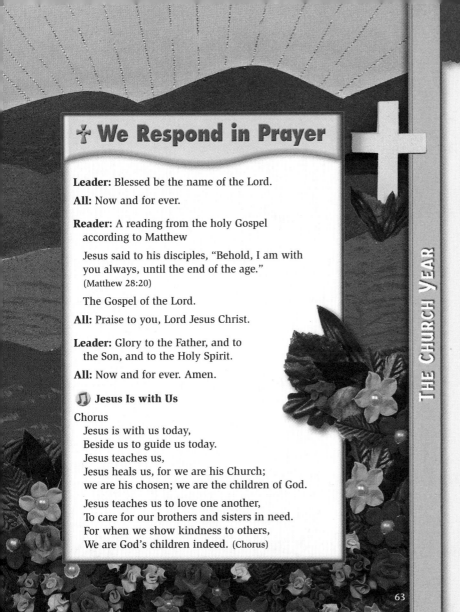

✝ We Respond in Prayer

Leader: Blessed be the name of the Lord.

All: Now and for ever.

Reader: A reading from the holy Gospel according to Matthew

Jesus said to his disciples, "Behold, I am with you always, until the end of the age." (Matthew 28:20)

The Gospel of the Lord.

All: Praise to you, Lord Jesus Christ.

Leader: Glory to the Father, and to the Son, and to the Holy Spirit.

All: Now and for ever. Amen.

🎵 **Jesus Is with Us**

Chorus
Jesus is with us today,
Beside us to guide us today.
Jesus teaches us,
Jesus heals us, for we are his Church;
we are his chosen; we are the children of God.

Jesus teaches us to love one another,
To care for our brothers and sisters in need.
For when we show kindness to others,
We are God's children indeed. (Chorus)

THE CHURCH YEAR

63

PREPARING TO PRAY

The children will listen to Scripture and respond in song.

• Let the children know that they are about to learn a song that will help us express our belief that Jesus is with us today and always.

• Play the CD or cassette of "Jesus Is with Us." Then invite the class to sing along as the song is played a second time.

• Add rhythm instruments.

• Have a reader and a leader prepare their parts in the prayer service.

The Prayer Space
• Gather the following items: a seasonal wreath of flowers, straw, or branches; a framed picture of Jesus; a white candle; a bright table covering.

 This Week's Liturgy
Visit **www.webelieveweb.com** for this week's liturgical readings and other seasonal material.

✝ We Respond in Prayer ___ minutes

• **Invite** the children to close their eyes and breathe deeply. Have them place their right hands lightly over their hearts and silently pray, "Jesus, I know you are with me."

• **Gather** in the prayer space. Light the candle, if allowed. Share *We Respond in Prayer*. When the leader prays "Glory to the Father . . ." all bow. Invite children to sing and play their instruments with enthusiasm because they believe that Jesus is with them always.

• **Conclude** by saying to the children "The Lord be with you." Remind them to respond, "And also with you." Then say, "Let us go in peace to love and serve the Lord." All respond: "Thanks be to God."

Name _____

Unscramble these words to reveal the names of
the Church year seasons.

NTEVAD   __ __ __ __ __ __

ARTSEE   __ __ __ __ __ __

OAYRNIRD EMIT   __ __ __ __ __ __ __ __ __ __ __

RHETE SAYD   __ __ __ __ __ __ __ __

SRAMTHCIS   __ __ __ __ __ __ __ __ __

ETLN   __ __ __ __

In the space below, write a riddle or a rhyme
about one of the seasons of the Church year.

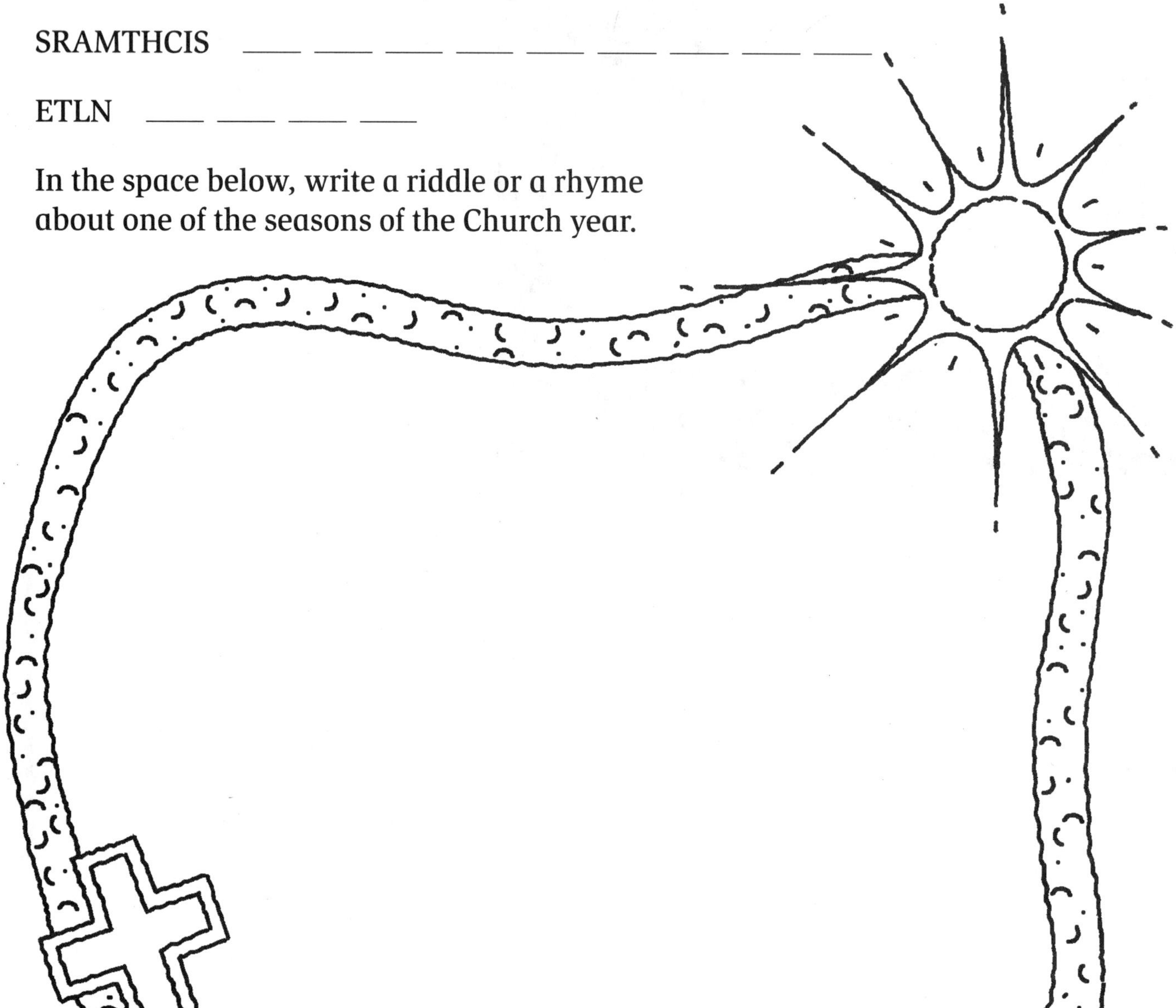

Individual Project

Distribute Reproducible Master 6 and explain the unscrambling activity. Do the first one together. (Answers: Advent, Easter, Ordinary Time, Three Days, Christmas, Lent) Print two examples of riddles and rhymes on the board, such as:

• When I arrive, everyone watches and waits for a blessed event. What season am I? (Advent)

• At Christmas Jesus came to save us. He was the Son that God himself gave us.

Share all responses and commend the children's work.

Group Project

Involve the third graders in writing and illustrating a Book of Blessings. Divide the book into six sections for Advent, Christmas, Lent, the Triduum, Easter, and Ordinary Time. Have the children design "cover" pages for each new section, using symbols for both the liturgical season and the natural season. The blessings for each season should focus on family and parish events. Together compile a list of possible blessings on the board. For example: A Blessing Before Going Christmas Shopping, A Blessing of the New Year, or A Blessing of the Lenten Rice Bowl. Have children work in pairs to compose simple blessings and illustrate them with symbols or scenes related to the season. Compile the book and share it with families.

HOME CONNECTION

Sharing Faith with My Family

Make sure to send home the family page (pupil page 64).

Encourage the children to involve their families in offering a family blessing before bedtime and in doing the "Around the Table" activity.

For additional information and activities, encourage families to visit Sadlier's

www.WEBELIEVEweb.com

PUPIL PAGE 64

Ordinary Time

Apart from those seasons having their own distinctive character, thirty-three or thirty-four weeks remain in the yearly cycle that do not celebrate a specific aspect of the mystery of Christ. Rather, especially on the Sundays, they are devoted to the mystery of Christ in all its aspects. This period is known as Ordinary Time.

(Norms Governing Liturgical Calendars, 43)

Overview

In this chapter the children will learn that, in Ordinary Time, we celebrate the life and teachings of Jesus Christ.

For Adult Reading and Reflection
You may want to refer to paragraphs 1163 and 1168 of the *Catechism of the Catholic Church*.

Catechist Background

What is your favorite gospel story? Why?

In the two-part season of Ordinary Time, we focus on the entire life of Jesus, his stories, and his teachings. The gospel readings on each numbered Sunday draw us deeper into the Christ-life to which we are called.

The term *ordinary*, in this context, does not mean unimportant. It refers to the ordered or counted Sundays in the two stretches of Ordinary Time. The first separates the seasons of Christmas and Lent. The second follows the Easter Season and lasts until Advent begins.

Ordinary Time provides us with the opportunity to appreciate each Sunday as a celebration of Christ's Resurrection and the unfolding of the new creation. We are reminded that "The day of Christ's Resurrection is both the first day of the week, the memorial of the first day of creation, and the 'eighth day,' on which Christ after his 'rest' on the great sabbath inaugurates the 'day that the Lord has made'" (CCC 1166).

As we celebrate the Eucharist each Sunday in this our longest liturgical season, we give thanks for the Lord's Day. As catechists, we go forth to inspire another generation to keep Ordinary Time holy by living a sacramental life centered on Christ.

How will you deepen your own appreciation o Ordinary Time?

Lesson Planning Guide

Lesson Steps	Presentation	Materials

1 WE GATHER

page 65 **Introduce the Season**	• Read the *Chapter Story*. • Introduce Ordinary Time. • Proclaim the words on the banner.	• bright green chalk • list of family and class birthdays in each season
page 66	• Answer questions about the Church's seasons.	

2 WE BELIEVE

pages 66–67 *In Ordinary Time, we celebrate the life and teachings of Jesus Christ.*	• Read and discuss the season of Ordinary Time. Make a list of events in the life of Jesus. Act out a favorite one.	

3 WE RESPOND

page 68	• Read and discuss the text about Saint Peter Claver. • Introduce the Exaltation of the Holy Cross.	• Saint Peter Claver statue or portrait • cross or crucifix
page 69 **We Respond in Prayer**	• Share the story of the cross. ♪ Honor the holy cross in song and prayer.	• prayer space items: reminders of Jesus and his teachings (fish net, yeast, boat, vine, wheat and weeds) and index cards ♪ "We Sing Your Glory," Bernadette Farrell, #6, Grade 3 CD
Guide pages 70A–70B **We Respond in Faith**	• Explain the individual Ordinary Time project. • Explain the Ordinary Time group project. • Discuss the Sharing Faith with My Family page.	• copies of Reproducible Master 7 • green markers, crayons, or colored pencils • butcher paper, paint supplies, markers • Family Book, pp. 22–23

For additional ideas, activities, and opportunities: Visit Sadlier's **www.WeBelieveweb.com**

Focus on Life

Chapter Story

At last it was lunchtime. Barry hurried into the cafeteria to join Cesar, R. J., Cathy, and Maria. They were all soccer players and both the boys' and girls' teams would be playing on Saturday morning.

"Finally, it's Friday," Barry said as he slid his tray on to the already crowded table. "Practice starts right after school and Coach Stetson wants us to work on heading corner kicks. That'll give us an edge over Hawthorne School."

Like a high-speed pass, Barry's enthusiasm spread across the table. Everyone started talking at once about game strategies and how their teams would definitely defeat their opponents. Then Cathy added a new level of excitement by telling them that her father had offered to take all five of them to a pro soccer game on Sunday.

"Wow! That's great!" said Cesar. "What time do we have to be ready?"

"Well, that's the hard part," Cathy replied. "It's a long trip so Dad wants to get started at 6 A.M."

Everyone agreed that they could make it at that time. But Barry suddenly remembered that his grandparents were coming on Saturday and the whole family was going to 9 A.M. Mass on Sunday. His parents had made reservations at Grandma's favorite restaurant for breakfast after Mass.

"I know," Barry thought. "This Sunday isn't anything special. I mean, it's not like it's Christmas or Easter. Maybe Mom and Dad will let me miss Mass just this once. I wonder."

▶ *What do you think Barry should do? Why?*

Ordinary Time

Advent | Christmas | Ordinary Time | Lent | Three Days | Easter | Ordinary Time

"Lord, it is good
to give thanks to you."

Responsorial Psalm, Eighth Sunday
in Ordinary Time

65

Catechist Goal

• To emphasize that, in Ordinary Time, we celebrate the life and teachings of Jesus Christ.

Our Faith Response

• To pray in thanksgiving

ADDITIONAL RESOURCES

Book   *I Want to Be Jesus*, Carol Camp-Twork, Ave Maria Press, 1999. This book presents 150 gospel plays for children, following the Church year cycle.

Video   *The Story of Jesus for Children*, Inspirational Films, 1979. This is a drama of Jesus' life as seen through the eyes of children. Use the Ministry segment. (20-minute segment of 62-minute tape)

To find more ideas for books, videos, and other learning material, visit Sadlier's

www.WE BELIEVE web.com

Lesson Plan

Introduce the Season ___ minutes

• **Pray** together the prayer Jesus taught us, "Our Father . . ."

• **Read** or tell the *Chapter Story*. Call on volunteers to tell what they think Barry should do and why. Make it clear that going to Mass on Saturday is not a good option on this particular weekend. Find out what children think of Barry's "excuse" that it was not a "special Sunday" like Christmas or Easter.

• **Explain** that the term *ordinary* often means that there is nothing special about a person, place, or thing. But when it comes to the seasons of the Church year,

ordinary has a different meaning. Print *Ordinary Time* on the board in bright green chalk. Explain that it refers to the longest season on the Church calendar. It has thirty-three or thirty-four Sundays in it. We call them "ordinary" but each one is special. Ask: *Why do you think every Sunday is special?* (It is the Lord's Day; we gather for Mass; Sunday is the day Jesus rose from the dead.)

• **Ask** children to find out in what season of the Church year each member of the family has his or her birthday. Have them bring a list to class for class prayer.

• **Stand** and pray "Lord, it is good/to give thanks to you." (Divide at slash mark and pray as Side 1 and Side 2.)

Lesson Materials

- list of family and class birthdays in each season
- Saint Peter Claver statue or portrait
- cross or crucifix
- Grade 3 CD
- copies of Reproducible Master 7
- green markers, crayons, or colored pencils
- butcher paper, paint supplies, markers

Teaching Tip

Parish Calendars

Duplicate copies of the parish calendar and help the children identify the autumn Sundays of Ordinary Time. Point out any special events children and their families might enjoy. This might be a good time to find Catholic calendars or parish calendars for any families who may not have one at home. If there are none to be found, search the Web site of the National Council of Catholic Bishops for liturgical notes to send home weekly. Or search "Liturgical Calendars, Roman Catholic."

In Ordinary Time, we celebrate the life and teachings of Jesus Christ.

WE GATHER

Can you remember the names of all the seasons in the liturgical year?

Which season is the Church in right now?

WE BELIEVE

Ordinary Time is a special time in the Church. During this season, we celebrate everything about Jesus! We hear about his teaching, his love, and his forgiveness. We also learn to be his followers.

Ordinary Time is the longest season of the Church year. It lasts about thirty-three or thirty-four weeks. It is called Ordinary Time because the weeks are "ordered," or named in number order. For example, the First Sunday in Ordinary Time is followed by the Second Sunday in Ordinary Time, and so on.

On the Sundays of Ordinary Time, and on the weekdays, too, the priest wears green vestments. Green is a sign of new life and hope.

On Sundays and weekdays in Ordinary Time, we learn about Jesus and his teachings by listening to the Scripture readings. Sometimes we hear events in the life of Jesus. Sometimes we hear a story Jesus told.

66

Lesson Plan

WE GATHER ___ minutes

Focus on Life Have children work with partners in listing their responses to the *We Gather* questions. Then make a master list on the board, calling on volunteers to name the seasons and to identify the current season. Teach the rhyme: A-C-L-T-E-O-T, Let's learn the seasons, if you please. Then as each of the initials is called out (with the last two together) have volunteers name the Church seasons in order.

- **List** each season in a row across the board. Ask for the names of class members born in each season. Does Ordinary Time have the greatest number of class birthdays? Suggest that children might want to wear something green the week of their Ordinary Time birthdays. Have a volunteer name three ways we can try to be

more like Jesus in our daily lives (pray, love others, work for peace and justice). Ask children to decide how they will be peacemakers in their families this week.

WE BELIEVE ___ minutes

- **Ask** a volunteer to read aloud the *We Believe* statement. Invite the children to read the first two paragraphs of *We Believe* to find out: *What do we learn about during Ordinary Time?* (life and teachings of Jesus; to be his followers) Then ask: *How long is the longest season of the Church year?* (thirty-three or thirty-four weeks) Have the third paragraph read aloud and emphasize that green is the color of new life and hope.

🏃 Together make a list of some of the events in the life of Jesus and a list of some stories he told.

_____

_____

_____

_____

Then in groups talk about your favorite events or stories. Act out one for the rest of the class.

During Ordinary Time, we learn more about Jesus and his teachings so that we can become more like him. Jesus shares himself with us in the sacraments. As Jesus did, we pray, love others, and work for justice and peace.

ORDINARY TIME

67

ACTIVITY BANK

Multiple Intelligences
Bodily/Kinesthetic

Suggest that children choose one of the following ways of expressing with their bodies giving thanks to God: form a body sculpture, do a dance, use physical gestures, or do a pantomime.

The Saints
Getting to Know Our Champions

The feast days of the saints are woven throughout the season of Ordinary Time. This is a fruitful time to introduce the children to a number of saints whose stories they may not yet know. Use resources like *Saints of the Seasons for Children* (Ethel Pochocki, St. Anthony Messenger Press 1989). Tell the stories of saints like Vincent de Paul, Frances Xavier Cabrini, Rose of Lima, Hedwig, and the twins Cosmas and Damian.

• **Discuss** the on-page photos. Ask: *How are these people living according to Jesus' teachings?* Say: *Pretend you are in the crowd listening to Jesus. What do you hear him saying?* (Accept reasonable responses like, "Love one another. Be just and fair.")

• **Invite** the children to complete the reading and point out the answers to these questions: *How do we learn about Jesus and his teachings?* (by listening to the Scripture readings at Mass on Sundays) *Why do we learn about Jesus?* (to become more like him)

🏃 **Form** small groups to do the activity. As a class, make a list of events and stories from the life of Jesus. Encourage each group to choose one story to act out for the entire class. (Try to avoid duplications.)

Quick Check

✔ *What do we celebrate during Ordinary Time?* (everything about Jesus)

✔ *What do we learn from the Scripture readings?* (about the life of Jesus and his teachings)

CONNECTION

To the Arts

Using library and Internet sources, share with the children a wide variety of art prints depicting crosses and crucifixes. Have them point out the differences among Latin, Greek, Maltese, Celtic, and Tau crosses. Find out which crosses are most appealing to the children and why.

To Faith and Media

Ask students to name one or two of their favorite TV shows. Then invite them to be "Jesus Values Spotters" the next time their favorite shows come on. Ask them to watch for values like: love, forgiveness, making peace, being fair, helping the poor, being truthful. Have them share their findings.

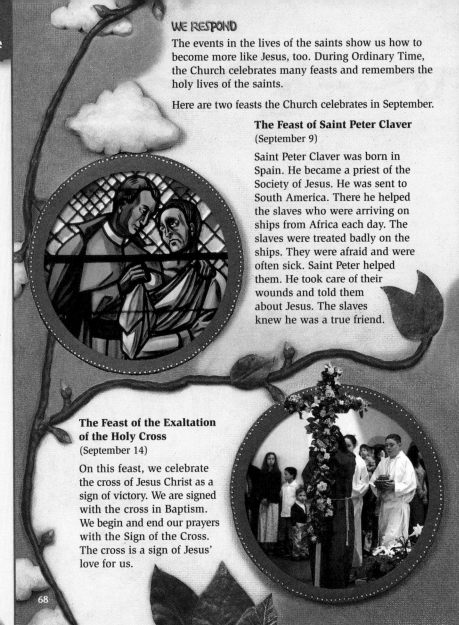

WE RESPOND

The events in the lives of the saints show us how to become more like Jesus, too. During Ordinary Time, the Church celebrates many feasts and remembers the holy lives of the saints.

Here are two feasts the Church celebrates in September.

The Feast of Saint Peter Claver
(September 9)

Saint Peter Claver was born in Spain. He became a priest of the Society of Jesus. He was sent to South America. There he helped the slaves who were arriving on ships from Africa each day. The slaves were treated badly on the ships. They were afraid and were often sick. Saint Peter helped them. He took care of their wounds and told them about Jesus. The slaves knew he was a true friend.

The Feast of the Exaltation of the Holy Cross
(September 14)

On this feast, we celebrate the cross of Jesus Christ as a sign of victory. We are signed with the cross in Baptism. We begin and end our prayers with the Sign of the Cross. The cross is a sign of Jesus' love for us.

68

Lesson Plan

WE RESPOND   ___ minutes

Connect to Life Take a survey of the first names, middle names, and baptismal names represented in the class. List all the recognizable saints' names on the board. Explain that in Ordinary Time we celebrate the feasts of many saints—one of whom we will learn about today.

• **Ask** a volunteer to read aloud the *We Respond* paragraph introducing the saints' feasts of Ordinary Time. Recall that we learn how to become more like Jesus first from the Scriptures. Now we will learn more about becoming like Jesus by meeting a special saint.

• **Introduce** Saint Peter Claver with a statue or portrait. Explain that he is the patron saint of all Catholic missions among the African American people of the world. Then have the children read the text to discover why Saint Peter Claver has been given that title. (He cared for African slaves in South America.)

• **Explain** the Exaltation of the Holy Cross. Display a decorative cross or crucifix. Find out how many children have crosses in their own rooms or in their homes. Have children read about the Feast of the Exaltation (Honoring) of the Holy Cross. Ask: *When do we pray the Sign of the Cross?* (in Baptism; at Mass; when we begin and end our prayers)

• **Share** this prayer. Have a volunteer hold the cross aloft. Pray together: *Jesus, we honor your holy cross by which you saved the world.* Then pray the Sign of the Cross slowly and reverently.

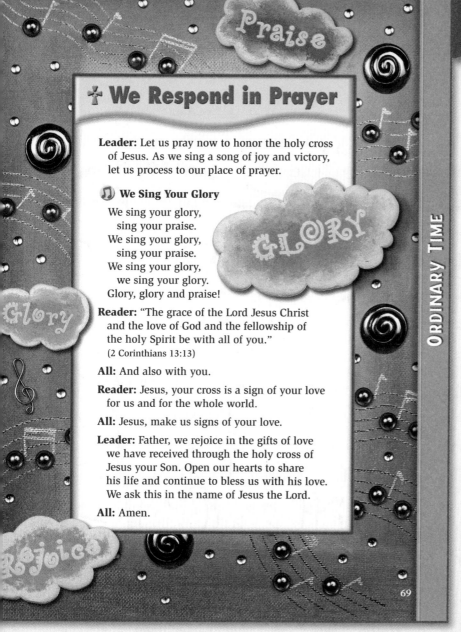

✝ We Respond in Prayer

Leader: Let us pray now to honor the holy cross of Jesus. As we sing a song of joy and victory, let us process to our place of prayer.

🎵 **We Sing Your Glory**

We sing your glory,
    sing your praise.
We sing your glory,
    sing your praise.
We sing your glory,
    we sing your glory.
Glory, glory and praise!

Reader: "The grace of the Lord Jesus Christ and the love of God and the fellowship of the holy Spirit be with all of you."
(2 Corinthians 13:13)

All: And also with you.

Reader: Jesus, your cross is a sign of your love for us and for the whole world.

All: Jesus, make us signs of your love.

Leader: Father, we rejoice in the gifts of love we have received through the holy cross of Jesus your Son. Open our hearts to share his life and continue to bless us with his love. We ask this in the name of Jesus the Lord.

All: Amen.

69

ORDINARY TIME

PREPARING TO PRAY

The children will process to the prayer space while singing. They will listen to Scripture and respond in prayer.

• Teach the song, "We Sing Your Glory."

• Select and prepare children who will serve as leaders with you, and a reader. Have the leaders and reader practice their parts.

• Distribute index cards and have children write one way they will be signs of the love of Jesus for others this week.

The Prayer Space

• Place items that will bring to mind stories of Jesus and his teachings (fishing net, wool, yeast, boat, vine, wheat and weeds).

📖 **This Week's Liturgy**
Visit **www.webelieveweb.com** for this week's liturgical readings and other seasonal material.

✝ We Respond in Prayer ___ minutes

• **Call** on volunteers to tell what feast we celebrate on September 14 in Ordinary Time (Exaltation of the Holy Cross). Explain that the word *exaltation* means to honor, praise, or raise on high.

• **Tell** this story to help the children understand why we exalt the holy cross of Jesus: *Over two thousand years ago a baby was born in Bethlehem. And that baby was the only Son of God. His name was _____. (Have children fill the blank.) When Jesus grew up, he left his home in Nazareth to do the work of God his loving Father. He cured the sick, made friends with sinners, helped the poor, and told everyone wonderful stories of God's love for them. Many people loved and followed Jesus because _____* (Accept all reasonable responses.) *But some important*

people did not believe in Jesus and did not trust him. They feared that he had come to take their power away. And they wanted to follow their own way instead of God's will. So they arrested Jesus, punished him, and had him nailed on a cross. (Be silent for a moment.) But three days later, when his friends went to visit his tomb, what did they find? _____ (He had risen from the dead.) Alleluia! And Jesus' friends remembered what he had told them: "No one has greater love than this, to lay down one's life for one's friends" (John 15:13).

• **Form** a procession at the back of the room. Have a volunteer hold aloft the large cross and lead the procession to the prayer space. Pray together *We Respond in Prayer*. Conclude by having children place their signs of love cards on the table.

Name _____

Color all the X spaces green. Print in the Jesus frame what we learn about him in Ordinary Time.

The power of Gods Love active in the world
Ending of sentence ideas
Helping other Donate time giving to charity
Helping Friends and neigbors

Thechers Help teach
Fr. Dave   - Parents

Faith means - U believe without seeing

Reflect + Pray
I am sad   mad   affarid Haveing fun with friends

Major Difference Between Jesus Resurection
Lazzarus raising from the Dead

Stay awake Be prepaird Keep eyes open
for opportunite to serre God and other in works
of mercy

Draw a circle to depict the seasons

We believe Paragraph

Divide into groups ~~to~~ read a season silently
the read aloud

	A	Ordinary Time
1 Print OrdnayTime	1 mission	Life + teacheing of Jesus
2 Foind out Bdays	2 apostle	Jesus Healed Blind men~~et~~ and
	3 Gospel	He ~~followed~~
	D	
	1 Martyrs	
	3 Heaven	

$\frac{1}{2}$ Print Ordinary Time

Its the Longest season in church Calender
          33 or 34 Sundays

3   Why is it special

B Days   1 the Lords day   We gather for mass

in Curch   2 Sunday is the day Jesus rose from the Dead

Calender Year

                    4 week
Advan~~et~~   ~~to~~ day Before Christmas

Christmas

Odinary time   Ordinary Time Teaches us

Lent   40 days How to live our lives Daily

Easter

Ordnay Time

Individual Project

Distribute Reproducible Master 7 and green markers, crayons, and colored pencils. Have children color all the X spaces green to highlight the hidden season. Invite them to print in the frame around the Jesus portrait what we learn about him during this season. Encourage them to display their work at home and explain its meaning to their families. Ask: *Why is green the color of Ordinary Time?* (because it is the color of life and hope)

Group Project

Have the children form several small groups that will work together on making Jesus Profiles. Provide large sheets of butcher paper, paint supplies, and markers. Draw in pencil a profile of Jesus standing or sitting. Around the perimeter of the profile, invite the children to print titles or descriptions of the Jesus stories they recall or remember from the New Testament. Have them use markers and leave spaces between titles like *The Good Shepherd* and *Jesus Hugs the Little Children*. In the center of the profile, the children may paint a scene representing one of the stories. Display the completed profiles side by side and have the artists explain their work.

HOME CONNECTION

Sharing Faith with My Family

Make sure to send home the family page (pupil page 70).

Encourage the children to involve their families in the "Around the Table" activities of praying for peace, sharing meals with lonely people, and visiting a shrine. Remind them to pray the Our Father together with their families.

For additional information and activities, encourage families to visit Sadlier's

www.WEBELIEVE.web.com

ASSESSMENT

In the *We Believe* program each core chapter ends with a review of the content presented, and with activities that encourage the children to reflect and act on their faith. The review is presented in two formats, standard and alternative.

Each unit is also followed by both standard and alternative assessment. The standard test measures basic knowledge and vocabulary assimilation. The alternative assessment allows the children another option—often utilizing another learning style—to express their understanding of the concepts presented.

Using both forms of assessment, perhaps at different times, attends to the various ways children's learning can be measured. You can also see the Grade 3 *We Believe* Assessment Book for:

• standard assessment for each chapter

• alternative assessment for each chapter

• standard assessment for each unit

• alternative assessment for each unit

• a semester assessment which covers material presented in Units 1 and 2

• a final assessment which covers material presented in Units 1, 2, 3, and 4.

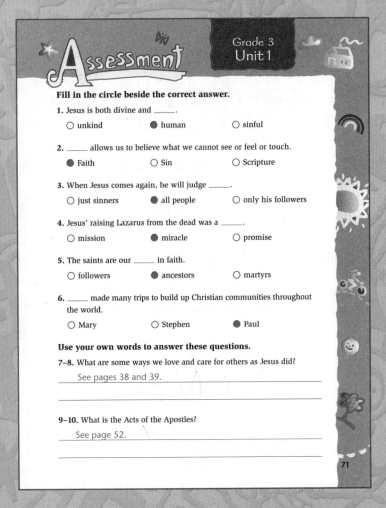

Grade 3
Unit 1

Fill in the circle beside the correct answer.

1. Jesus is both divine and _____.
   ○ unkind   ● human   ○ sinful

2. _____ allows us to believe what we cannot see or feel or touch.
   ● Faith   ○ Sin   ○ Scripture

3. When Jesus comes again, he will judge _____.
   ○ just sinners   ● all people   ○ only his followers

4. Jesus' raising Lazarus from the dead was a _____.
   ○ mission   ● miracle   ○ promise

5. The saints are our _____ in faith.
   ○ followers   ● ancestors   ○ martyrs

6. _____ made many trips to build up Christian communities throughout the world.
   ○ Mary   ○ Stephen   ● Paul

Use your own words to answer these questions.

7–8. What are some ways we love and care for others as Jesus did?
   See pages 38 and 39.

9–10. What is the Acts of the Apostles?
   See page 52.

71

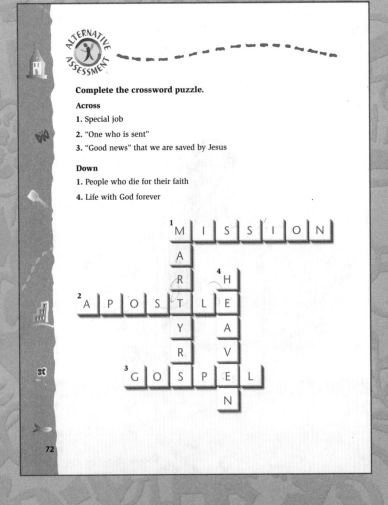

ALTERNATIVE ASSESSMENT

Complete the crossword puzzle.

Across
1. Special job
2. "One who is sent"
3. "Good news" that we are saved by Jesus

Down
1. People who die for their faith
4. Life with God forever

72

We Are Members of the Church

UNIT 2

73

CLASS CONNECTION

Point out the unit title to the children. Ask them what they think they will be learning more about in this unit. Have a class discussion preparing the children for this unit.

HOME CONNECTION

Sharing Faith as a Family

Sadlier *We Believe* calls on families to become involved in:

• learning the faith
• prayer and worship
• living their faith.

Highlighting of these unit family pages and the opportunities they offer will strengthen the partnership of the Church and the home.

For additional information and activities, encourage families to visit Sadlier's

www.WeBelieveweb.com

UNIT 2 SHARING FAITH as a Family

Turn Down the Sound

An important aspect of teaching children to pray is helping them to be quiet. This means turning down the sound internally as well as externally.

External quiet. We live in a noisy world. Television, cell phones, computers, background music, and traffic are just some of the sources of sound that engulf us. It becomes such a part of our routine that we often become immune to it. Help your child embrace the joy of silence by introducing a daily "quiet time" in your home. Turn off all electronic media for a set period of time. Encourage everyone to take part in a quiet activity, such as reading or working a puzzle. You are likely to find the family looking forward to and wanting to extend this "quiet time."

Internal quiet. As these external times of quiet are achieved, help your child develop ways of being still. Before turning out the lights at bedtime, spend time together, eyes closed, thinking over the best part of the day. During the day, go outside with your child, perhaps to a park or garden. Sit in silence together, and savor the feeling of interior peace.

Cultivated as a habit, the ability to be quiet is one that will give rise to deeper and richer prayer—both for your child and for you. Are you ready for it?

What Your Child Will Learn in Unit 2

In Unit 2, the children will come to more of an understanding that they are members of the Church. The four marks of the Church (one, holy, catholic, and apostolic) are explained, as are the images of the Church as the people of God and as the Body of Christ. The children will learn the Apostles' Creed as well as ways that the Church guides us—especially through Catholic social teaching. Prayer is another focal point in Unit 2. The children will understand the types of prayer, and the difference between liturgical and private prayer. They will see how the Church continues the prayer of Jesus throughout the world. There is an entire chapter devoted to the parish. The children will discover the parish as a family in Christ and appreciate the various ministries as well as the purposes of a parish. Lastly, Unit 2 talks about the meaning and types of vocations found in the Church. The emphasis here is on the fact that, whether one is single, married, in the priesthood, or a religious brother or sister, God calls each one of us to lead a life of holiness.

Plan & Preview

▶ This unit's *Family Pages* offer prayer cards that can be taped to the refrigerator door for all to see and pray. You will need scissors to cut out the prayer, one per chapter, and transparent tape.

The Universal Prayer

Lord, I believe in you: increase my faith.
I trust in you: strengthen my trust.
I love you: let me love you more and more.
I am sorry for my sins: deepen my sorrow.

Guide me by your wisdom,
Correct me with your justice,
Comfort me with your mercy,
Protect me with your power.

I want to do what you ask of me:
In the way you ask,
For as long as you ask,
Because you ask it.
Amen.

(attributed to Pope Clement XI, edited version)

From the Catechism

"Authority, stability, and a life of relationships within the family constitute the foundations for freedom, security, and fraternity within society."
(*Catechism of the Catholic Church*, 2207)

Bible Q & A

Q: My child will be learning about Jesus at prayer. What can I read to him to help him understand the meaning of prayer?
—*Scottsville, Kentucky*

A: Prayer is a vital part of Jesus' message. To learn more, read Matthew 6:5–8 and 7:7–11 as well as Philippians 4:4–7.

Note the Quote

"Prayer in my opinion is nothing else than an intimate sharing between friends; it means taking time frequently to be alone with Him who we know loves us."
Saint Teresa of Avila

74

Chapter 8 The Church Has Four Marks

Overview

In this chapter the children will learn about the four marks of the Church, which are its special characteristics.

Doctrinal Content	For Adult Reading and Reflection *Catechism of the Catholic Church*
The children will learn:	Paragraph
• Jesus chose the apostles to lead the Church. 765	
• The pope and bishops are the successors of the apostles. 880	
• The Church is one and holy. 823	
• The Church is catholic and apostolic. 857	

bishops (p. 77)
dioceses (p. 77)
pope (p. 77)
marks of the Church (p. 78)

Catechist Background

In what way do I rely on the Church to help me live a holy life?

At Mass, as we pray the Nicene Creed, we profess our belief in the one holy catholic and apostolic Church.

We also believe that the four marks or chief characteristics of the Church do not exist in a vacuum. They stand out as benchmarks when Catholics demonstrate a oneness that welcomes diversity and works for unity with other Christians. The Church bears witness to holiness by reaching out to sinners who need God's mercy and compassion in their lives. The Church is catholic when all its members expand thinking in narrow ways—"my Church, my diocese, my parish"—and start envisioning the Church as large enough to share its gospel with the whole world. The Church is apostolic because we believe the pope and bishops are successors of the apostles. All Catholics participate in this apostolic charism by sharing the good news with others, especially the poor. The marks of the Church define it as one, holy, catholic, and apostolic. Yet we are called to continue growing in each of these characteristics. The Church, under the Spirit's inspiration, teaches the way.

How can I expand my vision of the Church?

Lesson Planning Guide

Lesson Steps	Presentation	Materials

① WE GATHER

page 75 **Prayer** **Focus on Life**	• Pray the words of Scripture. • Respond with cards and gestures. • Discuss leaders of groups.	For prayer space: Bible, candles, holy water, globe, and picture of the pope and bishops

② WE BELIEVE

page 76 *Jesus chose the apostles to lead the Church.*	• Read and discuss the text about Jesus' choice of apostles. Write the apostles' message about Jesus. • Pray together.	• medium-sized rocks
page 77 *The pope and bishops are the successors of the apostles.*	• Read the text about the pope and bishops. Share what you know about your bishop, your diocese, and the pope. • Read and discuss *As Catholics.*	
page 78 *The Church is one and holy.*	• Read about the Church as one and holy. Illustrate answer to the question.	• large cardboard ring • scissors, glue, construction paper • copies of Reproducible Master 8 • drawing paper and markers
page 79 *The Church is catholic and apostolic.*	• Read and discuss the text about the Church as catholic and apostolic.	

③ WE RESPOND

page 79	Illustrate one of the four marks of the Church.	
page 80 **Review**	• Complete questions 1–5. Work on the *Assessment Activity.*	• Chapter 8 Test in Assessment Book, pp. 15–16 • Chapter 8 Test in Test Generator • Review & Resource Book, pp. 19–21
page 81 **We Respond in Faith**	Complete the *Reflect & Pray* activity. • Review *Remember* and *Key Words.* • Read about Blessed Pope John XXIII in *Our Catholic Life.* • Discuss **Sharing Faith with My Family.**	• Family Book, pp. 24–26

For additional ideas, activities, and opportunities: Visit Sadlier's www.WeBelieveweb.com

75B

Name _____

Help these third graders find the marks of the Church. Look for the marks of the Church on the cobblestones. Color those stones gold. Then color the rest of the picture.

apostolic

catholic

pray

joy

holy

mission

Church

song

one

love

peace

apostle

Connections

To Catholic Social Teaching

Call to Family, Community, and Participation
To emphasize the four marks of the Church—one, holy, catholic, and apostolic—tell the children that they can be applied to their own families and local communities. Suggest that striving for unity within their families or neighborhoods means working together. For example, the children and their families could participate in a community clean up of a park or take part in a block party or parish picnic. Elicit suggestions from the children for further ideas.

To Stewardship

The Church is called to be *catholic*, or *universal*. With this characteristic in mind, our call to be stewards extends beyond families, parish communities, and neighborhoods. We are called to share resources with all people. Invite a missionary priest, brother, sister, or layperson to visit your group. Have that person share stories about the country where he or she has served. If possible, ask your children to collect school supplies or other basic supplies needed in that country.

FAITH and MEDIA

▶ Invite the pastor to your parish room for a visit. Encourage children to ask questions about his work in the parish. Photograph the visit and post a brief story along with photos on your parish web page.

▶ Have the children send e-mail messages of thanks and friendship to our Holy Father. The Vatican site is a link on your program site: www.webelieveweb.com.

▶ Bring several copies of the diocesan paper to show to the children. Print out photos of your bishop and any letters or columns written by him as chief teacher of the diocese.

▶ Some dioceses have Web sites. If yours does, visit it. Help children to find their own parish and its leaders listed on this Web site.

Meeting Individual Needs

English Language Learners

Children whose second language is English may benefit during this lesson from additional graphics and visual aids. When speaking of Saint Peter or the apostles, hold up or point to a picture. Do the same when referring to the pope or other Church leaders. The visual association with the English words and title will aid comprehension.

ADDITIONAL RESOURCES

Book   *Bible for Today's Family, New Testament.* American Bible Society, 1991. Written in readable language, with multi-cultural art. The child can read Luke 5–6.

Video   *The Story of Jesus for Children.* CA Inspirational Films Inc, 1979. Well done drama through the eyes of children. Use segment on the choosing of the apostles. (6 minute segment of 62 minute tape)

To find more ideas for books, videos, and other learning material, visit Sadlier's

www.WeBelieveweb.com

Focus on Life

Chapter Story

Marcus was helping his oldest brother, James, pack his suitcase. "James, James, I got it to close! I sat on that old suitcase and turned the lock. We're done!" Marcus said, so pleased he had helped his brother that he almost forgot that in only forty-eight hours, James would be far, far away from home.

James was the oldest of five brothers, and Marcus was the youngest. James had just finished college. Even though James was busy with his part-time job, his friends, and sports, he always found time for his youngest brother. Sometimes James would show up unexpectedly at Marcus's baseball games. He had even helped coach the third-grade basketball team.

James was going to Guatemala, a country that was very far away, and Marcus would miss him very much. In Guatemala, James would work with a missionary group that helped families learn about Jesus. The mission group planned to help the people build houses, too. One evening, James had explained to his family the ways that the group hoped to make a difference. Marcus understood. He even told his family, "Maybe some day, I'll go to Guatemala, too!"

Marcus was proud of James. He liked to listen to James practice speaking Spanish, and he admired James for wanting to help people. James had promised that he would write his youngest brother a letter every week. Marcus knew that the letters would come just as James said. James always kept his promises, whether he was in Guatemala or in their own hometown. James was just that kind of brother.

▶ *Describe what James is like.*

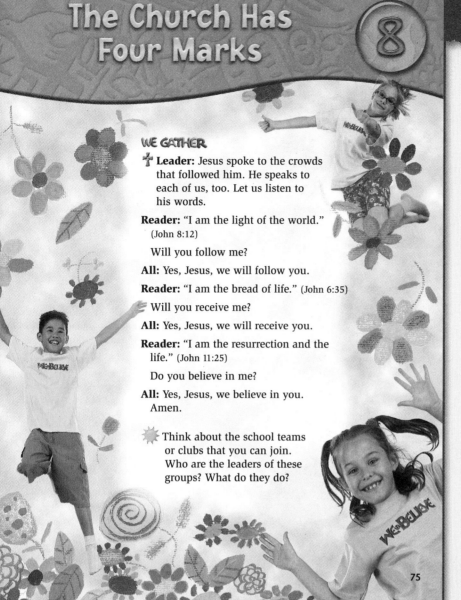

WE GATHER

✝ **Leader:** Jesus spoke to the crowds that followed him. He speaks to each of us, too. Let us listen to his words.

Reader: "I am the light of the world." (John 8:12)

Will you follow me?

All: Yes, Jesus, we will follow you.

Reader: "I am the bread of life." (John 6:35)

Will you receive me?

All: Yes, Jesus, we will receive you.

Reader: "I am the resurrection and the life." (John 11:25)

Do you believe in me?

All: Yes, Jesus, we believe in you. Amen.

☀ Think about the school teams or clubs that you can join. Who are the leaders of these groups? What do they do?

75

PREPARING TO PRAY

The children will pray by using the words of Saint John. They will respond in complementary gestures and words.

• Select four children to place the four items representing the marks of the Church in the prayer space.

• Tell the children that you will take the leader's part. Allow the reader time to rehearse his or her part. Practice the group response.

The Prayer Space

• Gather items representing the marks of the Church: a candle (for oneness), holy water (for holiness), a globe (for catholicity) and a picture of the pope and bishops (for apostolicity). Make a label for each item identifying the particular mark of the Church.

📖 **This Week's Liturgy**
Visit **www.webelieveweb.com** for this week's liturgical readings and other seasonal material.

Lesson Plan

WE GATHER
____ minutes

✝ **Pray**

• Call the children to the prayer space.

• Name each of the four marks of the Church, and signal the children to place their items on the table.

• Have the children open their books to the prayer on page 75.

• Pray the leader's part, and invite the reader and the children to follow.

☀ Focus on Life

• Invite the children to name school teams or clubs that they can join. Discuss the leaders of these groups and what they do as leaders.

• Share the *Chapter Story* on guide page 75E.

Home Connection Update

Invite the children to share experiences using Chapter 7 family page. Ask: *Did you and your family have an opportunity to pray for world peace or share a special meal with someone who may be lonely?*

Catechist Goal

• To present the four marks of the Church—one, holy, catholic, and apostolic

Our Faith Response

• To recognize ways in which our parishes show the Catholic Church is one, holy, catholic, and apostolic

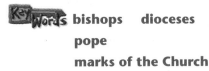 **bishops   dioceses   pope   marks of the Church**

Lesson Materials

• medium-sized rock
• large ring cut from cardboard
• scissors, glue, and construction paper
• copies of Reproducible Master 8

As Catholics...

The Pope

Tell children that the pope heads the Church and guides us to live in the way that God wants us to live. Ask a volunteer to read the list of the pope's work aloud. Discuss with children his important contributions.

WE BELIEVE
Jesus chose the apostles to lead the Church.

One of Jesus' apostles was named Simon. Jesus changed Simon's name to Peter, which means "rock." Jesus chose Peter to be the leader of the apostles. He told Peter, "You are Peter, and upon this rock I will build my church." (Matthew 16:18)

The apostles are Peter, Andrew, James and John (sons of Zebedee), Philip, Bartholomew, Thomas, Matthew, James (the son of Alphaeus), Thaddeus, Simon, and Judas Iscariot. Later Matthias took the place of Judas.

After Jesus' Ascension the apostles told the people all that Jesus had said and done. They traveled from place to place teaching what Jesus had taught them.

In every location the apostles gathered the baptized into communities. The Church grew, and the first members of the Church looked to Peter and the apostles as their leaders.

Look at the picture on page 77. In the space, write something you think the apostle told people about Jesus.

What will you tell people you know about Jesus?

76

Lesson Plan

WE BELIEVE   _____ minutes

Have a volunteer read aloud the statement. Read aloud the first two paragraphs. Show the children a medium-sized rock. Ask: *In what ways was Peter like a rock?* Try to elicit reasons why Jesus changed his apostle's name from Simon to Peter. Stress that the name Peter means *rock* and that Jesus wanted to build his Church on a strong foundation like a rock. Have volunteers read aloud the remaining paragraphs.

Invite the children to imagine what the work of an apostle must have been like. Use the title *The Work of an Apostle* and make two columns (label the first column with a minus sign, and the second column with a plus sign). Write the children's responses for both

columns (negative: encountering danger, traveling great distances, and so on) and (positive: serving Jesus, helping to form the early Church, and so on).

Invite the children to look at the picture on page 77. Encourage them to write a message that the apostles may have used to tell others about Jesus.

Ask for volunteers read aloud the statement and the paragraphs that follow. Emphasize the following points:

• The pope is the bishop of the diocese of Rome, Italy.

• The pope is the successor of Saint Peter.

• Bishops continue to lead the Church today just as the apostles did. They lead areas known as dioceses.

The pope and bishops are the successors of the apostles.

Like Jesus, the apostles chose leaders to succeed them. A *successor* is one who succeeds, or takes the place of, another. These new leaders would take the place of the apostles and continue their work.

The apostles gave these leaders the same authority that Jesus had given to them. Strengthened by the Holy Spirit, these leaders became the successors of the apostles.

As time passed each of these leaders was given the title of bishop. **Bishops** are the successors of the apostles. The bishops continue to lead the Church. They lead local areas of the Church called **dioceses.**

The **pope** is the bishop of the diocese of Rome in Italy. He continues the leadership of Peter. Together with all the bishops, he leads and guides the whole Catholic Church.

Talk about what you know about your bishop, your diocese, and the pope.

Find out more about the pope and Vatican City. Check the Vatican Web site at www.vatican.net.

Key Words

bishops (p. 250)
dioceses (p. 250)
pope (p. 253)

As Catholics...

The pope lives in Vatican City, in Rome, Italy. He is the leader of the whole Catholic Church. So in a way the whole world is his parish. He goes to places around the world to teach the good news of Jesus Christ and to seek peace. He encourages people to treat one another with respect. He also asks for help for those who are in need.

77

ACTIVITY BANK

Curriculum Connection

Art

Activity Materials: shoe boxes, construction paper, clay, contact or shelf paper, medium-sized rocks

Jesus compared Peter to a rock. He chose Peter to lead the early Church because of these characteristics. Gather medium-sized rocks. Ask the children to put together shoebox dioramas that illustrate the calling of Saint Peter by Jesus. Encourage them to add construction paper or clay figures of Jesus and Saint Peter to the scene. Suggest two or three Scripture verses for them to use. For example: Mark 1:17; Matthew 16:18; John 21:15. Write the verse on paper and attach it to the diorama. Remind the children that we can imitate the rock-like faith of Saint Peter in our own lives.

Explain: The word *dioceses* is a term that some children may not have heard before. Pronounce the term slowly and define it: local areas of the Church led by bishops. Then identify the diocese to which your parish belongs.

Discuss with children what they know about their bishop, their diocese, and the pope. If possible, visit the Vatican Web site.

Divide the group into smaller groups. Have them review the duties of the pope and bishops. Remind them that parishioners also carry out the work of the Church. Have each group act out a brief skit in which it imagines the bishop is going to visit the parish to celebrate its 75th anniversary. Have each group perform its skit.

Quick Check

✔ *Whom did Jesus choose to lead the Church?* (the apostles)

✔ *Name an important way that the apostles helped the early Church.* (They taught people about Jesus; they baptized people and gathered them into communities.)

Teaching Note

A Cheer for the Church

Children enjoy chanting and clapping, and the words in this lesson lend themselves to this activity. Try these. Stress each syllable.

Ask: *What are the marks of the Church?*
one (3 claps)
holy (2 claps)
catholic (1 clap)
and apostolic.
(Repeat three times. At the end add: *CHURCH!*)

The Church is one and holy.

The Church is one, holy, catholic, and apostolic. We call these characteristics the **marks of the Church**.

The Church is *one*, a community called together by God. Through the Church, God strengthens us to live and worship together.

All members of the Church are united by Baptism. We gather to celebrate the sacraments. We share with one another and serve together.

The Church is *holy*. God is all good and holy. God shares his holiness with the Church. Through Baptism all members of the Church receive a share in God's life. This share in God's life makes us holy.

As members of the Church we grow in holiness when we celebrate the sacraments. We also grow in holiness when we love God and others as Jesus did.

What is one way the Church is a community?

marks of the Church (p. 252)

78

Lesson Plan

WE BELIEVE (continued)

Have a volunteer to read aloud the statement on page 78. Ask volunteers to read the paragraphs. Emphasize the following important points:

• The Church is one faith community that is united by Baptism.

• All Catholics share in God's holiness through their Baptism.

• Receiving the sacraments and doing good works helps us grow in holiness.

Encourage the children work in pairs. Ask them to trace each other's hands on construction paper and then cut out the outlines and write their names on them. Point out that their hands are of different sizes and shapes, but they will become part of a larger whole when they are connected together to make a wreath of hands. Glue the hands to a large ring cut from cardboard. Stress that this activity shows that they are all different but they are all united and parts of the one Church.

Gather the children in the prayer space to identify the objects on the table that symbolize the oneness of the Church and its holiness. Invite them to say a silent prayer of thanks for their Church community.

The Church is catholic and apostolic.

The Church is catholic. The word *catholic* means "universal." The Church is open to all people. It is universal.

Jesus sent his apostles out to every part of the world. They spread the gospel to everyone, and the Church continued to grow. Even today people everywhere are invited and welcomed to become members of the Church. There are Catholics on every continent and in every country.

The Church is *apostolic*. The word *apostolic* comes from the word *apostle*. Jesus chose the apostles to be the first leaders of the Church. Their mission was to teach the good news and to baptize believers. By Baptism all members of the Church share in the work of spreading the good news of Christ.

The bishops continue the mission of the apostles in three very important ways.

- They *teach*. The bishops are the official teachers of the Church. They make sure that the members of the Church know and believe the teachings of Jesus.
- They *lead*. The bishops are the main leaders of the Church.
- They *sanctify*. The bishops work to make the people of God holy. They do this through prayer, preaching, and the celebration of the sacraments.

WE RESPOND

Draw a picture to show one of the four marks of the Church.

79

ACTIVITY BANK

Liturgy
Christian Unity Octave

An *octave* means eight. (An octave in a musical scale means eight notes.) Every year, for eight days in January, the Church prays for unity among all Christians. With the children, you may want to plan eight days of prayer for unity right now! The Franciscan Friars of the Atonement (Graymoor, New York) post information about these days of prayer, with a suggested intention for each day, on their Web site. This octave was first prayed and preached by the founder of this community. The Franciscan Sisters of the Atonement also share this special mission of prayer and action for unity.

Invite a volunteer to read aloud the statement on the top of page 79. Have the children work in pairs and read and highlight important words in the paragraphs. Ask: *What does the word* catholic *mean?* (universal; all people are welcomed to become members of the Church). *What does the word* apostolic *mean?* (comes from the apostles; to be sent to teach the good news and baptize new members). Read aloud the last paragraph with its bulleted items. Write on the board the words *teach, lead,* and *sanctify*. Stress that these are responsibilities of the bishops.

Distribute copies of the Reproducible Master 8 to reinforce their recognition of the four marks of the Church.

WE RESPOND ____ minutes

Invite the children to draw a picture to illustrate one of the four marks of the Church. Encourage the children to tell the group why they chose to draw what they did.

CHAPTER TEST

Chapter 8 Test is provided in the Grade 3 Assessment Book.

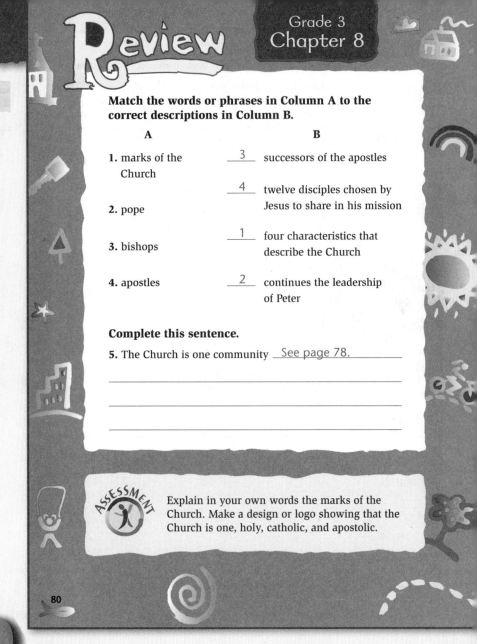

Match the words or phrases in Column A to the correct descriptions in Column B.

A	B
1. marks of the Church	__3__ successors of the apostles
2. pope	__4__ twelve disciples chosen by Jesus to share in his mission
3. bishops	__1__ four characteristics that describe the Church
4. apostles	__2__ continues the leadership of Peter

Complete this sentence.

5. The Church is one community ___See page 78.___

_____

_____

_____

ASSESSMENT

Explain in your own words the marks of the Church. Make a design or logo showing that the Church is one, holy, catholic, and apostolic.

80

Lesson Plan

 ___ minutes

Chapter Review Explain to the children that they are going to check their understanding of what they have learned. Then have the children complete questions l–4. Have the children brainstorm to complete question 5 in their books.

Assessment Activity This activity offers another way of reviewing the chapter—in this case making a design or logo. Explain that a logo is a distinctive trademark similar to one they might see on brand name shirts or sports equipment. List a few sample logos. Ask them to think about different kinds of distinctive lettering that they could use, such as bubble letters. Then,

provide the children with strips of tagboard and markers. Write the names of the marks of the Church on the board. Ask children to explain the meaning of each of these marks. Then invite them to make a design or logo that illustrates each mark of the Church.

 ___ minutes

Reflect & Pray Read the introduction aloud to the children. Ask them to think about ways the Church grew during the time of the apostles. Invite the children to share their answers. Have them complete the prayer and pray it quietly to themselves.

Reflect & Pray

Describe how the Church grew during the time of the apostles.

_____

_____

Jesus, I believe in you and love you. Help me to live as a loving member of the Church. Help me especially to

_____

_____

Key Words

bishops (p. 250)
dioceses (p. 251)
pope (p. 253)
marks of the Church (p. 252)

Remember

- Jesus chose the apostles to lead the Church.
- The pope and bishops are the successors of the apostles.
- The Church is one and holy.
- The Church is catholic and apostolic.

OUR CATHOLIC LIFE

Blessed Pope John XXIII

Angelo Roncalli became Pope John XXIII at 76 years of age. No one thought he would do much. But he surprised everyone with his energy and great spirit. He called the bishops from all over the world to gather together in Rome. This meeting was known as the _Second Vatican Council_. The pope and bishops worked together to strengthen the one, holy, catholic, and apostolic Church. They called the Church to reach out to other religions and especially to the poor. The council called us to be God's people.

HOME CONNECTION

Sharing Faith with My Family

Make sure to send home the family page (text page 82).

Encourage the children to post the refrigerator prayer card so that the entire family can notice it.

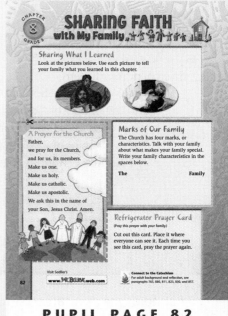

PUPIL PAGE 82

For additional information and activities, encourage families to visit Sadlier's

www.WEBELIEVEweb.com

Key Words Review the _Key Words_ and have the children write a sentence for each word.

Remember Review the four statements. Help the children to understand that these beliefs about Church leaders and the marks of the Church can make a difference in their lives. Ask them to consider how these beliefs make a difference in their lives and in the life of the Church.

Our Catholic Life Read the text aloud. Remind the children that all popes are successors to Saint Peter. All popes do their best to lead the Church and help it grow in grace and love. Tell the children that one Holy Father, Blessed Pope John XXIII, helped people everywhere. He especially helped the Church to be one, holy, catholic, and apostolic.

Plan Ahead for Chapter 9

Prayer Space: photos of family members, parish leaders, the pope and bishop, world leaders who work for justice

Lesson Materials: copies of Reproducible Master 9, Grade 3 CD, crayons and markers, posterboard

Overview

In Chapter 8, the children learned about the marks of the Church: one, holy, catholic, and apostolic. In this chapter, the children will learn more about the Church and the ways in which the Church teaches us.

Doctrinal Content	For Adult Reading and Reflection *Catechism of the Catholic Church*
The children will learn:	Paragraph
• The Church is the Body of Christ and the people of God.	782, 789
• We profess our faith through the Apostles' Creed.	194
• The Holy Spirit guides the Church.	798
• The Church continues to teach the true message of Jesus.	771

Key Words

Apostles' Creed (p. 85)
justice (p. 87)

Catechist Background

What helps me as a catechist to respond faithfully to the call of Jesus in my everyday life?

The Apostles' Creed was the first creed proclaimed and accepted by the early Church. In its emphasis on Father, Son, and Spirit, it is Trinitarian. Its focus on the life, death, and Resurrection of Jesus makes it Christocentric. In its simplicity, it encompasses a full expression of our faith.

This faith is grounded, through the incarnation, in the person of Jesus Christ—sent by the Father, conceived by the Holy Spirit, born, suffered, died, buried, and risen. This reality of Jesus Christ shapes our understanding of ourselves as the Church, the Body of Christ.

Every time we receive the Eucharist, we receive the Body of Christ. Christ becomes part of us. And we become part of that sacred Body of Christ as well. As the Body of Christ, the Church, we carry the Lord into our lives and our world.

Near the end of the Apostles' Creed, we say, "I believe in the Holy Spirit, the holy Catholic Church, the communion of saints." We believe not only in the Spirit. We believe also that this same life-giving Spirit is present in the Church, in us, each one of its members. We believe that the Holy Spirit planted the seed of holiness in the entire Church.

We believe that the Spirit is with us, that we can help and encourage one another, that we are truly the Body of Christ in the world, and that the love of Christ impels us to do his work, to teach his message, to extend his mercy to all.

When are you most grateful to be Catholic?

Lesson Planning Guide

Lesson Steps	Presentation	Materials

 1 WE GATHER

Lesson Steps	Presentation	Materials
page 83 ✚ Prayer **Focus on Life**	• Pray together. 🎵 Respond in song. • Name good things about being a member of your family or class.	For the prayer space: photos of family members, parish leaders, pope, bishop, and world leaders 🎵 "They'll Know We Are Christians," # 7, Grade 3 CD

2 WE BELIEVE

page 84 *The Church is the Body of Christ and the people of God.* 📖 *1 Corinthians 12:14–21*	• Read and discuss the Body of Christ and people of God in the text. 🚶 Answer the question.	• copies of Reproducible Master 9
page 85 *We profess our faith through the Apostles' Creed.* *Apostles' Creed*	• Read and discuss the importance of the Apostles' Creed. 🚶 Talk about ways to show our belief. • Pray the Apostles' Creed.	• crayons and markers • poster board
page 86 *The Holy Spirit guides the Church.*	• Read and discuss ways the Holy Spirit teaches and guides the Church. 🚶 Share what you have learned about Jesus and the Church.	
page 87 *The Church continues to teach the true message of Jesus.*	• Read and discuss the text about Catholic social teachings. • Read about Saint Francis and Saint Clare in *As Catholics*.	

3 WE RESPOND

page 87	🚶 Reflect on the questions and complete the activity.	
page 88 **Review**	• Complete questions 1–5. 🚶 Work on *Assessment Activity*.	• Chapter 9 Test in Grade 3 Assessment Book, pp. 17–18 • Chapter 9 Test in Test Generator • Review & Resource Book, pp. 22–24
page 89 **We Respond in Faith**	• Complete the *Reflect & Pray* activity. • Review *Remember* and *Key Words*. • Read and discuss Catholic Charities USA in *Our Catholic Life*.	• Family Book, pp. 27–29

For additional ideas, activities, and opportunities: Visit Sadlier's **www.WeBelieveweb.com**

Name _____

From Jesus' teachings about justice, we learn that
we have many _____ and _____.

Use the code here to figure out the missing
words. First write the letters above the numbers.
Then write two examples of each on the lines.

I	E	R	S	H	B	G	O	N	T	P	L
1	2	3	4	5	6	7	8	9	10	11	12

PEACE AND JUSTICE

Be FAIR!

and

___ ___ ___ ___ ___ ___
 3   1   7   5   10   4

___ ___ ___ ___ ___ ___ ___ ___ ___ ___ ___ ___ ___ ___ ___ ___
 3   2   4   11 8   9   4   1   6   1   12 1   10 1   2   4

_____

_____

_____

_____

Connections

To Community

As the children learn about justice and taking care of the world around us, discuss with them various community helpers who apply these ideals in their daily lives. For example, you may wish to talk about the work of social workers, teachers, healthcare workers, police officers, firefighters, and so on. Point out that these community helpers do God's work by caring for the needs of his people. Ask volunteers what they would like to be or do to promote peace and justice when they grow up.

To Liturgy

Help the children to recognize that our Catholic beliefs are expressed at Mass in a variety of ways. Point out that in the Nicene Creed we express our basic beliefs as Catholics. When we listen carefully to the Scripture readings we show our belief that Scripture is God's word. Encourage the children to pay attention to other expressions of faith during Mass.

FAITH and MEDIA

▶ After reading about the letters that the pope writes to the whole Church and the whole world, and about the decisions made by the pope and the bishops working together, you might mention again that the texts of the pope's letters and other Church documents are available in many different languages on the Vatican Web site. Remind the children that this is an example of the Church's use of media, and that it also demonstrates the great power of the Internet, a medium of mass communication that anyone, even a third grader, can use to send the same message at the same time to people all around the world.

Meeting Individual Needs

English Language Learners

Children for whom English is a second language may have difficulty understanding the reading material in the chapter. For these children, paraphrase a passage in the text once it is read. Ask frequently if there are any questions.

ADDITIONAL RESOURCES

Book *Saint Francis,* Brian Wildsmith, Wm. B. Eerdmans Publishing Company, 1996. Story of the life of Saint Francis of Assisi is told from the saint's point of view.

Video *Saints for Kids, Vol. 1, St. Francis of Assisi,* Pauline Books and Media, 1998. Animated portrayal of a carefree young man who gave up wealth to follow Jesus. (4 minute story of 15 minute tape)

To find more ideas for books, videos, and other learning material, visit Sadlier's

www.WeBelieveweb.com

Chapter Story

It was the last inning, and the score was 6–5. The Cougars were losing another game, and this was their last turn at bat. They hadn't won a game all year, and they didn't have many games left. It looked like the team was destined for last place again this year.

"Batter up!" came the umpire's voice. Steve went up to bat. He had struck out twice already today. It didn't look good. Strike one, two, three. You're out!

Janay got up to bat. She looked nervously back at her team. She didn't want to make another out, or the team might get mad. Steve looked at Janay's worried face. Suddenly he had an idea. He started to cheer for Janay. Tommy and Jen looked at Steve. "I guess it couldn't hurt to cheer a little bit," said Jen.

One by one, the teammates began joining in the cheer. Janay began to relax and smile. And suddenly—CRACK! The ball went sailing into left field. A base hit! The teammates looked at one another. Had their cheering made the difference?

Tommy was up next. So the team cheered for Tommy. It seemed to be their only hope. Strike one. Strike two. It wasn't looking good. But just when the team was getting nervous, Steve stood up and yelled out the team cheer. Before anyone knew what had happened, Tommy hit a home run, bringing Janay home. The Cougars had finally won a game!

"Good hit, Janay!" "Way to go, Tommy!" The team was so excited. But Tommy and Janay looked at their teammates. "We couldn't have done it without your cheering," they said. "This was definitely the best game of the year. Our teamwork saved the game!"

▶ *How is the Church like a "team"?*

The Church Teaches Us

9

WE GATHER

✝ **Leader:** God, we are your people.

All: We are your Church.

Leader: Keep us faithful to you.

All: We are your faithful followers.

Leader: Help us to do your work on earth.

All: We want to share your good news with others.

♫ **They'll Know We Are Christians**

We will walk with each other,
We will walk hand in hand,
We will walk with each other,
We will walk hand in hand,
And together we'll spread the news
that God is in our land.
And they'll know we are Christians
  by our love, by our love,
Yes, they'll know we are Christians
  by our love.

 Name some good things about being a member of your family or your class.

83

PREPARING TO PRAY

The children will pray a brief litany. They will respond in a song.

• Review the words and melody of the song "They'll Know We Are Christians," #7, Grade 3 CD.

• Choose a prayer leader.

• Invite the children to place their family photographs in the prayer space.

The Prayer Space

• Display photographs of parish leaders, the pope and bishop, and world leaders or those that work for justice in the world.

📖 **This Week's Liturgy**
Visit **www.webelieveweb.com** for this week's liturgical readings and other seasonal material.

Lesson Plan

WE GATHER   ___ minutes

✝ Pray

• Have the children open their books to the opening prayer.

• Pray the Sign of the Cross together.

• Pray the litany.

• Sing the song. You may want to have the children hold hands as you process around the room while singing the song. Sing until you have circled the room at least once.

☀ Focus on Life

• Invite children to name good things about being a member of their family or their class. Help the children to understand that the Church is a huge group of people who believe in and love Jesus Christ.

• Share the *Chapter Story* on guide page 83E.

Home Connection Update

Encourage the children to share experiences in using the Chapter 8 family page. Ask: *How did family members react to the prayer for the Church on the refrigerator prayer card?*

Catechist Goal

• To teach that the Church is the Body of Christ and the people of God and that the Holy Spirit guides the Church

Our Faith Response

• To appreciate that each person is an important member of the Church and to profess our faith in the Apostles' Creed

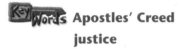 **Apostles' Creed**
justice

Lesson Materials

• copies of Reproducible Master 9

Teaching Tip
Individual Work

When the opportunity or option presents itself, encourage individuals to work alone on an activity or project in your group. This time to work independently is a valuable complement to the group and cooperative learning styles featured in their classes.

WE BELIEVE
The Church is the Body of Christ and the people of God.

📖 1 Corinthians 12:14–21

Saint Paul explained to the people that the Church is the *Body of Christ* on earth. All the parts in a person's body work together. The ear does not say, "Because I am not an eye I do not belong to the body." The eye does not say to the hand, "I do not need you." (1 Corinthians 12:16, 21) Each part of the body needs all the other parts.

Like a human body, the Church has many parts, or members. One part cannot say to another, "I do not need you!" or "You are not like me, so you do not belong." Everyone in the Church is an important part of the Body of Christ. We are united through our love for and belief in Jesus Christ.

God has chosen us to be his children, brothers and sisters of Jesus. Through our Baptism, we are brought into the Church. In the New Testament the Church is described as "God's people." (1 Peter 2:10) As the *people of God*, we try our best to love God and love one another. We try to share the good news of Jesus with everyone in the world.

✖ Look at the pictures. How are these people showing that they are the people of God?

_____

_____

_____

_____

84

Lesson Plan

WE BELIEVE ___ minutes

📖 **Have** a volunteer read aloud the first statement. Have volunteers read aloud the next three paragraphs of text and Scripture. Emphasize the following points:

• The Church is like a human body because it has many parts that all need each other and are all important.

• As God's children, we try to love one another and share Jesus' good news.

• We are the people of God, members of the Church.

Draw a large, simple outline of a human body on the board. Ask: *Who is in the Body of Christ?* (the pope, the bishops, priests, all baptized people all over the world, the saints, and those who have died). Write responses in the outline. Then ask: *Whom do you know personally in*

the Body of Christ? (Elicit names of the pastor, teachers, family, friends, themselves, and so.) Write names in the outline. End by praying for all of the people in the Body of Christ, especially for those who need it most.

✖ **Ask** the children look at the pictures on the page and discuss ways that they show that they are the people of God.

Have a volunteer read aloud the statement on page 85. Read the text below the Apostles' Creed. Point out that our beliefs were written down long ago so that the Catholic Church would have them forever. Also, stress the importance of the last sentence of the last paragraph.

We profess our faith through the Apostles' Creed.

Apostles' Creed

I believe in God, the Father almighty,
   creator of heaven and earth.

I believe in Jesus Christ, his only
   Son, our Lord.
He was conceived by the power
   of the Holy Spirit
   and born of the Virgin Mary.
He suffered under Pontius Pilate,
   was crucified, died, and was buried.
He descended to the dead.
On the third day he rose again.
He ascended into heaven,
   and is seated at the right hand
   of the Father.
He will come again to judge
   the living and the dead.

I believe in the Holy Spirit,
   the holy catholic Church,
   the communion of saints,
   the forgiveness of sins,
   the resurrection of the body,
   and the life everlasting.
Amen.

We state our belief in the Blessed Trinity: God the Father, God the Son, and God the Holy Spirit.

We state our belief that God the Son, the second Person of the Blessed Trinity, became one of us and died to save us.

We state our belief in the holy catholic Church that Jesus gave us. When we pray the Apostles' Creed we say together as the Church that we are one in faith and love.

Key Word
Apostles' Creed
(p. 250)

As the Church grew, the beliefs about Jesus and his teachings were written down in statements called *creeds*. One of the first creeds is called the **Apostles' Creed**. It is based on the teachings of Jesus Christ and the faith of the apostles.

Each time we pray the Apostles' Creed, we profess our faith. To *profess* means "to state what we believe."

With a partner talk about the ways we show our Catholic beliefs.

85

ACTIVITY BANK

Faith and Media

Advertising the Catholic Faith
Activity Materials: magazine advertisements, markers, construction paper

Talk about advertisements. Ask: *What is their purpose?* (to encourage people to buy or join something) Explain that they will be making similar advertisements for the Catholic faith. These should include the key beliefs of the Church, along with reasons for being a member of the Church. Make sure the advertisements include pictures and words.

Community

Sharing the Apostles' Creed
Activity Materials: construction paper, markers or crayons

Give the children a copy of the Apostles' Creed and construction paper on which to paste the Creed and decorate it. Have each child explain the Apostles' Creed to an older family member or another adult.

Write *I believe in . . .* on the board. Read the Apostles' Creed together. Ask the children to name the three Persons of the Trinity that the Creed lists after these words. Leave this information on the board.

Ask the children for suggestions on how their lives can reflect Catholic beliefs. Help them to think of ways that they can show their Catholic beliefs through their everyday actions. (Answers might include: looking for God in everyone, being aware of God's presence, and being respectful and helpful to all God's children)

Quick Check

✔ *How did Saint Paul explain the Church to the first Christians?* (He said the Church is the Body of Christ on earth.)

✔ *Why do we pray the Apostles' Creed?* (to profess our Catholic faith and beliefs)

The Holy Spirit guides the Church.

Jesus knew it would be difficult for the apostles to remember everything he had taught them. So he promised the apostles that "the holy Spirit that the Father will send in my name–he will teach you everything and remind you of all that [I] told you." (John 14:26) With the help of the Holy Spirit, the apostles were able to speak the truth about Jesus.

Today the Holy Spirit continues to guide the Church. The Holy Spirit guides the pope and bishops to teach the truth about Jesus. They do this by their words, writings, and actions. The pope and the bishops are the official teachers for the whole Church.

At certain times the pope gathers together all the bishops throughout the world. They make important decisions about the Church's faith and life.

Often the pope writes letters to the Church and to the whole world. These letters are about Catholic beliefs and how to live as Catholics in the world today.

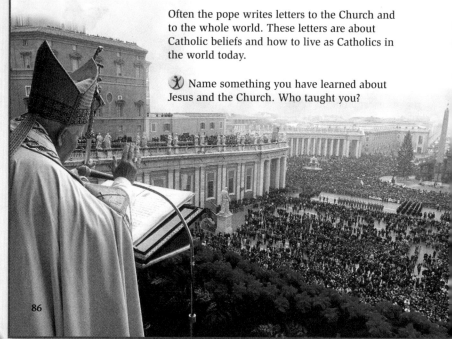

🧑 Name something you have learned about Jesus and the Church. Who taught you?

86

Teaching Tip
Teachers of the Faith

Make a bulletin board about people who teach the Catholic faith. Title it: *Teachers of the Catholic* faith. Add pictures of the pope and bishops, your priests and deacons, catechists from your school, and family members. Point out that these are some of the people who work to ensure that the children learn what it means to be members of the Catholic Church.

As Catholics...

Saints Francis and Clare

Read and discuss the lives of Saints Francis and Clare. Francis gave up everything to teach about Jesus and to help the poor. Clare gave up everything to pray for God's people. Ask: *Can we give up something to pray for and help those in need?*

Lesson Plan

WE BELIEVE (continued)

Read aloud the statement. Have the children silently read and underline important points in the following paragraphs. Emphasize the following points:

• The Holy Spirit has been sent by Jesus to guide the apostles.

• The Holy Spirit helps Church leaders today, as the apostles were taught long ago, to teach the truth of Jesus.

• Today, the pope and bishops are the official teachers of the Church.

Direct the children's attention to the photographs. Ask the children the name of the pope and where he lives. Point out the importance of the decisions that the pope and bishops make. Point out the many people being blessed by the Pope. Remind them that, with the pope and bishops, we are God's people.

🧑 **Have** children complete the activity. Stress that learning about faith requires listening, studying, and then putting into practice what has been taught.

Ask a volunteer to read aloud the statement on page 87. Have the children highlight or underline the bulleted items as you read them. Read the remaining paragraphs. Emphasize the following points:

The Church continues to teach the true message of Jesus.

The Church teaches what Jesus taught:

• God loves and cares for everyone.

• We are to love God with our whole heart.

• We are to love our neighbors as ourselves.

Some of the Church's teaching is known as *Catholic social teaching*. This teaching tells us that we are all made in God's image and have certain human rights. For example, we all have the right to life, food, housing, and safety. We have the right to be educated and to be treated equally.

These human rights are an important part of justice. **Justice** is treating everyone fairly and with respect. The justice that Jesus taught reminds us that we are all part of the human family. What helps or hurts one part of the family affects everyone.

We all have certain responsibilities to one another. For example, we have a responsibility to live together in peace. We have a responsibility to share the good things of the world. We have a responsibility to respect and care for one another.

WE RESPOND

What can you do this week to treat everyone fairly at home?

_____

in school?

_____

in your parish?

_____

Francis of Assisi was the son of a rich merchant. In his twenties, Francis felt God calling him to a different way of life. Francis gave up his wealth and began to live a simple, poor life. He fasted, prayed, and helped the poor. He preached to people about following God. Other men joined Francis and shared his life of fasting, poverty, and peace. In 1210 Francis began a religious community now known as the Franciscans.

Also born in Assisi, Clare heard Francis preach. She wanted to live a simple, poor life for Christ like Francis did. She devoted her life to God. With the help of Francis, Clare began a religious order of nuns that is known as the Poor Clares. Both communities continue to serve the needs of God's people.

Saint Francis' feast day is October 4, and Saint Clare's is August 11.

justice (p. 251)

87

ACTIVITY BANK

Curriculum Connection
Language

Have each child write a thank-you note to someone who has taught him or her about the Catholic faith. Say: *Write what that person has taught you and why it is important to you.*

Catholic Social Teaching
Call to Family, Community, and Participation
Activity Materials: magazines, scissors, glue

Have a group discussion about some ways that the Catholic Church has affected the lives of the children all over the world. (staffing schools and parish religious education programs, instruction in the sacraments, staffing hospitals) Have children cut out pictures and words from religious magazines to show ways the Church has made a difference in the lives of young people growing in the faith. Use these clippings to make a group collage entitled *Our Catholic Faith*.

• Catholic social teaching tells us that we are all made in God's image and have rights.

• Our human rights include the right to life, food, clothing, housing, and education. We also have the right to be treated fairly and equally and be safe from danger.

• Our responsibilities to others include living together in peace, sharing the good things of the world, and respecting and caring for all living things.

Distribute Reproducible Master 9. Have children complete the blanks (rights, responsibilities), and list two examples.

WE RESPOND ___ minutes

Ask children to write things that they can do this week to treat people fairly. Encourage volunteers to share their responses.

Conclude the lesson by giving the children a few minutes to pray silently for those who need help and those who have the power to help them.

CHAPTER TEST

Chapter 9 Test is provided in the Grade 3 Assessment Book.

Review

Write T if the sentence is true. Write F if the sentence is false.

1. The Church is the Body of Christ on earth.   T

2. Justice is a statement of beliefs.   F

3. The Holy Spirit helps the pope and bishops teach the truth about Jesus and our Catholic faith.   T

4. We have a responsibility to care only about the Catholics in our diocese.   F

Complete this sentence.

5. Catholic social teaching tells us _See page 87._

_____

_____

_____

_____

_____

ASSESSMENT Make a poster to show that the Church is the Body of Christ. Explain why every person is important.

Lesson Plan

Review ___ minutes

Chapter Review Explain to the children that they are going to check their understanding of what they have learned. Have them complete questions 1–4. Have them answer question 5 in their books. Allow them to go back and review the Catholic social teaching in their textbooks.

Assessment Activity This activity challenges the children to think of the Body of Christ in their own ways, at their own levels of understanding.

We Respond in Faith ___ minutes

Reflect & Pray Elicit a response to the questions. Invite a volunteer to read the prayer. Remind the children that the Holy Spirit is with us at all times, but there are certain times when we especially need guidance. Encourage the children to write about a specific time on the provided lines. Invite volunteers to share their responses with the group.

 Key Words Read the definitions for the *Key Words* from the chapter and ask children to say what word you are defining. Then challenge the children to make up their own sentences that correctly use the key words.

Reflect & Pray

What are some ways that you can act with justice in school? at home?

Jesus sent the Holy Spirit to guide us and to help us to remember his teachings.

Holy Spirit, be with me and guide me, especially when

_____

_____

Key Words

Apostles' Creed (p. 250)
justice (p. 251)

Remember

- The Church is the Body of Christ and the people of God.
- We profess our faith through the Apostles' Creed.
- The Holy Spirit guides the Church.
- The Church continues to teach the true message of Jesus.

OUR CATHOLIC LIFE

Catholic Charities USA

Justice is why Catholic Charities USA helps over ten million needy people throughout the United States each year. At food pantries, the group offers free bags of groceries for those in need. They offer counseling, daycare programs, and job training. They also work for justice for all people. Catholics can participate in the work of Catholic Charities USA by volunteering their time and by donating food, clothing, and money.

HOME CONNECTION

Sharing Faith with My Family

Make sure to send home the family page (text page 90).

Encourage the children to share with family members the Church's teachings on justice.

PUPIL PAGE 90

For additional information and activities, encourage families to visit Sadlier's

www.WeBelieveweb.com

Remember Invite the children to gather once again in the prayer space. While they are gathered, read each of the *Remember* statements aloud. Ask the children to explain what they have learned in the accompanying lesson. Also, ask children to locate items in the prayer spaces that relate to the statements or lesson.

Our Catholic Life Read aloud the text. Ask the children to identify ways they can be a part of such a charity. Give examples of other charitable organizations, such as the Saint Vincent de Paul Society. Remind the children that we have a responsibility to take care of one another, and this is a good way to do so.

Plan Ahead for Chapter 10

Prayer Space: crucifix or a statue of Jesus, recording of soft instrumental music

Materials: construction paper, magazines, catalogs, copies of Reproducible Master 10

Chapter 10 The Church Prays

Overview

In Chapter 9 the children learned about the Church. In this chapter they will learn about the ways Catholics listen and talk to God in prayer.

Doctrinal Content	For Adult Reading and Reflection *Catechism of the Catholic Church*
The children will learn:	Paragraph
• Jesus teaches his followers how to pray.	2759
• We can pray with others or by ourselves.	2655
• There are different kinds of prayer.	2626–2638
• The Church prays at all times.	2186

Key Words

prayer (p. 92)
synagogue (p. 92)
liturgy (p. 93)
pilgrimages (p. 95)

Catechist Background

When and where do I pray?

It might be helpful to think of the Church's prayer as a great river. At the depths of this river, always flowing, is liturgical prayer: the Mass, the sacraments, and the Liturgy of the Hours. At every moment of every day, all across the world, this great river of prayer is always accessible. We live from its depths.

We, as individuals, submerge our own prayer—our own praises and needs, joys and sorrows—into this great river of prayer. When we pray, we find ourselves carried along, buoyed up, by this abundant river, so much greater and deeper than ourselves.

Sometimes this river of prayer is quiet and peaceful. Sometimes it is choppy and turbulent, marked by unexpected rapids. Sometimes the river seems to dry up altogether, and we find ourselves in a vast desert! But then, by the grace of God, the river bubbles up again, a gift—just as Moses was given water from the rock with a tap of his rod.

Once Jesus cried out, "Whoever believes in me, as scripture says:

'Rivers of living waters will flow from within him'" (John 7:38).

Then follows an author's note: "He said this in reference to the Spirit that those who came to believe in him were to receive. There was, of course, no Spirit yet, because Jesus had not yet been glorified" (John 7:39).

Now Jesus is the Rock we tap with our rod of faith. From him flows the Spirit, the source of all prayer. In that Spirit, our prayer of faith, both liturgical and personal, opens to us the waters of life from within.

And in the Spirit we cry, "*Abba,* Father!" (Romans 8:15).

How can I share my prayer with others?

Lesson Planning Guide

Lesson Steps	Presentation	Materials

1 WE GATHER

Lesson Steps	Presentation	Materials
page 91 ✝ **Prayer** ☀ **Focus on Life**	• Pray together and use hand gestures. • Name ways to stay in touch.	For the prayer space: crucifix or statue of Jesus; recording of soft instrumental music

2 WE BELIEVE

Lesson Steps	Presentation	Materials
page 92 *Jesus teaches his followers how to pray.*	• Read and discuss the text about prayer and Jesus' teaching of the Our Father. 🧍 Tell about the Our Father. • Pray the Our Father together.	
page 93 *We can pray with others or by ourselves.*	• Read and discuss the text about the liturgy and different ways to pray. 🧍 Illustrate one way your family likes to pray.	• construction paper • magazines or catalogs
page 94 *There are different kinds of prayer.*	• Read and discuss the text about different kinds of prayer. 🧍 Identify types of prayer.	• copies of Reproducible Master 10
page 95 *The Church prays at all times.*	• Read and discuss the Liturgy of the Hours, pilgrimages, and the Mass as the greatest prayer. • Read and discuss the prayer posture in *As Catholics.*	

3 WE RESPOND

Lesson Steps	Presentation	Materials
page 95	🧍 Act out some ways your parish prays.	
page 96 **Review**	• Complete questions 1–5. 🧍 Work on *Assessment Activity.*	• Chapter 10 Test in Assessment Book, pp. 19–20 • Chapter 10 Test in Test Generator • Review & Resource Book, pp. 25–27
page 97 **We Respond in Faith**	🧍 Complete the *Reflect & Pray* activity. • Review *Remember* and *Key Words.* • Read and discuss general intercessions in *Our Catholic Life.* • Discuss **Sharing Faith with My Family.**	• Family Book, pp. 30–32

For additional ideas, activities, and opportunities: Visit Sadlier's  www.WeBelieveweb.com

Name _____

Under each heading write what you will include in your prayer. Use your prayer list to help you talk to God every day.

My Prayer List

Prayers of Praise	Prayers of Thanksgiving	Prayers of Intercession
_____	_____	_____
_____	_____	_____
_____	_____	_____
_____	_____	_____
_____	_____	_____
_____	_____	_____

Prayers of Petition	Prayers of Blessing
_____	_____
_____	_____
_____	_____
_____	_____
_____	_____

Connections

To Liturgy

As the children explore different types of prayer, talk about the variety of prayers prayed during Mass. Use a missal or the missalette used in church to guide the children through the Mass. Choose an example of each type of prayer (praise, thanksgiving, intercession, sorrow, blessing) ahead of time. Read those Mass prayers aloud. Allow volunteers to suggest which type of prayer each Mass prayer is.

To Family

Invite the children to discuss how prayer is shared in their families. Ask them to share the different times their families pray together, such as before and after meals or in the evening. Encourage them to initiate family prayer in their homes. Suggest that they pray the rosary as a family. Remind them that the beginning of a family car trip is a good time to pray the rosary together.

FAITH and MEDIA

▶ To enhance this chapter, you might show the children a variety of prayer-centered Internet sites. There are sites where one can find the words of the Lord's Prayer, the Apostles' Creed, and other prayers in languages ranging from English, French, and Spanish to Vietnamese, Wolof, and Navajo. On other sites one can find searchable, date-specific compilations of the prayers of the Liturgy of the Hours. Still other sites, such as the Irish Jesuits' *Sacred Space*, offer daily prayers and Scripture readings in a variety of languages.

Meeting Individual Needs

Children With Visual or Hearing Needs

Sometimes visual and hearing problems in children go undiagnosed because the children assume that their poor vision or hearing is normal. From time to time, ask, *Is anyone finding it hard to see what is on the board?* Or: *What's on the board?* Also ask: *Is anyone having a hard time hearing me?* Seat these children in the front. If you suspect a problem, speak to the children' parents about it.

ADDITIONAL RESOURCES

Book *Playing and Praying with God: Guided Meditations for Children*, Rita A. Brink, Paulist Press, 1996. Leader-led meditations root the child in faith and Scripture.

Video *The Angel's Prayer Lesson*, Twenty-Third Publications. A young girl teaches children how to offer prayers of praise, thanksgiving, petition, and sorrow. (12 minutes)

To find more ideas for books, videos, and other learning material, visit Sadlier's

www.WEBELIEVEweb.com

Focus on Life

Chapter Story

Jess woke early. She was concerned about Gramps. Mom had said that he was very sick. Jess prayed, "Please, God, take care of Gramps."

On the way to school, Jess noticed the beautiful flowers blooming all over town. Their smiling little faces cheered her up. She prayed, "O God, you made our beautiful world. You are so wonderful!"

At school, the girls were jumping rope. Jess loved to jump rope! One girl was already jumping when Jess cut in and jumped, too! Sarah yelled at her for jumping out of turn. Jess was sorry immediately and said so. She prayed, "Please forgive me, God. I didn't think before I acted."

At dinner that evening, Jess and her family bowed their heads and prayed, "Bless us, O Lord, and these your gifts . . ." Jess ate lots of macaroni and cheese!

That night, Mom got a phone call. She hugged Jess and told her that Gramps was much better. Together, they prayed, "Thank you God, for your care for all of us, especially Gramps."

▶ *Can you name five kinds of prayer in this story?*
(in order: intercession, praise, petition, blessing, thanksgiving)

The Church Prays

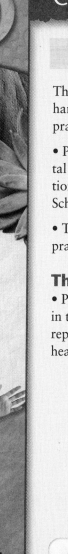

WE GATHER

✝ **Leader:** Be still and quiet. Place your hands on your knees with your palms up.

Talk to God in your heart. Tell him anything you wish. Ask God for what you need, and ask his blessing on those you love.

All: (Pray quietly.)

Leader: Lift up your hands as a sign of your prayer rising to God.

All: Let my prayer be incense before you. (Psalm 141:2a)

 When someone you love is far away, how can you stay in touch?

91

PREPARING TO PRAY

The children will pray quietly and use hand gestures to accompany their prayer.

• Play a recording of soft instrumental background music. Some suggestions are Pachabel's *Canon* in D and Schubert's *Impromptu* in G Flat.

• Tell the children you will lead the prayer.

The Prayer Space

• Place a crucifix or a statue of Jesus in the middle of the prayer table to represent our Lord Jesus Christ, who hears our prayers.

📖 **This Week's Liturgy**
Visit **www.webelieveweb.com** for this week's liturgical readings and other seasonal material.

Lesson Plan

WE GATHER
—— minutes

✝ **Pray**

• Explain that quiet music helps us to calm down and be still. Begin the music.

• Remind the children that incense is a sign of prayer. The smoke rises, just as our prayers rise to God. Incense has a beautiful perfume. Our prayers are beautiful to God.

• Have the children use the gestures as part of their prayer. Pray the Sign of the Cross and lead the prayer.

• You may want to ask the children to pray aloud for particular people or needs. After each prayer, ask all to lift up their hands and pray the psalm refrain on page 91.

☀ **Focus on Life**

• Ask the children how they stay in touch with people. Help them to see that prayer is a way to stay in touch with God.

• Share the *Chapter Story* on guide page 91E.

Home Connection Update

Encourage the children to share experiences using the Chapter 9 family page. Ask volunteers to share what their family did with the justice activity.

Catechist Goal

• To present that Jesus taught his followers how to pray and to explore ways we can pray

Our Faith Response

• To choose ways we can pray as followers of Jesus and members of the Church

 **prayer   synagogue**
liturgy   pilgrimages

Lesson Materials

• construction paper
• magazines or catalogs
• copies of Reproducible Master 10
• newspaper clippings about pilgrimages

Teaching Tip
Brainstorming

"Brainstorming" allows children to contribute their own ideas to a group. Each child's response is listed on the board. Brainstorming is a helpful tool when you are looking for a variety of ideas, such as, identifying options for a group project. Each contribution is accepted and not judged as right or wrong.

WE BELIEVE
Jesus teaches his followers how to pray.

Jesus is the son of God. Jesus is divine because he is God. He is also Mary's son. Jesus is human like us in every way except he is without sin.

Jesus had to learn how to walk, talk, read, and write. Mary and Joseph also taught Jesus how to talk to God in prayer. **Prayer** is listening and talking to God.

Jesus prayed in the **synagogue**, the gathering place where Jewish people pray and learn about God. Jesus also worshiped in the Temple in Jerusalem. Other times he went off by himself to pray. Sometimes he prayed with his family or his disciples.

The disciples wanted to learn how to pray as Jesus did. One day they said to him, "Lord, teach us to pray." (Luke 11:1) So Jesus taught them this prayer:

Our Father, who art in heaven,
hallowed be thy name;
thy kingdom come;
thy will be done on earth
as it is in heaven.
Give us this day our daily bread;
and forgive us our trespasses
as we forgive those who trespass
against us;
and lead us not into temptation,
but deliver us from evil. Amen.

This prayer is the Lord's Prayer. We also call it the Our Father. It is the greatest example of prayer for the Church.

Use your own words to tell what we pray for when we pray the Lord's Prayer.

92

Lesson Plan

WE BELIEVE ___ minutes

Read aloud the statement and the first four paragraphs. Explain that, at home with Mary and Joseph, Jesus learned the Jewish heritage of prayer. Jesus prayed the psalms of Israel with other faithful Jews at the synagogue and at the Temple in Jerusalem. Tell the children that in Saint Luke's Gospel there are beautiful examples of prayer. Foremost is Mary's *Magnificat* in Luke 1:46–55. When Jesus was presented in the Temple by Mary and Joseph, Simeon was moved by the Spirit to pray and bless God (Luke 2:29–32). Emphasize that these prayers show the variety of ways Jewish people prayed to God.

Read together the Lord's Prayer.

Have the children explain the meaning of the prayer that Jesus taught us.

Pray the Our Father. Point out that the Our Father or the Lord's Prayer "is truly the summary of the whole gospel (CCC 2761).

Ask a volunteer read aloud the statement on page 93. Invite pairs of children to read the two paragraphs to each other. Ask them to think of various times when people come together to worship God. Have them list their answers as well as their own ideas on a sheet of paper. Share ideas.

We can pray with others or by ourselves.

We often come together to worship God. We gather with others to celebrate the **liturgy**, the official public prayer of the Church. Each celebration, such as the Mass and the sacraments, is an action of the whole Church. Together as the Church, we worship the Blessed Trinity. We pray with Christ and with the whole Church, the Body of Christ.

Sometimes we pray alone just as Jesus did. We call this personal prayer. We can pray at any time and in any place. We can pray prayers such as the Our Father and the Hail Mary. We can also pray with our own words. God listens to us when we pray. He knows what we need.

✵ Draw one way your family likes to pray.

Key Word

prayer (p. 253)
synagogue (p. 253)
liturgy (p. 251)

93

ACTIVITY BANK

Multicultural Connection
Prayer Around the World

Various cultures have their own traditions and rituals concerning prayer. Invite someone from a culture different from yours or your group's to talk to the class about prayer. Ask your guest to share ways people from that culture traditionally pray. If he or she speaks a language other than English, invite your visitor to say a prayer in that language.

Curriculum Connection
Language Arts

Encourage the children to keep track of their prayer life for a set period of time. Have them keep a log or journal to record the various times (morning prayer, meal blessing, family rosary) and ways that they pray (alone, with the family, with the parish). At the end of the time period ask the children if they see patterns in their prayer log. Ask: *Did anything surprise you?*

Tell the children that God listens to us when we pray. He will always answer our prayers by giving us what we need.

Ask the children to cut pictures of doors from old magazines and catalogs. Paste them on construction paper. Place the doors in the prayer space.

Gather in the prayer space. Point out the doors that decorate the space. Remind the children that prayer is like a knock at the door. Read aloud: "I tell you, ask and you will receive; seek and you will find; knock and the door will be opened to you." (Luke 11:9). Invite the children to offer prayers of petition to God. To each petition have the children respond: *Lord, hear our prayer.*

Quick Check

✔ *What is prayer?* (listening and talking to God)

✔ *What did Jesus do when the disciples wanted to learn how to pray?* (He gave them the words of the Lord's Prayer to teach them how to pray.)

✔ *Who listens to us when we pray?* (God)

Teaching Note

Pilgrimages

Pilgrimages are journeys to sacred places to pray and do penance. They have always been popular with the people of all the major world religions. Christians frequently visit places of importance in the life of Jesus, such as Jerusalem, Nazareth, and Bethlehem. Catholics also go to sites of apparitions of Mary, such as Fatima in Portugal and Lourdes in France.

As Catholics...

The Prayer Posture

Read aloud the text. Invite the children to share their answers to the final question. Suggest that the children try different prayer postures, for example, arms upraised with palms up during a prayer.

There are different kinds of prayer.

Think of a time when something was so beautiful or amazing that it made you think "Wow!" That feeling can become a *prayer of praise.* "O God, you are wonderful!"

Think of a time when you passed a difficult test or when you felt better after being sick. You felt grateful that God had been so good to you. You said, "Thank you so much, O Lord!" This is a *prayer of thanksgiving.*

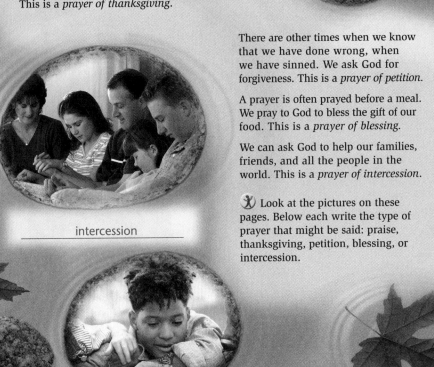

intercession

praise

94

There are other times when we know that we have done wrong, when we have sinned. We ask God for forgiveness. This is a *prayer of petition.*

A prayer is often prayed before a meal. We pray to God to bless the gift of our food. This is a *prayer of blessing.*

We can ask God to help our families, friends, and all the people in the world. This is a *prayer of intercession.*

Look at the pictures on these pages. Below each write the type of prayer that might be said: praise, thanksgiving, petition, blessing, or intercession.

Lesson Plan

WE BELIEVE (continued)

Have a volunteer read aloud the statement on page 94. Ask the children to read the text in small groups. Have them list the different types of prayer as they read.

- prayer of praise
- prayer of thanksgiving
- prayer of petition
- prayer of blessing
- prayer of intercession

Ask each group to make up and pray one type of prayer together.

Use the pictures to identify the type of prayer.

Distribute Reproducible Master 10. Encourage the children to write their own reasons to pray.

Ask a volunteer read aloud the statement on page 95. Form five groups. Assign each group a paragraph. Have them read the paragraph and discuss the information they have read. Ask each group to report the main points of its paragraph.

The Church prays at all times.

Did you know that the Church is always at prayer? In one part of the world, children are beginning their school day by praying. Yet at the same time in another part of the world, children are saying their prayers before going to bed.

There are special prayers called the Liturgy of the Hours. These prayers are prayed seven different times during the day. So somewhere in the world, people are always praying the Liturgy of the Hours.

If we could travel around the world, we would be able to pray in different languages and in different ways. For example, in some countries, people pray by taking part in dances.

Other people would be praying by walking through the streets in processions. In some countries, we would see people praying at shrines set up along the roads. In other places, we would see people making journeys to holy places. These prayer-journeys are called **pilgrimages**.

The greatest prayer of the Church is the Mass. The Mass is the celebration of the Eucharist, the sacrament of the Body and Blood of Christ. It unites us all and leads us to live as Jesus' disciples.

WE RESPOND

In groups talk about some of the ways your parish prays. How do these ways help people to grow closer to God? Act out one of these ways for the rest of the class.

Key Word

pilgrimages (p. 252)

blessing

petition

95

As Catholics...

We can pray with our bodies. We show respect for Jesus present in the Eucharist by genuflecting or bowing before the tabernacle. During Mass we pray by standing, kneeling, and sitting. At other times we pray with hands folded or with arms open wide. Sometimes people even pray by dancing!

How do you pray?

ACTIVITY BANK

Liturgy
General Intercessions
Activity Materials: missals or missalettes

Bring in missals or missalettes and point out where the general intercessions occur in the Mass. (after the Creed is said at Mass) Talk about the different versions of intercessions. Invite the children to write their own intercessions. Pray these in the classroom or arrange for the intercessions to be used at a school or parish Mass.

Multiple Intelligences
Bodily-Kinesthetic

Liturgical gestures and dance are ways of offering praise to God. Invite volunteers to develop their own liturgical dance to a favorite hymn or piece of service music. Ask the children what kind of prayer they want to express. Encourage them to share what they prepared. Consider incorporating some of these dances or gestures into future group prayers.

Emphasize the following points:

• The Liturgy of the Hours is prayed at various times of the day.

• At every moment of the day, Catholics are united in celebrating Mass and the sacraments.

• There are many different prayer customs in the Church throughout the world. One of them is a pilgrimage, a prayer-journey.

WE RESPOND _____ minutes

Ask the children to think about ways the parish prays.

Act out possible ways for the parish to pray together.

Pray Conclude the lesson by praying the Our Father. (Try praying with hands upraised, palms up.) Ask the children to imagine they are on a pilgrimage as they pray. Stress that Christians are never alone on their prayer-journeys. Jesus is always with them.

CHAPTER TEST

Chapter 10 Test is provided in the Grade 3 Assessment Book.

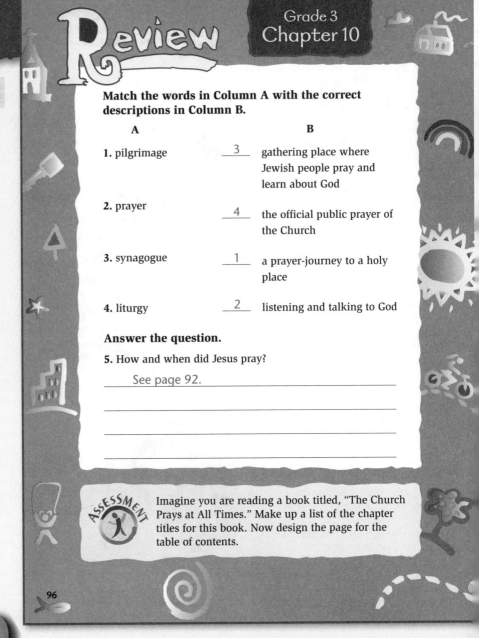

Review

Match the words in Column A with the correct descriptions in Column B.

A		B
1. pilgrimage	_3_	gathering place where Jewish people pray and learn about God
2. prayer	_4_	the official public prayer of the Church
3. synagogue	_1_	a prayer-journey to a holy place
4. liturgy	_2_	listening and talking to God

Answer the question.

5. How and when did Jesus pray?

See page 92.

_____

_____

_____

ASSESSMENT Imagine you are reading a book titled, "The Church Prays at All Times." Make up a list of the chapter titles for this book. Now design the page for the table of contents.

96

Lesson Plan

 __ minutes

Chapter Review Explain to the children that they are now going to check their understanding of what they have learned. Have the children complete questions 1–4. Have them read and answer question 5 in their textbooks. Invite them to share their answers.

Assessment Activity This review activity is meant to offer another way to assess what the children have learned. Review the activity directions with the children. Encourage them to look through books in the classroom if they need help creating a table of contents. When their project is complete, have volunteers tell why they chose their chapter titles. Place the finished activity in a portfolio of their work.

 __ minutes

Reflect & Pray Read aloud the introduction. Give the children time to think about and then write their ending. Gather in the prayer space. Pray the first part of the prayer aloud together. Pause to allow the children to offer their ending silently.

🔑 **Key Words** Invite the children to make fill-in-the-blank sentences for each *Key Word*. Have them read their sentences aloud and call on volunteers to give the correct answer using the *Key Words*.

Reflect & Pray

Jesus wants us to pray always. He is with us whenever we pray in his name. Finish the prayer.

Jesus, you are closer to me than I know. Be with me at all times. Especially help me to

_____

_____

_____

Key Words

prayer (p. 253)
synagogue (p. 253)
liturgy (p. 251)
pilgrimages (p. 252)

Remember

- Jesus teaches his followers how to pray.
- We can pray with others or by ourselves.
- There are different kinds of prayer.
- The Church prays at all times.

OUR CATHOLIC LIFE

General Intercessions

At every Mass, we pray the *general intercessions*. This is also called the *prayer of the faithful*. We remember the needs of the Church and all people in the world. We usually pray for: Church leaders and the whole Church; world leaders and world situations; our neighborhoods; the sick; and those who have died. Each person can also offer his or her own personal prayers.

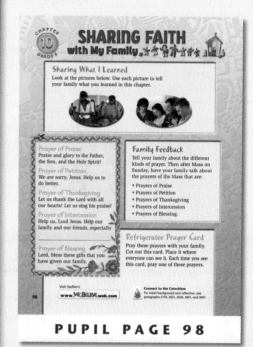

HOME CONNECTION

Sharing Faith with My Family

Make sure to send home the family page (text page 98).

Encourage the children to talk about different ways of praying with family members.

SHARING FAITH with My Family

CHAPTER 10 GRADE 3

Sharing What I Learned
Look at the pictures below. Use each picture to tell your family what you learned in this chapter.

Prayer of Praise
Praise and glory to the Father, the Son, and the Holy Spirit!

Prayer of Petition
We are sorry, Jesus. Help us to do better.

Prayer of Thanksgiving
Let us thank the Lord with all our hearts! Let us sing his praise!

Prayer of Intercession
Help us, Lord Jesus. Help our family and our friends, especially

Prayer of Blessing
Lord, bless these gifts that you have given our family.

Family Feedback
Tell your family about the different kinds of prayer. Then after Mass on Sunday, have your family talk about the prayers of the Mass that are:

- Prayers of Praise
- Prayers of Petition
- Prayers of Thanksgiving
- Prayers of Intercession
- Prayers of Blessing

Refrigerator Prayer Card
Pray these prayers with your family. Cut out this card. Place it where everyone can see it. Each time you see this card, pray one of these prayers.

Visit Sadlier's
www.WEBELIEVEweb.com

Connect to the Catechism
For adult background and reflection, see paragraphs 2750, 2651, 2626, 2691, and 2807.

98

PUPIL PAGE 98

For additional information and activities, encourage families to visit Sadlier's

www.WEBELIEVEweb.com

Remember Invite a volunteer to read the statements aloud. Then play "Round Review." Have the children sit in a circle. Then ask a child to read aloud the first statement. The child to his or her left says one thing that was learned about the statement. The next child suggests something else that was learned. Play continues until a child cannot think of any further examples, in which case he or she reads statement two and play continues.

Our Catholic Life Read the text aloud. Ask: *Do we pray the prayer of the faithful together or alone?* (Both, because we can add our own prayers silently and everyone together prays with us.) Suggest that, as a group, you compose general intercessions. Pray them together.

Plan Ahead for Chapter 11

Prayer Space: cans of food, pennies

Materials: small slips of paper, copies of Reproducible Master 11, pens and stationary

Overview

In Chapter 10 the children learned the ways in which we pray as Catholics. In this chapter they will gain a deeper understanding of the parish as a Catholic community and the various ways people serve in their parish.

Doctrinal Content	For Adult Reading and Reflection *Catechism of the Catholic Church*
The children will learn:	Paragraph
• We belong to a parish.	2179
• Many people serve our parish.	1348
• Our parish worships together.	2182
• Our parish cares for others.	2186

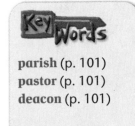

Key Words

parish (p. 101)
pastor (p. 101)
deacon (p. 101)

Catechist Background

How have my fellow parishioners supported me in my teaching ministry?

"And the Word became flesh
    and made his dwelling among us,
    and we saw his glory,
    the glory of the Father's only Son,
    full of grace and truth." (John 1:14)

We know that our lives are, deep down, full of grace and truth because they are filled with Christ, but sometimes parish life is not all that glorious. We may find this to be true more often than others, simply because we have accepted a mission in the parish that demands our time and talent on an on-going basis. Parish life is a "common life"—a life in community—and, while we profess a common faith, we are as individuals, very different!

If we step back a moment, we might find it just a bit amusing to watch these differences manifest themselves around the parish in various all-too-human ways. One parishioner has complete control of the parish coffee-pot. Another doesn't care if the roof falls in as long as nobody moves the kindergarten chairs. And the key to the supply closet? Just don't ask.

The glorious truth is that Jesus chose to live among us. He chose fallible human beings to carry on his work because that is the only kind of human beings there are. We will find him here, at home in our homes and at home in our parish, as we gradually learn to share our lives of faith with others, as we gradually learn to love one another. He will be with us especially when we, as a parish, reach out beyond our doors to welcome and strengthen our neighborhood, our town, and our world.

How do I show support for other ministries in my parish?

Lesson Planning Guide

Lesson Steps	Presentation	Materials

1 WE GATHER

page 99 ✝ **Prayer** ☀ **Focus on Life**	• Listen to Scripture. • Respond in prayer. • Discuss family get-togethers.	For the prayer space: cans of food, pennies

2 WE BELIEVE

page 100 *We belong to a parish.*	• Read and discuss the text about parish activities. 🏃 Illustrate a parish activity.	• small slips of paper
page 101 *Many people serve our parish.*	• Read about and discuss people who work in a parish. 🏃 Complete the activity. • Discuss ministries within the parish.	• copies of Reproducible Master 11
pages 102–103 *Our parish worships together.* *Our parish cares for others.*	• Read and discuss the text about celebrations within the Church. 🏃 Talk with the children about worshipping. Have them share their thoughts with the group. • Read and discuss the text regarding loving and serving one another. • Read and discusss pastoral administrators in *As Catholics*.	

3 WE RESPOND

page 103	🏃 Complete the acrostic about parish activities.	
page 104 **Review**	• Complete questions 1–5. 🏃 Work on *Assessment Activity*.	• pens and stationery • Chapter 11 Test in Grade 3 Assessment Book, pp. 21–22 • Chapter 11 Test in Test Generator • Review & Resource Book, pp. 28–30
page 105 **We Respond in Faith**	• Complete the *Reflect & Pray* activity. • Review *Remember* and *Key Words*. • Read and discuss "Caring for the Sick" in *Our Catholic Life*. • Discuss **Sharing Faith with My Family**.	• Family Book, pp. 33–35

For additional ideas, activities, and opportunities: Visit Sadlier's **www.WeBelieveweb.com**

99B

Name _____

Most parishes have groups that help others. What are some in your parish? What do they do?

Our Parish Cares for Others

Groups	What Do They Do?
_____	_____
_____	_____
_____	_____
_____	_____
_____	_____

Connections

To Community

Children learn in this chapter that "our parish cares for others." Guide them to the realization that many people in the community are lonely or sick, and would appreciate attention and care. Point out examples of parish programs and organizations that help people in the larger community. Remind the children of the positive influence the parish can have on the surrounding community.

To Scripture

In this chapter children will read the words of Jesus, "For where two or three are gathered together in my name, there am I in the midst of them" (Matthew 18:20). Be prepared to talk with the children about the many parish activities where people gather in his name. Stress that at the Eucharist, we gather as God's people to give him praise and thanksgiving.

FAITH and MEDIA

▶ To emphasize ways to use media to do Christ's work in the world, show the children examples of the Church's use of media at both the parish and diocesan levels.

▶ Bring several issues of the diocesan newspaper to class. Ask: *What do you learn about parish life?*

▶ If your diocese has a Web site, visit it with the children. If the site offers links to the Web sites of parishes in the diocese, visit several. If your diocese includes parishes whose parishioners come from different ethnic or national backgrounds, you might also look at these special customs and prayers.

▶ Bring to class as many issues of your own parish bulletin as possible. Encourage the children to read about the people who serve the parish and ways they serve.

Meeting Individual Needs

Children Who Daydream

Some children ease inner tension by "acting out." Others daydream. Most often, this is not a conscious choice, but simply a need for an active mind to "take a break." Never call attention to a daydreamer with a remark like "Lost in outer space?" This may provoke classmates to tease. Gently guide the child back to the lesson with a specific request, such as "Carla, will you read the last paragraph on page 72?"

ADDITIONAL RESOURCES

Books

A Peek Into My Church, Veronica Kelly, Wendy Good, and Ginny Pruitt, Whippersnapper Books, 1999. This book offers students an informative glance into the church community.

A Tour of Our Parish Church, Ikonographics, St. Anthony Messenger Press, 2000. Older students teach younger ones the names and meanings of objects of the Catholic faith.

To find more ideas for books, videos, and other learning material, visit Sadlier's

www.WE BELIEVE web.com

Focus on Life

Chapter Story

"I'm not going to Mass today," Molly said quietly.

"Why, Molly?" her mother inquired, as she placed her hand on the girl's forehead. "Are you sick?"

"No, I just don't care if I go to church. Nobody's going to miss me."

Mrs. Smith replied, "Molly, I'd like to tell you about a man who also thought he wasn't important. He played the piccolo in a very large orchestra. Many great musicians were part of this orchestra. But whenever they rehearsed, Pete the piccolo player would think to himself, 'All of these musicians play much better than I do. I don't think it matters if I play or not. I'm not important.' And so one day during practice, Pete lowered his piccolo and stopped playing."

"For a moment the great orchestra played on. But suddenly the conductor threw up his hands as a signal for silence. He boomed out across the stage, 'Where is my piccolo? Why have you stopped playing?' Pete hung his head in shame. How could he have thought that he wouldn't be missed? He knew now that he *was* important. The great orchestra needed even the little piccolo to make its music perfect."

Mrs. Smith gently reached for her daughter's hand as she said, "Molly, do you understand that just as Pete was needed in the orchestra, you are important to the parish? It's important to show our love for Jesus and for one another by coming together at Mass on Sunday. We want everyone there for the celebration!"

Molly quickly grabbed her coat and then hugged her mom. "Thanks Mom for helping me realize I'm important to our parish. Come on, we don't want to be late for Mass!

▶ *How does one person make a difference in celebrating as a faith community?*

The Parish Is Our Home

WE GATHER

✝ **Leader:** Let us listen to the words of Jesus.

Reader: "I have called you friends. As I have loved you, so you also should love one another." (John 15:15; 13:34)

All: Thank you, Jesus, for calling us to be your friends and followers in the Church.

Reader: "For where two or three are gathered together in my name, there am I in the midst of them." (Matthew 18:20)

All: Thank you, Jesus, for our parish where we can gather in your name.

Reader: "Whatever you did for one of these least brothers of mine, you did for me." (Matthew 25:40)

All: Thank you, Jesus, for inviting us to do your work on earth. Help us to see you in all those in need. Amen.

✹ When does your whole family get together? Why?

Thank You JESUS!

PREPARING TO PRAY

The children will listen to Scripture and respond in a prayer of thanks to Jesus.

• Choose children to place the items on the prayer table at the appointed time.

• Select a reader for the reading. Have the reader practice the readings with a partner.

• Tell the children that you will be the leader for this prayer.

The Prayer Space

• Gather items to remind children of parishioners who may be in need of help. Display cans of food to remember people who are hungry and pennies to remember those who are penniless, or poor.

📖 **This Week's Liturgy**
Visit www.webelieveweb.com for this week's liturgical readings and other seasonal material.

Lesson Plan

WE GATHER ___ minutes

✝ Pray

• Have the volunteers place the selected items on the prayer table.

• Begin with the Sign of the Cross. As the leader, say the first line of the prayer and then have reader proclaim the Scripture.

• Pray together.

• You may want to suggest that children bring cans of food to add to the ones in the prayer space. At the end of the week bring the cans to a food pantry.

Focus on Life

• Discuss times families get together, and the different reason for the get-togethers. Explain to the children that in this chapter they will learn about reasons why the parish gets together.

• Share the *Chapter Story* on guide page 99E.

Home Connection Update

Encourage the children to share their weekend experiences of completing the Chapter 10 family page. Inquire whether the prayer card was posted somewhere in their home.

Catechist Goal

- To explain that we belong to a parish and that there are many ways that we serve God and one another in our parishes

Our Faith Response

- To decide on ways to be active caring members of our parish

 **parish   pastor   deacon**

Lesson Materials

- small slips of paper
- copies of Reproducible Master 11

Teaching Note

Parish Community Experience

It is reasonable to assume that some of the children have had much experience in the parish community, while others have had little or none. Provide the children's parents with the name of the pastor and other parish leaders. If possible, show the children photographs of the parish leaders. Also describe in detail the parish's worship and social activities.

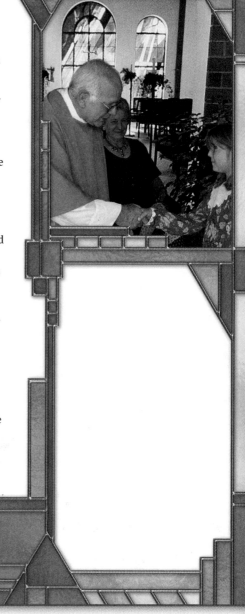

WE BELIEVE
We belong to a parish.

A parish is like a family. A **parish** is a community of believers who worship and work together. It is made up of Catholics who usually live in the same neighborhood. It is part of a diocese which is led by a bishop.

The members of a parish share the same faith in Jesus Christ. Parish members:

- come together to celebrate the Mass and other sacraments
- come together to pray, learn, and grow in faith
- work together to meet the needs of their parish
- welcome people who want to become members of the Church. These people learn from others about the Catholic faith. They prepare for the sacraments of Baptism, Confirmation, and Eucharist.

You belong to a parish. In your parish there are many ways to live and grow as a Catholic.

Draw or write about one time you took part in a parish activity.

100

Lesson Plan

WE BELIEVE ___ minutes

Have a volunteer read aloud the statement and the first paragraph on page 100. Explain to the children that the parish is much like a large tree. Draw a tree on the board. Write the word *diocese* under the tree and have children recall who is the leader of the diocese (the bishop). Write *parish* on the trunk of the tree and ask a child to explain what that word means. (A parish is a community of believers who worship and work together.)

Ask volunteers to read the second paragraph, the bulleted items, and remaining text. Next, have the children write their names on small slips of paper, and place them on the branches of the tree. Ask: *What important things unite the members of a parish?* (Faith in Jesus Christ and the teachings of the Church.)

Review the directions and have children complete the activity about taking part in parish life.

Have a volunteer read aloud the statement and the first paragraph on page 101.

Many people serve our parish.

Through our Baptism God calls each one of us. He calls us to do his work. This work is to bring the good news of Jesus Christ to others. Helping in our parish is a way to serve God and the Church.

A **pastor** is the priest who leads the parish in worship, prayer, and teaching. His most important work is to lead the parish in the celebration of the Mass. The parish might have other priests who work with the pastor. They also lead the parish in the celebration of the sacraments and in parish activities.

Sometimes the parish has a deacon. A **deacon** is a man who is not a priest but has received the sacrament of Holy Orders. He serves the parish by preaching, baptizing, and assisting the bishops and priests.

There are many ways of serving in your parish. These are called *ministries.* Some ministries are: catechist, director of youth services, director of social ministries, special minister of the Eucharist, director of music, altar server, and reader.

Can you name any other ministries? With a partner talk about how you and your family can help and serve your parish.

Key Words

parish (p. 252)
pastor (p. 252)
deacon (p. 250)

101

ACTIVITY BANK

Multiple Intelligences
Verbal-Linguistic

Use one of the Key Words *parish, pastor,* or *deacon* to show children how to write *cinquain* (five line) poetry. Guide the group to develop the poem by following these directions: line 1— one word that serves as the title of the poem; line 2—two words that describe the title word; line 3— three words that describe an action; line 4—four words that express a feeling; line 5— one word that refers back to the title word. Use the following as an example:

> *Pastor*
> *Loving, friendly*
> *He serves us*
> *He loves his parish*
> *Priest*

Write another in a large group. Then ask the children to work as partners to write a *cinquain* poem about a person or ministry in their parish.

Distribute copies of Reproducible Master 11. Help the children gather information for the chart. Tell them to list as many names as possible in the chart. Make an enlarged version of the chart to compile the responses from the children.

Read aloud the remaining paragraphs. Stress that the various ministries mentioned in the text complement the ordained minister of priest and deacon. Each in his or her way works to serve the parish and its people.

Complete the activity about ministries. Have the children work in pairs.

Quick Check

✔ *How are we important in the work of the parish?* (We can bring the good news of Jesus Christ to others by helping our parish.)

✔ *What are some of the ministries that serve the parish?* (Possible responses include: catechist, director of youth services, director of social ministries, special ministers of the Eucharist, director of music, and others.)

As Catholics...

Pastoral Administrators

Read the text to the children. Ask them to identify who helps with parish activities if there are not enough priests to serve all the parishes *(a pastoral administrator)*. Explain that a priest from another parish will be assigned to celebrate Mass and the other sacraments of the parish.

Teaching Note

The Early Christians

The early Christians shared all that they had with one another so that no one would go hungry. Read about them in the Acts of the Apostles. These Christians healed the sick and those disturbed by unclean spirits, even though many were imprisoned or beaten for doing so. Like early Church communities, Catholic parishes today show love and concern for people in need.

"Go in Peace to Love and Serve the Lord!"

Our parish worships together.

Celebrations are an important part of parish life. The Church has always gathered to celebrate the life, death, and Resurrection of Jesus. Participating in Mass is an important part of belonging to the Church.

Jesus said, "Where two or three are gathered together in my name, there am I in the midst of them." (Matthew 18:20) So when we gather as a parish, we are in the presence of Jesus. We gather to worship, to give thanks and praise to God.

Every time we celebrate Mass and the sacraments as a parish, we show our faith in Jesus. We show our love for him and for one another.

Name one thing you enjoy about worshiping with your parish.

Our parish cares for others.

Our parish worship encourages us to help others. At the end of each Mass, the priest or deacon says to us, "Go in peace to love and serve the Lord." We answer by saying, "Thanks be to God." But our real answer comes in our daily effort to help others.

102

Lesson Plan

WE BELIEVE (continued)

Write the following questions on the board. Have the children find the answers after reading the first statement on page 102 and the following text.

• *What is the great celebration of the Church?* (Mass)

• *Name the three things we celebrate in the life of Jesus.* (his life, death, and Resurrection)

• *What are some things we do when we gather to celebrate in our parish?* (worship, give thanks, and give praise to God)

Help the children memorize Matthew 18:20 by writing the verse on the board. Ask the children to look away while you erase one or two words. Invite the children to identify the missing words.

Have the children identify things that they enjoy about worshiping with their parish.

Have a volunteer read aloud the second statement on page 102. Ask a child to read the text.

Ask a volunteer to identify the Scripture quote on page 102.

We love and serve the Lord and others by:

- studying and learning more about our Catholic faith
- sharing the good news
- sharing what we have—our money, our time, and our talents—with one another
- caring for those in need—the sick, the poor, and the hungry
- making peace with others, even those who hurt us
- working for justice by treating all people fairly and with respect
- protecting the rights of people who cannot stand up for themselves.

St. Joseph the Worker Clean-Up Come Join Us!

All these actions are not just nice things to do. They are ways to show that we are true followers of Jesus Christ and members of his Body, the Church.

WE RESPOND

What kinds of things take place in your parish? List some of these things using the letters below.

P raising God together at Mass (sample)
A _____
R _____
I _____
S _____
H _____

As Catholics...

Some parishes do not have priests to serve them. So the bishop of the diocese selects a *pastoral administrator* to serve the parish. This administrator leads parish activities. He or she guides the parish in religious education and prayer. However, the bishop always assigns a priest to celebrate Mass and the other sacraments at these parishes.

Do you know of any parishes with a pastoral administrator?

103

ACTIVITY BANK

Multiple Intelligences
Bodily-Kinesthetic
Teach the children the following chant:

I am the Church! You are the Church!
We are the Church together!
All who follow Jesus, all around the world!
Yes, we are the Church together.

Ask them to think of a series of body movements to express the chant. Have them do the movements with the chant.

Curriculum Connection
Art
Activity Materials: drawing paper
Ask the children to draw a scene of people worshiping and participating at Mass. Have them include thought bubbles for several of the people in the drawing and write positive thoughts that those parishioners might be thinking. Display their drawings.

Divide the class into seven groups. Assign each group one of the seven bulleted items in the section. Have them devise and perform skits that display the behavior described. After each group performs its skit, identify which bulleted item the group was illustrating. Read aloud the final paragraph. Remind the children that kind, helpful actions are a way for them to show their commitment to the Church and to Jesus.

WE RESPOND
_____ minutes

Connect to Life Ask volunteers to share their responses about various things that take place in their parishes.

Have the children complete the acrostic activity. If there is time, ask volunteers to role-play one of their responses.

Pray together the following prayer:

Jesus, show us how to help others. When others see the things we do, we show them that we are members of your Body, the Church. Amen.

CHAPTER TEST

Chapter 11 Test is provided in the Grade 3 Assessment Book.

Review

Write the word to complete the sentences.

1. A _____parish_____ is a community of believers who worship and work together.

2. The priest who leads a parish is called the _____pastor_____.

3. Different ways of serving in a parish are called _____ministries_____.

4. At the end of Mass, the priest or deacon sends us out to love and _____serve_____ the Lord.

Complete this sentence.

5. In our parish, we See pages 100–103. _____

_____

_____

_____

_____

ASSESSMENT

Imagine a new family has joined your parish. Write at least three things you think they should know about your parish. How could you welcome them into your parish?

104

Lesson Plan

_____ minutes

Chapter Review Ask a volunteer to read aloud the directions. Remind the children that they will use what they have learned this week to complete sentences 1–4. Have them complete sentence 5 by first thinking about their own parish. Ask them to share their written responses.

Assessment Activity Read the directions to the activity. Before the children begin to write, ask: *How does it feel to be in a new school or parish?* (You probably miss your old friends, you do not feel as if you belong; you hope others will be friendly to you.) Suggest that the children write their responses in the form of a letter welcoming a new family to their school or parish.

_____ minutes

Reflect & Pray Ask the children to reflect on what they have learned this week about being members of a parish community. Then direct the children to the prayer and ask a volunteer to read it aloud. Gather the children in the prayer space and invite them to share their finished prayers with the class.

Key Words Write the three *Key Words* on the board and encourage the children to write brief definitions of each word. Ask volunteers to share their answers. Then invite the children to write a brief paragraph that uses the three words correctly.

Reflect & Pray

The parish is a community. What have I learned from my parish about being a member of the Church?

Finish this prayer.

Loving Father,
we belong to each other
just as we belong to you, our God.
Through our parish family, teach us to

_____

_____

Key Words

parish (p. 252)
pastor (p. 252)
deacon (p. 250)

Remember

• We belong to a parish.
• Many people serve our parish.
• Our parish worships together.
• Our parish cares for others.

OUR CATHOLIC LIFE

Caring for the Sick

Throughout history the Catholic Church has been a leader in caring for the sick. In the United States alone, there are almost six hundred Catholic hospitals.

Whenever we care for the sick, we show our respect for life. Our actions show that every human being has dignity because we are made in God's image. Catholic hospitals always try to protect human dignity—from the first moment of life to the last moment.

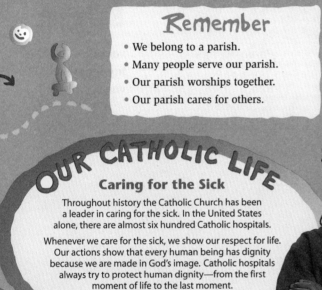

HOME CONNECTION

Sharing Faith with My Family

Make sure to send home the family page (text page 106).

Encourage the children to pray for their parishes with family members.

PUPIL PAGE 106

For additional information and activities, encourage families to visit Sadlier's

www.WE BELIEVE.web.com

Remember Ask the children to divide a regular sheet of notebook paper into four sections, and write one of the four doctrinal statements in each section. Then have them write three things they learned in the lesson that correspond to each statement. Say: *You can include prayer space items that relate to specific doctrinal sentences.*

Our Catholic Life Read aloud the text. Remind the children that Catholic hospitals are carrying on the work of the early Christians who helped so many sick people. Pray for those who work in all hospitals.

Plan Ahead for Chapter 12

Prayer Space: symbols of Baptism (candle, bowl of water, white garment), a parish bulletin

Materials: copies of Reproducible Master 12, Grade 3 CD, parish bulletin or diocesan newspaper

Chapter 12 · God Calls Us to Holiness

Overview

In Chapter 11 the children learned about the parish as a worshiping and caring community of faith. In this chapter the children will learn that God calls each of us to holiness.

Doctrinal Content	For Adult Reading and Reflection *Catechism of the Catholic Church*
The children will learn:	Paragraph
• God calls each of us.	1213
• God calls everyone to be holy.	825, 1719
• God calls some men to be priests.	1565
• God calls some people to religious life.	915

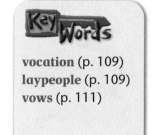

Key Words

vocation (p. 109)
laypeople (p. 109)
vows (p. 111)

Catechist Background

How did I choose my vocation? How did my vocation choose me?

"It was not you who chose me, but I who chose you and appointed you to go and bear fruit that will remain" (John 15:16).

A vocation springs forth from our true identity in God. To a great extent it expresses our gifts and talents, but in some cases it uncovers gifts and talents never before revealed! From the first tentative steps—into religious life or the priesthood, into a married relationship or into independent single living—we have a sense, a grace from the Holy Spirit, that "This is right." Even when we falter, or dig in our heels, something (grace again) pulls us forward.

Some find vocations within vocations. Someone is called to marriage, then further called to catechize. Another is called to live a single life and devote time to a particular volunteer effort. Another, a religious, discovers a call to music ministry or adult faith development. A vocation is not only a particular path but also ongoing response to a creative God.

What can all this mean to third graders? A pervasive question for this age is, "What do you want to be when you grow up?" Now is the time to learn of the wonderful choices available in service to God and others. Now is the time to explore, through books or videos, the lives of the saints and the contemporary lives of those who have said yes to God in a particular way of life.

Now is the time to find people in your community who can share their vocation stories with your group. And while you are searching for stories of the called and the chosen, do not forget to tell your own!

How can I say yes to God today?

Lesson Planning Guide

Lesson Steps	Presentation	Materials

1 WE GATHER

page 107 ✝ **Prayer** ☀ **Focus on Life**	• Listen to Scripture. ♫ Respond in song. • Discuss children's answers to, "What do you want to be when you grow up?"	For the prayer space: symbols of Baptism (white candle, bowl of water, white garment); parish bulletin ♫ "Only a Shadow" #8, Grade 3 CD

2 WE BELIEVE

page 108 *God calls each of us.*	• Read and discuss the text about vocation. 🏃 Talk about people in your parish who follow their vocations.	
pages 108–109 *God calls everyone to be holy.*	• Read and discuss laypeople and their vocations. 🏃 Role-play different vocations of laypeople. Use the pictures to complete the activity.	
page 110 *God calls some men to be priests.*	• Read and discuss the text about priestly vocation. • Make a word web about a priest's vocation.	
pages 110–111 *God calls some people to religious life.*	• Read and discuss vows of religious. • Read and discuss deacons in *As Catholics*.	• copies of Reproducible Master 12

3 WE RESPOND

page 111	🏃 Write a prayer asking God's help to all Church members to live out their vocations.	• parish bulletin or diocesan newspaper
page 112 **Review**	• Complete questions 1–5. 🏃 Work on *Assessment Activity*.	Additional Resources: • Chapter 12 Test in the Grade Assessment Book, pp. 23–24 • Chapter 12 Test in Test Generator • Review & Resource Book, pp. 31–33
page 113 **We Respond in Faith**	• Complete the *Reflect & Pray* activity. • Review *Remember* and *Key Words*. • Read and discuss *Our Catholic Life*. • Discuss **Sharing Faith with My Family**.	• Family Book, pp. 36–38

For additional ideas, activities, and opportunities: Visit Sadlier's **www.WeBelieveweb.com**

107B

Name _____

Imagine yourself twenty years from today. You are a **priest, brother, sister,** or **layperson.** What are you doing? What is your everyday life like? In what ways are you carrying on the mission of Jesus Christ? How are you helping people?

Choose one of the vocations written above in dark black type. Then write a paragraph about yourself in the future as a priest, brother, sister, or layperson. Draw a picture of yourself as you live this vocation. Then color the frame.

How could you respond to God's call?

Looking into the Future

_____

_____

_____

_____

_____

_____

_____

_____

Connections

To Vocations

As Catholics we believe that God calls each of us to live a life in union with God and in service to our neighbor. In this chapter the children will learn about the call to serve God and neighbor through a vocation within the Church as a priest, deacon, religious brother or sister, or layperson. Throughout the chapter remind the children that God calls each one of us. Encourage them to be open to God's call to service.

To Saints

Responding in faith to our baptismal call is central to our understanding of our vocation. The saints were ordinary women and men who tried to listen and respond to God's call throughout their lives. They became extraordinary because of the ways they lived their lives in response to God's call. For example, Saint Joseph was asked by God to care for Mary and Jesus. He answered God's call faithfully. Encourage the children to think about saints whose lives illustrate this kind of listening and responding to God.

FAITH and MEDIA

▶ You might show the children some of the ways the Church uses the Internet to help people discern whether or not they have been called to Holy Orders or to the religious life. The Internet is now one of the main places to go to find out more about vocations.

▶ As part of your discussion of God's call to some men to be priests, you might visit the "Vocations" area of your diocesan Web site with the children. You might also explore the sites of orders of priests such as the Jesuits and the Franciscans. You might also visit the Web sites of other religious communities, including contemplative communities, to show the children pictures of these men and women as they go about their lives of work and prayer.

Meeting Individual Needs

English Language Learners

Children for whom English is not a first language may find it difficult to write responses in English. Encourage these children to write their responses in their native language first, and then provide them with help translating the words into English. If possible, have these children work with partners who are fluent in both languages.

ADDITIONAL RESOURCES

Book *Victor Finds His Vocation,* Miriam Laderman and Susan Brindle, Precious Life Books, 2000. A grumpy cricket travels to faraway lands in the suitcase of a newly ordained priest.

Video *Mother Teresa—Seeing the Face of Jesus,* Morning Light Media, St. Louis, MO, 1998. Shows how Mother Teresa saw the face of Jesus in the sick and dying, and gave her life to this work. (35 min.)

To find more ideas for books, videos, and other learning material, visit Sadlier's

www.WE BELIEVE web.com

Focus on Life

Chapter Story

Amanda's mom was waiting for her as the after-school program was dismissed. She immediately noticed that her daughter Mandy was not her usual skipping self.

"Mandy, what's wrong?" asked Mom.

Mandy sighed. "I have a big assignment for next Monday. I have to write about a person I admire."

"Really?" asked Mom. "Let's think about that a little."

They got into the car, buckled up, and began the drive home. Mandy stared out the window from her place in the back seat and sighed again.

When they stopped at a light, her mother suggested, "What about dad's friend Father Tim? He's a priest in Bolivia. You remember that we mail his Christmas present right after Halloween?" Mandy's dad had read aloud letters from Father Tim. Father Tim really loved his work with the people of Bolivia.

Then Mandy thought about Sister Carol. She was a sister at the hospital. Their class had raised money and given new stuffed animals to the children's ward. They all brought the toys to the hospital to-gether. Sister Carol met them and showed them a video about Saint Victor's Hospital. She laughed and joked and seemed very happy.

Mandy's mom interrupted her thoughts. "We have to stop a minute at the grocery store. I am baking two apple pies this Saturday—one for the parish bake sale and one for our Sunday dinner—and we are all out of apples!"

Mandy thought about all the good things her mom did for her and for other people, too. She made pies. She helped with homework. She read stories. She helped solve problems. "Mom," said Mandy. "I think I found the person I admire!"

▶ *After reading this story, how would you define a hero?*

God Calls Us to Holiness

12

WE GATHER

✝ **Leader:** Let us listen to the word of God.

Reader: A reading from the first Letter of Saint John

"Beloved, if God so loved us, we also must love one another. No one has ever seen God. Yet, if we love one another, God remains in us, and his love is brought to perfection in us." (1 John 4:11, 12)

The word of the Lord.

All: Thanks be to God.

🎵 **Only a Shadow**

The love we have for you, O Lord,
Is only a shadow of your love for us;
Only a shadow of your love for us,
Your deep abiding love.

Our lives are in your hands,
Our lives are in your hands.
Our love for you will grow, O Lord;
Your light in us will shine.
Your light in us will shine
'Til we meet face to face.

 What would you say if someone asked you, "What do you want to be when you grow up?"

107

PREPARING TO PRAY

The children will listen to Scripture about God's love abiding in us. They will respond in song.

• Choose one child to be the prayer reader. Allow the child time to read over his or her part.

• Practice singing or saying the song, "Only a Shadow," #8, Grade 3 CD.

The Prayer Space

• Place items in the prayer space that will remind the children of their baptismal call, such as the symbols of Baptism (candle, bowl of water, white garment). Also include a parish bulletin.

📖 **This Week's Liturgy**
Visit **www.webelieveweb.com** for this week's liturgical readings and other seasonal material.

Lesson Plan

WE GATHER ___ minutes

✝ **Pray**

• Invite the children to gather together in the prayer space.

• Have the reader proclaim the Scripture.

• Sing the song.

• Remind the children that both water and the shell are symbols of Baptism. (a shell made of precious metal is sometimes used to pour baptismal water over the head of the one being baptized.)

☀ **Focus on Life**

Ask children if they have ever thought of what they wanted to do in life. Explain that God calls each of us to holiness. We choose a way in life to follow God and to show love for God and others.

• Share the *Chapter Story* on guide page 107E.

Home Connection Update

Ask the children to share experiences of using the Chapter 11 family page. Ask: *Were the family members able to share a special meal?*

107

Catechist Goal

• To teach that God calls each of us to be holy and to serve him in a particular way

Our Faith Response

• To choose ways we can grow in holiness and respond to God's call

 vocation   laypeople   vows

Lesson Materials

• parish bulletin
• copies of Reproducible Master 12

Teaching Note

Vocations and Sacraments

Review the sacraments with the children as you introduce the concept of vocations. Explain that as our relationship with God deepens, we are better able to understand how we are being called to love and serve him and to serve our brothers and sisters in Christ. Emphasize that Matrimony and Holy Orders are sacraments that celebrate vocations of service to our faith community.

WE BELIEVE
God calls each of us.

In Baptism God calls all of us to love and to serve him. This is the mission we share as members of the Church. Our mission is to learn from Jesus and to continue his work in the world. We are called to show others who Jesus is so they will love and follow him, too.

A **vocation** is God's call to serve him in a certain way. Each baptized person has a vocation to love and serve God. There are specific ways to follow our vocation: the married life, the single life, the priesthood, and the religious life.

None of us lives our vocation alone. We live it as a member of the Church.

With a partner talk about people in your parish who follow their vocations to serve God. Give some examples of how they do this.

God calls everyone to be holy.

Most Catholics live out their vocation as laypeople. **Laypeople** are baptized members of the Church who share in the mission to bring the good news of Christ to the world.

108

Lesson Plan

WE BELIEVE ___ minutes

Ask a volunteer read aloud the first statement. Ask volunteers to read the text and the *Key Word* definition. Have the children discuss possible ways they can hear God's call in their own lives. (Possible responses: through prayer, conversations with others, learning from life experiences.) Emphasize the following points:

• In Baptism we were joined to Christ and to one another as members of God's family. As members of God's family we are responsible for carrying out Jesus' mission in the world.

• God calls each of us to love and serve him and to serve our brothers and sisters in Christ's name. This is our vocation, our work of service.

Invite the children to look at the pictures in their texts. List on the board the types of vocations and service portrayed. Remind the children that we each have a baptismal call to love and service. Ask: *How do we know what God is asking us to do today?* (from our parents, our teachers, inspiration of the Holy Spirit during prayer and while participating at Mass and in the sacraments)

Have children work in pairs to complete the activity.

Some laypeople are called to the vocation of married life. A husband and wife show Jesus to the world by the love that unites them. One important way they live out their vocations is by teaching their family to pray and to follow Jesus Christ.

Some laypeople live their vocation as single people in the world. They, too, answer God's call by living their lives as Jesus did. They use their time and talents to serve others.

Key Words

vocation (p. 253)
laypeople (p. 251)

God calls all people to holiness. Our holiness comes from sharing God's life. To live a life of holiness means to share the good news of Jesus and help to build up God's Kingdom. We do this when we:

• tell others in our parish, our school, and our workplace about Jesus

• treat others as Jesus did

• care for those in need

• help others to know that God's life and love are alive in the world.

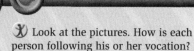 Look at the pictures. How is each person following his or her vocation?

Draw a way you follow God's call right now.

109

ACTIVITY BANK

Curriculum Connection
Social Studies
Activity Materials: chart paper

Invite the children to think of jobs performed by different people in their community (examples: mayor, teacher, police officer, librarian, banker, storekeeper). Help the children understand that these people are not just doing their jobs. They are responding to God's call by serving the rest of the community. Have the children work together to make a two-column chart. In the first column they will list various workers in the community. In the second column they will list the ways the people serve the community by their work.

Have a volunteer read aloud the second statement on page 108. Ask volunteers to read the next paragraphs and bulleted text.

Form teams of two to four children. Ask the teams to develop and act out skits showing laypeople leading lives of holiness. Encourage the children to take ideas for their skits from the pictures on the text pages and from the list of ways to build up God's Kingdom. Congratulate them on their presentations.

Complete the activity after discussing the pictures on the pages.

Quick Check

✔ *What mission are we committed to by our Baptism?* (to continue the mission of Jesus by loving and serving God and one another)

✔ *Who has a vocation?* (Every baptized person has a vocation to love and serve God in a specific way.)

Invite the children to pray silently to God for help in leading a holy life. Remind the children that becoming a holy person means cooperating with God's grace and responding in love and service.

As Catholics...

Deacons

Read aloud the text. Invite volunteers to answer the questions. Share answers. You might like to make up a group prayer in which you mention by name the deacons known to you and the children. As an encouragement and a thank-you, send a copy of your prayer to each deacon mentioned.

Teaching Note

The Religious Life

Religious life in a community has its roots in the early years of the Church. Laymen and women felt a deep yearning to live their lives completely for God and the Church. Usually they chose to do this by joining together with others to live in communities shaped by a particular way of living the gospel. This led to many different religious orders and congregations.

God calls some men to be priests.

Some men are called by God to serve as priests. When a man follows this call, he accepts a special ministry within the Church. In the sacrament of Holy Orders, he is ordained to the priesthood by a bishop.

Priests promise not to marry. This allows them to share God's love with all people and to go wherever the bishop sends them.

How have the priests in your parish helped you learn about Jesus?

Ask God to help them to continue their work in the Church.

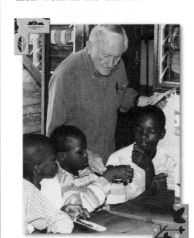

God calls some people to religious life.

Some Church members follow Jesus Christ in the religious life. They are priests, brothers, or sisters who belong to religious communities. They share their lives with God and others in a special way.

As members of their religious communities they make **vows**, or promises to God. The vows usually are chastity, poverty, and obedience. Those in religious life promise to:

- live a life of loving service to the Church and their religious community. By not marrying they can devote themselves to sharing God's love with all people.

110

Lesson Plan

WE BELIEVE (continued)

Ask a volunteer read aloud the first statement on page 110. Have the students with partners read the text to each other. Have them explain any new terms in their own words. Invite the children to discuss similarities among the work of laypeople, priests, and those in religious life, and to describe the differences among these vocations.

Write the word *priest* on the board and circle it. Then draw lines radiating from the circle, and ask the children to tell you what they have learned about priests and the things they do. Write the responses on the lines. To connect this lesson to the previous lesson about laypeople, draw a diagram comparing the two groups.

Discuss with children ways the priests in your parish have helped them to learn about Jesus.

Gather in the prayer space. Pray the Sign of the Cross and this prayer for an increase in vocations to the priesthood:

Jesus Christ, you came to us as our high priest and saved us. Call men worthy to serve as you did to the priesthood and to the service of God's people. Amen.

Ask a volunteer to read the second statement on page 110. Have the children take turns to read aloud the remaining text and bulleted items.

Discuss religious life with children. Say: *Most religious live in communities (convents, friaries, monasteries) where they live and pray together. Women and men in such*

- live simply as Jesus did and own no personal property.

- promise to listen carefully to God's direction in their lives and to go wherever their religious community sends them to do God's work.

Those in religious life serve the Church in many different ways. Some live alone; others live in community. Some live apart from the world so they can pray all the time. Others combine prayer with a life of service as teachers, social workers, missionaries, doctors, and nurses.

As Catholics...

A deacon is a man who is ordained in the sacrament of Holy Orders. A bishop ordains him as a special minister to the people. He lays his hands on the man and asks the Holy Spirit to strengthen him in preaching, baptizing, and serving the Church.

Does your parish have a deacon? What does he do in your parish?

Key Word

vows (p. 253)

WE RESPOND

The Church needs the help and support of people in every vocation. Each vocation is important for the growth of the Church.

 Write a prayer asking God to help all Church members in their vocations.

_____

_____

_____

_____

ACTIVITY BANK

Curriculum Connection
Mathematics

Ask the children to write the following column headings across a sheet of paper: *name, single, married, priest or deacon, religious.* Have them list the names of their families in the *name* column and check the correct vocation columns for each member. Combine the information from the children's graphs into a class graph to show the vocations represented in the families of the entire class.

Multiple Intelligences
Spatial

Activity Materials: markers, drawing paper

Have the children draw a house with many windows. Label the house *holiness.* Discuss ways to be holy or to show holiness and write one way in each window of the house. (pray; go to Mass; receive the sacraments; get along with others; be honest; share; be joyful.)

---

communities are often involved in teaching, hospital work, social work, and similar jobs. Some religious, such as cloistered nuns and monks, live in communities in which they dedicate themselves to a life of prayer and work. Others, called hermits, live alone and apart from the world.

WE RESPOND ___ minutes

Connect to Life Read aloud the text about the Church and vocations.

 Allow the children time to write their prayers.

Distribute copies of Reproducible Master 12. Encourage the children to use their imagination as they think about the world twenty years from now and ways God might be calling them to live.

Pray Begin by praying the Sign of the Cross. Invite volunteers to pray their prayers written in the activity.

Review

CHAPTER TEST

Chapter 12 Test is provided in the Grade 3 Assessment Book.

Write T if the sentence is true. Write F if the sentence is false.

1. A job is the invitation to serve God in the Church in a special way. _____F_____

2. Laypeople are baptized members of the Church who share in the mission to bring the good news of Christ to the world. _____T_____

3. Those in religious life make vows, or promises to God. _____T_____

4. Bishops ordain priests through the sacrament of Confirmation. _____F_____

Answer the questions.

5. What is a vocation? Why do we say that everyone in the Church has a vocation?

See pages 108 and 109.

_____

_____

This week, read a Catholic newspaper or your parish bulletin. Find at least one person who is serving the Church. Write a short paragraph about this person. Tell what he or she is doing to follow Jesus and to help others grow in holiness.

112

Lesson Plan

 ___ minutes

Chapter Review Tell the children that they are going to check their understanding of what they have learned. Have them complete questions 1–4. Then have them read and answer the two-part question 5. Ask them to check and share their answers.

Assessment Activity Read the directions. Invite the children to pick one from among the Catholic periodicals and church bulletins that you have brought to class. When everyone has found someone to write about and written a short paragraph, ask volunteers to share their reports with the class.

 ___ minutes

Reflect & Pray Read aloud the text. Ask the children to reflect on what it means to say: *This is mine!* (Possible answers: I own this; I treasure this.) Share your own thoughts on what it means to be called and to belong to God. Invite the children to complete the prayer, and encourage them to answer God's call.

Key Words Review the *Key Words* with the children. Invite them to write sentences using the key words correctly.

Reflect & Pray

In the Bible, God tells us, "I have called you by name: you are mine." (Isaiah 43:1) How does this make you feel? How can you convince others that they, too, are important to God?

Lord, you have called me by name. Help me to answer your call this week by

_____

_____

_____

Key Words

vocation (p. 253)
laypeople (p. 251)
vows (p. 253)

Remember

- God calls each of us.
- God calls everyone to be holy.
- God calls some men to be priests.
- God calls some people to religious life.

OUR CATHOLIC LIFE

Helping Poor People

The saints are examples of holiness. They show us how to follow Jesus. Martin de Porres was born in Lima, Peru, in 1579. During his childhood he was not always treated with respect. But he learned how to treat others with respect.

When he grew up, Martin became a religious brother. He spent each day caring for poor children and for the sick and homeless. We can follow Jesus with all our hearts as Saint Martin did.

HOME CONNECTION

Sharing Faith with My Family

Make sure to send home the family page (text page 114).

Encourage the children to make a family vocation tree at home.

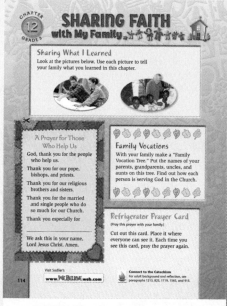

PUPIL PAGE 114

For additional information and activities, encourage families to visit Sadlier's

www.WeBelieveweb.com

Remember Have the children number the *We Believe* statements 1–4. Ask volunteers to share three things they have learned for each statement. Then invite the children to point out items in the prayer space and explain how the items relate to or symbolize things they have learned this week.

Our Catholic Life Read the text aloud. Then invite the children to share stories about the lives of other saints. After each, invite the class to share what we can learn from that saint's life.

Plan Ahead for Chapter 15

Prayer Space: sign "The Sacraments Are Signs of God's Love for Us," name cards, objects used with seven sacraments.

Materials: examples of sacramentals (holy water, medals, rosary) (option), large picture of Jesus, welcome sign, Grade 3 CD, copies of Reproducible Master 15, construction paper, markers

Advent

Advent has a twofold character: as a season to prepare for Christmas when Christ's first coming to us is remembered; as a season when that remembrance directs the mind and heart to await Christ's Second Coming at the end of time.

(Norms Governing Liturgical Calendars, 39)

Overview

In this chapter the children will learn that the season of Advent helps us prepare for the coming of the Son of God.

For Adult Reading and Reflection
You may want to refer to paragraphs 524 and 1171 of the *Catechism of the Catholic Church*.

Catechist Background

How do you experience joyful expectation during Advent?

Advent is the season of our preparation for Christ's coming: past, present, and future. In joyful expectation, we prepare to celebrate the birth of Jesus Christ at Christmas, his presence in our lives today, and his final coming at the end of time.

Like the prophets who foretold the Messiah's advent, we prayerfully watch and wait. "When the Church celebrates the *liturgy of Advent* each year, she makes present this ancient expectancy of the Messiah, for by sharing in the long preparation for the Savior's first coming, the faithful renew their ardent desire for his second coming" (CCC 524).

The four weeks of Advent prepare us to rejoice in the Incarnation:

"And the Word became flesh
    and made his dwelling among us" (John 1:14).

The Son of God was made man to save us and to reveal the Father's love for us. He became flesh in order that we might, as 2 Peter 1:4 testifies, "come to share in the divine nature." By our communion with him, we become sons and daughters of God.

Through the liturgical readings of Advent, the prophets call us to prepare the way of the Lord. And Jesus himself commands, "Be watchful! Be alert!" (Mark 13:33). The Church responds with prayer and worship, reconciliation and peacemaking, almsgiving and the works of justice.

In what new way will you prepare for Christ's coming?

Lesson Planning Guide

Lesson Steps	Presentation	Materials

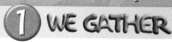

1 WE GATHER

page 115 **Introduce the Season**	• Read the *Chapter Story*. • Introduce the Advent season. • Proclaim the words on the banner.	• photo of Father Mychal Judge, if possible • 8½" x 11" poster board (2 for each child) • tape, purple chalk
page 116	🎵 Sing the song.	🎵 "Prepare the Way," Christopher Walker, #9, Grade 3 CD

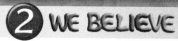

2 WE BELIEVE

pages 116–117 *The season of Advent helps us to prepare for the coming of the Son of God.*	• Read and discuss the season of Advent. 🏃 Complete the path activity.	

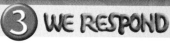

3 WE RESPOND

page 118	• Identify the signs of the Advent season. • Introduce the Advent saints. 🏃 Form groups to act out saints' stories.	• simple props, costume pieces, crown-making materials • buns (optional)
page 119 **We Respond in Prayer**	• Listen to Scripture. 🎵 Respond in prayer and song.	• prayer space items: Advent wreath, Advent calendar, oil lamp or night light, Bible, purple table covering 🎵 "Do Not Delay," Anne Quigley, #10, Grade 3 CD
Guide pages 120A–120B **We Respond in Faith**	• Explain the individual Advent project. • Explain the Advent group project. • Discuss the **Sharing Faith with My Family** page.	• Reproducible Master 13 • markers • balloons, T-shirts, kites, streamers • Family Book, pp. 39–40

For additional ideas, activities, and opportunities: Visit Sadlier's **www.WeBelieveweb.com**

Focus on Life

Chapter Story

Wherever he went, Father Mychal Judge, a Franciscan priest, was always well prepared. In his pocket he carried a stack of prayer cards. One side of the card said: "Lord, take me where you want me to go. Let me meet whom you want me to meet. Tell me what you want me to say, and keep me out of your way." On the other side of the card was a prayer for peace, courage, and wisdom.

Father Judge needed those special qualities because he was a chaplain for the New York City Fire Department. He was often in danger when he went to the scene of a fire with the other firefighters. Each day they had to be ready if a fire broke out anywhere in their area. Father Judge always told the firefighters, "Do you want to hear the Lord laugh? Just tell him your plans for tomorrow." That was his way of saying that only God knew what they might be facing tomorrow.

One of those tomorrows was September 11, 2001. Father Judge rushed to the scene of the disaster at the Twin Towers of the World Trade Center. He was praying for the injured and dying firemen when falling debris killed him. His brother firefighters carried his body to a nearby church. They covered him with a white cloth, and placed his priest's stole, his helmet, and his chaplain's badge on his chest.

A Baptist chaplain who worked with Father Judge passed out two thousand copies of Father Judge's prayer card on September 11. Later he had these words added to the back of the card: "An angel is asking: 'Do you want to hear the Lord laugh?' And then saying with a bright Irish smile: 'Just tell him your plans for tomorrow.'" That "angel" was Father Mychal Judge, who was always ready to serve God and whoever needed him.

▶ *How do you think Father Judge showed that he was always prepared to do whatever God asked of him?*

Advent

Advent | Christmas | Ordinary Time | Lent | Three Days | Easter | Ordinary Time

"Prepare the way of the Lord, make straight his paths."

Luke 3:4

115

Catechist Goal

• To emphasize that the season of Advent helps us prepare for the coming of the Son of God

Our Faith Response

• To decide on one way to prepare the Lord's way

ADDITIONAL RESOURCES

Book *Saint Francis and the Christmas Donkey*, Robert Byrd, Dutton Books, 2000. A donkey serves Mary and the newborn Jesus.

Video *Following Jesus Through the Church Year: Advent Roads*, Twenty-Third Publications, 1991. Krispin travels through the four weeks of Advent, guided by Advent symbols. (10 minutes)

To find more ideas for books, videos, and other learning material, visit Sadlier's

www.WEBELIEVEweb.com

Lesson Plan

Introduce the Season ___ minutes

• **Pray** the Sign of the Cross and offer this day's lesson to the Lord.

• **Read** or tell the *Chapter Story* about Father Mychal Judge. If possible, display a few articles with photos of Father Judge. At the end of the story, call on volunteers to name the ways they think this brave chaplain was always prepared to do whatever God asked of him. (Possibilities: always carrying his prayer cards to distribute, asking God to direct him daily, serving as a fire department chaplain where he could be called on night and day, his humor about planning for tomorrow)

• **Print** the word *Advent* in purple letters on the board. Let children know that they will be learning more about this beautiful season. Find out whether anyone knows what the word Advent means (*coming*). Ask: *Whom do you think is coming?* (Jesus) *How do you think we might get ready for his coming?* (Accept all reasonable answers.)

• **Have** the children work with partners to trace each other's feet on poster board. Ask them to carefully cut out their footprints. On the right foot, have them print *Prepare*. On the left foot, have them print *the Way*. Tape these Advent reminders to the floor to make a path to the prayer space.

• **Pray** the poster prayer on this page.

The season of Advent helps us prepare for the coming of the Son of God.

Lesson Materials
- Grade 3 CD
- simple props, costume pieces, crown-making materials
- buns (optional)
- bells and rhythm instruments
- Reproducible Master 13
- markers
- balloons, T-shirts, kites, streamers

Teaching Note

The Second Coming

In this lesson a brief reference is made to the Second Coming of Jesus Christ. This refers to the triumph of Christ's Kingdom at the end of the world when he will come again to judge the living and the dead.

WE GATHER

🎵 **Prepare the Way**

Prepare the way
for the coming of God.
Make a straight path
for the coming of God.

WE BELIEVE

The word *Advent* means "coming." Each year during Advent we prepare to celebrate the first coming of the Son of God. We prepare to celebrate the birth of Jesus Christ at Christmas.

During Advent, we rejoice that Jesus is our Savior. He is the Son of God sent to save us from sin. We remember that God's people waited many, many years for the Savior to come. During those years of waiting, God spoke to his people through the prophets. The prophets told the people to prepare for the Savior.

116

Lesson Plan

WE GATHER ___ minutes

Focus on Life Call on volunteers to role-play the following situations: 1) Your mother sends you on an errand and you get sidetracked by some friends; 2) Your family makes a vacation trip to a faraway place and the driver gets lost; 3) A mouse enters a maze but there is no cheese to lead him out. Have the children contrast these situations with making a straight path.

• **Explain** that during Advent we try to make a straight path for Jesus in our lives. Invite the children to read aloud the lyrics for "Prepare the Way." Play the Grade 3 CD. Then sing the song together.

WE BELIEVE ___ minutes

• **Have** volunteers read aloud the first two paragraphs of *We Believe*. Ask volunteers to write on the board the meaning of Advent (coming), and what we prepare to celebrate during Advent (the birth of Jesus). Call on other volunteers to write why God sent his Son to us (to save us from sin), and who told the people how to prepare for Jesus' coming (the prophets).

• **Ask** children to review the four ways the prophets told the people to prepare the way of the Lord. Have partners choose one way and pantomime it for the class. Seek specific ways the children can carry out these practices.

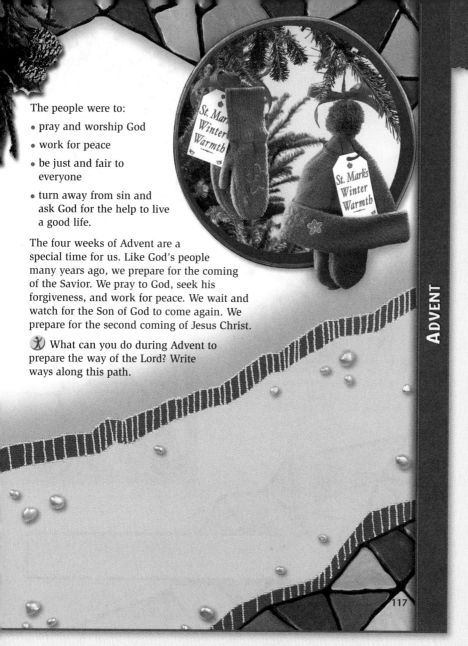

The people were to:

- pray and worship God
- work for peace
- be just and fair to everyone
- turn away from sin and ask God for the help to live a good life.

The four weeks of Advent are a special time for us. Like God's people many years ago, we prepare for the coming of the Savior. We pray to God, seek his forgiveness, and work for peace. We wait and watch for the Son of God to come again. We prepare for the second coming of Jesus Christ.

What can you do during Advent to prepare the way of the Lord? Write ways along this path.

ADVENT

117

ACTIVITY BANK

Family

Advent Recipes

Activity Materials: recipes for Saint Lucy Day buns, Saint Nicholas Day cookies

Download from the Internet recipes for Advent feast day recipes for children to take home. Encourage them to have their families make these treats for sharing with others. Ask children to bring in additional recipes from their own families.

Parish

Advent Activities

Activity Materials: parish calendar of seasonal events; construction paper, markers

Have the children copy from parish Advent calendars the times and places of any special events like an Advent Wreath Workshop, Advent Evening Prayer, or a Christmas bazaar. Ask the children to make invitations to these events for their families.

• **Print** *Watch* and *Wait* on the board. Invite ideas about ways the children might practice being Advent lookouts who watch for signs of Advent. Suggest: sitting quietly to observe the changes in the weather of this season; watching for ways people show God's love; observing signs of Advent in our parish church.

• **Complete** the reading of *We Believe* text. Emphasize that these four weeks of Advent are a time to prepare to celebrate the birth of Jesus and to prepare for the second coming of Christ at the end of time.

Explain the activity and offer help as needed.

Quick Check

✔ *What do we do during Advent?* (prepare for the coming of Jesus)

✔ *How do we prepare the way of the Son of God?* (by praying and working for peace, seeking forgiveness, watching and waiting)

Chapter 13 • Advent

CONNECTION

To Community

One of the ways we prepare for the coming of the Savior is by being signs of God's love for others. This may be done through prayer, almsgiving, or works of service. Make a list of community organizations serving people in need. Find out how the children can volunteer their help or support. If there is a day care center for families, the children might collect toys or books for the children. Follow through on one community project.

To Liturgy

To help the children become more familiar with the Gospel readings of Advent, check each Sunday's Lectionary for the proper cycle (A, B, C). Consider learning by heart one of the following: Matthew 1: 18–24, Luke 1:26–38, or Luke 1:39–45. Prepare to tell the children one of these stories, and encourage them to learn the stories as well.

WE RESPOND

The Church honors saints all year long. Here are some saints that we honor during Advent. They help us to rejoice in the coming of the Lord. Their lives help us to see that the Lord is near.

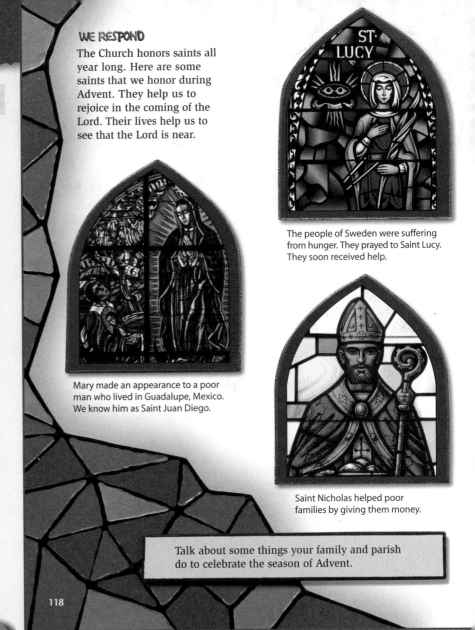

The people of Sweden were suffering from hunger. They prayed to Saint Lucy. They soon received help.

Mary made an appearance to a poor man who lived in Guadalupe, Mexico. We know him as Saint Juan Diego.

Saint Nicholas helped poor families by giving them money.

Talk about some things your family and parish do to celebrate the season of Advent.

118

Lesson Plan

WE RESPOND _____ minutes

- **Find** out what signs of the season the children have noticed at home, at school, in the community, or in the media. List or sketch these on the board. Again print the words: *Watch* and *Wait*.

- **Read** aloud the opening paragraph of *We Respond* section. Ask: *How do the saints help us during Advent?* (Their lives help us see the Lord is near and rejoice.)

- **Ask** three volunteers to introduce the Advent saints by reading aloud the next three paragraphs. After each paragraph, have the entire group name the saint(s).

- **Give** the following thumbnail sketches to amplify the stories of the Advent saints:

- Saint Nicholas was a bishop who helped the poor. He came by night and left his gifts secretly.

- Our Lady of Guadalupe imprinted her own image on the cloak of Saint Juan Diego so he could convince the bishop that Mary had actually appeared to him. Mary was dressed as a Native Mexican.

- Saint Lucy was a martyr who died for her faith. She is represented in Sweden by a young girl or woman dressed in a white robe, a red sash, and a leafy crown with five candles.

- **Form** three groups, one for each Advent saint. The Lady of Guadalupe group will include Saint Juan Diego. Provide simple props, costume pieces, and crown-making materials. Help each group prepare a mini-skit about its saint.

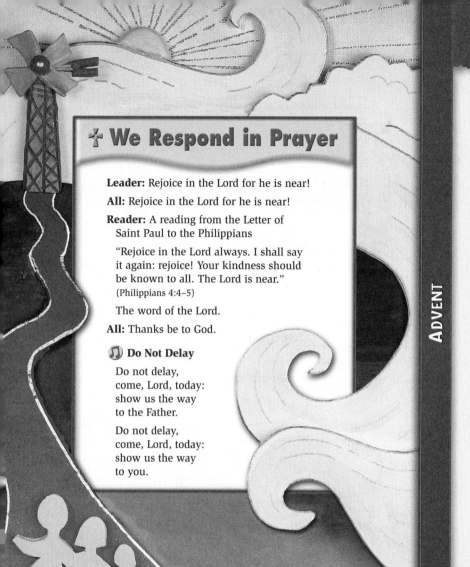

✝ We Respond in Prayer

Leader: Rejoice in the Lord for he is near!

All: Rejoice in the Lord for he is near!

Reader: A reading from the Letter of Saint Paul to the Philippians

"Rejoice in the Lord always. I shall say it again: rejoice! Your kindness should be known to all. The Lord is near."
(Philippians 4:4–5)

The word of the Lord.

All: Thanks be to God.

🎵 **Do Not Delay**

Do not delay,
come, Lord, today:
show us the way
to the Father.

Do not delay,
come, Lord, today:
show us the way
to you.

ADVENT

119

PREPARING TO PRAY

The children will listen to Scripture and respond in prayer and song.

• Choose a volunteer to read Scripture and another volunteer to be the prayer leader. Have them prepare their parts.

• Gather bells and other rhythm instruments.

• Teach the song "Do Not Delay."

The Prayer Space

• Place in the prayer space these items: an Advent wreath, an Advent calendar, an oil lamp or a night light, a Bible on a purple table covering.

 This Week's Liturgy

Visit **www.webelieveweb.com** for this week's liturgical readings and other seasonal material.

✝ We Respond in Prayer ___ minutes

• **Invite** the children to close their eyes and breathe deeply. Ask them to silently pray within themselves, "Come, Lord Jesus."

• **Ask** whether any of the children's families make any special foods during Advent such as cookies or fruit cakes to be given as gifts. Ask: *Does anyone's family make "Lucia cats"?* Explain that "Lucia cats" or *lussekatter* are Saint Lucy buns served on her feast day December 13. These yeast and saffron buns are curled in the shape of a sleeping cat. Show a picture (or have actual buns to be shared after the prayer service).

• **Using** the Grade 3 CD, teach the song "Do Not Delay." Then add the bells and other rhythm instruments. Have bell ringers "punctuate" each of the opening "Rejoice" lines at the beginning of the prayer service on this page.

• **Gather** in one corner. Follow the path to the prayer space. Spend a few quiet moments reflecting on the seasonal items. Then ask the leader to begin the prayer. After the song, if saffron or other buns are available, share them in memory of Saint Lucy.

Name _____

On each paving stone write one way to make a straight path for the Lord during Advent. Then complete the action statement at the bottom of the page.

Today I will make a straight path for the Lord by

_____

We Respond in Faith

Individual Project

Distribute Reproducible Master 13. Have the children fill in and color the paving stones to make a straight path for the coming of the Savior. Ask them to complete the action statement at the bottom of the page.

Group Project

Brainstorm numerous ways in which the children might spread the Advent message, "Be prepared." Ways to consider include: large purple balloons with white letters attached to entrances; T-shirts with alphabet transfers to spell out the message; kites; paper streamers; book covers; posters; a mural; an Advent Web site. Form small groups and work out several ways of communicating the Advent message.

Be Prepared

Sharing Faith with My Family

Make sure to send home the family page (pupil page 120).

Encourage the children to involve their families in the Advent Gifts activity. Discuss the possible "gifts of kindness" they will offer. Remind them to pray the Family Prayer with their families.

For additional information and activities, encourage families to visit Sadlier's

www.WeBelieveweb.com

Christmas

Next to the yearly celebration of the Paschal Mystery, the Church holds most sacred the memorial of Christ's birth and early manifestations. This is the purpose of the Christmas season.

(Norms Governing Liturgical Calendars, 39)

Overview

In this chapter the children will learn that the Christmas season is a special time to celebrate that God is with us.

For Adult Reading and Reflection
You may want to refer to paragraphs 1171 and 525 of the *Catechism of the Catholic Church*.

Catechist Background

How do you extend Christmas beyond December 25th?

During the Christmas season, the Church celebrates with joy the wondrous exchange by which "Man's Creator has become man, born of the Virgin. We have been made sharers in the divinity of Christ who humbled himself to share in our humanity" (CCC 526).

Extending from Christmas Day to the Baptism of the Lord, this season commemorates "the beginning of our redemption," as we pray in the Christmas Vigil Mass (Prayer Over the Gifts). In his coming as an infant in a manger, the Son of God and Savior of the world makes manifest heaven's glory. By his poverty and vulnerability, Jesus teaches us that "To become a child in relation to God is the condition for entering the kingdom" (CCC 526).

The Savior, revealed first to simple shepherds, is manifested to the Gentiles in the adoration of the wise men (magi). They have sought and found the king of the nations among the people of Israel. In the Church's celebration of Epiphany on the Second Sunday after Christmas, we anticipate Christ's coming in glory at the end of the world. (The word epiphany comes from the Greek *epiphainesthai* meaning "to appear.") In prayer and worship, we "await the blessed hope, the appearance of the glory of the great God and of our savior Jesus Christ" (Titus 2:13).

How will you manifest or show forth the Son of God in your own life?

Lesson Planning Guide

Lesson Steps	Presentation	Materials

1 WE GATHER

Lesson Steps	Presentation	Materials
page 121 **Introduce the Season**	• Read the *Chapter Story*. • Introduce the Christmas season. • Sing the refrain from, "Go Tell It on the Mountain."	• red chalk • book of Christmas carols (optional)
page 122	• Discuss the questions about waiting for someone special.	

2 WE BELIEVE

Lesson Steps	Presentation	Materials
pages 122–124 *The Christmas season is a special time to celebrate that God is with us.* 📖 *Luke 2:1–11*	• Read and discuss the season of Christmas and the birth of our Savior, Jesus. • Form tableaux. 🏃 Write original songs. • Read and discuss the saints' days celebrated during the Christmas season. • Brainstorm ways to follow the example of the Christmas saints.	• optional: CD instrumental carols • star badges • sources (books or Internet) on Christmas saints

3 WE RESPOND

Lesson Steps	Presentation	Materials
page 124	• Share a favorite Christmas poem. 🏃 Complete drawings of parish celebrations.	• your choice of a favorite Christmas poem
page 125 **We Respond in Prayer**	• Explain short litany of Saints Stephen, John, and the Holy Innocents. • Respond in prayer.	• prayer space items: manger scene, with Holy Family, shepherds, and angels. Hang a star or light over manger. • a small flashlight for each child
Guide pages 126A–126B **We Respond in Faith**	• Explain the individual Christmas season project. • Explain the Christmas season group project. • Discuss the **Sharing Faith with My Family** page.	• Reproducible Master 14 • treats • markers • poster paints, crayons, paint brushes, large sheets of drawing paper • Family Book, pp. 41–42

For additional ideas, activities, and opportunities: Visit Sadlier's www.WEBELIEVEweb.com

Focus on Life

Chapter Story

"I wish all these sheep would run away somewhere," Daniel muttered to himself. He didn't really mean it. But grumbling made him feel better about being hungry, thirsty, dirty, and tired. It had been his first day tending the flock with his father and brothers. They had been moving the flock from one pasture to another, so there had been very little time to rest.

When the last plump ewe had finally been counted and the sheep-fold door was securely closed, Daniel sat down by the doorkeeper's fire. He opened his leather bag and pulled out all the food his mother had packed for him: a flat loaf of barley bread, a piece of dried fish, a bunch of juicy grapes, and two fat figs. Daniel wanted to stuff all the food into his mouth at once. But he had to wait for his father and brothers to join him.

It was already dark. In the distance, Daniel heard the high pitched laughing sound of hyenas. He moved closer to the fire and made sure his slingshot was hanging from his belt. He was relieved when the rest of the family arrived. His father blessed the food and everyone ate together.

Daniel was about to fall asleep when suddenly a great light filled the sky. "Look!" he shouted. "It's an angel!" The other shepherds stared in disbelief. But the splendid angel assured them they had nothing to fear. He had come to announce the birth of a Savior—right in Bethlehem! Then a whole crowd of angels began singing. And Daniel fell down on his knees, thanking God for the sheep. Without them, he would never have been out in this starlit field hearing the greatest news of all!

▶ *What changed Daniel's mind about being a shepherd?*

Christmas

"Today is born our Savior, Christ the Lord!"
Responsorial Psalm, Christmas Mass at Midnight

121

Chapter 14 • Christmas

Catechist Goal

• To introduce the Christmas season as a special time to celebrate that God is with us.

Our Faith Response

• To celebrate the Son of God.

ADDITIONAL RESOURCES

Videos *Following Jesus Through the Church Year: Christmas Crossroads,* Twenty-Third Publications, 1991. Krispin, lost in Bethlehem, reaches the stable after Jesus has left. (10 minutes)

A Good and Perfect Gift, Franciscan Communications, 1992. This touching story of the answer to a child's Christmas prayer leads us to look at how we treat others. (25 minutes)

To find more ideas for books, videos, and other learning material, visit Sadlier's

www.WeBelieve.web.com

Lesson Plan

Introduce the Season ___ minutes

• **Pray** together the Sign of the Cross and repeat the lesson's opening verse.

• **Read** or tell the story of Daniel, the young shepherd, who witnesses a surprising event on his first night in the fields. If possible, display pictures of Middle Eastern shepherds and provide background information that can be found in *The Land & People Jesus Knew,* by J. Robert Teringo (Bethany House, 1985). After telling the story, ask the children to provide an ending for the story.

• **Ask** volunteers how many days their birthday lasts,

or the Fourth of July. Then ask how many days Christmas lasts. Print in red chalk: Christmas Season, December 25 to January ____. Look at the current Church calendar to find the date of the Baptism of the Lord. Fill in and count together how many days Christmas lasts.

• **Encourage** the children to identify ways they can remind themselves each day that Christmas is an entire season. They might decide to: give small gifts of love each day, go caroling, or begin each day by praying, "Today is born our Savior, Christ the Lord!"

• **Pray** by singing only the refrain of "Go, Tell It on the Mountain," the traditional African-American spiritual.

121

Lesson Materials

• star badges

• CD instrumental carols (optional)

• a favorite Christmas poem

• sources on Christmas saints (books or Internet)

• a small flashlight for each child

• Reproducible Master 14

• treats

• markers

• poster paints, crayons, brushes, large sheets of drawing paper

Teaching Tip

Seasonal Music

To raise awareness of the ongoing Christmas season, you might decide to play various CDs of Christmas music each day while children are involved in activities. Instrumental music played quietly will support rather than distract from the activity.

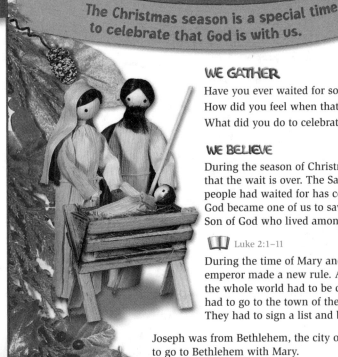

The Christmas season is a special time to celebrate that God is with us.

WE GATHER

Have you ever waited for someone? How did you feel when that person arrived? What did you do to celebrate?

WE BELIEVE

During the season of Christmas we celebrate that the wait is over. The Savior that God's people had waited for has come. The Son of God became one of us to save us. Jesus is the Son of God who lived among us.

📖 Luke 2:1–11

During the time of Mary and Joseph, the emperor made a new rule. All the people of the whole world had to be counted. All men had to go to the town of their father's family. They had to sign a list and be counted.

Joseph was from Bethlehem, the city of David. So he had to go to Bethlehem with Mary.

"While they were there, the time came for her to have her child, and she gave birth to her firstborn son. She wrapped him in swaddling clothes and laid him in a manger, because there was no room for them in the inn." (Luke 2:6–7)

There were shepherds in the fields nearby. The angel of the Lord came to them and said:

"Do not be afraid; for behold, I proclaim to you good news of great joy that will be for all the people. For today in the city of David a savior has been born for you who is Messiah and Lord. You will find an infant wrapped in swaddling clothes and lying in a manger." (Luke 2:10–12)

122

Lesson Plan

WE GATHER ___ minutes

Focus on Life Invite volunteers to respond to the *We Gather* questions. Tell about a time when you waited for someone special. Share how the waiting affected your experience of the person's arrival. Have the children recall that Advent is a season of watching and waiting for the coming of the Son of God.

WE BELIEVE ___ minutes

• **Have** a volunteer read aloud the *We Believe* statement. Then read or paraphrase the opening paragraph of *We Believe*. Focus on our belief that Jesus is the Son of God who came to live among us. This is what we celebrate during the Christmas season.

• **Ask** the children to read silently the entire story from Luke 2:1–11. If available, play quietly a seasonal instrumental CD. After the reading, ask: *Why did Mary and Joseph travel to Bethlehem?* (because people had to be counted in the hometown of Joseph's family). *Why was Jesus placed in a manger?* (no room in the overcrowded inn because of the census). Finally, ask: *What news did the shepherds receive from the angels?* (A Savior has been born for all the people.) Then have children read the final paragraph to discover the meaning of *Emmanuel* (God with us).

• **Explain** to the children that they will form a tableau for each scene of the gospel story. *Scene 1*: a group pose of Mary and Joseph traveling to Bethlehem with

Jesus is our Lord and Messiah. During Advent and Christmas we hear Jesus called Emmanuel. The name *Emmanuel* means "God with us." This is what we are celebrating during Christmas: God is with us today, now, and forever.

One way we share the joy of Christmas is through music. Write your own song to tell others the good news that Jesus is with us. Use a tune you know or make up one of your own.

_____

_____

_____

CHRISTMAS

ACTIVITY BANK

Multicultural Awareness
First Star
Activity Materials: foil, scissors, fishing line

In Poland a Christmas Eve tradition is to watch for the first star of the night. The first to spot it cries, "The star!" and everyone knows that Advent is over and Christmas has begun. The star is called *gwiazdka* or little star. Have the children make little stars and hang them around the room.

Parish
Church Visit
Activity Materials: disposable camera

Take children on a tour of the parish church to photograph all the signs of the season. Take turns with the camera. Use the photos to decorate a bulletin board. The children might also write thank-you notes to the liturgical committee and others who help to decorate the parish church.

others. *Scene 2*: the birth of Jesus. *Scene 3*: the angelic announcement to the shepherds. Select three narrators for these scenes. Distribute the star badges to the various characters (a large blue star for Mary, gold for Joseph, white for angels, green for shepherds). As the story is read aloud, each tableau is formed and held until the scene changes.

Explain the directions to the *We Believe* activity. Tell the children that in Wales an annual Christmas carol writing competition is held. Village choirs compete to provide the best music in honor of the Lord Jesus. Help the children write their own Christmas songs using familiar or original melodies.

Quick Check

✔ *What do we celebrate in the Christmas season?* (God is with us)

✔ *Why did Jesus become one of us?* (to save)

CONNECTION

To Catholic Social Teaching

Call to Family, Community, and Participation

Our faith tradition emphasizes that human beings achieve fulfillment in community rather than in excessive individualism. Encourage the children and families to participate in community events (parties, concerts, plays) as part of their seasonal celebration.

To Faith and Media

Seasonal editions of comic strips and cartoons like *Peanuts, The Family Circus, Dennis the Menace, B.C., It,* and *Frank and Ernest* often communicate Christian beliefs. Have students search for examples and share them with the class.

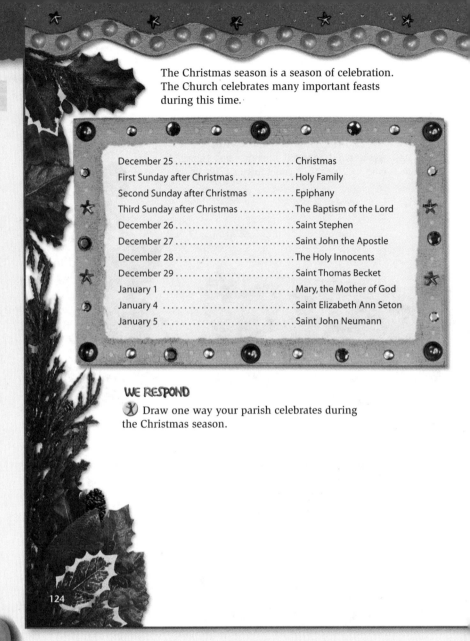

The Christmas season is a season of celebration. The Church celebrates many important feasts during this time.

December 25	Christmas
First Sunday after Christmas	Holy Family
Second Sunday after Christmas	Epiphany
Third Sunday after Christmas	The Baptism of the Lord
December 26	Saint Stephen
December 27	Saint John the Apostle
December 28	The Holy Innocents
December 29	Saint Thomas Becket
January 1	Mary, the Mother of God
January 4	Saint Elizabeth Ann Seton
January 5	Saint John Neumann

WE RESPOND

Draw one way your parish celebrates during the Christmas season.

124

Lesson Plan

WE BELIEVE (continued)

• **Generate** enthusiasm in the children for the entire Christmas season with all its saints' days and other feasts. Have eleven different children read aloud the list of feasts in the text. Ask volunteers to point out the feasts that celebrate Jesus or Mary or the Holy Family (the first four plus January 1). Note that the others all celebrate saints of the season.

• **Form** nine small groups or sets of partners. Assign each one of the feasts from Holy Family to Saint John Neumann (omitting Holy Innocents). Provide simple library or Internet sources on saints and seasonal feasts. (See *Children's Daily Prayer* by Elizabeth McMahon Jeep, Liturgy Training Publications.) Help children to prepare brief oral reports about the feast or the saint. Then list

on the board ways the children can follow the example of the Christmas season saints.

WE RESPOND ___ minutes

Connect to Life Share any favorite Christmas poems, rhymes, or songs other than carols. Consider teaching the children the final verse of Christina Rossetti's "A Christmas Carol" or read aloud with musical cadence the anonymous "A Carol" ("He came all so still"). Encourage the children to bring in copies of any of their favorite poems of the Christmas season.

Call attention to the *We Respond* activity. Brainstorm ideas and give the children time to complete their drawings.

✠ We Respond in Prayer

Leader: We thank you, God, for the lives of your holy people. Be with us as we ask their prayers for us.

All: Blessed be God for ever.

Reader: Saint Stephen was a deacon. He was the first to give his life for his faith in Jesus.

Saint Stephen,

All: Pray for us.

Reader: Jesus chose John to be an apostle. Saint John was the author of one of the four gospels. He wrote that God is love.

Saint John,

All: Pray for us.

Reader: King Herod did not want Jesus the Savior to live. He ordered all the baby boys two years of age and under to be killed! We call them the Holy Innocents. Their lives remind us of God's great gift of life.

Holy Innocents,

All: Pray for us.

Leader: Jesus shares God's gift of life with each of us. Praise God!

All: Blessed be God for ever.

CHRISTMAS

125

PREPARING TO PRAY

The children will pray a litany of Christmas saints, Saint Stephen, Saint John, and the Holy Innocents.

• Select three readers and ask them to prepare for their parts in the prayer.

• Distribute rhythm instruments to accompany carol or song at beginning and end of litany (optional). Practice as needed.

The Prayer Space

• In the prayer space place a manger scene with the Holy Family, the shepherds, and assorted animals and angels. Hang a star or a light over the manger.

 This Week's Liturgy

Visit **www.webelieveweb.com** for this week's liturgical readings and other seasonal material.

✝ We Respond in Prayer ___ minutes

Invite the children to close their eyes and breathe deeply. Ask them to silently pray within themselves, "Emmanuel, God with us."

• **Guide** a brief sharing on how children are aware of Emmanuel, God with us in their daily lives. Do they know that Jesus is present with them at morning prayer, at breakfast, in the smile of a family member, in the beauty of the natural world, in the love of a pet, in the Blessed Sacrament? Have them name other ways in which they know Jesus is with them.

• **Explain** that the litany we will pray today reminds us that God is with us in difficult times, too. Saint Stephen and the Holy Innocents gave their lives for Christ. But Saint John reminds us in his gospel that God loves us no matter what!

• **Darken** the room as able. Process to the prayer space singing "Away in a Manger" or another carol.

• **At** the prayer space, ask the children to be silent for a few moments while reflecting on the manger scene. Pray: Today is born our Savior, Christ the Lord!

• **Pray** the on-page litany.

• **Conclude** with another carol or appropriate song.

Name _____

Complete the Christmas acrostic by writing something you have learned about each word below. Color the letters with decorative colors.

Christ _____

Holy Family _____

Rejoice _____

Innocents _____

Shepherds _____

Today _____

Mary _____

Angels _____

Savior _____

We Respond in Faith

Individual Project

Distribute Reproducible Master 14. Offer help in to the children to complete the acrostic sentences. Remind children that they can write anything they learned about in this chapter. Have them exchange completed papers and share their sentences. If time allows, distribute markers for coloring the decorative letters. Offer treats during this project.

Group Project

As a seasonal art project, provide the children with: poster paints, crayons or cray-pas, paint brushes, and large sheets of drawing paper. Display assorted crèche scenes on a bulletin board for inspiration. Invite the children to draw their own versions of the crèche or manger scene. They may include all the figures or focus only on a few. The process of crayon resist involves drawing with crayons and pressing down hard to achieve a waxy look. Light colors are more effective. Then paint with darker colors over the drawing. Display the completed works.

HOME CONNECTION

Sharing Faith with My Family

Make sure to send home the family page (pupil page 126).

Encourage the children to involve their families in making a Christmas scrapbook of special seasonal memories. Remind them to make a calendar of the Christmas season with their families.

For additional information and activities, encourage families to visit Sadlier's

www.WeBelieveweb.com

PUPIL PAGE 126

ASSESSMENT

In the *We Believe* program each core chapter ends with a review of the content presented, and with activities that encourage the children to reflect and act on their faith. The review is presented in two formats, standard and alternative.

Each unit is also followed by both standard and alternative assessment. The standard test measures basic knowledge and vocabulary assimilation. The alternative assessment allows the children another option—often utilizing another learning style—to express their understanding of the concepts presented.

Using both forms of assessment, perhaps at different times, attends to the various ways children's learning can be measured. You can also see the Grade 3 *We Believe* Assessment Book for:

• standard assessment for each chapter

• alternative assessment for each chapter

• standard assessment for each unit

• alternative assessment for each unit

• a semester assessment which covers material presented in Units 1 and 2

• a final assessment which covers material presented in Units 1, 2, 3, and 4.

Assessment Grade 3 Unit 2

Match the words in Column A with the correct descriptions in Column B.

A	B
1. vocation	__4__ promise to God
2. prayer	__2__ listening and talking to God
3. Apostles' Creed	__5__ the official public prayer of the Church
4. vow	__1__ God's call to serve him in a certain way
5. liturgy	__3__ Christian statement of beliefs

Write T if the sentence is true. Write F if the sentence is false.

6. __T__ Catholic social teaching tells us that we have a responsibility to share the good things of the world.

7. __T__ The bishops of the Church are the successors of the apostles.

8. __F__ The Lord's Prayer is also called Our Prayer.

9. __T__ One mark of the Church is that it is *catholic,* which means "universal."

10. __F__ Priests, sisters, and brothers who belong to religious communities make vows of poverty, chastity, and justice.

127

ALTERNATIVE ASSESSMENT

Find ten words related to prayer in the puzzle. Use these words to tell your group about prayer.

B	I	N	P	G	L	I	T	N	G	I	L
L	T	K	R	H	T	V	H	T	R	H	I
E	L	U	A	L	K	R	A	B	S	L	S
S	I	N	I	G	I	O	N	I	L	G	T
S	N	L	S	S	V	L	K	R	H	G	E
I	N	T	E	R	C	E	S	S	I	O	N
N	G	L	I	T	L	I	G	L	N	D	I
G	L	W	O	R	S	H	I	P	Y	L	N
L	R	I	V	I	N	G	V	I	N	G	G
I	S	O	T	A	L	K	I	N	G	O	N
P	E	T	I	T	I	O	N	I	O	N	I
L	R	L	I	T	U	R	G	Y	L	G	Y

128

The Church Leads Us in Worship

UNIT 3

129

UNIT 3 SHARING FAITH as a Family

What Media Violence Does to Kids

By age eighteen, American children have witnessed approximately 200,000 acts of violence on television alone. Add video games, movies, and music lyrics, and the number escalates dramatically. The impact on children is enormous. Here are just some of the reasons why parents and teachers need to be vigilant about children's exposure to media violence.

Violence in American media tends to be justified, that is, it is often carried out by the "good guy" against the "bad guy." Children quickly learn that this is an acceptable way to solve problems. This is hardly the message of the Gospel!

Most young children are unable to separate fantasy from reality. Thus,

the computer graphics that make a movie dinosaur so life-like entertains adults while it terrifies children.

In the same manner, a child may see the repeated footage of a catastrophe on a news program as a new event each time. This raises their level of fear and anxiety to greater heights. Therefore, limit your child's exposure to graphic news footage. During times of national or local crises, they need reassurance. Talk to them honestly, and let them know that you are doing everything possible to make sure they are safe.

It is up to parents to teach children to love one another and to respect the precious gift of life.

Note the Quote
"He who has courage and faith will never perish in misery."

Anne Frank

From the Catechism
"The family is the 'domestic church' where God's children learn to pray 'as the Church' and to persevere in prayer."
(*Catechism of the Catholic Church*, 2685)

Eucharistic Prayer
God of power and might,

we praise you through your Son, Jesus Christ,

who comes in your name.

He is the Word that brings salvation.

He is the hand you stretch out to sinners.

He is the way that leads to your peace.

God our Father,

we had wandered far from you,

but through your Son you have brought us back.

You gave him up to death

so that we might turn again to you

and find our way to one another.

(Eucharistic Prayer for Masses of Reconciliation II)

What Your Child Will Learn in Unit 3

A presentation of the seven sacraments begins Unit 3. The children will be able to describe the sacraments of Christian Initiation (Baptism, Confirmation, Eucharist), the sacraments of Healing (Penance and Reconciliation, and Anointing of the Sick) and the sacraments at the Service of Communion (Matrimony and Holy Orders). The children will more fully realize that the Mass is the celebration of the Eucharist. The four parts of the Mass are then explained. These are the Introductory Rites, the Liturgy of the Word, the Liturgy of the Eucharist, and the Concluding Rite. The last two chapters of Unit 3 concentrate on the sacraments of healing: Penance and Reconciliation, and the Anointing of the Sick.

Plan & Preview

▶ Your child will be making a thank-you card to share with the entire family. Have a sheet of construction paper or drawing paper on hand. *(Chapter 16 Family Page)*

▶ You might want to obtain a photograph of someone special who has died in your family for use in the "Remembering Someone Special" activity. *(Chapter 19 Family Page)*

130

CLASS CONNECTION

Point out the unit title to the children. Ask them what they think they will be learning more about in this unit. Have a class discussion preparing the children for this unit.

HOME CONNECTION

Sharing Faith as a Family

Sadlier *We Believe* calls on families to become involved in:

• learning the faith

• prayer and worship

• living their faith.

Highlighting of these unit family pages and the opportunities they offer will strengthen the partnership of the Church and the home.

For additional information and activities, encourage families to visit Sadlier's

www.WeBelieveweb.com

Chapter 15 · We Celebrate the Sacraments

Overview

In Chapter 12, the children learned that we are called to serve God in our particular vocations. In this chapter, the children will learn about the seven sacraments as the special signs of God's love.

Doctrinal Content	For Adult Reading and Reflection *Catechism of the Catholic Church*
The children will learn:	Paragraph
• The Church celebrates the sacraments. .1113	
• Baptism, Confirmation, and Eucharist are the sacraments of Christian initiation. 1212	
• Reconciliation and Anointing of the Sick are sacraments of healing. 1421	
• Holy Orders and Matrimony are sacraments of service to others. 1534	

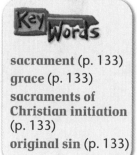

Key Words

sacrament (p. 133)
grace (p. 133)
sacraments of Christian initiation (p. 133)
original sin (p. 133)

Catechist Background

When have you experienced God's love in a real and meaningful way?

Some moments are so sacred that through them we experience God in real and meaningful ways. In our daily lives, this might happen through an encounter with another person, in awe of nature, by reading the Bible or in praying. There are many signs of God's love and presence among us.

When the Church celebrates the sacraments, we experience God in real and effective ways. "The sacraments are efficacious signs of grace, instituted by Christ and entrusted to the Church, by which divine life is dispensed to us" (CCC 1131). Jesus gave us the sacraments so that we, too, might participate in the life and love of God.

Assured of this gift of grace, the Church celebrates seven sacraments. In the sacraments of Christian initiation—Baptism, Confirmation, and Eucharist—new members are initiated into the fullness of life with God and membership in the Church. Through the sacraments of healing—Penance and Anointing of the Sick—Christians are restored and reconciled to God and strengthened when we are seriously ill. In the sacraments of service—Matrimony and Holy Orders—we witness and celebrate the vocations of married people and of bishops, priests, and deacons.

In each of the sacraments, we celebrate and participate in the liturgical action. However, in each, it is Christ who is always present and by his power makes the sacraments efficacious signs, that is, they truly effect what they signify. When we respond in faith, God's grace truly changes us.

How do I keep myself open to receiving the effects of God's grace in my life?

Lesson Planning Guide

Lesson Steps	Presentation	Materials

① WE GATHER

page 131
✚ **Prayer**

☀ **Focus on Life**

- Listen to Scripture.
- 🎵 Respond in song.
- Discuss neighborhood signs and their importance.

For the prayer space: placard about sacraments, names of sacraments on cards, objects used with sacraments
🎵 "Jesus Is with Us," Owen Alstott, #11, Grade 3 CD

② WE BELIEVE

page 132
The Church celebrates the sacraments.

- Read and discuss the seven sacraments as special signs.
- Discuss the meaning of grace.
- 🏃 List sacraments already received.
- Read and discuss *As Catholics*.

- large picture of Jesus
- "Welcome Friends" sign
- examples of sacramentals (holy water, medals, rosaries) (option)

page 133
Baptism, Confirmation, and Eucharist are the sacraments of Christian initiation.

- Read and discuss the sacraments of initiation and original sin.
- 🏃 Discuss parish celebrations of the sacraments of initiation.

page 134
Reconciliation and Anointing of the Sick are sacraments of healing.

- Read and discuss Jesus' healing ministry and the sacraments of healing.
- 🏃 Reflect on the question about forgiveness, and love and care of the sick.

page 135
Holy Orders and Matrimony are sacraments of service to others.

- Read and discuss Holy Orders and Matrimony as sacraments of service.

- copies of Reproducible Master 15

③ WE RESPOND

page 135

- 🏃 Draw or write about joining with friends in the celebration of the sacraments.

page 136
Review

- Complete questions 1–5.
- 🏃 Work on *Assessment Activity*.

- construction paper, markers
- Chapter 15 Test in Assessment Book, pp. 31–32
- Chapter 15 Test in Test Generator
- Review & Resource Book, pp. 34–36

page 137–138
We Respond in Faith

- Complete the *Reflect & Pray* activity.
- Review *Remember* and *Key Words*.
- Read and discuss *Our Catholic Life*.
- Discuss Sharing Faith with My Family.

- Family Book, pp. 43–45

For additional ideas, activities, and opportunities: Visit Sadlier's 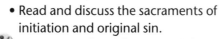 **www.WeBelieve.web.com**

Name _____

Complete the chart below. In column l, show whether the sacrament is a sacrament of initiation, a sacrament of healing, or a sacrament of service. In column 2, color the picture reminding you of the sacrament. In column 3, write a sentence that tells about the sacrament. The first sacrament is begun for you.

God Shows His Love for Us Through the Seven Sacraments

	TYPE OF SACRAMENT	PICTURE OF SACRAMENT	SENTENCE ABOUT SACRAMENT
Baptism	I		_____ _____
Confirmation			_____ _____
Holy Eucharist			_____ _____
Reconciliation (Penance)			_____ _____
Anointing of the Sick			_____ _____
Holy Orders			_____ _____
Matrimony			_____ _____

Connections

To Catholic Social Teaching

Life and Dignity of the Human Person
Remind the children that the sacrament of Anointing of the Sick honors the dignity of the human person, no matter what the person's physical condition. We can participate in ensuring the dignity of individuals by reaching out to those who are ill and unable to be with the parish community. Whether it is a classmate or a parishioner, we can help them feel more connected by sending cards, e-mail, and remembering them in our prayers.

To Parish

Point out to the children that the parish offers many opportunities to prepare for the reception of the sacraments. Bring in a copy of a parish bulletin and tell the children about the various sacramental preparation programs that the parish offers.

FAITH and MEDIA

▶ You might scan photographs of the children and members of their families receiving the sacraments. Post these on the parish or school Web site. Remind the children that this activity is another example of a way we can use media—in this case, the media of photography and the Internet—to share aspects of our faith life with others.

▶ In connection with the sacrament of Holy Orders, tell the children that they can find information about the topic from the diocese or archdiocese on the Internet.

Meeting Individual Needs

English Language Learners

Children whose primary language is not English would benefit from paired readings of the text pages. Introducing as many pictures as possible at the beginning of the chapter will encourage each child to attach meaning to the new vocabulary words and concepts that they encounter. Allow time for the children to review materials with a study buddy or class coach.

ADDITIONAL RESOURCES

Book *A Child's Journey: The Christian Initiation of Children*, Rita Burns Senseman, St. Anthony Messenger Press, Cincinnati, OH, 1998. This book helps adults understand a child's journey to the sacraments.

Video *The Sacraments for Children: An Introduction to the Seven Sacraments for Middle-Grade Children*, Liguori, Liguori, MO, 1989. Fr. Hain and children learn the meaning and symbols of sacraments. (60 min.–8 segments)

To find more ideas for books, videos, and other learning material, visit Sadlier's

www.WE BELIEVE web.com

Focus on Life

Chapter Story

It was September again, and Eliza Beth Morley was going to a new school. Her mom traveled a great deal for her company, so Eliza Beth, or E. B. as everyone called her, had lived in many different places. She had attended six different schools so far. But E.B. had a feeling that this new school was going to be special.

For one thing, Mr. Prochaska was her teacher. This was his first year of teaching. He had just come to the United States from Europe where he had been a scientist. He promised that his class would do a lot of experiments. At recess, he organized soccer games for the third graders. He told jokes, and he asked the children to help him learn more about American customs and holidays.

E.B. thought that the children at her school were really friendly. In the first week, Darla Jones had already invited her over to her house to play. And on Saturday, she'd be going to Jennifer's birthday party!

E.B. was so happy to feel that she belonged. Her mom was glad. She said that she was going to try to get a job that didn't involve so much travel, so that E.B. could stay at this school.

This week, Mr. Prochaska's third grade class was in charge of the "Welcome Back to School Assembly." They decorated the hall and chose the songs for the special day.

At the end of the assembly, the principal announced, "Would all of our newcomers, children and staff, please come to the front?"

E.B. felt a little shy, but she saw that the other new children were walking to the front of the auditorium. Mr. Prochaska followed them. Then the third grade class circled around the newcomers and sang "A Circle of Love." E.B. knew that, at last, she belonged.

▶ *What are some words and actions that make people feel welcome?*

We Celebrate the Sacraments

WE GATHER

✝ **Leader:** God loves us very much. Let us thank God for all the ways he shows his love for us. Let us thank God for sending his Son.

Reader: "For God so loved the world that he gave his only Son, so that everyone who believes in him might not perish but might have eternal life." (John 3:16)

All: Thank you, God, for giving us your Son, Jesus. Amen.

🎵 **Jesus Is with Us**

Jesus is with us today,
beside us to guide us today.
Jesus teaches us, Jesus heals us,
for we are his Church;
we are his chosen;
we are the children of God.

 What are some signs that you see in your neighborhood? Tell why each one is important.

131

PREPARING TO PRAY

The children will listen to the good news that God so loved the world he sent his only Son. They will respond in song.

• Select a prayer leader and allow him or her to practice.

• Tell the children you will be the reader. Then practice the song.

• Choose seven children to carry sacramental reminders.

The Prayer Space

• Make a placard with *The Sacraments Are Signs of God's Love for Us* and place it in the prayer space.

• Invite volunteers to write the names of the sacraments on name cards.

• Gather reminders of the sacraments: candle, act of contrition, bread, red paper flame, dish of olive oil, two gold rings (real or paper), white stole (paper or long white scarf).

📖 **This Week's Liturgy**
Visit **www.webelieveweb.com** for this week's liturgical readings and other seasonal material.

Lesson Plan

WE GATHER ____ minutes

✝ Pray

• Have the prayer leader pray the Sign of the Cross.

• Proclaim the Scripture.

• Sing the song.

• After the children have finished singing "Jesus Is With Us," instruct the seven children to place their reminders of the sacraments respectfully in the prayer space next to the name card of the sacrament with which it is associated. Help the child place it by explaining the meaning of each reminder. Have the rest of the children respond with "Thank you, Jesus, for the sacrament of _____."

Focus on Life

• Have the children discuss the signs they see in their neighborhood and tell why each is important.

• In this chapter, the children will learn about the seven sacraments as special signs of God's love.

• Read the *Chapter Story* on guide page 131E. Discuss the welcoming words and actions in the story.

Home Connection Update

Encourage the children to share their weekend experiences in using the Chapter 12 family page. Ask: *What did you learn about your family by making the Vocation Tree?*

Catechist Goal

• To introduce the sacraments as the special signs that the Church celebrates

Our Faith Response

• To appreciate the gift of the sacraments and their importance in our lives

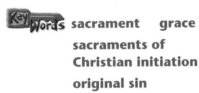 **sacrament   grace**

sacraments of Christian initiation

original sin

Lesson Materials

• examples of sacramentals (holy water, medals, rosary) (option)
• picture of Jesus and "Welcome" sign
• copies of Reproducible Master 15
• construction paper, markers

As Catholics...

Sacramentals

Read aloud the text. Ask volunteers to describe the kinds of sacramentals that might be present in their homes. Show the sacramentals you have brought and explain their meaning.

WE BELIEVE

The Church celebrates the sacraments.

Every day we can see all kinds of signs. A sign stands for or tells us about something. A sign can be something we see or something we do.

Jesus often pointed to ordinary things to help us to learn more about God. He spoke about birds, wheat, and even wildflowers as signs of God's love. Jesus' actions were signs of God's love, too. He held children in his arms. He touched people and healed them. He comforted sinners and forgave them.

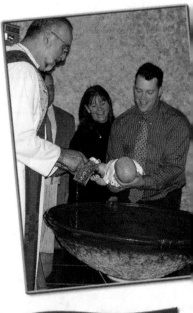

The Church celebrates seven special signs. We call these signs sacraments. A **sacrament** is a special sign given to us by Jesus through which we share in God's life and love. The seven sacraments are Baptism, Confirmation, Eucharist, Penance and Reconciliation, Anointing of the Sick, Holy Orders, and Matrimony.

Through the power of the Holy Spirit, we receive and celebrate God's own life and love in the sacraments. Our share in God's life and love is called **grace**. Through the power of grace, we grow in holiness. The sacraments help us to live as Jesus' disciples.

As Catholics...

Sacramentals are blessings, actions, and special objects given to us by the Church. They help us to respond to the grace we receive in the sacraments. Blessings of people, places, and food are sacramentals. Actions such as making the sign of the cross and the sprinkling of holy water are sacramentals. Some objects that are sacramentals are statues, medals, rosaries, candles, and crucifixes.

Name a sacramental that is part of your life at home.

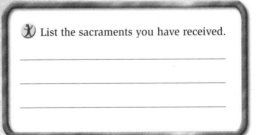

List the sacraments you have received.

_____

_____

_____

Lesson Plan

WE BELIEVE _____ minutes

Have a volunteer read aloud the *We Believe* statement. Ask a volunteer to read the two *We Believe* paragraphs. Point out that Jesus used ordinary things in natures such as birds, wheat, and flowers to teach about God's love. Have volunteers continue reading the remaining paragraphs. Emphasize these points:

• Actions as well as objects can be signs.

• While on earth, Jesus showed us signs of God's love by welcoming and blessing the children, healing the sick, and forgiving sinners.

• The Church celebrates seven special signs called the sacraments. These sacraments are Baptism, Confirmation, Eucharist, Penance and Reconciliation, Anointing of the Sick, Holy Orders, and Matrimony.

Have the children list the sacraments they have already received. Refer to the photos throughout the lesson that show the sacraments being celebrated.

Display a large picture of Jesus or a poster with the name Jesus on the chalkboard. Place a sign that has *Welcome Friends* under the Jesus picture or poster. Write each child's name on the sign.

Baptism, Confirmation, and Eucharist are the sacraments of Christian initiation.

We are joined to Jesus and the Church through the **sacraments of Christian initiation**: Baptism, Confirmation, and Eucharist. Another word for *initiation* is *beginning*. Through the sacraments of Christian initiation, a new life of grace begins in us.

In Baptism the Church welcomes us. We become children of God and members of the Church. Each of us is born with **original sin**, the first sin committed by the first human beings. Through Baptism God frees us from original sin and forgives any sins we may have committed. God fills us with grace, his life and love.

In Confirmation we are sealed with the Gift of the Holy Spirit. The Holy Spirit gives us strength and courage to live as disciples of Jesus.

In the Eucharist we praise and thank God the Father for sending his Son, Jesus. We receive Jesus' Body and Blood in Holy Communion. We grow closer to Jesus and all the members of the Church.

Key Words

sacrament (p. 253)

grace (p. 251)

sacraments of Christian initiation (p. 253)

original sin (p. 252)

In groups talk about how your parish celebrates the sacraments of Christian initiation.

133

ACTIVITY BANK

Faith and Media
Memories of the Sacraments
Activity Materials: photographs of sacramental celebrations; optional clothesline and clothespins

The sacraments are a vital part of Catholic life. To get a visual sense of the sacraments, encourage the children to bring in photographs of themselves or family members receiving one of the sacraments. Allow time for the children to share their photographs. Post pictures on a classroom clothesline with clothespins during the study of the sacraments. Ask parents for permission to post some of their family's photographs in your classroom or on the parish Web site. Suggest that the children write captions to accompany their pictures that are posted on the Web site.

Have a volunteer read aloud the *We Believe* statement on page 133. Ask volunteers to read sections of the text. Stress that the sacraments of Christian initiation welcome us into the Church and bring us more fully into the Church's life. Point out that in Baptism we are freed of original sin. This is God's gift that allows us to share in his divine grace. Confirmation provides the strength and courage necessary to live as a disciple of Jesus. In the Eucharist, we receive the Body and Blood of Christ. We grow closer to Jesus and all the members of the Church.

Invite the children to form small groups and talk about the celebrations of the sacraments of initiation in their parishes.

Quick Check

✔ *What are the seven special signs that the Church celebrates?* (sacraments)

✔ *Name the sacraments that you have received.* (Answers will vary, but the majority of third graders will probably have received Baptism, Reconciliation, and Eucharist. Ask the students to name the other four sacraments.)

✔ *What are the sacraments of Christian initiation?* (Baptism, Confirmation, and Eucharist)

Reconciliation and Anointing of the Sick are sacraments of healing.

During his ministry Jesus healed many people. Sometimes he did this when he cured them of their sicknesses. At other times Jesus forgave people their sins.

Jesus gave the Church the power to continue his healing work. The Church does this especially through two sacraments: Reconciliation and Anointing of the Sick. These sacraments are called sacraments of healing.

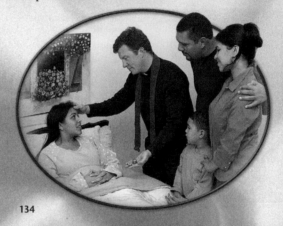

In the sacrament of Reconciliation, we confess our sins to the priest and promise to do better. In the name of God, the priest forgives our sins. Our relationship with God and others is healed.

In the sacrament of the Anointing of the Sick, the priest lays his hands on the sick. He blesses them with holy oil and prays for their health. They are strengthened in their faith and sometimes their bodies are healed. They receive the peace of Christ.

Think about someone you need to forgive or someone you know who is sick. What can you do to show them your love and care?

134

Teaching Note
Bulletin Board

Make a bulletin board that celebrates the children' Baptisms. Ask them to bring in baptismal or baby pictures. Make a caption that reads *The Church Welcomed You*. Ask each child to cut out a flower, place the picture in the center of the flower and write his or her baptismal dates on the leaves of the flower. If you would like, have classmates guess the identity of each baby.

Lesson Plan

WE BELIEVE (continued)

Have a volunteer read aloud the *We Believe* statement on page 134. Read aloud the first *We Believe* paragraph. (At this time you might want to share with the group Luke 5:17–25, the healing of the paralytic.)

Read aloud the remaining paragraphs of the *We Believe* text. Refer to the photos on text page 134. Emphasize the following:

• Jesus gave the Church the power to continue his healing work.

• The sacraments of Reconciliation and Anointing are the sacraments that heal us.

• Both sacraments celebrate God's love and forgiveness.

Have the children quietly reflect on the question.

Read aloud the *We Believe* statement on page 135. Have the children work with a partner to read and highlight the *We Believe* paragraphs. Emphasize the following:

• The sacraments of Holy Orders and Matrimony are special signs of service to God and the Church.

• Bishops and priests are ordained to serve the people of God by preaching the good news and celebrating the sacraments with them. Deacons are ordained to serve the dioceses, especially people who are in need.

Holy Orders and Matrimony are sacraments of service to others.

Through Baptism God calls each one of us to be a sign of his love to others. We each have a vocation to serve God and the Church. The Church celebrates two sacraments that are special signs of service: Holy Orders and Matrimony.

In the sacrament of Holy Orders, certain men are ordained to serve the Church as deacons, priests, and bishops. This sacrament gives them the grace to live out their vocation of service in the Church.

Bishops serve the Church by leading a larger community of faith called a diocese. They lead their dioceses in service, teaching, prayer, and sacraments. Under their guidance, priests also carry on the ministry of Jesus.

Priests usually serve in parishes. They lead the celebration of the sacraments, guide the people they serve, and reach out to those who are in need. Some priests teach in schools.

Along with the bishop and priests, deacons are ordained to serve their dioceses. Deacons do many things to help in their parish worship. They also have a special responsibility to serve those who are in need.

In the sacrament of Matrimony, or Marriage, the love of a man and woman is blessed. They are united in the love of Christ. The husband and wife receive the grace to help them to be faithful to each other. The sacrament also helps the couple to share God's love with their family. They grow in holiness as they serve the Church together.

WE RESPOND

✖ Draw or write how you and your friends join in the celebration of the sacraments.

135

ACTIVITY BANK

Parish
Invitation into the Church
Activity Materials: paper and markers

Talk with parish leaders to learn ways children can assist in welcoming new members into the Church as they receive the sacraments of Christian initiation.

Family
Sacramental Trees
Activity Materials: small tree branch, sand, flowerpot, ribbons, artifacts related to the sacraments

Each family can make a tree of symbols related to sacraments that they or their family members have received. They would use a small tree branch placed in a pot of sand and adorn the tree with pictures of sacramental ceremonies, announcements, Mass folders, and so on.

• Through the sacrament of Matrimony, husbands and wives are strengthened by God to love and respect each other, share love with their families, and to serve others together. (Refer to the photo of the couple celebrating the sacrament. Explain the symbolism of the rings.)

Explain the hierarchy of the Church. Draw concentric circles on the board. Write the word *pope* in the center, followed by *archbishop*, *bishop*, *priest*, and *deacon* in subsequent circles. Point out that a *bishop* leads the parishes within his *diocese*.

WE RESPOND ___ minutes

Connect to Life Invite the children to illustrate or write how they and their friends would join together in the celebration of the sacraments. Share their work and compliment the students on their creativity.

Distribute copies of Reproducible Master 15. Have the children work on the activity now or work on it at home. Direct them to use the letter **I** for a sacrament of initiation, **H** for healing, and **S** for service.

Grade 3
Chapter 15

CHAPTER TEST

Chapter 15 Test is provided in the Grade 3 Assessment Book.

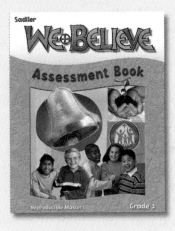

Sadlier
We Believe
Assessment Book

Reproducible Masters   Grade 3

Use the words in the box to complete the sentences.

Matrimony Anointing of the Sick sacrament
Reconciliation   Eucharist

1. A ___sacrament___ is a special sign given to us by Jesus through which we share in God's life and love.

2. Baptism, Confirmation, and ___Eucharist___ are the sacraments of Christian initiation.

3. Anointing of the Sick and ___Reconciliation___ are sacraments of healing.

4. Holy Orders and ___Matrimony___ are sacraments of service to others.

Finish this sentence.

5. Through the sacraments _we receive and celebrate_ _God's own life and love. (See page 132.)_

ASSESSMENT

Make a booklet of the sacraments you have celebrated. Describe each sacrament. Include drawings that show the celebration of the sacrament. Decorate the cover of your book.

136

Lesson Plan

___ minutes

Chapter Review Read aloud the directions. Have the children complete sentences 1–4. Brainstorm possibilities to question 5, then ask them to complete the sentence. Ask volunteers to share their responses.

Assessment Activity When the children do this activity, suggest that they include a description of the sacrament as well as drawings that show the celebration of the sacrament. Encourage them to design covers for their booklets. Include the booklet as part of the children's portfolios.

___ minutes

Reflect & Pray Remind the children of the sacraments and their importance in our lives. Ask them to answer the question and complete the prayer.

Key Words Write scrambled versions of the *Key Words* on the chalkboard. Have the children unscramble the words and write a sentence that shows the meaning of the words. Ask them to share their sentences in small groups.

Remember Have the children underline the seven sacraments in the *We Believe* statements. Have them close their texts and name the seven sacraments.

We Respond in Faith

Reflect & Pray

What are some of the ways God shares his life and love with us?

_____

Jesus, help me to be a sign of God's love in today's world. Help me to

_____

Key Words

sacrament (p. 253)
grace (p. 251)
sacraments of Christian initiation (p. 253)
original sin (p. 252)

Remember

• The Church celebrates the sacraments.

• Baptism, Confirmation, and Eucharist are the sacraments of Christian initiation.

• Reconciliation and Anointing of the Sick are sacraments of healing.

• Holy Orders and Matrimony are sacraments of service to others.

Martyrs for the Faith

In 1980 four American Catholic women, Sister Ita Ford, M.M., Sister Maura Clarke, M.M., Sister Dorothy Kazel, O.S.U., and Jean Donovan were killed in El Salvador. These women died as they had lived, serving God and the Church.

A _martyr_ is someone who dies for his or her faith. Christian martyrs give their lives as a sign of God's love to others. Many martyrs have already been declared saints by the Church. Some day these four women may be officially declared saints, too.

HOME CONNECTION

Sharing Faith with My Family

Make sure to send home the family page (text page 138).

Encourage the children to enjoy coloring the sacrament reminders for the sacraments of Baptism and Confirmation with family members.

PUPIL PAGE 138

For additional information and activities, encourage families to visit Sadlier's

www.WeBelieve.web.com

Our Catholic Life Explain that three of the women were members of religious orders. Sisters Ita Ford and Maura Clarke were Maryknoll Sisters of Saint Dominic. (M.M. stands for Maryknoll Missioner.) Sister Dorothy Kazel was an Ursuline Sister. (O.S.U. stands for Order of St. Ursula.) Jean Donovan was a laywoman. Ask the children to pray for all those who suffer now because of their faith.

Family Page Note Explain that the reminder for Baptism shows the cross, a candle flame, and ripples of water. The reminder for Confirmation shows a dove. This is a symbol of the Holy Spirit. (Another is a flame of fire.) The dove carries an olive branch, a symbol of peace.

Plan Ahead for Chapter 16

Prayer Space: mini-loaves of bread, grapes, card with eucharistic symbols

Materials: copies of Reproducible Master 16, calendar, chart paper, markers, magazines

Chapter 16 Celebrating Eucharist: The Mass

Overview

In Chapter 15 the children learned that there are seven sacraments. In this chapter, they will continue to learn about the sacrament of the Eucharist.

Doctrinal Content	For Adult Reading and Reflection *Catechism of the Catholic Church*
The children will learn:	Paragraph
• Jesus celebrated Passover and the Last Supper.	1340
• The Mass is a sacrifice and a meal.	1323
• We take part in the Mass.	1348
• We celebrate Mass each week.	1343

Key Words

Passover (p. 141)
Eucharist (p. 141)
Mass (p. 141)
sacrifice (p. 141)
assembly (p. 142)

Catechist Background

How do I honor the memory of important people in my life who have died?

There are many ways in which we invoke and honor the memory of a person who has died. We tell stories about the person. We imitate them in our own lives. We do the things that they asked us to do. When we celebrate and participate at the Mass, we do all this and more to remember Jesus.

The Last Supper that Jesus shared with his disciples was a special Jewish feast called Passover. Passover is celebrated through a meal in which the Jewish people recall how they went from slavery to freedom. Participants in the Passover celebration remember the Exodus event as their own personal history.

As participants in the new Passover of Christ we remember his dying and rising, and in faith, we do everything in "memory of him." Our eucharistic meal is a sacrifice of praise and thanksgiving through Christ to the Father.

At the Last Supper, Jesus transformed the meaning of the Passover meal by changing the bread and wine into his very Body and Blood.

Then, he called upon his disciples to celebrate this meal in his memory. We believe that, whenever we celebrate the Mass, Jesus is truly present to us in his Body and Blood in the Eucharist. The Eucharist is "a sacrament of love, a sign of unity, a bond of charity, a Paschal banquet" (CCC 1323).

The Mass is also a sacrifice, an offering and a participation in the passion of Jesus. We recall Jesus and his passion not simply as history, but as a person and an event that have the power to change us still. We are called to be active participants at Mass not only in the words and actions of the prayer and ritual but also in all that the Mass makes present to us. Our participation in the Eucharist transforms us, making us more like Christ.

How can I remember Jesus in my life?

Lesson Planning Guide

Lesson Steps	Presentation	Materials

① WE GATHER

| page 139
  Prayer

  Focus on Life | • Listen to Scripture.
 • Respond in prayer.
 • Share responses to the questions about special times with special meals. | For the prayer space: small table, white covering, card with eucharistic symbols, mini-loaves of bread, grapes |

② WE BELIEVE

pages 140–141 *Jesus celebrated Passover and the Last Supper.* 📖 *Matthew 26:26–28*	• Read and discuss the Passover feast and Jesus giving us the Eucharist at the Last Supper. 🏃 Write what we can be thankful for at the Eucharist.	
page 141 *The Mass is a sacrifice and a meal.*	• Read and discuss the Mass as sacrifice and meal. 🏃 Act out the meaning of the Mass.	
page 142 *We take part in the Mass.*	• Read and discuss the assembly's participation in the Mass. 🏃 Discuss ways to encourage others to participate at Mass. • Read and discuss *As Catholics*.	
page 143 *We celebrate Mass each week.*	• Read and discuss Sunday and holy days of obligation, and other feasts.	• calendar • copies of Reproducible Master 16

③ WE RESPOND

page 143	🏃 Send a message inviting parishioners to take part in the Mass.	
page 144 **Review**	• Complete questions 1–5. 🏃 Work on *Assessment Activity*.	• chart paper, markers, magazines • Chapter 16 Test in Assessment Book, pp. 33–34 • Chapter 16 Test in Test Generator • Review & Resource Book, pp. 37–39
page 145–146 **We Respond in Faith**	• Complete the *Reflect & Pray* activity. • Review *Remember* and *Key Words*. • Read and discuss *Our Catholic Life*. • Discuss **Sharing Faith with My Family**.	• Family Book, pp. 46–48

For additional ideas, activities, and opportunities: Visit Sadlier's **www.WeBelieveweb.com**

Name _____

After Holy Communion we offer prayers of thanksgiving and joy.

✝ **Prayer After Communion**

Jesus, Son of God,
  thanks and praise to you.

Jesus, Good Shepherd,
  thanks and praise to you.

Jesus, Lamb of God,
  thanks and praise to you.

Jesus, Bread of life and love,
  thanks and praise to you.

Jesus, Source of strength and joy,
  thanks and praise to you.

Thank you, Jesus,
  for your life in mine.

Help me live your good news of
  love and peace.

(from Sadlier's *Prayers and Practices for Young Catholics*)

Write your own prayer to say after you receive Holy Communion. Then color the picture of Jesus.

_____
_____
_____
_____
_____
_____
_____
_____
_____
_____

Connections

To Liturgy

As the children learn about participating in the celebration of the Mass, encourage them to add ways we can actively prepare for worship. (For example: by allowing enough time to get ready, by reviewing ways to act reverently in church, by finding our places in the missalette or Mass sheet.) Stress that celebrating the Mass brings us closer to God and to one another.

To Scripture

Many of the hymns sung at Mass are based upon the words of Scripture. Bring in a parish missalette or hymnal and have the children notice the reference to the biblical text usually given with the hymn. You might want to look up the text in the Bible to compare it to the words used in the hymn.

FAITH and MEDIA

▶ After the children have learned about the holy days of obligation in the United States, you might go online as a class to find descriptions and pictures of holy day celebrations in other countries. You might do this as part of the optional research activity.

▶ As the children work on their plans for magazine stories about the Eucharist, you might recall your discussions earlier in the year about the responsibilities of those who work in media.

Meeting Individual Needs

English Language Learners

Directions for assignments could be frustrating for a child with limited English proficiency. Invite classmates to help limited English speakers who need additional directions, clarification of directions, or help in understanding the vocabulary used in the lesson.

ADDITIONAL RESOURCES

Videos *The Story of Jesus for Children,* Inspirational Films, Inc., San Clemente, CA, 1979. From this excellent drama of Jesus' life through children's eyes, use the segment about the Last Supper. (7 min. segment of 62 min. tape)

Why Do We Go to Mass on Sunday? Ikonographics, St. Anthony Messenger Press, Cincinnati, OH, 2000. Children learn why celebrating Sunday Mass as a community is vital to our faith. (13 min.)

To find more ideas for books, videos, and other learning material, visit Sadlier's

www.WeBelieve.web.com

Focus on Life

Chapter Story

When Carlo came home from school on Monday afternoon, his mom and dad were home! Aunt Monica had stayed with him while his parents spent the weekend hunting for mushrooms.

Carlo's family liked to eat mushrooms, especially morel mushrooms. Morels only grew in certain areas and at certain seasons. For one weekend in the spring, Carlo's parents drove up north, where they would pick as many morels as they could find.

"Hi, Dad!" Carlo called.

"Carlo! We did it again—ten bushels of morels! Look at them! Your mom even kept searching and picking when it began to rain," his father said.

Carlo sat at the kitchen table and watched his father clean handfuls of morels in the sink, then fry them in butter in a pan on the stove. Carlo's father then took four thin steaks from the refrigerator and placed them in the pan with the mushrooms. He smiled at Carlo. The kitchen quickly filled with a delicious aroma. Carlos began to set the table.

Soon Carlo, his parents, and Aunt Monica were seated around the table. His father proudly gave each of them a steak and a big spoonful of mushrooms. They all bowed their heads for the blessing. Then Carlo ate one morel. He had never tasted anything so delicious.

"Mom, Dad, thank you. This is the greatest meal I've ever had," Carlo said.

His parents happily said, "You're welcome!" and began eating, too. The kitchen was filled with good conversation as Carlo's family savored their wonderful meal together.

▶ *What did Carlo's parents do to prepare such a special family meal? How did Aunt Monica and Carlo help?*

Celebrating Eucharist: The Mass

WE GATHER

✝ **Leader:** Everything good that we have is God's gift to us. Think quietly about what God has given you.

Reader: "Give thanks to the LORD, who is good, whose love endures forever." (Psalm 106:1)

All: We thank you, O God!

Reader: "You are my God, I give you thanks; my God, I offer you praise."(Psalm 118:28)

All: We thank you, O God!

Many people celebrate special times with special meals. When have you and your family done this? What made the celebration special for you?

139

PREPARING TO PRAY

The children will listen to and respond to a psalm of thanksgiving to God.

• Tell the children you will lead the prayer.

• Choose two children to read the Scriptures, one reader for each psalm verse. Allow the children time to practice reading their parts.

The Prayer Space

• Place a white covering on the prayer table.

• Display a card decorated with eucharistic symbols that reads *The Mass is a sacrifice and a meal* in the prayer space. (Symbols might be a chalice and host or wheat and grapes.)

• Place mini-loaves of bread and grapes on the small table.

📖 **This Week's Liturgy**

Visit **www.webelieveweb.com** for this week's liturgical readings and other seasonal material.

Lesson Plan

WE GATHER ____ minutes

✝ **Pray**

• Gather in the prayer space, and have the children open their books to page 139.

• Lead the opening prayer.

• Have the readers proclaim the psalm verses.

 Focus on Life

• Share the *Chapter Story* on guide page 139E. Discuss special times and meals families enjoy together.

• In this chapter, the children will learn about the sacrament of the Eucharist and its celebration.

Home Connection Update

Review the activities on the Chapter 15 family page. Ask: *How will you display your sacrament reminders at home?*

Catechist Goal

• To present that Jesus gave us the Eucharist at the Last Supper and that the Mass is a sacrifice and a meal

Our Faith Response

• To appreciate why we actively participate in the celebration of the Mass

 **Passover   Eucharist**
Mass   sacrifice
assembly

Lesson Materials

• calendar
• copies of Reproducible Master 16
• chart paper, markers, magazines

Teaching Note

The Sabbath Day

The Jewish Sabbath is celebrated from Friday evening at sundown until Saturday evening. We celebrate the Lord's Day on Sunday in remembrance of the Resurrection of Jesus. We follow the Jewish tradition in beginning our celebration the night before, on Saturday evening, and ending it on Sunday evening.

WE BELIEVE
Jesus celebrated Passover and the Last Supper.

Throughout their history, Jewish people have celebrated important events with special meals. On the feast of **Passover**, the Jewish people celebrate their freedom from slavery in Egypt. They remember that God "passed over" the houses of his people, saving them. They remember that God protected them from the suffering that came to Egypt.

On the night before he died, Jesus celebrated the Passover meal with his disciples in a new way. This meal that Jesus celebrated is called the Last Supper.

Matthew 26:26–28

While Jesus and his disciples ate, Jesus took bread and blessed it. He then broke it and gave it to his disciples saying, "Take and eat; this is my body." (Matthew 26:26) Then Jesus took a cup of wine and gave thanks. He gave the cup to his disciples saying, "Drink from it, all of you, for this is my blood." (Matthew 26:27, 28)

At the Last Supper Jesus told his disciples to bless and break bread in his memory. He gave us the **Eucharist**. The Eucharist is the sacrament of Jesus' Body and Blood. At each celebration of the Eucharist, the Church follows Jesus' command to "Do this in memory of me." (Luke 22:19)

140

Lesson Plan

WE BELIEVE ___ minutes

Have a volunteer read the *We Believe* statement. Pair each child with a partner. Have them read and highlight points in the *We Believe* paragraphs. Assign each pair one paragraph for which they are to write a question. When finished, have them share questions and answers.

Point out the picture of the Last Supper in the text, which some children will probably recognize. Ask them whether they know what the picture portrays. Explain that Jesus celebrated the Last Supper with his disciples. Ask a volunteer to share the meaning of the word *Passover*. Ask: *How are Passover and the Last Supper related?* (The Last Supper was the last time that Jesus celebrated the Passover meal.)

Explain to the children that the word *eucharist* means "to give thanks." The word refers to the sacrament of Jesus' Body and Blood. The word *eucharist* is also another word for the celebration of the Mass. During the *Eucharist* the Church gives thanks for everything God has given us.

Invite the children to write what they can thank God for at the Eucharist.

Have a volunteer read aloud the *We Believe* statement on page 141. Have volunteers read aloud the *We Believe* paragraphs. Emphasize the following:

• The celebration of the Eucharist is also called the Mass.
• The Mass is a sacrifice and a meal.

The word *eucharist* means "to give thanks." At the celebration of the Eucharist, the Church gives thanks for all that God gives us.

 Write what you can thank God for at the celebration of the Eucharist.

_____

_____

The Mass is a sacrifice and a meal.

The greatest gift God has given to us is his Son, Jesus. Jesus' greatest gift is giving up his life for us. The Church remembers Jesus' death and Resurrection at the Eucharist.

The celebration of the Eucharist is also called the **Mass**. The Mass is a sacrifice. A **sacrifice** is a gift offered to God by a priest in the name of all the people. Jesus offered the greatest sacrifice of all–his own body and blood on the cross. By his sacrifice Jesus reconciles us with God and saves us from sin.

Key Words

Passover (p. 252)
Eucharist (p. 251)
Mass (p. 252)
sacrifice (p. 253)

The Mass is also a meal. We remember what Jesus did at the Last Supper. He changed bread and wine into his Body and Blood. At Mass we receive his Body and Blood in Holy Communion. We are strengthened to live out our faith.

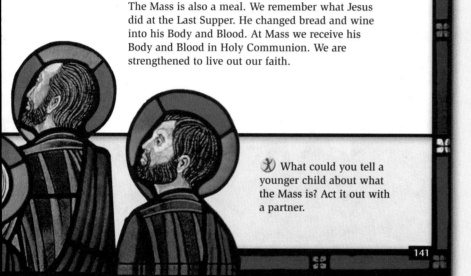

 What could you tell a younger child about what the Mass is? Act it out with a partner.

141

• Jesus' sacrifice reconciles us to God and saves us from sin. We receive Christ's Body and Blood in Holy Communion.

 Have the children act out what they would tell a younger child about the Mass.

Quick Check

✔ *What is the Eucharist?* (The sacrament of Jesus' Body and Blood. It is also another word for the celebration of the Mass.)

✔ *What is the Mass?* (a sacrifice and a meal during which we give thanks and praise to God.)

We take part in the Mass.

The Mass is a celebration. It is the Church's great prayer of thanksgiving and praise. It is important that each of us participate in the celebration.

We gather as the assembly. The **assembly** is the people gathered to worship in the name of Jesus Christ.

We can all:

- pray the responses
- sing praise to God
- listen to the readings and the homily
- pray for needs of the community
- offer the sign of peace to others
- receive Holy Communion.

The priest who leads us at the Mass is called the *celebrant*. Many parishes have deacons who serve at the Mass. Greeters and ushers welcome us and help us to find seats. During the Mass they collect our donations. Altar servers help the priest before, during, and after Mass.

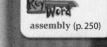

Key Word

assembly (p. 250)

As Catholics...

Altar servers are men, women, boys, and girls who serve at the altar. They light the altar candles. They lead the entrance procession at the beginning of Mass. They may help the priest and deacon receive the gifts of bread and wine. They lead everyone out of church at the end of Mass.

Find out how boys and girls can become altar servers.

As Catholics...

Altar Servers

As you read the section aloud, ask the children to listen for ways that altar servers participate in the Mass. Encourage the children to become altar servers if this is allowed at their age in the parish.

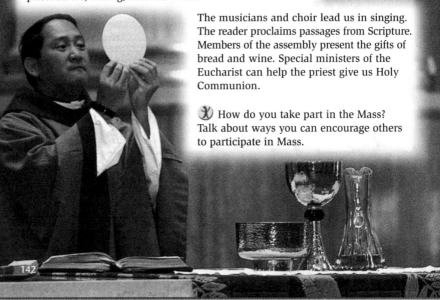

The musicians and choir lead us in singing. The reader proclaims passages from Scripture. Members of the assembly present the gifts of bread and wine. Special ministers of the Eucharist can help the priest give us Holy Communion.

How do you take part in the Mass? Talk about ways you can encourage others to participate in Mass.

142

Lesson Plan

WE BELIEVE (continued)

Read aloud the *We Believe* statement. Have a volunteer read the first two *We Believe* paragraphs. Stress the importance of active participation during Mass. Write the word *assembly* on the board or chart paper. Have the children make a word web that describes their thoughts on the word.

Point out to the students the bulleted items in the third *We Believe* paragraph. Encourage them to look for all of the different opportunities for people to participate in Mass. Ask them to underline each sentence describing how people can participate.

Stress the word *celebrant* in the fourth paragraph and its referring to the priest and his special role at the Mass. Draw the students' attention to the other people—deacons, greeters, ushers, altar servers (refer to the *As Catholics* text on the page), musicians, choir, and special ministers of the Eucharist—who contribute to the celebration of the Eucharist.

Invite the children to talk about ways they can encourage others to participate in the Mass.

Read aloud the *We Believe* statement on page 143. Ask volunteers to read the paragraphs under *We Believe*. Stress that Sunday is our great holy day of celebration.

We celebrate Mass each week.

Sunday is our great holy day. It is the day on which Jesus Christ rose from the dead. The Resurrection of Jesus took place on "the first day of the week." (Matthew 28:1)

In our parishes we come together at Mass each Sunday or Saturday evening. We give praise and thanks to God. Celebrating the Eucharist together is the center of Catholic life. That is why the Church requires all Catholics to take part in the weekly celebration of the Mass. We are also required to participate in Mass on special feasts called *holy days of obligation.*

There are many other important feast days in the Church. One of these is the feast of Our Lady of Guadalupe, which we celebrate on December 12. On these feasts and on every day of the year, we can take part in the Eucharist.

WE RESPOND

Send a message inviting people in your parish to take part in the Mass.

Holy Days of Obligation

Solemnity of Mary, Mother of God
(January 1)

Ascension
(when celebrated on Thursday during the Easter season)

Assumption of Mary
(August 15)

All Saints' Day
(November 1)

Immaculate Conception
(December 8)

Christmas
(December 25)

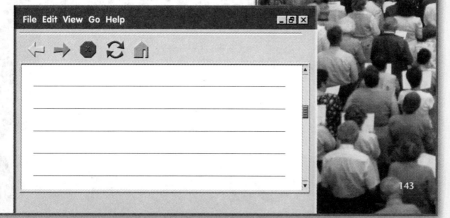

143

ACTIVITY BANK

Parish

Celebrating the Mass Together
Activity Materials: *invitations*

Invite the children and their families to attend Mass together as a group during the year. Send a special invitation to each family. Have them sit together. Have the children carry a class banner during the presentation of the gifts. Encourage families to get to know one another by inviting them to stay for a get-together.

Ask: *Why is this so?* (Sunday is the day Jesus rose from the dead. The first Christians celebrated the Resurrection from Saturday evening to Sunday evening.) It is the Resurrection of Jesus Christ for which we give praise and thanks to God at the Eucharist. Point out that the holy days of obligation require Catholics to take part in the celebration of the Mass.

Use the chart of the holy days of obligation on text page 143 in order to mark each one on a calendar. Highlight each of these special days with a sticker or symbol. Display the calendar in a prominent place in the classroom. (A fuller explanation and treatment of the holy days of obligation and the precepts of the Church appears in Grade 4 of the *We Believe* program.)

WE RESPOND ___ minutes

Connect to Life Have the children complete the *We Respond* activity. Stress that their message may strengthen someone's relationship with God. Ask volunteers to share their messages.

Distribute copies of the Reproducible Master 16. Have the children begin to work on writing their own prayers and coloring in the picture of Jesus. This activity can be finished at home.

CHAPTER TEST

Chapter 16 Test is provided in the Grade 3 Assessment Book.

Write the answer to each question.

1. What Jewish feast did Jesus celebrate at the Last Supper?

Jesus celebrated Passover. (page 140)

2. What do we call the sacrament of the Body and Blood of Christ?

The Eucharist is the sacrament of the Body and Blood of Christ. (page 140)

3. The Mass is a meal. What else is it?

The Mass is also a sacrifice. (page 141)

4. What do we call the people gathered to worship in the name of Jesus Christ?

The assembly is the people gathered to worship in the name of Jesus Christ. (page 142)

5. Why do Catholics celebrate Mass each Sunday or Saturday evening?

See page 143.

 ASSESSMENT The feature story for a magazine is "The Eucharist: Why Is It Important?" What would you write in this story? What pictures would you use?

144

Lesson Plan

 Review ___ minutes

Chapter Review For the first four questions, have the children work with a partner. Have each pair take turns asking and answering the four questions. Check their answers. Then have them read and answer question 5. Ask volunteers to share their answers.

Assessment Activity This activity is meant to offer another way of reviewing what the children learned. The activity has each child develop a story for a magazine that explains the importance of the Eucharist. Encourage the children to draw or cut and paste pictures to enhance their feature stories. Place this story in a portfolio of the child's work.

 **We Respond in Faith** ___ minutes

Reflect & Pray Encourage the children to share their answers to the first question. Give the children time to finish the prayer.

Key Words Continue to allow the children to work in groups. Encourage them to discuss each *Key Word* with their group and agree on a definition for each word. Then invite them to write the meaning, in their own words, on the board.

Reflect & Pray

Jesus is present to us at Mass. What does this mean to you?

_____

_____

Jesus, I believe that you are with us when we come together in your name. This week, at Mass, help me

_____

_____

Key Words

Passover (p. 252)
Eucharist (p. 251)
Mass (p. 252)
sacrifice (p. 253)
assembly (p. 250)

Remember

- Jesus celebrated Passover and the Last Supper.
- The Mass is a sacrifice and a meal.
- We take part in the Mass.
- We celebrate Mass each week.

OUR CATHOLIC LIFE

Our Contributions Count

Catholics have always given money for the needs of the Church and the poor. At Mass our donations are collected during the preparation of the gifts. The money collected helps the parish meet its needs. It also is used to help others in need: for example, those who are sick or those who are victims of earthquakes, fires, or floods.

When you put your own donations in the basket at Mass, remember—your contribution counts. You are following Jesus by sharing what you have with others.

HOME CONNECTION

Sharing Faith with My Family

Make sure to send home the family page (text page 146).

Ecourage the children to color the picture of the sacrament of the Eucharist with family members. Remind the children that the large cup is called a *chalice*, the plate is called a *paten*, and the small round pieces of consecrated Bread are called *Hosts*.

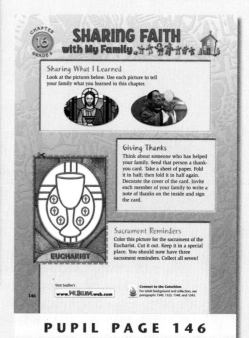

PUPIL PAGE 146

For additional information and activities, encourage families to visit Sadlier's

www.WeBelieveweb.com

Remember Write each of the *We Believe* statements on chart paper. Form four groups. Have the children write explanations and thoughts about the statements on the chart paper. After three minutes signal the children to move to a new key point. Continue until all groups have had time at each statement. As a class, discuss what has been written for each.

Our Catholic Life Read aloud the text. List things that the parish needs to maintain itself, such as electricity and heat. Then make a list of things that poor people and disaster victims may need, including clothing, shelter, and medical care. Help the children to understand there are many ways that the offerings of the parishioners are used.

Plan Ahead for Chapter 17

Prayer Space: parish bulletin, missalette, Bible, bread and chalice

Materials: Grade 3 CD, copies of Reproducible Master 17, poster paper, markers, index cards

Chapter 17 We Worship at Mass

Overview

In Chapter 16 the children learned about the celebration of the Eucharist. In this chapter the children will learn about the parts of the Mass and how we are sent forth from Mass to serve God and other people.

Doctrinal Content	For Adult Reading and Reflection *Catechism of the Catholic Church*
The children will learn:	Paragraph
• We gather to praise God.	1359
• We listen to God's word.	1349
• We receive Jesus Christ.	1355
• We go out to love and serve the Lord.	1694

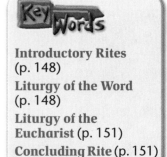

Key Words

Introductory Rites (p. 148)

Liturgy of the Word (p. 148)

Liturgy of the Eucharist (p. 151)

Concluding Rite (p. 151)

Catechist Background

What are some of the rituals that mark my day?

We participate in many daily rituals. Some are as mundane as washing and dressing ourselves. Others are more significant, like the ritual we may use to begin class with the children. For most of us, these daily rituals are essential for helping us, and those we teach, proceed smoothly through the day.

Just as we establish an order in our daily lives, so too the Mass also has an order that enables us to actively respond and participate. According to the Second Vatican Council, "This full and active participation by all the people is the aim" of all liturgical worship (*Constitution on the Sacred Liturgy,* 14). The order of the Mass was established early on in Christian Tradition and has been maintained throughout the Church's history. The order of Mass begins with the Introductory Rites, the time for gathering and preparation. During this time, we confess our sins and give praise for God's mercy in the "Gloria." The Liturgy of the Word follows, in which we listen to God's word proclaimed and are called to respond by making that word part of

our daily lives. After the homily, we profess our faith in the Creed and present our needs to God in the general intercessions.

The second part of the Mass, the Liturgy of the Eucharist, begins with the presentation of the gifts of bread and wine at the altar. The Eucharistic prayer follows, when, by the power of the Holy Spirit and the words and actions of the priest, the bread and the wine are transformed into the Body and Blood of Christ. The mystery by which this happens is called *transubstantiation*. We pray the Lord's Prayer, offer one another a sign of peace, and then approach the altar to receive Holy Communion. Finally, we celebrate the Concluding Rite, the final prayers that send us forth "to love and serve the Lord."

How can I more fully participate in the Mass?

Lesson Planning Guide

Lesson Steps	Presentation	Materials
① WE GATHER		
page 147 ✝ **Prayer** ☀ **Focus on Life**	🎵 Pray in song. • Discuss getting ready for some things and how to prepare.	For the prayer space: a church bulletin, a missalette, and Bible; bread and a chalice 🎵 "Jesus, We Believe in You," Carey Landry, #12, Grade 3 CD
② WE BELIEVE		
page 148 *We gather to praise God.* *The Roman Missal*	• Read about the parts of the Introductory Rites. 🧍 Discuss what happens during the Introductory Rites.	
pages 148–149 *We listen to God's word.* *The Roman Missal*	• Read and discuss the parts of the Liturgy of the Word. 🧍 Write a prayer to pray at Mass.	
page 150 *We receive Jesus Christ.* *The Roman Missal*	• Read and discuss the Liturgy of the Eucharist and its parts. 🧍 Discuss ways to be united to Christ and one another.	• missalette
page 151 *We go out to love and serve the Lord.*	• Read and discuss the Concluding Rite. • Read and discuss *As Catholics.*	• copies of Reproducible Master 17
③ WE RESPOND		
page 151	🧍 Write responses to situations.	
page 152 **Review**	• Complete questions 1–5. 🧍 Work on *Assessment Activity.*	• poster paper and markers • index cards • Chapter 17 Test in Grade 3 Assessment Book, pp. 35–36 • Chapter 17 Test in Test Generator • Review & Resource Book, pp. 40–42
page 153–154 **We Respond in Faith**	• Complete the *Reflect & Pray* activity. • Review *Remember* and *Key Words.* • Read and discuss *Our Catholic Life.* • Discuss *Sharing Faith with My Family.*	• Family Book, pp. 49–51

For additional ideas, activities, and opportunities: Visit Sadlier's **www.WeBelieveweb.com**

Name _____

Imagine that you have been asked to design a panel of
stained glass to hang in your church. Have the panel
illustrate the celebration of Mass and Holy Communion.
In the space below draw your scene or design. Use any of
the actions or symbols discussed in class, or choose others
that you think of. Color your drawing. After you finish,
draw a design of black lines over your picture to make it
look like a stained-glass window.

Connections

To Liturgy

As the children learn about the different parts of the Mass, have them explore their understanding of each aspect. Help them to see that the coming together as a community to worship God and to receive Holy Communion is a positive, joyful event. You may wish to distribute missalettes and have the children point out the words of praise and joy in the liturgy, as well as words which speak of our obligation to love others.

To Community

Explain to the children that the Mass is a time of thanksgiving to God. It brings us closer to God and helps us to understand his teachings as well as his love for us. We, in turn, are called to love and care for others. Discuss ways that the children can make the teachings at Mass a part of their lives every day. Tell of the joy that we can have when we are more Christian in our thoughts, words, and actions towards others. Have the children brainstorm ways in which they can love and serve their community in God's name.

FAITH and MEDIA

▶ Obtain an age-appropriate video that explains the various parts of the Mass. Consider inviting a priest to watch the video with the children and answer any questions they might have. You might also introduce the children to the CD-ROM *We Go to Church* (available from Sadlier). This is an easy-to-use, interactive children's guide to the different parts of the Mass complete with music, spoken readings, and an assortment of activities.

▶ During this week you might suggest to the children that they look for images of the Mass on television, in movies, and in magazines. Remind them, as they think about these media representations of the Mass, to remember what they've learned about the need for accuracy and truth in media.

Meeting Individual Needs

Children with Attention Deficit Disorder

Children with Attention Deficit Disorder often do not have the ability to focus for long periods of time or to focus during long pages of text or lengthy discussions. Divide the lessons into different types of instruction. Use visual aids and hands-on activities whenever possible. Allow the children to use drama or music when appropriate. A larger variety of instructional methods will help them to remain focused and retain the material.

ADDITIONAL RESOURCES

Book *Kate from Philadelphia: The Life of Saint Katharine Drexel for Children,* Patricia E. Jablonski, Pauline Books and Media, Boston, MA, 2001. Tells Katharine's story as a missionary sister.

Video *Grandma's Bread,* St. Anthony Messenger Press, Cincinnati, OH, 1985. The touching tale of a grandmother who helps her grandchild understand the meaning of Holy Eucharist. (62 min.)

To find more ideas for books, videos, and other learning material, visit Sadlier's

www.WeBelieveweb.com

Focus on Life

Chapter Story

Amanda left school feeling very confident. In her class today they were talking about being a good Christian. Amanda was sure she had that well under control. After all, she went to Mass every Sunday, loved her religion class, and even sang in the choir. How could she possibly be a better Catholic?

Then she noticed two of her classmates ahead of her. They had taken a second grader's book and were holding it up, just out of his reach. He was in tears because they were laughing at him and teasing him. Amanda crossed the street and tried to ignore them as she walked past. Suddenly the words from her class that day came to her. "Jesus wants me to be a disciple of peace and love," Amanda said to herself. She realized that she was not doing what a disciple of Jesus should do.

Amanda gathered her courage and crossed the street. She approached the two and said, "Terry and Craig, give that boy his book back!"

"Go away, Amanda!" said Terry.

"We're just having some fun!" said Craig. However, Craig grudgingly gave the book to the younger boy.

Craig and Terry were irritated with Amanda. "Why did you do that?" Terry asked.

"Don't you remember our lesson from today, Terry?" she replied. "We are supposed to help others, not hurt them." Terry and Craig looked at Amanda a bit sheepishly.

When Amanda got home, she noticed that her portable CD player was on the coffee table in the living room. That meant that her little sister, Kate, had gone into her room and taken it. Amanda was angry and went to find Kate.

▶ *What do you think Amanda did next?*

We Worship at Mass (17)

WE GATHER

✝ **Leader:** Let us pray by singing.

🎵 **Jesus, We Believe In You**

Chorus
Jesus, we believe in you;
we believe that you are with us.
Jesus, we believe in you;
we believe that you are here.

We believe that you are present with us here
as we gather in your name. (Chorus)

We believe that you are with us at all times,
and your love will guide our way. (Chorus)

Leader: Jesus, thank you for your presence in
our lives,

All: today and always. Amen.

☀ What are some things you get ready for?
How do you prepare?

147

PREPARING TO PRAY

In joyful song, the children will
express their belief in Jesus.

• Take the role of leader.

• Practice the song "Jesus, We Believe
in You," #12 on the Grade 3 CD.

The Prayer Space
• Display a church bulletin, missalette
or hymn book, and Bible.

• Place bread and a chalice (goblet or
wineglass) on a table to represent the
Eucharist.

📖 **This Week's Liturgy**
Visit **www.webelieveweb.com** for
this week's liturgical readings and
other seasonal material.

Lesson Plan

WE GATHER ___ minutes

✝ **Pray**

• Invite the children to pray.

• Remind the children that the words of the song help
them to profess their faith in Jesus' presence.

• Sing song.

• Continue the prayer by asking children to add
their own prayers, beginning with, "Jesus, thank you
for . . ." The response to each is "today and always.
Amen."

 Focus on Life

• Discuss "getting ready" and ways to prepare.

• In this chapter, the children will learn about the parts
of the Mass and ways to prepare to participate in them.

• Read the *Chapter Story* on guide page 147E. Discuss
the ways Christians can put into practice what they
learn about their faith.

Home Connection Update

Ask the children to share experiences using
the Chapter 16 family page. Ask: *Were you
able to use it in weekend discussions or activities with your family members?*

Catechist Goal

• To describe the way we prepare to give thanks and praise to God throughout the parts of the Mass

Our Faith Response

• To identify the ways that we can live out the Mass in love and service of the Lord

 Introductory Rites
Liturgy of the Word
Liturgy of the Eucharist
Concluding Rite

Lesson Materials

• copies of Reproducible Master 17
• missalette
• poster paper and markers
• index cards

Teaching Tip

Supportive Classroom Communities

Listening to children and giving them your undivided attention is an important part of letting them know that you are genuinely interested in them. Make your classroom one of comfort and safety. Your small acts of kindness can make a difference!

Key Words
Introductory Rites (p. 251)
Liturgy of the Word (p. 252)

WE BELIEVE
We gather to praise God.

The first part of the Mass is called the Introductory Rites. In the **Introductory Rites** we become one as we prepare to listen to God's word and to celebrate the Eucharist.

We gather together as members of the Church, the Body of Christ. We sing an opening song of praise to God. Then the priest welcomes us as God's people. With the priest we make the sign of the cross. The priest reminds us that Jesus is present among us.

The priest invites us to remember that we need God's forgiveness. We think about the times that we might have sinned. We tell God that we are sorry and ask for forgiveness.

On most Sundays of the year, we sing or say the "Gloria." We praise and bless God for his great love and care. This hymn of praise begins with: "Glory to God in the highest."

🧒 Think about your parish's celebration of the Mass last week. With a partner talk about what happened in the Introductory Rites.

We listen to God's word.

The **Liturgy of the Word** is the part of the Mass when we listen and respond to God's word.

148

Lesson Plan

WE BELIEVE _____ minutes

Have a volunteer read aloud the first *We Believe* statement. Ask volunteers to read aloud the *We Believe* paragraphs. Emphasize the following points:

• We begin by gathering together and praising God in song.

• We are welcomed by the priest and pray the Sign of the Cross together.

• We ask for forgiveness in the *Lord, have mercy* and/or the *Confiteor* (I confess . . .).

• We sing or say the *Gloria* on Sundays and special days (not sung during seasons of Advent and Lent).

• The priest invites us to join him in prayer and we respond "Amen."

🧒 **Invite** the children to talk with a partner about what happens during the Introductory Rites. Afterwards, share ideas as group.

Read aloud the second *We Believe* statement. Have the children work with partners. Have them read and highlight the We Believe paragraphs. Emphasize the following points:

• On other days besides Sundays and feast days, there may be only two readings. The second reading is always a gospel reading. Ask: *Is this reading from the Old or New Testament?* (New Testament)

• During Lent, a season of repentance, we do not sing the Alleluia before the gospel because Alleluia is used to express joy. Instead, we sing another gospel acclamation.

On Sundays and other special days, there are three readings from Scripture. The first reading is usually from the Old Testament. After this reading we sing or say a psalm from the Old Testament. Then the second reading is from the New Testament. The readers end the first and second readings with: "The word of the Lord." We respond: "Thanks be to God."

The third reading is from one of the four gospels: Matthew, Mark, Luke, or John. The gospel reading is very special. We hear about the life and teachings of Jesus.

Before the gospel reading we show we are ready to hear the good news of Jesus Christ. We do this by standing and singing the Alleluia. The deacon or priest then proclaims the gospel. To proclaim the gospel means to announce the good news with praise and glory. At the end of the gospel the deacon or priest says: "The Gospel of the Lord."

We respond: "Praise to you, Lord Jesus Christ."

After the gospel reading, the priest or deacon gives the homily. The homily helps us to understand what the three readings mean in our lives. Then we all stand and state our belief in God by saying the creed.

In the *general intercessions,* also called the prayer of the faithful, we pray for our Church and our world. We ask God to help our leaders, our family and friends, all those who are sick and in need, and all those who have died.

Who would you like to pray for at Mass this week? Write a prayer for them here.

_____
_____
_____
_____
_____

149

ACTIVITY BANK

Family
Family Prayer Lists
Activity Materials: paper and pens or pencils

At the end of the Liturgy of the Word, the priest calls us to pray for others. Encourage children and their families to establish a family prayer list. Hang the list in a family room or gathering place in the house. As family members' needs arise, write them on the list. Have the family pray from the list at mealtime, when going to bed, or whenever they pray. By praying for one another, family members become more aware of one another's needs and makes them more united. Encourage the children and their families to make it a part of their everyday lives. Remind the children to include prayers of thanksgiving as well as requests for help.

• The Book of the Gospels is a formal book of the Church that contains the gospel readings for Sundays, feasts days, and other special days. The priest or deacon traces the sign of the cross on this book and on his forehead, lips, and heart before proclaiming the gospel.

Stress the importance of the homily as a way to understand the Scripture readings and apply them to our lives. Point out that the proclamation of the creed and the general intercessions gives the assembly the opportunity to profess its faith and then call upon God to help the Church and the whole world.

Encourage the children to write their prayers and to pray them during the week.

Quick Check

✔ *What is the purpose of the Introductory Rites?* (to join us together and help us prepare to listen to God's word and celebrate the Eucharist)

✔ *What is the Liturgy of the Word?* (the part of the Mass when we listen and respond to God's word)

✔ *What are the general intercessions?* (prayers in which we pray for our Church and our world, and for those in need)

The Blessed Sacrament

Read aloud the text. Discuss why the Blessed Sacrament is kept in the tabernacle. If possible, take the children to the place where the tabernacle is located in the church. Review the practice of genuflection (kneeling briefly on the right knee before entering the pew). Give the children time to pray to Jesus in the Blessed Sacrament.

We receive Jesus Christ.

During the **Liturgy of the Eucharist** the bread and wine become the Body and Blood of Christ, which we receive in Holy Communion. The altar is prepared for this part of the Mass. Members of the assembly bring forward our gifts of bread and wine and our gifts for the Church and the poor.

The priest then asks God to bless and accept the gifts we will offer. We also offer our whole lives to God. Now the *eucharistic prayer* begins. It is the great prayer of praise and thanksgiving. The priest prays this prayer in our name to the Father through Jesus Christ. Through this prayer we are united with Christ.

The priest recalls all that God has done for us. We sing a song that begins: "Holy, holy, holy Lord."

The priest then says and does what Jesus said and did at the Last Supper. Through these words and actions of the priest, by the power of the Holy Spirit, the bread and wine become the Body and Blood of Christ. This part of the eucharistic prayer is called the *consecration*. Jesus is truly present in the Eucharist. This is called the *real presence*.

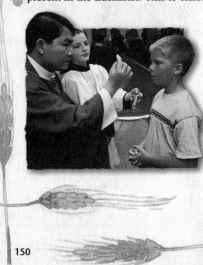

At the end of the eucharistic prayer, we say or sing "Amen." Together we are saying "Yes, we believe."

Next we pray together the Lord's Prayer, the Our Father. We offer one another a sign of peace to one another. The priest then breaks the Bread while the "Lamb of God" prayer is sung.

Then we all come forward to receive Holy Communion. We sing as we go to receive to show our unity with one another. After communion we all sit in silence.

🧑 In groups talk about ways we can show that we are united to Christ and one another.

150

Lesson Plan

WE BELIEVE (continued)

Have a volunteer read aloud the *We Believe* statement. Read aloud the first *We Believe* paragraph. Stress that in the Liturgy of the Eucharist the bread and wine become the Body and Blood of Christ. Explain that the prayer, "Christ has died. Christ is risen. Christ will come again" is one of four Memorial Acclamations that may be used during the eucharistic prayer. Use a missalette and recite the other three acclamations for the children. Ask the children to repeat each one after you.

Draw the children's attention to the artwork and photos on page 150. Ask: *Who is the Lamb of God?* (Jesus is the Lamb of God.) *Why are there grapes, wheat, bread and wine?* (Grapes become wine, wheat becomes bread. We offer the bread and wine at Mass.) *How do all these refer to the Eucharist?* (The bread and wine become the Body and Blood of Christ.)

Emphasize that Jesus is truly present in the Eucharist. Through the words and actions of the priest during consecration and by the power of Holy Spirit, the bread and wine become the Body and Blood of Christ.

🧑 **Encourage** the children to talk about ways they can show that they are united to Christ and one another.

We go out to love and serve the Lord.

As the Mass ends we are encouraged to share the good news of Jesus with others. The last part of the Mass is the Concluding Rite. The **Concluding Rite** reminds us to continue praising and serving God each day.

The priest says a final prayer thanking God for the Eucharist we have celebrated. He blesses us, and we make the sign of the cross. Then the priest or deacon, in Jesus' name, sends us out into the world. He says, "Go in peace to love and serve the Lord." We answer, "Thanks be to God."

We leave the church singing. With the help of the Holy Spirit, we try to help people who are in need. We do what we can to make our world a more loving and peaceful place. We try to treat others as Jesus would.

WE RESPOND

How could we love and serve others in these situations? Write your ideas.

• A family member is really tired.

We could:

_____

• A classmate is being "picked on."

We could:

_____

As Catholics...

After Holy Communion, the remaining consecrated Bread, or Hosts, are put in a special place in the Church called the *tabernacle*. The Eucharist in the tabernacle is known as the *Blessed Sacrament*. The Blessed Sacrament can be taken to people who are dying and to those who are sick.

Jesus Christ is truly present in the Blessed Sacrament. Catholics honor Jesus' real presence by praying before the Blessed Sacrament.

The next time you are in church, kneel and pray to Jesus in the Blessed Sacrament.

Key Words

Liturgy of the Eucharist (p. 252)

Concluding Rite (p. 250)

151

Read aloud the *We Believe* statement on page 151. Have volunteers read aloud the *We Believe* paragraphs. Stress the blessing given by the priest is in the name of the Blessed Trinity. Point out that in God's name we are sent out to bring peace and justice to our homes, school, and neighborhoods.

WE RESPOND ___ minutes

Connect to Life Have the children respond to the two situations in the *We Respond* activity. Encourage the children to keep in mind their commitment to God and their ability to do good works in the world. Have the children come together and discuss their responses.

Distribute copies of the Reproducible Master. Review the directions and ask the children to describe stained-glass windows they have seen. If possible, take them to church and let them view the stained-glass windows there. Encourage them to recall what they have learned about the liturgy as they complete their work.

Catholic Social Teaching

Option for the Poor and Vulnerable
Activity Materials: items to donate to the homeless

Sometimes people feel that they have no where to turn for help. A homeless person or family is actually nomadic in our society. In desperate straits, they take shelter in centers offered by civic and religious outreach services. Contact a homeless shelter near you. These shelters are often in need of items such as socks, basic hygiene packets, clothing, and so on. Obtain a list of some of the items needed. Then organize a drive for the homeless. Ask your children to donate certain items and encourage them to work together to assemble the items to be delivered to the homeless shelter.

CHAPTER TEST

Chapter 17 Test is provided in the Grade 3 Assessment Book.

Write T if the sentence is true. Write F if the sentence is false.

1. The first part of the Mass is called the Liturgy of the Word.   T

2. We learn about the life and teachings of Jesus in the gospel reading.   T

3. The Liturgy of the Eucharist gets us ready to listen to God's word.   F

4. The Concluding Rite reminds us to continue to praise God and to serve God and his people each day.   T

Answer the question.

5. How do we live out the Mass all through the week?
   See page 151.

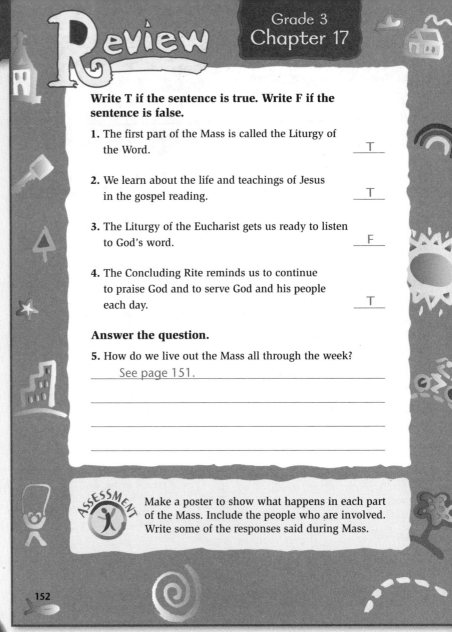

ASSESSMENT

Make a poster to show what happens in each part of the Mass. Include the people who are involved. Write some of the responses said during Mass.

152

Lesson Plan

Review   ___ minutes

Chapter Review Tell the children that they are going to check their understanding of what they have learned. Have children complete questions 1–4. Have them answer the questions, then make the false sentences true. First brainstorm answers, then have them complete question 5 in their texts. Ask them to share their answers.

Assessment Activity Read the assessment directions and check for understanding of the task. Distribute the large poster paper and markers. When the children have completed their posters that show what happens during each part of the Mass, have them share their work. You may want to display the posters in the parish hall or other appropriate place.

We Respond in Faith   ___ minutes

Reflect & Pray Read the questions and ask the children to write their answers. Have them work in pairs or small groups. After the children have discussed these answers among themselves, share the ideas as an entire group. Ask the children to finish the prayer and pray it silently in their hearts.

 **Key Words** Distribute index cards to children. Have children copy each *Key Word* on one side of their card. Ask them to flip the card over and write their own definition for that term. Then have children check themselves by comparing their definitions with the text definition and making the necessary corrections. Form the group into pairs and have them use the index cards as flash cards.

Reflect & Pray

At the end of Mass, we are sent out to love and serve. What does this mean to you?

_____

_____

Complete this prayer.

Jesus, I believe in you and

_____

_____

Key Words

Introductory Rites
(p. 251)
Liturgy of the Word
(p. 252)
Liturgy of the Eucharist
(p. 252)
Concluding Rite
(p. 250)

Remember

- We gather to praise God.
- We listen to God's word.
- We receive Jesus Christ.
- We go out to love and serve the Lord.

Our Catholic Life

Saint Katharine Drexel

Katharine Drexel decided to use her inheritance to help others. She worked for the equal rights of Native Americans and African Americans.

In 1891, Katharine started a religious community called the Sisters of the Blessed Sacrament. She believed strongly that Jesus invites all people to join the Church and to take part in the Eucharist. Because of the efforts of Katharine and her sisters, many Native Americans and African Americans are active members of the Church today.

Sharing Faith with My Family

Make sure to send home the family page (text page 154).

Encourage the children to color and cut out their sacrament reminders with the help of family members.

PUPIL PAGE 154

For additional information and activities, encourage families to visit Sadlier's

www.WeBelieveweb.com

Remember Have the children read aloud the four statements. Have them discuss the major points expressed in each statement. Then invite the children to the prayer space. Ask them to name each item on the table and how it relates to or symbolizes what they have learned from the week's lessons.

Our Catholic Life Read about Saint Katharine Drexel aloud to the group. Ask children to reflect on her life and the times in which she took up her cause. Discuss ways Saint Katharine Drexel demonstrated love for others in her life. The Sisters of the Blessed Sacrament have a Web site on which pictures and historical materials about Saint Katharine Drexel can be found. For a link to this and other useful Web sites, go to www.webelieveweb.com.

Plan Ahead for Chapter 18

Prayer Space: Bible, copy of an Act of Contrition, crucifix

Materials: copies of Reproducible Master 18, scissors and crayons, stationery, colored pens, markers, Grade 3 CD (option)

Overview

In Chapter 17 the children learned about the Mass. In this chapter, the children will learn how we celebrate God's forgiveness in the sacrament of Penance and Reconciliation.

Doctrinal Content	For Adult Reading and Reflection *Catechism of the Catholic Church*
The children will learn:	Paragraph
• We make the choice to love God.	1428
• God is our forgiving Father.	1439
• The sacrament of Reconciliation has several parts.	1450–1460
• The Church celebrates the sacrament of Reconciliation.	1469

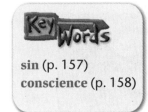

Key Words

sin (p. 157)
conscience (p. 158)

Catechist Background

When in my life have I experienced the need for forgiveness and reconciliation?

When our relationships are broken, we desire to be reconciled, to make things right again. We want to forgive and be forgiven.

When our relationship with God is broken, we desire reconciliation and forgiveness.

This awareness that we need to seek forgiveness comes from our conscience. Our conscience tells us when we have turned away from God through sin.

Sometimes our turning away is complete and we commit a mortal sin. Sometimes our breach is less serious, a venial sin. In either case, we approach God in order to ask forgiveness and to be reconciled to him in the sacrament of Penance.

No matter what we have done to strain our relationship with God, we are assured that God forgives us. God, in turn, asks that we forgive others. "In refusing to forgive our brothers and sisters, our hearts are closed and their hardness makes them impervious to the Father's merciful love" (CCC 2840).

In the parable of the prodigal son, Jesus shows us that God's attitude toward us, even when we sin, is like that of the loving Father. He not only welcomes us back; he wants to throw us a party!

The sacrament of Penance is very much like the encounter between the prodigal son and his father. In the sacrament, we examine our conscience, confess our sins to the priest, receive a penance, and are absolved from our sins. When celebrated in a communal celebration, we rejoice together that God has indeed forgiven us. Even when celebrated individually, the sacrament of Penance is a celebration with the community, the Church. When sin is forgiven and relationships are healed, we rejoice.

How can God's forgiveness flow from me to others?

Lesson Planning Guide

Lesson Steps	Presentation	Materials
① WE GATHER		
page 155 ✟ **Prayer** ☀ **Focus on Life**	• Pray in quiet reflection. • Respond with an Act of Contrition. • Answer questions about making choices.	For the prayer space: tablecloth, Bible, crucifix, copy of an Act of Contrition
② WE BELIEVE		
page 156 *We make the choice to love God.*	• Read about and discuss mortal and venial sins. 🧍 Write one way to show love our love for God today.	• copies of Reproducible Master 18 • scissors and crayons
page 157 *God is our forgiving Father.* 📖 *Luke 15:11–32*	• Read and discuss the story of the lost son and God's forgiveness, and God as a forgiving Father. 🧍 Talk about people forgiving one another.	
page 158 *The sacrament of Reconciliation has several parts.*	• Read and discuss conscience and the parts of the sacrament of Reconciliation. 🧍 Write one reason we celebrate the sacrament of Reconciliation.	
page 159 *The Church celebrates the sacrament of Reconciliation.*	• Read and discuss *As Catholics.* • Read and discuss chart on two ways to celebrate Reconciliation.	
③ WE RESPOND		
page 159	• Discuss ways to thank God for forgiveness. 🎵 Sing the song "Jesus, Jesus." (option)	• sentence strips 🎵 "Jesus, Jesus," Carey Landry, #14, Grade 3 CD (option)
page 160 **Review**	• Complete questions 1–5. 🧍 Work on *Assessment Activity.*	• stationery, colored pens and markers • Chapter 18 Test in Assessment Book, pp. 37–38 • Chapter 18 Test in Test Generator • Review & Resource Book, pp. 43–45
page 161–162 **We Respond in Faith**	• Complete the *Reflect & Pray* activity. • Review *Remember* and *Key Words.* • Discuss **Sharing Faith with My Family.**	• Family Book, pp. 52–54

For additional ideas, activities, and opportunities: Visit Sadlier's www.WeBelieveweb.com

Name _____

Color and cut out the door hanger. Display it in your room to help you remember to celebrate God's forgiveness in the sacrament of Reconciliation.

Write the dates and times that the sacrament of Reconciliation is celebrated in your parish on the lines provided.

The Sacrament of Reconciliation

"Peace I leave with you."
(John 14:27)

_____

_____

_____

_____

Connections

To Catholic Social Teaching

The Call to Family, Community, and Participation
Explain to the children that a hallmark of the Catholic community is a willingness to forgive. Our celebration of the sacrament of Reconciliation can signify clearly that we are reconciled to God and one another. A parish Reconciliation service gives us a wonderful opportunity to celebrate God's forgiveness and his healing presence in the community.

To Liturgy

Encourage the children to think about the meaning of the phrase, *Forgive us our trespasses as we forgive those who trespass against us*, in the Our Father. Remind them that this special prayer was given to us by Jesus himself (Luke 11: 1–4). Discuss as a group the meaning of this phrase from the Lord's Prayer.

FAITH and MEDIA

▶ As the children learn about the sacrament of Reconciliation, you might help them set up a "media library" featuring books, videos, and CDs of stories, poems, and songs on the theme of forgiveness and healing. If possible, allow the children to take the materials home to share. Invite the children to write short reviews of the materials as they use them. Then place the children's reviews in a file, either physical (an index-card file) or virtual (the school Web site), for others to share.

▶ You might ask the children whether they have seen any videos of the Lost Son story or read versions of it in books. Encourage the children to read and view different versions. Ask: *How would you tell this story today?*

Meeting Individual Needs

Children with Visual Needs

Help the children who are visually challenged to better understand the sacrament of Reconciliation by providing a church tour complete with hands-on experiences. Ask a sensitive, mature child helper to assist the child in touring the church and examining the reconciliation room used in this sacrament. Encourage the visually challenged child to ask questions and request assistance as needed.

ADDITIONAL RESOURCES

Videos
Parables for Kids, Volume 1, Pauline Books and Media, Boston, MA, 2001. Stories of forgiveness that include The Lost Sheep, The Prodigal Son, The Sower, and others. (22 min.)

The Prodigal Son, Nest Entertainment, Irving, TX, 1988. The story of a wayward son who is reunited with his father and family emphasizes God's love and joy at the return of the sinner. (30 min.)

To find more ideas for books, videos, and other learning material, visit Sadlier's

www.WeBelieveweb.com

Focus on Life

Chapter Story

Maurice had a prized possession: a fielder's glove that somehow always helped him grab those almost impossible line drives! That's why he had doubts about lending his glove to his brother, Randy.

"Don't worry, your glove will be in good hands!" Randy called out as he ran down to the baseball field.

In the second inning, the downpour began. Everyone ran for cover. Randy ran to the coach's van without even glancing at his brother's glove, lying on the park bench.

That evening Maurice asked, "Hey, Randy, did you put my glove back in my room?"

"Oh, no, the glove! I must have left it at the park!" Randy moaned.

"I'm never talking to you again!" Maurice shouted as he slammed the door to his room.

Later, Maurice heard a knock on his door. It was Randy. "Maurice, I've found the glove," Randy said. "If it's ruined, I'll buy you a new one. I promise I will."

Maurice held the wet, soggy glove in his hand. Randy really did seem sorry. Maurice knew his brother hadn't meant to ruin the glove, so he couldn't stay angry. "C'mon, Mom's making pizza!" Maurice said. "Race you to the table!"

▶ *How does Randy show he is sorry? How does Maurice let Randy know that he forgives him?*

Celebrating Penance and Reconciliation

WE GATHER

✝ **Leader:** Sit quietly. Think about the last few days. Sometimes our actions and words do not show love. How have you acted with your family and friends? Let us pray an act of contrition together.

All: My God,
I am sorry for my sins with all my heart.
In choosing to do wrong and failing to do good,
I have sinned against you whom I should love above all things.
I firmly intend, with your help,
to do penance,
to sin no more,
and to avoid whatever leads me to sin.
Our Savior Jesus Christ suffered and died for us.
In his name, my God, have mercy.

☀ Think about an important choice you had to make. What did you think about before choosing? How did you know whether you made the right choice?

155

PREPARING TO PRAY

The children will spend a few moments in quiet reflection. They will respond by praying an Act of Contrition.

• Tell the children you will open the prayer with a period of reflection.

• Explain to the children that they will use the quiet moments for personal reflection.

The Prayer Space
• Place a purple tablecloth on the prayer table.

• Display a crucifix and a copy of the Act of Contrition.

📖 **This Week's Liturgy**
Visit **www.webelieveweb.com** for this week's liturgical readings and other seasonal material.

Lesson Plan

WE GATHER ___ minutes

✝ **Pray**
• Gather in the prayer space.

• Spend a few moments discussing the art and photos. (Girl pushed classmate; now she is sorry and is asking for forgiveness.)

• Speak the opening remarks.

• Invite the children to reflect quietly.

• Pray the Act of Contrition.

☀ **Focus on Life**
• Ask the children to think about their choices.

• In this chapter, the children will learn about celebrating God's forgiveness in the sacrament of Reconciliation.

• Read the *Chapter Story* on guide page 155E. Relate the actions of the characters in the story to the theme of forgiveness presented in the lesson.

Home Connection Update
Review the activities on the Chapter 17 family page. Ask: *How did you and other members in the family enjoy coloring the sacrament cards?*

155

Catechist Goal

• To teach that we can choose to love God our forgiving Father

Our Faith Response

• To appreciate God's willingness to forgive us when we are truly sorry and to celebrate his mercy and forgiveness in the sacrament of Reconciliation

Key Words sin   conscience

Lesson Materials

• Grade 3 CD (option)
• copies of Reproducible Master 18
• scissors, crayons
• sentence strips
• stationery, colored pens, markers

Teaching Tip

A Peaceful Classroom Atmosphere
    Find time during the busy classroom day to set aside a moment for your children to reflect quietly. Encourage the children to put their heads down, visit the prayer space, or listen to music. Promote this peaceful atmosphere by personally participating in these meaningful moments of peace.

WE BELIEVE
We make the choice to love God.

God wants us to love him, ourselves, and others. This is God's law. When we live by the Ten Commandments and follow Jesus' example we obey God's law.

However, there are times we do not live the way Jesus wants us to live. We freely choose to do what we know is wrong. We commit a sin. **Sin** is a thought, word, or action that is against God's law. Sin is always a choice. That is why mistakes and accidents are not sins.

Some sins are very serious. These serious sins are mortal sins. A *mortal sin* is:

• very seriously wrong
• known to be wrong
• freely chosen.

People who commit mortal sin turn away completely from God's love. They choose to break their friendship with God. They lose the gift of grace, their share in God's life and love.

Not all sins are mortal sins. Sins that are less serious are *venial sins*. People who commit venial sins hurt their friendship with God. Yet they still share in God's life and love.

Write one way you can show that you have chosen to love God today.

_____

_____

156

Lesson Plan

WE BELIEVE   ___ minutes

Read aloud the *We Believe* statement and the first two *We Believe* paragraphs. Write the word *sin* on the board. Have the children highlight or underline its definition in their texts. Have a volunteer read aloud the third paragraph. Pause for a moment. Then read aloud the final two *We Believe* paragraphs. Stress the difference between mortal sin and venial sin.

Invite the children to write one way they can choose to love God today.

Read aloud the *We Believe* statement on page 157.

Have several volunteers read aloud the different roles of the story of the Lost Son. (If time permits, ask volunteers to act it out.) Emphasize these points:

• Like the lost son, many of us make unwise or wrong choices. When we realize what we have done, we want to express our sorrow and be forgiven.

• In this gospel story, the father joyously forgave his son who had left home and squandered his money. He rushed out to welcome him home, hugged him, and gave a great feast. (Refer to the artwork on pages 156–157.)

• Like the forgiving father in the story, God always welcomes us when we return to him in Reconciliation. Because we express our sorrow and ask for his mercy, God forgives us and welcomes us back into his friendship.

Encourage the children to talk about people forgiving one another.

sin (p. 253)

God is our forgiving Father.

Jesus told this story to help us to understand God's love and forgiveness.

Luke 15:11–32

A rich man had two sons. One son wanted his share of the father's money. He wanted to leave home and have some fun. His father was sad, but he let his son have the money.

The son went away and began to spend his money. He used his money on all kinds of things. Soon all his money was gone.

The son found himself poor, dirty, hungry, and without friends. He thought about his father and his home. He decided to go home and tell his father that he was sorry.

When the father saw his son, he was so happy. The father rushed out and hugged him. The son said, "Father, I have sinned against heaven and against you; I no longer deserve to be called your son." (Luke 15:21)

But the father wanted everyone to know his son had come home. The father shouted to his servants, "Let us celebrate with a feast." (Luke 15:23)

Jesus told this story to show that God is our loving father. He is always ready to forgive us when we are sorry.

We receive God's forgiveness through the Church. Our relationship with God and the Church is made strong through the sacrament of Reconciliation.

Talk about times people forgive each other.

157

Quick Check

✔ *What is a sin?* (a thought, word, or action that is against God's law)

✔ *What is the difference between a venial and mortal sin?* (A mortal sin is a very serious sin. A venial sin is less serious.)

The sacrament of Reconciliation has several parts.

Examining our conscience is the first step in preparing for the sacrament of Reconciliation. Our **conscience** is God's gift that helps us know right from wrong.

When we examine our conscience, we ask ourselves whether or not we have loved God, others, and ourselves. We think about the things we have done and whether they were right or wrong. This examination of conscience helps us to know and to be sorry for our sins.

Contrition, confession, penance, and absolution are always part of the sacrament of Reconciliation.

Contrition is being sorry for our sins and firmly intending not to sin again. *Confession* is telling our sins to the priest. The priest may talk to us about the way we can love God and others.

A *penance* is a prayer or action that shows we are sorry for our sins. Accepting the penance shows that we are willing to change the way that we live. *Absolution* is God's forgiveness of our sins through the actions and words of the priest. The priest extends his hand and forgives us. He ends by saying,

"Through the ministry of the Church may God give you pardon and peace, and I absolve you from your sins in the name of the Father, and of the Son, † and of the Holy Spirit."

🧍 Write one reason why the Church celebrates the sacrament of Reconciliation.

_____

158

• **contrition** •

• **confession** •

Key Word

conscience (p. 250)

As Catholics...

Many parishes have a separate space for celebrating the sacrament of Reconciliation. This is a special place where you meet the priest for individual confession and absolution. You can choose how you want to talk with the priest. You can sit and talk to him face-to-face or kneel behind a screen.

In your parish, where do you celebrate the sacrament of Reconciliation?

As Catholics...

Special Places for Reconciliation

Take the children to church to see where the sacrament of Reconciliation is celebrated. Emphasize that parishes offer the option of celebrating Reconciliation face-to-face with the priest, or talking to the priest from behind a screen. Assure the children that the priest may never, *ever*, tell anyone what is said during the confession of sins. This is called *the seal of confession*.

Lesson Plan

WE BELIEVE (continued)

Read aloud the first two *We Believe* paragraphs. Stress that the examination of conscience is a necessary preparation for celebrating the sacrament of Reconciliation. This period of reflection helps us to know where we have failed to love God and neighbor, and to be sorry for our sins.

Have a volunteer read aloud the *We Believe* statement. As you read aloud the *We Believe* paragraphs (beginning with the third), have the children highlight the words in their texts that are in italics (*contrition, confession, penance, absolution*).

🧍 **Ask** the children to write one reason we celebrate the sacrament of Reconciliation.

Read aloud the *We Believe* statement on page 159 and the first *We Believe* paragraph.

Ask volunteers to read the text and discuss the major differences between celebrating individually and celebrating with the community. Stress that both ways of celebrating Reconciliation require individual confession of sins and absolution by the priest.

Write the characteristics of each kind of penance service on sentence strips. Make three columns on the board labeled *Celebrating with the Community, Celebrating Individually,* and *Both.* Have volunteers read the sentence strips and tape them under the correct column on the board.

The Church celebrates the sacrament of Reconciliation.

The sacrament of Reconciliation is a celebration of God's love and forgiveness. Here are two ways the Church celebrates the sacrament of Reconciliation.

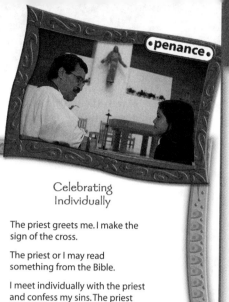
•penance•

Celebrating with the Community

We sing an opening hymn and the priest greets us and prays an opening prayer.

We listen to a reading from the Bible and a homily.

We examine our conscience and pray an act of contrition. We pray the Our Father.

I meet individually with the priest and confess my sins. The priest talks to me about loving God and others. He gives me a penance.

The priest extends his hand and gives me absolution.

After everyone has met with the priest, we join together to conclude the celebration. The priest blesses us, and we go in the peace and joy of Christ.

Celebrating Individually

The priest greets me. I make the sign of the cross.

The priest or I may read something from the Bible.

I meet individually with the priest and confess my sins. The priest talks to me about loving God and others. He gives me a penance.

I pray an act of contrition.

The priest extends his hand and gives me absolution.

Together the priest and I give thanks to God for his forgiveness.

I pray an act of contrition.

WE RESPOND

How can you thank God for his forgiveness after celebrating the sacrament of Reconciliation?

•absolution•

159

ACTIVITY BANK

Liturgy
The Penitential Rite

Encourage the children to pay close attention to the part of the Mass called the Penitential Rite. In this part of the Mass, the prayer community joins together to ask God for his mercy and forgiveness. Urge the children to recall their sins briefly and ways they can do better whenever they participate in this special rite.

WE RESPOND ___ minutes

Connect to Life Have the children consider how they would complete the *We Respond* statement.

(At this time, you may want to play the song "Jesus, Jesus" from the Grade 3 CD. The music and words for the song can be found in Sadlier's *We Believe* Program Songbook.)

Distribute copies of Reproducible Master 18. Encourage the children to be creative in coloring their door hangers. Have them complete their work in class or at home.

CHAPTER TEST

Chapter 18 Test is provided in the Grade 3 Assessment Book.

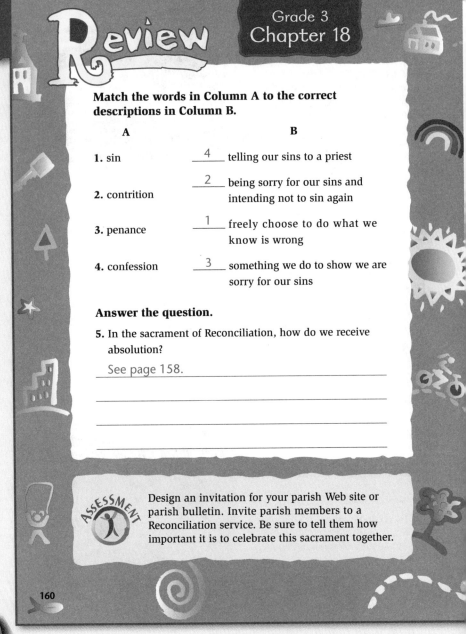

Review

Match the words in Column A to the correct descriptions in Column B.

A	B
1. sin	__4__ telling our sins to a priest
2. contrition	__2__ being sorry for our sins and intending not to sin again
3. penance	__1__ freely choose to do what we know is wrong
4. confession	__3__ something we do to show we are sorry for our sins

Answer the question.

5. In the sacrament of Reconciliation, how do we receive absolution?

See page 158.

_____

_____

_____

ASSESSMENT Design an invitation for your parish Web site or parish bulletin. Invite parish members to a Reconciliation service. Be sure to tell them how important it is to celebrate this sacrament together.

160

Lesson Plan

 ___ minutes

Chapter Review Have the children match the columns. Have them exchange books with a partner and check his or her answers, while volunteers give the correct answers aloud. Discuss the response to question 5 together, then have the children answer question 5 in their books. Ask volunteers to read their answers aloud.

Assessment Activity This activity offers another way of reviewing the learning of the children—in this case, designing an invitation to a parish Reconciliation service to be posted on the church Web site or in the parish bulletin. Offer the children various kinds of stationery and colored pens and markers to use in designing their invitations.

 ___ minutes

Reflect & Pray Read the introduction aloud to the children. Say: *Think about ways the choices that you make show your love for God and others. Explain what Jesus' forgiveness helps you to do.* Give the children time to complete their responses.

Key Words Ask the children to work in pairs to review the definitions of the *Key Words: sin* and *conscience.* Suggest that they provide examples and scenarios that help them to remember the meanings of these words.

Remember Review the *We Believe* statements. Help the children to understand what differences these beliefs about Jesus make in their lives and in the

Reflect & Pray

There are many choices that I have to make in my life. How do the choices that I make show my love for God and others?

_____

_____

Jesus, your forgiveness helps me

_____

_____

Key Words

sin (p. 253)
conscience (p. 250)

Remember

- We make the choice to love God.
- God is our forgiving Father.
- The sacrament of Reconciliation has several parts.
- The Church celebrates the sacrament of Reconciliation.

OUR CATHOLIC LIFE

An Example of Forgiveness

In 1980, Pope John Paul II wrote a letter to the whole Church. This letter reminded people that God is merciful and forgiving. Six months later, the pope was nearly killed when Mehmet Ali Agca shot him. Although Pope John Paul II was seriously wounded, he publicly forgave Agca. Later the pope visited with his attacker in prison. The pope personally forgave the man who had tried to kill him. The pope's willingness to forgive is an example to all of us. We are called to forgive those who hurt us.

HOME CONNECTION

Sharing Faith with My Family

Make sure to send home the family page (text page 162).

Encourage the children to involve family members in making a "I am sorry" card and in coloring and cutting out the sacrament reminder for the sacrament of Reconciliation.

PUPIL PAGE 162

For additional information and activities, encourage families to visit Sadlier's

www.WeBelieveweb.com

Church. Gather in the prayer space. Say: *Reflect on what you have learned about the sacrament of Reconciliation this week.* Then pray:

Dear God, help us to make good choices.
Keep us on your path of love.
When we stray, help us to be sorry for our sins.
Let me remember to ask for your forgiveness often in the sacrament of Reconciliation.
Thank you for your life-giving gift of forgiveness.
Amen.

Our Catholic Life Read the story of Pope John Paul II forgiving his attacker for seriously wounding him. Ask children to respond to the pope's visit to his attacker and to his public forgiveness of the man who tried to assassinate him. Ask: *What lesson is the pope teaching all people about forgiveness?*

Plan Ahead for Chapter 19

Prayer Space: crucifix

Materials: Grade 3 CD (option), copies of Reproducible Master 19, construction paper, markers

Chapter 19 We Pray for Healing and Eternal Life

Overview

In Chapter 18 the children learned more about the sacrament of Reconciliation. In this chapter, the children will learn about the strength and healing that we receive through the sacrament of the Anointing of the Sick.

Doctrinal Content	For Adult Reading and Reflection *Catechism of the Catholic Church*
The children will learn:	Paragraph
• Jesus cared for and healed the sick.	1503
• The Church heals us in Jesus' name.	1511
• We believe in eternal life with God.	1681
• The Church celebrates eternal life with God.	1684

Key Words

oil of the sick (p. 165)
eternal life (p. 167)
funeral Mass (p. 167)

Catechist Background

Recalling a time when I was sick, what were my needs during that illness?

When we are sick, we become more vulnerable. Sometimes we can care for ourselves. But even then, it is nice to have people looking after us. When the illness is more serious, it is imperative that we have others caring for us.

The Church continues the ministry of Jesus by caring for those who are sick. "She believes in the life-giving presence of Christ, the physician of souls and bodies." (CCC 1509) In the sacrament of the Anointing of the Sick, those who are sick are offered strength, comfort, courage, and healing.

The Anointing of the Sick can be part of the Last Rites, along with the sacraments of Penance and Eucharist (called *Viaticum*). But the recipient of the sacrament of Anointing need not be dying. In fact, we are encouraged to celebrate the sacrament of Anointing when we face a serious illness, an operation, or physical difficulties in old age. If

serious illness recurs, the sacrament can be repeated. Like all of the sacraments, the Anointing of the Sick is a celebration with the whole Church, acknowledging Jesus' healing presence among us.

However, sometimes sickness does lead to death. And while death is often experienced by us as a loss, as Christians we know through our faith that death is more than simply a fact of life, it is a continuation of life. We know that Christ's Resurrection holds the promise of eternal life. In the risen Jesus we will live forever in the company of God and the saints.

How can I help those in mourning take comfort in Jesus' promise of eternal life?

Lesson Planning Guide

Lesson Steps	Presentation	Materials

① WE GATHER

page 163 ✚ **Prayer** ☀ **Focus on Life**	♪ Pray in song. • Discuss feelings of being helped when hurt or sick.	For the prayer space: white tablecloth, crucifix, list of those who are ill ♪ "Walking Up to Jesus," by Paule Freeburg, DC, and Christopher Walker, #15 Grade 3 CD

② WE BELIEVE

page 164 *Jesus cared for and healed the sick.* 📖 *Mark 10:46–52*	• Discuss Jesus' healing work or ministry among the people. 🚶 Act out the gospel story.	
page 165 *The Church heals us in Jesus' name.*	• Discuss the sacrament of Anointing of the Sick. 🚶 Write one way to bring comfort and hope to others.	
page 166 *We believe in eternal life with God.*	• Discuss eternal life, heaven, hell, and purgatory. 🚶 Name some ways our choices show that we are God's friends. • Read and discuss *As Catholics*.	
page 167 *The Church celebrates eternal life with God.* *Order of Christian Funerals*	• Read about and discuss the funeral Mass.	

③ WE RESPOND

page 167	🚶 Design a card to send to a person in need of comfort and hope. ♪ Pray in song. (option)	• construction paper, markers ♪ "We Are Marching/Siyahamba," #16 Grade 3 CD (option) • copies of Reproducible Master 19
page 168 **Review**	• Complete questions 1–5. 🚶 Work on *Assessment Activity*.	• Chapter 19 Test in Assessment book, pp. 39–40 • Chapter 19 Test in Test Generator • Review & Resource Book, pp. 46–48
page 169–170 **We Respond in Faith**	• Complete the *Reflect & Pray* activity. • Review *Remember* and *Key Words*. • Read and discuss *Our Catholic Life*. • Discuss **Sharing Faith with My Family**.	• Family Book, pp. 55–57

For additional ideas, activities, and opportunities: Visit Sadlier's  www.WeBelieveweb.com

Name _____

Haiku is a form of poetry that follows a strict pattern of syllables. In haiku, there are three lines of poetry. The first line has five syllables. The second line has seven syllables. The third line has five syllables.

> Lord, I trust in you.
> Comfort me in time of need.
> Please heal my sad heart.

Look at another example of a haiku about the healing of Jesus.

> Good Shepherd of love,
> Jesus, who leads and guides us,
> Grant us your healing.

Now write a haiku that expresses your faith in God and your trust in Jesus to help you in times when you need healing. Draw an illustration below the poem.

Line 1 (five syllables) _____

Line 2 (seven syllables) _____

Line 3 (five syllables) _____

Connections

To Catholic Social Teaching

Life and Dignity of the Human Person
In 1 John 4:7–8 we read that we need to have love in our lives. Discuss different ways we can show our love for others. Encourage the children to pray for others who are in need of God's healing, whether they know these people or not. Suggest that the children also tell others that they are praying for them. Remind them that our ages are not important, but our actions are. Anyone can go to God in prayer at any time. Urge the children to show their love for others through prayer.

To Liturgy

As the children learn about the Anointing of the Sick, eternal life, and the funeral Mass, focus their attention on ways to care for the sick or elderly. Remind them that we pray for the sick in a special way at Mass. Most parishes also post the names of those that are ill or hospitalized in the church bulletin and urge the entire parish to pray for them. Eucharistic ministers bring the Eucharist to parishioners who are ill and not able to attend Sunday Mass.

FAITH and MEDIA

▶ Consider inviting your pastor or another priest to speak to the class this week about the sacrament of the Anointing of the Sick. Help the children prepare suitable questions beforehand. With the speaker's permission, you might also videotape the presentation to use as a teaching tool.

▶ You might post the children's haiku (Reproducible Master 19) on the parish Web site.

Meeting Individual Needs

Children with Musical Talent

There are children in your religion class who have been blessed with music talent. Provide these children with the opportunity to perform for the rest of the class. Let the talents of others in science, writing, or math be used to enhance what is discussed in the group.

ADDITIONAL RESOURCES

Video   *A Place Prepared: Helping Children Understand Death and Heaven,* Paraclete Press, 2000. This video is for adults to help them explain death and the afterlife to children. (35 min.)

To find more ideas for books, videos, and other learning material, visit Sadlier's

www.WeBelieve.web.com

Focus on Life

Chapter Story

It was a beautiful spring day, and the entire class was excited and ready to play a game of kickball. The teams were chosen and the third grade teacher, Mrs. O'Neill, was the pitcher.

Kate's team was up first. There were two people already on base when Kate got up to kick. Mrs. O'Neill rolled the ball and Kate kicked the ball hard. It sailed into the outfield. The whole team was cheering as the three children were running around the bases. Kate was so excited. This was her best kick ever!

As Kate rounded second base she slipped and fell, breaking her fall with her left arm.

As everyone gathered around, Mrs. O'Neill checked and saw that Kate had a badly scraped knee, elbow, and hand.

Mrs. O'Neill asked Abby to help Kate get to the nurse's office.

Mrs. Harris greeted the girls warmly. She sat Kate down. As she took out a cloth and some antiseptic she explained, "This won't hurt much, Kate, and it will help to clean these scrapes." She worked carefully and did her job quickly. Then Mrs. Harris put some antibiotic cream on the wounds and placed bandages over them. "This will help keep your scrapes free of germs and allow them to heal."

After a few minutes Kate was ready to rejoin her class. "Thank you, Mrs. Harris. I feel better already!" exclaimed Kate as she ran out to join her class.

"You sure came back fast," said Mrs. O'Neill.

Kate nodded. "I sure did, Mrs. O'Neill. Our school nurse, Mrs. Harris, is the best. She's gentle, and always makes me feel better," said Kate.

Everyone agreed. Mrs. O'Neill said, "That is how it is with Jesus. He always watches over us. He takes care of us and heals us with love and care."

▶ *Who helped Kate when she got hurt?*

We Pray for Healing and Eternal Life

WE GATHER

✝ **Leader:** Jesus asked people to believe in him. He healed those who had faith in him. Let us rejoice and sing this song:

🎵 **Walking Up to Jesus**

So many people in the house with Jesus,
People, people, people come to see him!

Jesus looked, and said to the man who could not walk:
"Get up now. You are healed.
You can walk!
And all at once the man jumped up and everyone said, "OH!"

For he was walking in the house with Jesus,
Walking, walking,
walking up to Jesus!

 Think of a time when you felt hurt or sick. Who helped you? How did you feel after they helped you?

163

PREPARING TO PRAY

The children will sing a song about Jesus' healing those who come to him for comfort and peace.

• Practice opening song, "Walking Up to Jesus," #15 on the Grade 3 CD.

• Have the children place on the prayer table lists of friends, relatives, and classmates who are ill.

The Prayer Space
• Place a white covering on the table and a crucifix in the center.

📖 **This Week's Liturgy**
Visit **www.webelieveweb.com** for this week's liturgical readings and other seasonal material.

Lesson Plan

WE GATHER ___ minutes

✝ Pray

• Pray the Sign of the Cross and read aloud the opening paragraph.

• Sing the song.

☀ Focus on Life

• Invite the children to recall how it felt to be helped when sick or hurt.

• In this chapter, the children will learn about the strength and healing received in the sacrament of the Anointing of the Sick.

• Read the *Chapter Story* on guide page 163E. Relate Kate's experience of being helped to the lesson's theme of giving comfort and strength.

Home Connection Update

Ask the children to share experiences using the Chapter 18 family page. *Did you and family members make an "I am sorry" card? Did you or another family member use it?*

Catechist Goal

• To explain that Jesus cared for and healed the sick and that the Church continues Jesus' healing ministry in the sacrament of the Anointing of the Sick

Our Faith Response

• To identify the ways the sacrament of the Anointing of the Sick brings comfort and strength to those who receive it

 **Key Words** oil of the sick
eternal life
funeral Mass

Lesson Materials

• Grade 3 CD

• copies of Reproducible Master 19

• construction paper, markers

Teaching Note

Eternal Life

Perhaps the farthest thing from your children's minds is the mystery of eternal life. Yet, this lesson should give them confidence in God's love, now and forever. When the children hear of or face tragedy and loss, remind them that we live forever in God.

WE BELIEVE

Jesus cared for and healed the sick.

Jesus cared for all people. When those who were sick, hungry, poor, or in need reached out to him, Jesus comforted them. Sometimes he cured them of their illnesses. He gave them a reason to hope in God's love and care.

📖 Mark 10:46–52

Jesus was leaving a town with his disciples and a large crowd. A blind man named Bartimaeus was sitting by the side of the road. He called out to Jesus to have pity on him. People in the crowd told Bartimaeus to be quiet. But he kept calling out to Jesus anyway.

"Jesus stopped and said, 'Call him.' So they called the blind man, saying to him, 'Take courage; get up, he is calling you.' He threw aside his cloak, sprang up, and came to Jesus. Jesus said to him in reply, 'What do you want me to do for you?'

The blind man replied to him, 'Master, I want to see.' Jesus told him, 'Go your way; your faith has saved you.' Immediately he received his sight and followed him on the way." (Mark 10:49–52)

✲ Act out this gospel story.

Jesus listened to people who needed his help. Jesus often visited the homes of people who were sick. Wherever he went people asked Jesus to help and to heal them.

Jesus wants us to have his comfort and peace, too. No matter what our needs are Jesus gives us hope and the joy of his love.

164

Lesson Plan

WE BELIEVE ___ minutes

Read aloud the *We Believe* statement and the first *We Believe* paragraph.

📖 **Draw** attention to the story of Bartimaeus in Mark 10:46–52.

✲ **Explain** to the children that they are going to act out the story of Bartimaeus. Draw the children's attention to the artwork on page 164. Then have volunteers play the roles of Jesus, Bartimaeus, and the narrator. The rest of the class can be the disciples or members of the crowd following Jesus. Ask the children to reflect on what their characters, as well as other people around Jesus, might have been thinking and feeling as this scene was unfolding. Have them use this under-

standing of the characters to make their skits as realistic as possible. Congratulate them on their performance.

Have read aloud the last two *We Believe* paragraphs on page 164. Stress that during his public ministry or work, Jesus brought healing, hope, and joy into people's lives.

Read aloud the *We Believe* statement on page 165. Have volunteers read the *We Believe* paragraphs. Stress that the Church is concerned for our happiness and well being. If we are suffering a serious illness, we may receive the Anointing of the Sick, no matter what our age. In addition, we may receive this sacrament more than once. Emphasize the following points:

The Church heals us in Jesus' name.

Today the Church carries on Jesus' healing work. One of the most important ways is in the sacrament of the Anointing of the Sick. Through the sacrament those who are sick receive God's grace and comfort. The Holy Spirit helps them to trust in God's love. The Holy Spirit helps them to remember that God is always with them.

Any Catholic who is seriously ill may receive the Anointing of the Sick. Those in danger of death, for example, or those about to have a major operation are encouraged to celebrate this sacrament.

During this sacrament a priest uses the oil of the sick. The **oil of the sick** is holy oil that has been blessed by the bishop for use in the Anointing of the Sick.

Key Word

oil of the sick (p. 252)

A priest anoints the forehead of each sick person with this oil, saying:

"Through this holy anointing may the Lord in his love and mercy help you with the grace of the Holy Spirit."

The Anointing of the Sick is a sacrament for the whole Church. Family and parish members join with those who are sick in celebrating this sacrament.

At this sacrament we all pray that God will heal the sick. We also remember our own call to follow Jesus by loving and caring for people who are sick.

With a partner talk about some times people may need Jesus' comfort and hope. Write one way we can help them.

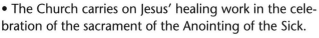

_____

_____

165

ACTIVITY BANK

Catholic Social Teaching
Call to Family, Community, and Participation

Remind the children that it is our responsibility as Catholics to pray for others. Encourage the children to remember their departed loved ones, the sick, and all those who need the healing of Jesus. Organize a group that offers its prayers for those who need healing in spirit and body.

Scripture Search
A Change of Heart
Activity Materials: Bible

Prepare a worksheet entitled "Change of Heart." Have the children work in groups of three and read one of the following passages: Acts 9:1–19 (Saul's Conversion); John 9:1–39 (Man Born Blind); and Matthew 8:5–13 (Centurion's Servant). Then ask the children to describe how encountering Jesus brought hope and healing and changed the lives of Saul, the man born blind, and the servant. Have each group share its findings with the entire class.

• The Church carries on Jesus' healing work in the celebration of the sacrament of the Anointing of the Sick.

• The sacrament is not only for the person who is ill but also for the family and the entire Church. We come together to ask for God's blessing. (Refer to the photos on the page.)

• The words of the Our Father remind us that we can put our complete trust in God's will. He will always care for us.

Encourage the children with their partners to write one way they can help bring comfort and hope to others.

Quick Check

✔ *What did Jesus do for those who were sick?* (He healed and cured the spirits and bodies of those who believed in him.)

✔ *In whose name does the Church continue the ministry of healing in the sacrament of Anointing of the Sick?* (in the name of Jesus)

We believe in eternal life with God.

Sometimes people may be so sick that they do not get better. We pray that they will not feel lonely and sad. We pray that they will trust in Jesus' promise to be with them always. Jesus will be with them at their death as he was during their life.

Death is not easy for us to understand or to accept. As Christians we do not see death as the end of life. We believe that our life continues after death, in a different way. We call this eternal life. **Eternal life** is living forever with God in the happiness of heaven.

When people choose to love and serve God and others, they will live with God forever. Heaven is life with God forever.

Some people choose not to love and serve God. Some people choose to break their friendship with God completely. Because of this choice, they separate themselves from God forever. Hell is being separated from God forever.

God does not want anyone to be separated from him. Yet many people who die in God's friendship may not be ready to enter the happiness of heaven. We believe these people enter into purgatory, which prepares them for heaven. Our prayers and good works can help these people so they may one day be with God in heaven.

Name some ways that the choices we make show God that we are his friends.

166

As Catholics...

Mass Cards

Read aloud the text. Encourage the children to be aware of when a Mass is offered with a special remembrance for a person who has died. Remind them to pray for that person along with their deceased loved ones.

As Catholics...

The Church encourages us to remember and pray for those who have died. One way we can do this is by having a Mass offered in their memory. A Mass card is given to the family of the person who has died. This Mass card lets the family know that a priest will be offering a Mass for their loved one. The family is given comfort knowing that the person who has died is being remembered.

Next time you are at Mass, remember to offer a prayer for a family member, relative, or friend who has died.

Lesson Plan

WE BELIEVE (continued)

Read Read aloud the *We Believe* statement. Ask volunteers to read aloud the *We Believe* paragraphs. Emphasize the following points:

• Death is not the end of life for a Christian.

• Eternal life is our life with God in heaven.

• The choices we make in our lives show our love and faithfulness to God. Our prayers and good works can help those in purgatory to find eternal life with God.

Ask the children to name some ways their choices can help show their friendship with God.

Have a volunteer read aloud the *We Believe* statement on page 167. Read the first *We Believe* paragraph. Have volunteers read the remaining *We Believe* paragraphs. Discuss what happens at the funeral Mass and how important it is to celebrate what God has done in the life of the person who has died. Stress that Christ's Resurrection is our promise from God that we also share in eternal life with him in heaven. Point out that our life in Christ begins with our Baptism and continues throughout our lives. Faith brings us to God to enjoy life with him in heaven.

Stress that the presence of our friends and family at a time of loss, as well as their prayers, can aid us and give us hope. We miss our loved ones, and we need to remember their lives and how they loved us. Refer to the photos on pages 166 and 167.

The Church celebrates eternal life with God.

No one can take away the sadness that we feel when someone we love dies. Even though we are sad, Catholics trust that this person will enjoy eternal life.

At a special Mass we thank God for the life of the person who has died. This Mass is called a **funeral Mass**. We gather as the Church with the family and friends of the person who has died. We pray that this person will share life with God forever.

The funeral Mass gives us hope. We are reminded that:

- at Baptism we were joined to Christ
- Jesus died and rose from the dead to bring us new life
- death can be the beginning of eternal life.

At the funeral Mass we pray that the person who has died will be joined to Christ in heaven. We celebrate our belief that everyone who has died in Christ will live with him forever. We give comfort to the person's family and friends by spending time and praying with them.

WE RESPOND

Design a card for someone who might need comfort and hope.

Key Words

eternal life (p. 251)
funeral Mass (p. 251)

ACTIVITY BANK

Curriculum Connection
Art

Activity materials: string or thread; beads, pasta, or other materials suitable for stringing.

Show the children that they can make a remembrance band to wear every day to help them remember that they are part of the eternal circle of God's love. Ask the children to share the meaning of the band with others and tell of God's love and his promise of life forever in Jesus.

Parish
Remembering the Dead

Ask the children to describe how the parish community celebrates All Souls' Day. What special reminders do we have in Church to help us pray for them? Have each child promise to pray for one person from the parish who has recently died.

167

WE RESPOND   ___ minutes

Have the children design their cards that would bring comfort and hope to people. Display these in the prayer space.

(At this time you may want to the play "We Are Marching/Siyhamba" from the Grade 3 CD. On the CD, the verse in English is followed by the same verse of the Zulu [African] song. The words for both are found in Sadlier's *We Believe* Program Songbook.)

Distribute copies of Reproducible Master 19. Help the children write a haiku prayer. Have them work with a partner to compose their haikus. These may be finished at home.

CHAPTER TEST

Chapter 19 Test is provided in the Grade 3 Assessment Book.

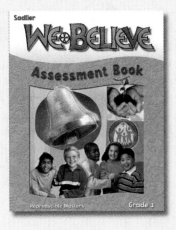

Fill in the blanks.

1. The Church continues Jesus' healing in the sacrament of the __Anointing of the Sick__.

2. In the sacrament of the Anointing of the Sick, the priest anoints a sick person with __the oil of the sick__.

3. __Eternal life__ is living forever with God in the happiness of heaven.

4. A __funeral Mass__ is a special Mass at which we thank God for the life of a person who has died.

Answer the question.

5. What is one way the funeral Mass reminds us of our Baptism?

   __See page 167.__
   _____
   _____
   _____

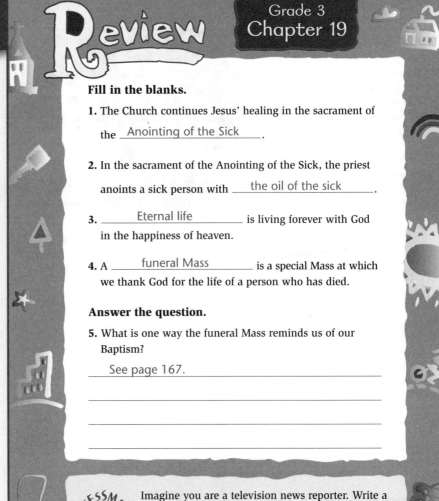

ASSESSMENT

Imagine you are a television news reporter. Write a news story to be shown on your local television station. In your news story describe what your parish can do to care for those who are sick and dying.

168

Lesson Plan

Review

___ minutes

Chapter Review Invite four volunteers to come to the board. After reading each fill-in-the-blank question, have them write their answers on the board. Discuss the answer to question 5 together. Then have the children answer question 5 in their texts. Ask volunteers to share their answers.

Assessment Activity This activity offers another way of reviewing the lesson with the children. Invite the pastor or a member of the parish staff to speak to the children. Ask the person to share how the parish cares for the sick and the dying. Afterwards, form groups to give presentations on what they have learned.

Sharing Faith in Class and at Home At this time you may want to work on pages 235–236 of Chapter 28. Refer to the *Lesson Planning Guide* on page 233B before you present these pages.

We Respond in Faith

___ minutes

Reflect & Pray Read the reflective activity aloud. Ask: *How does the Church bring Jesus' healing, comfort, and hope to those who need it?* Provide time for the children to complete their prayers and share responses.

 **Key Words** Invite children to participate in "Who Has the Key?" a game-show type review activity. Form small groups. Have them sit in a line on either side of you. Say a *Key Word*. Call on the first child who

We Respond in Faith

Reflect & Pray

The Church brings Jesus' healing, comfort and hope to those who need it. What do you think this means?

_____
_____

Loving God, where there is sadness, help me to

_____
_____

Key Words

oil of the sick (p. 252)
eternal life (p. 251)
funeral Mass (p. 251)

Remember

- Jesus cared for and healed the sick.
- The Church heals us in Jesus' name.
- We believe in eternal life with God.
- The Church celebrates eternal life with God.

OUR CATHOLIC LIFE

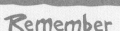

Pastoral Care for the Sick

By Baptism, Catholics are called to be concerned about others. Following the example of Jesus, we show respect for all people. In each of our parishes, help is provided to the sick, the elderly, and the dying. Priests, deacons, and special ministers of the Eucharist visit these people. They read from the Bible and pray together. Holy Communion is also offered during the visit. You can help by praying for those who are sick. You can also show your care by sending cards, by visiting, or by phoning. Remembering the sick in these special ways lets them know they are not forgotten.

HOME CONNECTION

Sharing Faith with My Family

Make sure to send home the family page (text page 170).

Encourage the children to ask their family members to pray for someone special who has died. Explain that OI on the sacrament card means *oleum infirmorum* (Latin for *oil of the sick*).

PUPIL PAGE 170

For additional information and activities, encourage families to visit Sadlier's

www.WEBELIEVEweb.com

signals, and ask him or her the answer. The group with the most correct answers wins.

Remember Review the statements. Help the children understand how these ideas are connected. Gather the children in the prayer space; direct their attention to the cards that depict Jesus as a source of comfort and healing. Ask them to relate these items to the statements and invite them to say a silent prayer for the sick of the parish.

Our Catholic Life Discuss our calling to care for others as Jesus did in his life. Talk about ways that children can help to care for the sick in their families and parishes.

Plan Ahead for Chapter 22

Prayer Space: globe, crucifix

Materials: Grade 3 CD, copies of Reproducible Master 22

Lent

Lent is a preparation for the celebration of Easter. For the Lenten liturgy disposes both catechumens and the faithful to celebrate the Paschal Mystery: catechumens, through the several stages of Christian initiation; the faithful, through reminders of their own baptism and through penitential practices.

(Norms Governing Liturgical Calendars, 27)

Overview

In this chapter the children will learn that the season of Lent is a time of preparation for Easter.

For Adult Reading and Reflection
You may want to refer to paragraphs 790 and 1436 of the *Catechism of the Catholic Church*.

Catechist Background

Do you find yourself welcoming Lent or wishing it away? Why?

In Lent as in Advent and most importantly at the Easter Vigil, the Church "re-reads and re-lives the great events of salvation history in the 'today' of her liturgy" (CCC 1095). We, the faithful, guided by the Holy Spirit, are given this seasonal opportunity to open ourselves to a conversion of heart and a renewal of our baptismal commitment.

Beginning on Ash Wednesday and ending before the Evening Mass of the Lord's Supper on Holy Thursday, Lent is our season of preparation for the Triduum and for Easter. These three seasons all together make up the paschal season of the Church. During Lent, the assembly of believers renews its faith in Jesus, God's only Son, through whom we have eternal life (John 3:16). By his cross, death, and Resurrection, Jesus saves us from sin and death.

These saving mysteries happened only once in historical time. However, they last forever as saving events that we continue to experience in the present. "Times, feasts, and seasons for celebration are observed so that through the liturgy the Church can be drawn into Christ's paschal mystery" (*The New Dictionary of Catholic Spirituality*, ed. Michael Downey, Liturgical Press, 1993, p. 607).

By the traditional practices of prayer, fasting and abstinence, penitence, and almsgiving, we can observe Lent as a fruitful time to recommit ourselves to Christian living.

What area of your life could use conversion of heart and renewal?

Lesson Planning Guide

Lesson Steps	Presentation	Materials

① WE GATHER

Lesson Steps	Presentation	Materials
page 171 **Introduce the Season**	• Read the *Chapter Story*. • Introduce the season of Lent. • Make a Lenten time line. • Proclaim the words on the banner.	• long strips of butcher paper (one for each child) • rulers, purple markers, scissors
page 172	• Discuss preparing for family get-togethers.	

② WE BELIEVE

Lesson Steps	Presentation	Materials
pages 172–174 *The season of Lent is a time of preparation for Easter.*	Listen to and sing the song. • Read and discuss the importance of Lent. • Read and discuss the sacraments connected to the season of Lent.	"Ashes," Tom Conry, #17, Grade 3 CD

③ WE RESPOND

Lesson Steps	Presentation	Materials
page 174	• Brainstorm ways to observe Lent. • Complete the Lenten faith and love chart. • Make baptismal shells.	• paper scallop shells or pattern • crayons or markers
page 175 **We Respond in Prayer**	• Discuss the importance of the sacrament of Reconciliation. • Listen to Scripture. • Respond in prayer and song.	• prayer space items: a Bible, a bowl of ashes, bowl of holy water, piece of rough fabric, a cactus, a large candle, purple table covering. • purple index cards "Ashes," Tom Conry, #18, Grade 3 CD
Guide pages 176A–176B **We Respond in Faith**	• Explain the individual Lenten project. • Explain the Lenten group project. • Discuss the Sharing Faith with My Family page.	• Reproducible Master 20 • markers and crayons • Family Book, pp. 58–59

For additional ideas, activities, and opportunities: Visit Sadlier's **www.WeBelieveweb.com**

Focus on Life

Chapter Story

As Mr. Delardi looked down from the stage, Carmela kept thinking, "Pick me! Pick me!" Many of the roles in the Easter play had already been taken. But Mr. Delardi had not yet chosen the angels. Carmela smiled and tried to look angelic.

The director smiled back and said, "Carmela, how would you like to be one of our angels?"

"Thanks, Mr. Delardi," she replied. "I'll do my best!" When Carmela told her parents about the play, they were happy for her but they wondered how she would find time for all the rehearsals. Carmela was a Girl Scout. She also had weekly piano and dance lessons. "No problem," she assured her parents. "I can handle it."

At first, Carmela never missed a single rehearsal. But as opening night drew near and rehearsals were held more often, she began to make excuses for being absent. "I already know my lines," she told herself. "I don't have to be there every single time."

On the night of the play, Carmela felt very confident—until the curtain went up! When she saw the full auditorium, she suddenly realized that she was not prepared at all! When Carmela missed her cue for her big line at the empty tomb, another angel had to say it for her: "Woman, why are you weeping?"

After the play, Carmela apologized to Mr. Delardi. He replied, "That's all right, Carmela. I know you had good intentions. Next year I'm sure I'll see you at all the rehearsals."

▶ *What do you think Carmela learned from her experience of being in the Easter play?*

Talk about Preparing for the play - easter

Lent

"Come to me heedfully,
listen, that you may have life."

Isaiah 55:3

171

Catechist Goal

• To present the season of Lent as a time of preparation for Easter

Our Faith Response

• To follow Jesus more closely this Lent

ADDITIONAL RESOURCES

Book *Saints of the Seasons for Children*, Ethel Marbach Pochocki, St. Anthony Messenger Press, 1989. Explore the unit on "Saints for the Journey: Lent/Easter."

Video *Following Jesus Through the Church Year: Lenten Lane*, Twenty-Third Publications, 1991. Krispin travels to Jerusalem because Jesus is celebrating the Passover there. (10 minutes)

To find more ideas for books, videos, and other learning material, visit Sadlier's

www.WEBELIEVEweb.com

Lesson Plan

Introduce the Season ___ minutes

• **Pray** together the Sign of the Cross and "Lord, have mercy. Christ, have mercy. Lord, have mercy."

• **Read** aloud the *Chapter Story* of Carmela and the Easter play. At the end of the story call on volunteers to tell what they think Carmela learned from her experience. Encourage the children to explain ways that Carmela can prepare for next year's Easter play.

• **Print** the jumble *NLET* on the board and have the children unscramble the letters to name the season. Explain that Lent begins on Ash Wednesday. It is a long period of preparation for Easter, and we must use each day well.

• **Ask** the children to describe the on-page art. *What does the dry ground mean?* (Lent) *What do the flowers mean?* (Easter is coming!) Ask the children to describe the action in the photo.

• **Invite** the children to make a personal Lenten time line. Explain that Lent has forty days, not counting Sundays. Refer to a calendar for this year's dates. The children can design and cut symbols for the special days of Lent: Ash Wednesday, the Sundays of Lent, Saint Valentine's and Saint Patrick's days. Use the time lines during Lent to mark off the weeks and days from Ash Wednesday to Holy Thursday.

• **Proclaim** the words in the banner under the photo.

Lesson Materials

- Grade 3 CD
- paper scallop shells or pattern
- crayons or markers
- purple index cards
- Reproducible Master 20

Teaching Note

Seasonal Symbols

Teach the symbols of the season: ashes (repentance or sorrow for sin), holy water (Baptism), burlap or sackcloth (repentance), cactus (desert), candle (prayer), and purple (Lent). Display an example of each Lenten symbol in the prayer space.

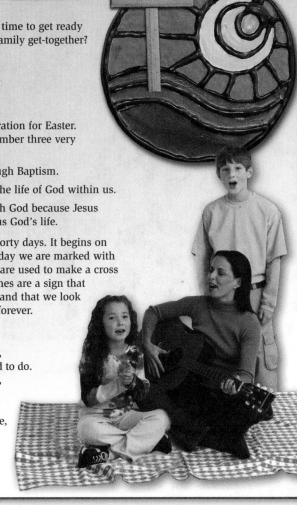

The season of Lent is a time of preparation for Easter.

WE GATHER

Have you had to take the time to get ready for a special event like a family get-together?

How did you prepare?

What did you do?

WE BELIEVE

Lent is our time of preparation for Easter. All during Lent, we remember three very important things:

- We belong to God through Baptism.
- We live now by grace, the life of God within us.
- We will live forever with God because Jesus died and rose to bring us God's life.

The season of Lent lasts forty days. It begins on Ash Wednesday. On this day we are marked with blessed ashes. The ashes are used to make a cross on our foreheads. The ashes are a sign that we are sorry for our sins and that we look forward to life with God forever.

♪ **Ashes**

We rise again from ashes,
from the good we've failed to do.
We rise again from ashes,
to create ourselves anew.
If all our world is ashes,
then must our lives be true,
an offering of ashes,
an offering to you.

172

Lesson Plan

WE GATHER ___ minutes

Focus on Life Ask partners to share their responses to the *We Gather* questions. Call on volunteers to share how they prepared for family gatherings or other events. Ask: *What exactly did you do? Make special food? Clean especially well? Decorate or make signs?* Help the children to realize that the extra effort we take to prepare for family gatherings, guests, or other events is an expression of our love and respect for those special people or events.

WE BELIEVE ___ minutes

• **Play** the song "Ashes" from the Grade 3 CD. Then invite the children to sing along. Ask: *What does this song tell us about Lent?* (During Lent, we rise from the ashes of good things we failed to do and begin again as God's new creation.)

• **Call** on a volunteer to read aloud the *We Believe* statement. Then have the children read silently the first two paragraphs of *We Believe* and highlight the three things we remember during Lent, how long Lent lasts, and what happens on Ash Wednesday. Share these responses.

• **Have** volunteers read aloud the remaining paragraphs of *We Believe* to discover what sacraments are especially important during Lent (Baptism, Reconciliation, and Eucharist). Call on the children to explain why each of these sacraments is so important to our getting ready for Easter. Emphasize the following points:

Lent is a special time for the Church. It is a special time to renew our Baptism. We remember the waters of Baptism that cleansed us from sin and brought us new life. We recall that in Baptism we were joined to Jesus and first received a share in God's life, grace. This is the grace we also receive in the Eucharist and the other sacraments.

Celebrating the sacraments of Reconciliation and the Eucharist is an important part of the season of Lent. The sacraments bring us into the wonder of Christ's death and Resurrection. We are strengthened by God's love and forgiveness. We are nourished by the Body and Blood of Christ.

LENT

Lent is a time to grow in faith. We think and pray about the life we have because Jesus died and rose for us. We think about what we believe as Christians. We pray with those who will celebrate the sacraments of initiation at the Easter Vigil.

173

ACTIVITY BANK

Mardi Gras
Activity materials: party hats, noise-makers

Find out whether the parish is sponsoring a Mardi Gras celebration on the Tuesday before Ash Wednesday. Encourage the children and their families to participate in the "Fat Tuesday" festivities. If there is no parish celebration, consider having a celebration with party hats, noise-makers, games, and refreshments.

Stewardship
Activity materials: poster board, crayons or paints

Lent is a good time to share with the third graders the biblical roots of the Church's teaching on stewardship. Have the children work in small groups to make a series of posters for display during the liturgical season. Have each group illustrate one Scripture passage like the following: 1 Peter 4:10 (good stewards); 1 Corinthians 4:2 (trustworthy stewards); Matthew 25:21 (faithful servant); Luke 21:3 (poor widow). Explain how these passages encourage us to use our time, talents, and resources to serve the Lord.

- The waters of Baptism washed away our sins, brought us new life, joined us to Jesus, gave us grace.
- Reconciliation strengthens us with God's love and forgiveness.
- Eucharist nourishes us with the Body and Blood of Christ.

Quick Check
✔ *What do we do during Lent?* (prepare for Easter)
✔ *What sacrament do we renew during Lent?* (Baptism)

CONNECTION

Liturgical Music

The Catholic Church is blessed with a wealth of traditional and contemporary liturgical music resources. Many of these hymns and songs are simple enough to be understood and sung by third graders. Among those that can be used for daily prayer are: "Lord, Who Throughout These Forty Days" and "The Glory of These Forty Days" (traditional); "Jesus, Remember Me" (Taizé), and "Hold Us in Your Mercy" (Tom Conry). You may want to find a recording of a simple *Kyrie eleison* (Lord, have mercy) to teach the children. Be sure to explain what the words mean.

During Lent we make a special effort to follow Jesus. We do this through prayer, penance, and acts of love and mercy. Doing these things during Lent helps us to renew our Baptism and gets us ready for the great Three Days.

Caring For Our Community
Catholic Diocese of Gary and Northwest Indiana Habitat for Humanity

OPERATION RICE BOWL
Catholic Relief Services

WE RESPOND

Talk together with your class about what you can do to grow in faith and love during Lent. Write some of the ideas suggested.

_____

_____

_____

_____

Look back at what you have written. Put a check beside the things you would like to do.

174

Lesson Plan

WE BELIEVE (continued)

• **Ask** a volunteer to read the paragraph at the top of the page. Then write the following headings on the board in large letters: *Think, Pray, Do Penance, Offer Love,* and *Mercy.*

WE RESPOND ___ minutes

Connect to Life Begin a process of brainstorming about specific ways in which the children can perform the above actions during Lent. Ask questions: *What might we think about? When? How might we pray? How can we do penance for the wrong we have done or the good we have failed to do?*

Read the directions for the *We Respond* activity. Say: *Can you remember some ideas we just spoke of? Write them on the lines. Now think: Which of these would you like to do for Lent? Ask the Holy Spirit to help you decide.* Ask the children to take a moment for silent prayer. Then have them check the one(s) they will do.

• **Distribute** paper scallop shells or shell outlines, scissors, and markers. Have the children trace the shells and/or cut out the scallop shapes. On the front of the shells have them print their names in decorative letters and write: *By my Baptism, I am joined to Jesus.* On the back, have them write their Lenten practice. Then have them display these shells on a bulletin board. (The scallop shell is a traditional symbol of Baptism.)

✝ We Respond in Prayer

Leader: O merciful God, you loved us so much you sent your Son to bring us life. Help us to believe in and follow him.

All: We believe!

Reader: A reading from the Gospel of John

"For God so loved the world that he gave his only Son, so that everyone who believes in him might not perish but have eternal life. For God did not send his Son into the world to condemn the world, but that the world might be saved through him." (John 3:16–17)

The Gospel of the Lord.

All: Praise to you, Lord Jesus Christ.

🎵 **Ashes**

Thanks be to the Father,
who made us like himself.
Thanks be to his Son,
who saved us by his death.
Thanks be to the Spirit
who creates the world anew
From an offering of ashes,
an offering to you.

LENT

175

PREPARING TO PRAY

The children will listen to Scripture and respond in quiet prayer and song.

• Tell the children you will be the prayer leader.

• Choose a volunteer to be the reader. Give this the child time to prepare the reading aloud.

• Practice the song, "Ashes," with the words given in the prayer service.

The Prayer Space

• In the prayer space place a Bible, a bowl of ashes, a bowl of holy water, a piece of rough fabric like burlap, a cactus, a large candle, and a purple table covering.

 This Week's Liturgy

Visit **www.webelieveweb.com** for this week's liturgical readings and other seasonal material.

✝ We Respond in Prayer ___ minutes

• **Invite** the children to recall what it means to be merciful (kind, compassionate, loving, forgiving). Remind them that because God has always loved us and shown his mercy toward us, he sent his only Son to save us from our sins. Ask: *How can we be merciful to others?*

• **Remind** the children that one of the most important ways to celebrate God's mercy is to participate in the sacrament of Reconciliation. Distribute index cards. Have the children write on the card the date and time of the parish celebration of the sacrament of Reconciliation. This can be posted at home. Or, with a parish priest, plan a celebration of this sacrament and invite families.

• **Gather** in the prayer space. Pray the Sign of the Cross. Serve as the prayer leader. After the reading, have the children extend their arms like a cross and silently tell Jesus that they will be merciful, loving, and forgiving like him. Close the prayer service with the song "Ashes," #18 on the Grade 3 CD.

Name _____

Complete each segment of this chart by writing one way
you will practice renewing your Baptism during Lent.
In the center oval, draw your own Baptism or a symbol
of Baptism.

Renew Your Baptism

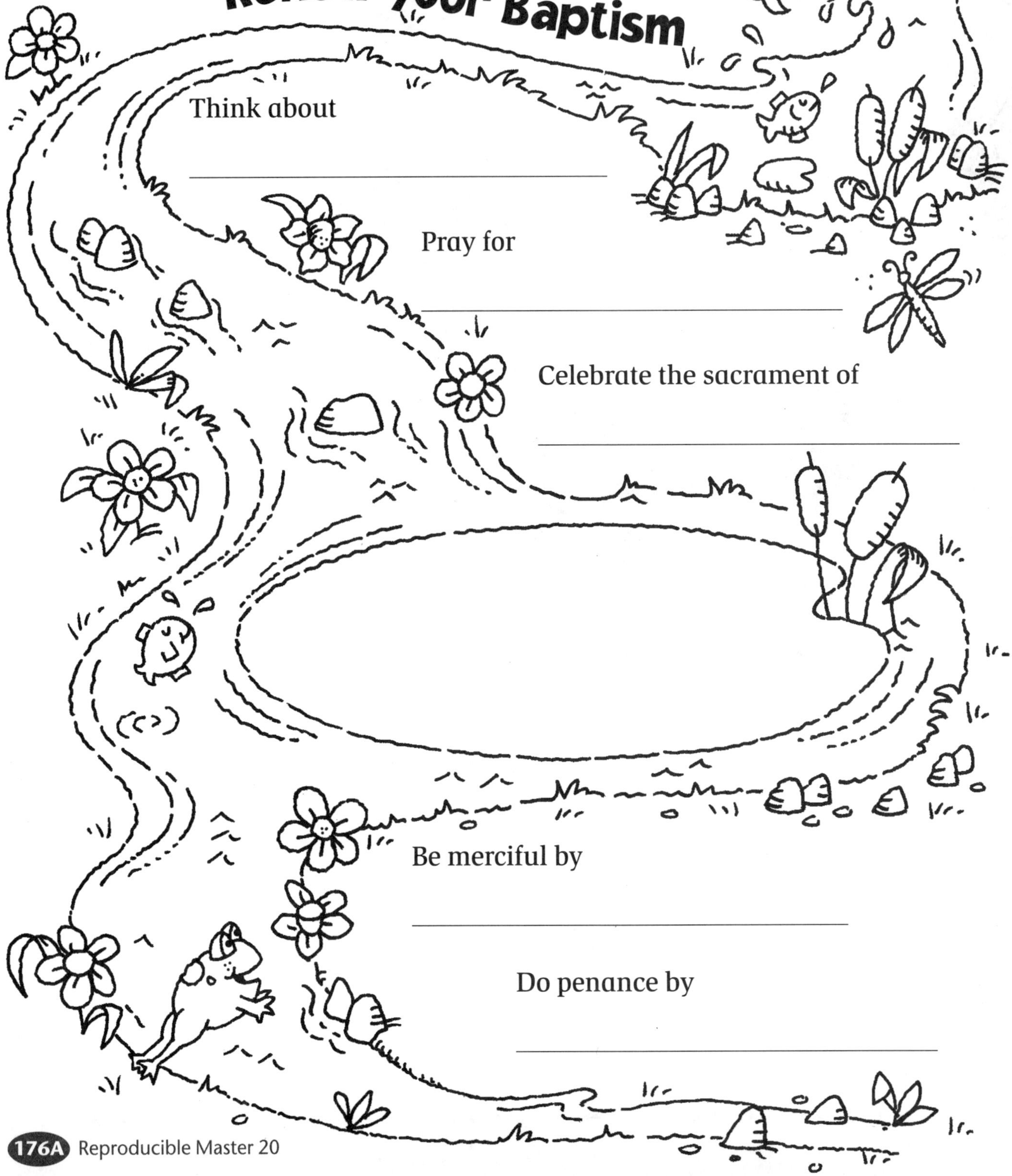

Think about

_____

Pray for

_____

Celebrate the sacrament of

_____

Be merciful by

_____

Do penance by

_____

We Respond in Faith

Individual Project

Distribute Reproducible Master 20 and markers. Explain the "Renew Your Baptism" activity. Note that the center oval is a space for a sketch of the child's Baptism or a drawing of a baptismal symbol. Suggest that if the children have pictures of their own Baptisms, they might cut out the center oval and fill it with a photo. Explain that each segment of the chart is to be filled in with one way of renewing their Baptism during Lent.

Group Project

Gather information from parish and community service organizations on projects the children might participate in or support. Their Web sites might also be helpful. Share this information with the children. Narrow the possible choices to three.

Have the children vote on which project or service they most want to help or do as a class. Make an action plan of when, where, how, for whom, and with whom they will accomplish this Lenten project.

During the project, keep a class journal of your efforts.

HOME CONNECTION

Sharing Faith with My Family

Make sure to send home the family page (pupil page 176).

Encourage the children to involve their families in the Prayers for Lent. These prayers can be added to the meal prayer each day of the week. Suggest that the children post the list in a special place at home as a reminder.

For additional information and activities, encourage families to visit Sadlier's

www.WeBelieveweb.com

PUPIL PAGE 176

The Three Days

Christ redeemed us all and gave perfect glory to God principally through his paschal mystery: dying he destroyed our death and rising he restored our life. Therefore the Easter Triduum of the passion and resurrection of Christ is the culmination of the entire liturgical year.

(Norms Governing Liturgical Calendars, 18)

Overview

In this chapter the students will learn that the Three Days celebrate Jesus' passing from death to new life.

For Adult Reading and Reflection
You may want to refer to paragraphs 1168 and 1096 of the *Catechism of the Catholic Church*.

Catechist Background

W**hat is your most memorable liturgical experience of the Three Days? Why?**

The celebration of the Triduum is the high point of the Church year. Lasting from Holy Thursday evening's Mass of the Lord's Supper to the evening of Easter Sunday, this brief but brilliant season is actually one great liturgy. Each day focuses on a particular aspect of the Paschal Mystery of the suffering, death, and Resurrection of the Lord.

At the Holy Thursday liturgy, the Church experiences itself as a "eucharistic people." The washing of the feet rededicates us to Christian service in response to Christ's command: "I have given you a model to follow, so that as I have done for you, you should also do" (John 13:15). By our partaking of the Body and Blood of Christ, we fulfill his desire that we "Take and eat" and "Drink from it, all of you" (Matthew 26: 26, 27).

The liturgy continues on Good Friday. Now the Church listens once again to the proclamation of the passion and venerates the holy cross as the sign of the world's salvation.

On Holy Saturday, at the Easter Vigil, the Church joyfully sings the "Easter Proclamation" *(Exsultet)*, praising the Passover Lamb who

"broke the chains of death
and rose triumphant from the grave."

The catechumens are welcomed into the Church through the sacraments of initiation, and the faithful renew their baptismal promises.

H**ow can you keep your usual observance of the Triduum and yet add (or discover) a new dimension this year?**

Lesson Planning Guide

Lesson Steps	Presentation	Materials
① WE GATHER		
page 177 **Introduce the Season**	• Read the *Chapter Story*. • Introduce the Three Days. • Proclaim the words on the banner.	
page 178	• Answer the questions about special times with families.	
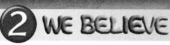 **② WE BELIEVE**		
pages 178–180 *The Three Days celebrate that Jesus passed from death to new life.*	• Read and discuss the Three Days as the greatest celebration of the Church. • Begin mural for the Three Days. • Welcome a guest to speak about the Three Days.	• mural paper hung on one wall, markers • construction paper • paper doll pattern for tracing • scissors, tape or glue • a guest speaker (priest, deacon, or a person initiated into the Church last year at the Easter Vigil) • crayons or markers
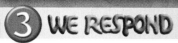 **③ WE RESPOND**		
page 180	🏃 Write or draw something to share with others about the Three Days.	
page 181 **We Respond in Prayer**	• Prepare to renew baptismal promises. • Bless each child with holy water.	• prayer space items: white candle, Bible, crucifix, flowering plant, white tablecloth, bowl of holy water, large white stole or cape • parish hymnal (optional)
Guide pages 182A–182B **We Respond in Faith**	• Explain the individual Three Days project. • Explain the Three Days group project. • Discuss the Sharing Faith with My Family page.	• Reproducible Master 21 • markers • poster board, paper and fabric scraps • scissors and glue • Family Book, pp. 60–61

For additional ideas, activities, and opportunities: Visit Sadlier's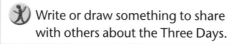

Focus on Life

Chapter Story

As Casey's parents rushed out the door, his mother turned to give him one last hug. "Don't worry, Casey," she assured him. "Grandma will be right over. And the next time you see me, your new baby sister will be in my arms." Casey wanted to hang on to his mom for a few more minutes. But his dad said, "Sorry, Son. We've got to get to the hospital right now."

Casey watched them drive away. He had mixed feelings about a baby sister. He was now in third grade and had always been an only child. He wondered if his parents would be so busy with the baby that they would forget about him. Casey was just starting to feel sorry for himself when Grandma arrived with a plate of chocolate-chip cookies. She would be spending the next three days with him while his mom was in the hospital and his dad was working.

When she saw the look on Casey's face, Grandma said, "What you need, my boy, is at least two cookies and a game of Chinese checkers." And before Casey could say a word, Grandma was already in the kitchen setting out the cookies and the game board. Casey bit into a cookie, grinned and said, "I hope I don't beat you too badly."

They spent the next three days together. Grandma made Casey feel much better about the new baby. They finished preparing the baby's bedroom. Then they went to the hospital to visit mom and meet the new baby, Angela Lee. His new sister was awfully red and wrinkled. But Casey loved her right from the start. He was glad that he had had time with Grandma to get ready for the newest member of the family. Maybe having a baby sister wouldn't be so bad after all.

▶ *Why was Casey glad that he had three days with his grandmother before his baby sister came home?*

The Three Days 21

"Most blessed of all nights,
chosen by God
to see Christ rising from the dead!"

Exsultet, Easter Vigil

177

Catechist Goal

• To present the Three Days as a celebration of Jesus' passing from death to life

Our Faith Response

• To praise the risen Lord

ADDITIONAL RESOURCES

Videos *The Story of Jesus for Children,* Inspirational Films, 1979. This is an excellent drama of Jesus' life and works through the eyes of children. Use the Holy Week segment. (20-minute segment of 62-minute tape)

Following Jesus Through the Church Year: Holy Week Crossing, Twenty-Third Publications, 1991. Krispin thinks his search for Jesus is over because Jesus has died. (10 minutes)

To find more ideas for books, videos, and other learning material, visit Sadlier's

www.WEBELIEVEweb.com

Lesson Plan

Introduce the Season ___ minutes

• **Pray** the Sign of the Cross and the acclamation "Christ has died. Christ is risen. Christ will come again."

• **Read** or tell the *Chapter Story* of Casey and the new member of his family. Emphasize that Casey's grandma helped him make the transition or crossover from being an only child to being an older brother.

• **Make** a chart on the board depicting stick figures in a church building with a cross on it. Over the church print *Lent*. About a foot away, sketch stick figures dancing and singing in a church with bells ringing. Over the church print *Easter*. Then ask: *Do you know how we cross* over from Lent to Easter? After volunteers respond, sketch a bridge from one church to the other. Depict a few figures on the bridge, headed toward Easter. Print *The Three Days* over the bridge. Explain that this is the season we will learn about this week.

• **Invite** the children to look at the photo. Explain: *This is the Easter candle. The priest is lighting it with new fire. It is a sign of Jesus' new life and Resurrection. The deacon will carry it into the church. Everyone in church is holding a small candle. Everyone will get a new little light from the big Easter candle.*

• **Proclaim** the words under the photo.

Lesson Materials

- mural paper hung on one wall, markers
- construction paper
- paper doll pattern for tracing
- scissors, tape or glue
- a guest speaker
- crayons or markers
- parish hymnal (optional)
- Reproducible Master 21
- poster board, paper and fabric scraps
- scissors and glue

Teaching Note

The Holiest Days of the Year

Although the three days of the Triduum are not holy days of obligation (except, of course, for Easter Sunday), Catholics who understand that the Church is celebrating the central mystery of our faith will not want to miss participating in the liturgy. By doing so, we are formed and shaped as a paschal people. We live the Paschal Mystery by fully experiencing these powerful celebrations on the holiest days of the year.

The Three Days celebrate that Jesus passed from death to new life.

WE GATHER

When have you celebrated a long weekend or holiday with your family?

What did you do or say that made it a special time to be with your family?

WE BELIEVE

The Three Days are the Church's greatest celebration. They are like a bridge. The Three Days take us from the season of Lent to the season of Easter.

Adoration before the Blessed Sacrament, Holy Thursday night

During the Three Days, we gather with our parish. We celebrate at night and during the day. The Three Days are counted from evening to evening. The first day starts on the evening of Holy Thursday. We remember what happened at the Last Supper. We celebrate that Jesus gave himself to us in the Eucharist. We remember the ways Jesus served others. We have a special collection for those who are in need.

178

Lesson Plan

WE GATHER   ___ minutes

Focus on Life Ask partners to share their responses to the *We Gather* questions. Then call on a few volunteers to tell about these special times with their families.

• **Explain** that during the Three Days, all over the world, followers of Jesus gather to celebrate his death and Resurrection. This time is the most special time of the year because we celebrate that Jesus died and rose for us.

WE BELIEVE   ___ minutes

• **Call** on a student to read aloud the *We Believe* statement. Emphasize that these Three Days are the greatest celebration of the Church year. Explain that the Three Days are counted from Holy Thursday evening to Easter

evening. Then have volunteers read aloud the *We Believe* paragraphs describing Holy Thursday, Good Friday, and Holy Saturday. Conclude with the Easter Sunday paragraph on the next page, page 179.

Draw attention to the photos. Remind the children that praying before the Blessed Sacrament is honoring Jesus in the Eucharist. Point out that the priest wears red on Good Friday to recall Jesus' suffering and death. Note the Easter candle and the Easter fire.

• **Form** four small groups to work on one panel of a mural:

◆ Holy Thursday (Last Supper, Eucharist, service)

◆ Good Friday (Jesus dies; we pray for the world)

On Good Friday, we remember the suffering and death of Jesus on the cross. In church, the altar is completely bare. We listen to the Bible readings that tell us about Jesus' death. We give special honor to the cross, and we praise God for the life that comes from Jesus' death. We pray for the whole world. Then we wait and pray.

Reading of the Passion, Good Friday

Easter candle lit by Easter fire, Easter Vigil

On Holy Saturday, we think about all that happened to Jesus. We pray that we might be joined to Jesus. We gather again as a community at night for the Easter Vigil. A fire is burning bright. The Easter candle is lit and we sing "Christ our light!"

We listen to many different stories from the Bible. We remember all the great things God has done for us. We sing with joy to celebrate that Jesus rose from the dead.

New members of the Church receive the new life of Christ in Baptism, Confirmation, and the Eucharist. We rejoice with them. This is the most important and the most beautiful night of the year! Holy Saturday turns into Easter Sunday.

179

THE THREE DAYS

ACTIVITY BANK

The Arts

Activity Materials: Christian art books or prints depicting the Three Days

The Last Supper, the passion and death of Jesus, and the Resurrection have fascinated artists over the centuries. Share with the students examples such as: Jacopo Bassano's *The Last Supper*, Raphael's *Christ Stumbling on the Road to Calvary*, and Mathis Grunewald's *The Resurrection*. Invite responses in dialogue and art.

Liturgy

Fast and Feast

Activity Materials: post-it notes, markers

Explain that the Church observes an Easter fast from the night of Holy Thursday to the night of the Easter Vigil. We fast from excess foods or special foods until we feast at Easter to celebrate the new life of Jesus. Have the children make *Fast* and *Feast* messages to post on refrigerator doors as family reminders.

◆ Holy Saturday ("Christ our light!"; new members receive new life of Christ)

◆ Easter Sunday (Jesus is risen, alleluia!; living new life).

Help the children as they sketch scenes and symbols illustrating the Three Days.

• **Have** the children trace a paper doll figure on construction paper to represent themselves. Ask them to cut them out, write their names on them and tape or glue them on the mural to show that they are following Jesus in these special days.

Quick Check

✔ *What do we celebrate on the Three Days?* (Jesus' passing from death to new life)

✔ *What are the Three Days a bridge between?* (Lent and Easter)

CONNECTION

Multicultural Connection

Explain that Maronite Catholics are Catholics who belong to the Maronite Catholic (Eastern) Church. They celebrate the liturgy in the Syriac or Arabic languages. They have a "Burial of the Cross" ritual on Good Friday. Invite the children to carry out their own ritual with original prayers. Bury the cross on Good Friday (or the last day you meet before Easter). After the Three Days, dig it up and decorate it with flowers and ribbons.

To Community

Share a community calendar listing events during the Three Days. Have the children design calendars for their families. Ask them to include times and places of: ecumenical services, sacred music concerts, parish suppers, Easter egg hunts or rolls, and any other events their families might participate in and enjoy.

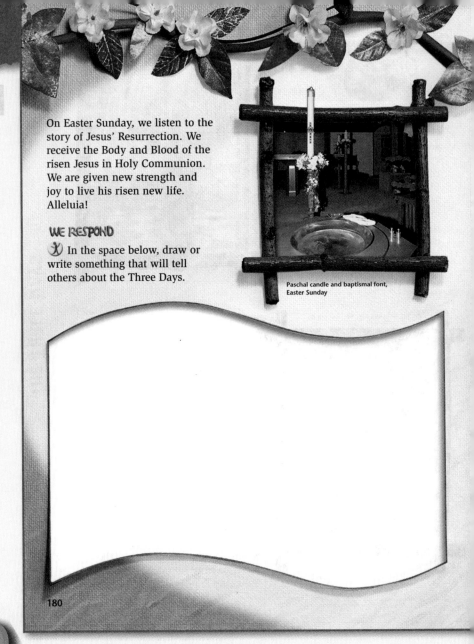

On Easter Sunday, we listen to the story of Jesus' Resurrection. We receive the Body and Blood of the risen Jesus in Holy Communion. We are given new strength and joy to live his risen new life. Alleluia!

WE RESPOND

In the space below, draw or write something that will tell others about the Three Days.

Paschal candle and baptismal font, Easter Sunday

180

Lesson Plan

WE BELIEVE (continued)

• **Welcome** a priest, deacon, or a person who was initiated into the Church last year at the Easter Vigil. Let the children know that the guest(s) will share the experience of the Three Days celebration last year and tell what was most meaningful to him or her. Give the children an opportunity to ask questions or make comments. Follow through with a thank-you card from the children.

• **Note** the photo. Compare this baptismal font to the font or pool in your parish. Tell the children that *pasch* and *paschal* mean "Easter." *Pasch* originally comes from the Hebrew *pesah,* meaning "Passover."

WE RESPOND ___ minutes

Connect to Life Using parish bulletins, newsletters, or the Web site, have the children decide on how they will participate in making the Three Days better known in the parish. Will they write a letter to parishioners? Draw a Three Days bridge chart? Compose an advertising slogan? Make posters? Guide students in carrying out this activity.

Prepare for the *We Respond* activity by reviewing what we celebrate during each of the days of the Three Days. You may want to add to your class mural at this time. Then give students time to write or draw something for each day: Holy Thursday, Good Friday, Easter Vigil or Easter Sunday.

✝ We Respond in Prayer

Leader: On the night before Easter Sunday, during the Easter Vigil, those who have been preparing for Baptism during Lent are baptized. They receive the new life Jesus won for us in his rising from the dead.

Each of you is baptized. You are children of God. Let us renew the promises our parents and godparents made for us at Baptism.

Leader: Do you believe in God our Father and creator?

Children: I do.

Leader: Do you believe in Jesus Christ who saved us through his dying and rising again?

Children: I do.

Leader: Do you believe in the Holy Spirit who guides the Church and who lives in each of us?

Children: I do.

Leader: This is what we believe. This is our faith. As a sign of that faith, come forward to be signed with the sign of the cross.

THE THREE DAYS

181

PREPARING TO PRAY

The children will renew their baptismal promises and will be signed with the cross by the leader.

• Tell the children you will be the prayer leader.

• Prepare the children to answer "I do" after question.

• Explain that you will bless each child and "clothe" each one with a "baptismal garment" (the white stole or cape).

• You may want to choose and practice a seasonal song from the parish hymnal to end the prayer service.

The Prayer Space

• Place a white candle, a Bible, a crucifix, a flowering plant, a white tablecloth, a bowl of holy water, and a large white stole or cape to recall the "baptismal garment."

 **This Week's Liturgy**

Visit **www.webelieveweb.com** for this week's liturgical readings and other seasonal material.

✝ We Respond in Prayer ___ minutes

• **Pray** Invite the children to close their eyes and breathe deeply. Ask them to pray within their hearts: "Come, Holy Spirit." Continue this contemplative prayer in silence for a minute or two.

• **Have** the children look at *We Respond in Prayer*. Ask a volunteer to read the first paragraph aloud. Explain that those who will be baptized at the Easter Vigil will make their baptismal promises for the first time. These are the same promises our parents and godparents made for us when we were baptized as infants. First, we make promises that we will say no to a sinful life. Then we profess our faith in God the Father, the Son, and the Holy Spirit. Invite students to silently read the promises.

• **Remind** the children that they were baptized in the name of Jesus Christ, who died and rose for them. Say: *Today you can proclaim your faith for yourself by answering "I do" to the questions in the prayer service.* (Go over the questions briefly to prepare the children to respond.)

• **Gather** in the prayer space in a semi-circle. Serve as the prayer leader. Invite all to stand for the renewal of baptismal promises. Then call each child forward in turn. Bless him or her with the holy water after placing the white stole or cape over the shoulders. Place your hand gently on the child's head and offer a silent prayer for him or her. When all have been blessed, share a seasonal song.

Name _____

In the circle, write a prayer to Jesus expressing your feelings about the Three Days. Decorate the corners with symbols of each celebration.

My Three Days Prayer

Holy Thursday

Good Friday

Easter Sunday

Holy Saturday

Individual Project

Distribute Reproducible Master 21 and markers. Explain to the children that they are to decorate the picture frame with symbols of each of the Three Days celebrations. For example: Holy Thursday might be symbolized by bread and wine, or a person receiving Holy Communion. Inside the frame, students are to write a prayer based on what they would like to say to Jesus about the Three Days in our Church year.

Group Project

Involve the children in assembling mosaic crosses using a wide assortment of paper and fabric scraps. Cut the crosses from poster board. Provide scissors and glue. Make a sample by cutting geometric shapes from gold, silver, and red foils. Cut shapes from decorative papers (wallpaper, contact paper) and bright solid color fabrics. Shapes may be pencil drawn on the cross and filled in with the mosaic pieces. Or the design may be worked out as the student assembles the pieces. Display the crosses in or around the prayer space.

HOME CONNECTION

Sharing Faith with My Family

Make sure to send home the family page (pupil page 182).

Encourage the children to involve their families in decorating the cross with Three Days scenes. Remind them to say the Family Prayer with their families.

For additional information and activities, encourage families to visit Sadlier's

www.WEBELIEVE.web.com

ASSESSMENT

In the *We Believe* program each core chapter ends with a review of the content presented, and with activities that encourage the children to reflect and act on their faith. The review is presented in two formats, standard and alternative.

Each unit is also followed by both standard and alternative assessment. The standard test measures basic knowledge and vocabulary assimilation. The alternative assessment allows the children another option—often utilizing another learning style—to express their understanding of the concepts presented.

Using both forms of assessment, perhaps at different times, attends to the various ways children's learning can be measured. You can also see the Grade 3 *We Believe* Assessment Book for:

• standard assessment for each chapter

• alternative assessment for each chapter

• standard assessment for each unit

• alternative assessment for each unit

• a semester assessment which covers material presented in Units 1 and 2

• a final assessment which covers material presented in Units 1, 2, 3, and 4.

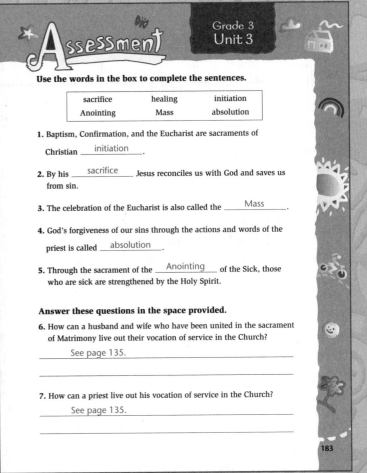

Assessment
Grade 3
Unit 3

Use the words in the box to complete the sentences.

sacrifice	healing	initiation
Anointing	Mass	absolution

1. Baptism, Confirmation, and the Eucharist are sacraments of Christian ___initiation___.

2. By his ___sacrifice___ Jesus reconciles us with God and saves us from sin.

3. The celebration of the Eucharist is also called the ___Mass___.

4. God's forgiveness of our sins through the actions and words of the priest is called ___absolution___.

5. Through the sacrament of the ___Anointing___ of the Sick, those who are sick are strengthened by the Holy Spirit.

Answer these questions in the space provided.

6. How can a husband and wife who have been united in the sacrament of Matrimony live out their vocation of service in the Church?

___See page 135.___

7. How can a priest live out his vocation of service in the Church?

___See page 135.___

183

ALTERNATIVE ASSESSMENT

The pictures show two of the four parts of the Mass.

Label the part shown in each picture and write a short description of it on the lines.

___See pages 148–149.___

Liturgy of the Word

___See page 150.___

Liturgy of the Eucharist

Choose one of these projects.

• Make a poster illustrating the seven sacraments.

• Imagine that your neighbor's good friend has just died. Write a letter of comfort to your neighbor.

184

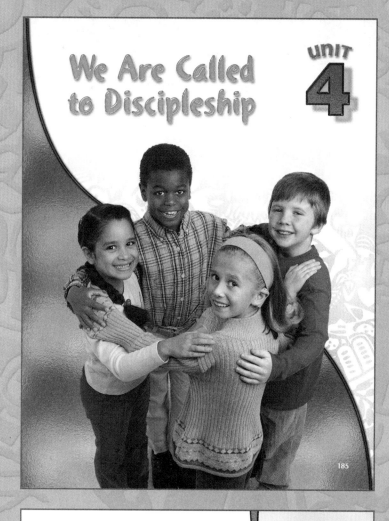

We Are Called to Discipleship

UNIT 4

185

UNIT 4 SHARING FAITH as a Family

Five Ways to Manage Conflict in the Home

Few homes are free from the presence of conflict. It is a part of learning how to relate to one another. Suppressing conflict can often add fuel to the fire. Here are five ways to manage conflict in the home so that it doesn't get out of hand.

1. Teach children to name their anger or hurt without accusing others. The use of "I" messages ("I feel," "I think") is an effective way to do this.

2. Parenthood does not equate with being a referee. Encourage your children to work out disagreements on their own. Agree to mediate only as a last resort.

3. Stick to the point. Arguments get out of hand when past hurts and unresolved issues get thrown into

the fray. Stay focused on solving the current source of conflict.

4. Don't repeat second or third-hand information. Relating what Grandma or Cousin Bob thinks of another person's actions is rarely helpful. Repeating someone else's words can make the situation more complicated.

5. Pick your battles. Let's face it—some things aren't worth the time and energy it takes to fight about them. Let go of insignificant issues, especially ones held onto out of pride or needing to be "right."

What Your Child Will Learn in Unit 4

Unit 4 challenges the children to appreciate and accept that we, as the followers of Jesus Christ, are all called to discipleship. In order to understand how we can live as disciples, the children will appreciate that the Church respects all people and religions. They will also discover that the Church is present throughout the world. This leads to a clear and comprehensive explanation of the Latin (or Roman) and Eastern Rites of the Catholic Church. To have the children continue to grasp the meaning of discipleship, the saints are presented as examples of holiness. No such discussion is complete without presenting Mary, the Mother of God. The children will learn ways they can honor Mary. Unit 4 concludes with an inspiring explanation of the Kingdom of God and how the Church and each one of us as its members can help the Kingdom of God grow every day.

Plan & Preview

▶ You might want to have available pieces or cardboard or stiff paper as well as a glue stick in order to make the trading cards that appear on each *Family Page* throughout the unit.

186

Captain Timothy Stackpole

A Story in Faith
Timothy Stackpole

It was one of those days in New York City that makes postcards. It was a great day to have off from work. Tim Stackpole certainly thought so. Tim had a way of enjoying a day and making others around him do the same. This morning it was his turn to teach Confirmation class at his local parish.

From the Catechism
"Becoming a disciple of Jesus means accepting the invitation to belong to *God's family,* to live in conformity with His way of life."
(*Catechism of the Catholic Church,* 2233)

So it was a surprise, a terrible shock, to hear the heart-stopping news that swept New York that September 11th morning.

Tim was a firefighter. He loved being a firefighter. Tim was one of the best. Six months before, Tim had fought his way back to active service after being badly burned in a major fire. Most people thought it would be impossible for Tim to return to the fire department he loved. "Impossible" was not in the vocabulary of Timothy Stackpole.

Now, Tim was rushing to the burning World Trade Center. Terrorists had aimed two hijacked planes into each of the Twin Towers' gleaming facades. Both were on fire. Both were filled with innocent people. Both needed the help and courage of firefighters like Timothy Stackpole.

Tim died there, giving his life to help others. There are many definitions for hero. Being called to be a disciple of Jesus Christ can take numerous forms. But on that burning day in September, Timothy Stackpole was the living example of both a courageous hero and a faithful disciple.

CLASS CONNECTION

Point out the unit title to the children. Ask them what they think they will be learning more about in this unit. Have a class discussion preparing the children for this unit.

HOME CONNECTION

Sharing Faith as a Family

Sadlier *We Believe* calls on families to become involved in:

• learning the faith
• prayer and worship
• living their faith.

Highlighting of these unit family pages and the opportunities they offer will strengthen the partnership of the Church and the home.

For additional information and activities, encourage families to visit Sadlier's

www.WEBELIEVEweb.com

Overview

In Chapter 19 the children learned that we can pray for healing in Jesus' name, especially in the sacrament of the Anointing of the Sick, and that we have eternal life in God. In this chapter the children will learn how we share in Jesus' mission as we live out his message of peace and justice each day.

Doctrinal Content	For Adult Reading and Reflection *Catechism of the Catholic Church*
The children will learn:	Paragraph
• Jesus brings God's life and love to all people.	543
• Jesus shares his mission with his disciples.	551
• The Church works for justice and peace.	2419
• We live out the good news of Jesus Christ.	2449

Catechist Background

Have you ever experienced injustice?

We live in a world that is in desperate need of good news. We know of illness, natural disasters, and situations of injustice. Jesus lived in such a world, too. He lived in an occupied land where people who were poor and ill walked the roads, begging for help. Jesus brought a message of hope to those on the margins of society.

As he began his ministry, Jesus chose a scriptural passage from the prophet Isaiah and declared himself to be the bearer of the glad tidings that Isaiah promised. Some of the people who heard him were scandalized; the message of a prophet is not often welcomed in his hometown. So, Jesus left Nazareth to begin his ministry.

Jesus empowered his disciples to participate in his mission and to announce the good news of God's salvation. After Jesus was crucified and risen, the disciples, filled with the Holy Spirit, boldly continued the work of Jesus.

We, too, are called to participate in the mission to proclaim good news to those in need. "From the Hebrew prophets to Christ's' description of the Last Judgment, the Scriptures are clear that we are called to help those in need and to oppose unjust and oppressive laws. The practice of charity and the pursuit of justice are linked and complementary duties" (*Sharing Catholic Social Teaching, p. 26*). The work of the Church is the work of justice. This work is accomplished only when we, as individual Christians, work with the Holy Spirit and with those who are Jesus' disciples today to seek to change situations of despair and oppression. Then our world will know the good news.

What is one action I can take to work toward ending an unjust situation?

Lesson Planning Guide

Lesson Steps	Presentation	Materials

① WE GATHER

page 187 ✝ **Prayer** ☀ **Focus on Life**	• Listen to and reflect on Scripture. • Respond in prayer. • Share times of being given an important job to do.	For the prayer space: decorative tablecloth, globe, crucifix

② WE BELIEVE

page 188 *Jesus brings God's life and love to all people.* 📖 *Luke 4:16–19*	• Discuss Jesus' mission to bring the good news to everyone. 🏃 Name ways to care for others.	
page 189 *Jesus shares his mission with his disciples.*	• Discuss the apostles' mission to continue the work of Jesus. 🏃 Name ways your parish shares the good news.	• copies of Reproducible Master 22 (option) • crayons or markers
page 190 *The Church works for justice and peace.*	• Discuss ways the Church works for justice and peace in the world. 🏃 Write slogans for justice and peace.	🎵 a song about peace (option)
pages 190–191 *We live out the good news of Jesus Christ.*	• Discuss actions of true disciples of Jesus. • Read and discuss *As Catholics.*	• construction paper with letters of word *disciple* • works of mission printed on index cards

③ WE RESPOND

page 191	🏃 Draw one way your family can bring love to others.	
page 192 **Review**	• Complete questions 1–5. 🏃 Work on *Assessment Activity.*	• Chapter 22 Test in Assessment Book, pp. 43–44 • Chapter 22 Test in Test Generator • Review & Resource Book, pp. 49–51
page 192 **We Respond in Faith**	• Review *Remember* and *Key Words.* • Complete the *Reflect & Pray* activity. • Read and discuss *Our Catholic Life.* • Discuss Sharing Faith with My Family.	• Family Book, pp. 62–64

For additional ideas, activities, and opportunities: Visit Sadlier's **www.WeBelieve.web.com**

187B

Name _____

Paste a photo or draw a picture of yourself next to Jesus.
Color the picture and complete the sentence. Display it
at home to help you remember that you are a disciple of
Jesus with a very important mission.

I, _____, am a disciple of Jesus.

My mission is to _____.

Connections

To Mission

Remind the children of these words of Jesus: "Whatever you did for one of these least brothers of mine, you did for me" (Matthew 25:40). Explain that Jesus told us to care for those who experience difficulties in life, such as the poor, sick, and lonely. When we do this, we also express our love for Jesus. (Some suggestions of what they can do: talk about their religion class with other children, encourage their families to volunteer at a soup kitchen or a thrift shop, visit the sick)

To Vocations

Remind the children that many people devote their lives to the mission of Jesus by serving as priests, brothers, and sisters. Emphasize that missionaries also include single or married people who serve Jesus and participate in mission work. Display mission magazines or posters that show how missionaries feed the hungry, provide medical care for the sick, teach the children, and preach God's word. Ask the children to ask Jesus to call more people to this necessary work.

FAITH and MEDIA

▶ As the children discuss the many ways we have today to share the good news of Jesus (*We Believe* activity), you might remind the class that the Church actively encourages us to use media to continue the work of Jesus in the world.

Meeting Individual Needs

Children with Linguistic Needs

If children in your class have difficulty with stuttering or mispronunciation, help them by fostering an environment of acceptance. Encourage them to speak in class. Gently repeat their words only if needed for clarity. Emphasize that you and your children are interested in what everyone in the class has to say. Require all children to treat each other with respect. Point out that Jesus always reached out to anyone who had difficulties. He expects us to do likewise.

ADDITIONAL RESOURCES

Book   *Following Jesus,* Lawrence G. Lovasik, Catholic Book Publishing, 1990. This book shows children that following Jesus means helping those in need.

Video   *The Acts of the Apostles,* CCC of America, 1998. This animated video shows how Jesus asked his followers to preach the good news throughout the land. (30 min.)

To find more ideas for books, videos, and other learning material, visit Sadlier's

www.WeBelieveweb.com

Focus on Life

Chapter Story

It was late Saturday morning. "Good morning, Sleepyhead!" Mom said with a smile as Tommy came into the kitchen. "I thought I'd let you sleep late today. You looked so tired after your soccer game yesterday."

"Yeah, I was pretty tired," Tommy agreed as he filled a cereal bowl and made room for himself at the cluttered kitchen table. "Mom, what are you doing with all this stuff?"

The table was filled with advertising circulars and small pieces of paper. His mom had been clipping coupons and making lists since early morning.

"We're having a barbecue pot-luck on Sunday," she replied. "I'm getting ready to go shopping. Would you like to come with me?"

"Sure, Mom," Tommy answered. "Who's coming on Sunday?"

"Just the neighbors," she answered. "It will be fun to sit, talk, and share some good food together. Each family is bringing a favorite dish, and we're providing the hamburgers and hot dogs."

"Are we inviting Juan and his family?"

"Who is Juan?" his mom asked.

"He's in my class at school. He just moved here from Mexico. He lives the next street over."

"So we have new neighbors! Let's stop and invite them on the way to the store. We can ask Juan's mother to bring her family's favorite dish. This will be a good way to welcome Juan's family to the neighborhood!"

▶ *How are Tommy and his mother planning to share with Juan and his family? What is your family's favorite dish? When do you share it?*

We Continue the Work of Jesus

WE GATHER

✝ **Leader:** Imagine that you are with the apostles. Jesus has just been crucified. You are praying together in a room.
(Pause)

All of a sudden, Jesus is standing in the room with you. He says,

Reader 1: "Peace be with you."
(John 20:19)

Leader: Think about the way you feel seeing Jesus again.
(Pause)

Now Jesus looks at you and says,

Reader 2: "As the Father has sent me, so I send you." (John 20:21)

Leader: What do you think Jesus means? Where is he sending you?
(Pause)

Let us pray together:

All: Jesus, we are listening to the message you have for each of us. You are sending us out to share the good news that you have saved us. Help us as we go out to share your love with others. Amen.

 Tell about a time when you were given something important to do. How did doing this help you, your family, or your friends?

187

PREPARING TO PRAY

The children will imagine that they are praying with the apostles who encountered the risen Jesus. They will respond in prayer.

• Tell the children you will be prayer leader.

• Choose two volunteers to be the readers. Provide time for the readers to prepare.

The Prayer Space
• Cover the prayer table.

• Place a globe and a crucifix on the prayer table.

📖 **This Week's Liturgy**
Visit **www.webelieveweb.com** for this week's liturgical readings and other seasonal material.

Lesson Plan

WE GATHER ____ minutes

✝ Pray

• Lead the prayer by praying the Sign of the Cross and reading the introductory paragraph.

• Have the readers proclaim the Scripture.

• Observe pauses where indicated. Give the children time to think about the questions after the second reading. Then pray the final prayer together.

☀ Focus on Life

• Discuss doing things that are important. This lesson is about the most important thing we do—continue the work of Jesus.

• Read the *Chapter Story* on page 187E. Ask: *What is important above welcoming others and sharing with them?*

Home Connection Update

Ask the children to discuss their experiences of sharing the family page from Chapter 19. Ask: *How did your family remember someone special who has died?*

Catechist Goal

• To explain Jesus' work and the ways the Church continues his work

Our Faith Response

• To name ways that we can carry on Jesus' work and share his good news

Lesson Materials

• copies of Reproducible Master 22, crayons or markers

• construction paper, markers

• index cards

• a song about peace (option)

Teaching Tip

Classroom Management

Build community and respect by encouraging children to work co-operatively in ways that bring out their best qualities. Vary children's work groups to help them to know different classmates. Emphasize that Jesus respected everyone and befriended those who felt left out.

WE BELIEVE

Jesus brings God's life and love to all people.

Jesus, the Son of God, had very important work to do. His mission was to bring God's life and love to all people.

📖 Luke 4:16–19

Jesus began his work among the people after he was baptized by his cousin John. In the synagogue in Nazareth, Jesus read these words from the prophet Isaiah.

"The Spirit of the Lord is upon me,
   because he has anointed me
      to bring glad tidings to the poor.
He has sent me to proclaim liberty to captives
   and recovery of the sight to the blind,
      to let the oppressed go free,
and to proclaim a year acceptable to
   the Lord." (Luke 4:16–19)

Jesus then went to many towns and villages telling people that God cared for and loved them. Jesus showed those who were poor or lonely that they were important. He healed people who were sick. He stood up for those who were treated unjustly. Jesus cared for the people's needs and taught his disciples to do the same.

Jesus offered others the peace and freedom that come from God's love and forgiveness. He shared God's love with them, and they believed.

✗ Jesus asks his disciples to care for the needs of others. Name one way you can do this.

188

Lesson Plan

WE BELIEVE   ___ minutes

Read aloud the *We Believe* statement and the first *We Believe* paragraph.

📖 **Have** volunteers read aloud the passage from Saint Luke. Emphasize the following points:

• As God's Anointed One, Jesus came to teach people to trust and hope in God.

• Jesus shared the good news with everyone, especially the poor and needy. Some people did not believe in Jesus' message and mission.

• Jesus spoke and acted on behalf of freedom and justice.

✗ **Have** children name ways to care for others.

Ask a volunteer to read aloud the *We Believe* statement on page 189. Have several volunteers read aloud the *We Believe* paragraphs. Ask: *What mission did Jesus give his apostles and disciples?* (to spread the good news to all nations) *In what way did the Holy Spirit help the apostles and disciples?* (The Holy Spirit strengthened and guided them) *Where did the apostles and disciples share the good news?* (in other lands and at home) *For what did Jesus work?* (for justice and peace) *What are we called by our Baptism to do?* (to learn Jesus' teachings and do his work)

Jesus shares his mission with his disciples.

Jesus gave his apostles a mission. Jesus asked the apostles to go to all nations and teach people about him. The apostles were to baptize all those who believed in him.

The Holy Spirit strengthened and guided the apostles. The apostles led the other disciples in doing the work of Jesus. This is the good news they shared:

• God made all people in his image.

• God loves and cares for everyone.

• God so loved the world that he sent his only Son who showed us how to live and saved us from sin.

• Jesus taught us to love God above all else and to love our neighbors as ourselves.

• Jesus worked for justice and peace and he asks all of us to do the same.

Through Baptism each of us is called to learn from Jesus' teachings and to share the good news of Jesus.

In groups name some ways your parish shares the good news of Jesus. Write them here.

_____

_____

_____

_____

189

ACTIVITY BANK

Faith and Media
Spreading the Good News

Activity Materials: optional costumes and videotaping equipment

Encourage the children to work together in small groups to produce skits about the mission of Jesus. Invite children to portray scenes of Jesus caring for the poor and lonely, healing the sick, and protecting the weak. Share a list of biblical stories that illustrate Jesus' mission such as Matthew 4:23, Mark 8:22–26, Luke 7:11–17, and John 1:5–15. If possible, videotape the skits. Show the video to the class and ask volunteers to summarize what their classmates have shared about the mission of Jesus. Encourage the children to reflect on why carrying out Jesus' mission is an important part of being Catholic.

Complete the activity about sharing the good news.

Distribute the copies of Reproducible Master 22. Read aloud the directions. Encourage the children to consider how they can use their talents to serve God's people. Help as needed to determine each one's mission. Remind them that Jesus is always with them to help them.

Quick Check

✔ *What did Jesus ask the apostles to do?* (to go to all nations and teach people about him)

✔ *What is Jesus' good news?* (God loves everyone, and he sent his only Son, Jesus, to show us how to live.)

189

The Church works for justice and peace.

Jesus taught that all people are created and loved by God. We are all made in God's image. So all people deserve to be treated fairly and with respect. Making sure this happens is one way the Church works for justice and peace in the world.

The pope and bishops teach us about the need to protect human life. In many ways they remind us to respect the rights of all people.

Our parishes serve those in need and work together to build better communities. In our families, schools, and neighborhoods, we live out Jesus' command to love others as he loves us.

The whole Church works for justice. We help to protect children, to care for the poor, and to welcome people who are new to our country.

ⓧ With a partner come up with a slogan to remind your class about the need for justice and peace.

We live out the good news of Jesus Christ.

As disciples of Jesus we are called to live out the good news and to work for peace and justice as Jesus did. To show we are disciples we can:

- love and obey our parents and those who care for us
- be a friend to others, especially those who feel lonely and left out
- help those who are treated unfairly

190

Teaching Note

Graphic Organizer

Use the board or poster board to make a flowchart to help children understand their roles in Jesus' mission. Title the flowchart *The Mission of Jesus*. Write the name of Jesus and draw a downward arrow pointing to the words *Disciples Live the Good News*. Then draw three arrows and list three ways that children can live out the mission of Jesus.

As Catholics...

Missionaries

Show pictures from Catholic magazine of priests, deacons, sisters, brothers, and lay people who share their faith and work to help others in the missions. Ask the children why missionaries are so important in the lives of those in need. If possible, invite someone who has missionary experience to speak to your children. Encourage the children to pray for the people who work as Jesus' missionaries.

Lesson Plan

WE BELIEVE (continued)

Have a volunteer read aloud the *We Believe* statement on page 190. Have the children, with partners, read and highlight the *We Believe* paragraphs. Emphasize the following points:

• The Church works to ensure that everyone in the world is treated fairly.

• The pope and bishops help us to respect the rights of all people.

• As followers of Jesus, it is our mission to work for justice and peace and live out his commandment to love one another.

ⓧ **Assign** partners and ask them to write slogans about peace and justice. Ask the children to share their slogans.

Read the *We Believe* statement on page 191. Have volunteers read the *We Believe* section. Ask: *What do true disciples do?* (They try to act as Jesus acted.) *How do we show that we are disciples?* (Answers will vary, but have the children highlight the bulleted phrases in their texts.)

Ask the children to work in pairs. Give each pair a piece of construction paper with one of the letters of the word *disciple* written on it. Have the children find words to describe a disciple, beginning with the letter they have been given. For example, suggest *daring* and *devoted* for D, and so on. Write an acrostic on the board, using the words suggested by volunteers. [option]

- treat everyone fairly and with respect
- learn about and care for people who need our help in this country and in the world.

As disciples of Jesus we do not work alone. Together with other Church members, we can visit those who are sick or elderly. We can volunteer in soup kitchens or homeless shelters. We can help those who have disabilities. We can help those from other countries to find homes and jobs and to learn the language. We can write to the leaders of our state and country. We can ask our leaders for laws that protect children and those in need.

WE RESPOND

Draw one way your family can bring Jesus' love to others.

As Catholics...

Both at home and in other countries, missionaries help to do the work of Jesus. They may be ordained priests and deacons, religious sisters and brothers, and single or married laypeople. Some missionaries serve as teachers, nurses, doctors, or social workers.

Some people spend their whole lives being missionaries. Others spend a month, a summer, or even a year or two doing missionary work.

Find out about some missionaries in your neighborhood.

191

ACTIVITY BANK

Multicultural Connection
Respect Around the World
Activity Materials: books and Web sites about other countries

Help the children understand that showing respect is important to people all around the world. Help them to research how other people show respect for one another. Invite staff members or children' parents from different ethnic backgrounds to tell your class about customs that show respect in their native countries.

Multiple Intelligences
Musical
Activity Materials: rhythm instruments (optional), tape recorder and cassette (optional)

Invite children to form small groups to make up songs about peace, justice, and respect. Invite the children to explain how the message of their songs relates to the mission of Jesus.

WE RESPOND   ___ minutes

Complete the *We Respond* activity about sharing Jesus' love as a family.

Have the following mission works printed on index cards: being a friend to a lonely person; welcoming a new neighbor from another country; showing respect and care to someone with a disability. Invite volunteers to choose a card and mime whatever work they have chosen. The children guess what is being enacted. Congratulate those who volunteer to mime before the group!

You may want to ask the children to share a sign of peace with one another and to sing a song about peace. Suggestions: "Let There Be Peace on Earth," "Peace Is Flowing Like a River," "The Prayer of St. Francis" (*We Believe* Songbook, page 162)

CHAPTER TEST

Chapter 22 Test is provided in the Grade 3 Assessment Book.

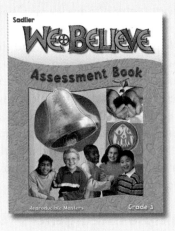

Circle T if the sentence is true. Circle F if the sentence is false.

1. We show we are disciples only when we participate in Mass.

   T   (F)

2. Jesus asks his disciples to continue his work.

   (T)   F

3. Only the pope and bishops share the good news and work for justice.

   T   (F)

4. Only some people deserve to be treated fairly and with respect.

   T   (F)

Answer the questions.

5. What was Jesus' mission? How did he carry it out?

   See page 188.

   _____

   _____

 ASSESSMENT Prepare a talk for children your age. Tell how you can work with others for justice and peace.

Lesson Plan

 Review ____ minutes

Chapter Review Tell the children that they will review what they have learned about the mission of Jesus. Have them answer the first four questions. If a statement is false, have them explain why it is incorrect. Ask for verbal responses to question 5. Then have the children complete question 5 in their texts. Share responses.

Assessment Activity Read aloud the directions. Encourage the children to brainstorm ways that they can work for peace and justice. Then invite them to prepare a talk that explains one way to do this. Allow them to work in pairs. Provide time for them to present their talks to the class. Save their written work.

 **We Respond in Faith** ____ minutes

Reflect & Pray Read aloud the opening line to the reflective activity. Discuss ways that the children can serve others and participate in the mission of Jesus. Then ask them to complete the sentence. Provide time for them to complete the prayer and share it.

Remember Review the *We Believe* statements. Remind the children that they have been given a very important task: to spread the good news of Jesus and continue his work. Gather in the prayer space. Encourage them to live out Jesus' message of peace and justice each day. Ask them to recall what they have learned about the mission of Jesus this week and how they intend to put what they have learned into practice.

Reflect & Pray

The way I can serve others is

_____

_____

Jesus, you gave your disciples a mission. Help me to

_____

_____

Remember

- Jesus brings God's life and love to all people.
- Jesus shares his mission with his disciples.
- The Church works for justice and peace.
- We live out the good news of Jesus Christ.

OUR CATHOLIC LIFE

Supporting Missionary Work

The Catholic Church Extension Society helps missionary work in the United States. It began in 1905. It receives many donations. The money that it donates goes to people and places that need it the most. In a recent year, seventy-four dioceses in thirty-four states received donations from the Catholic Church Extension Society.

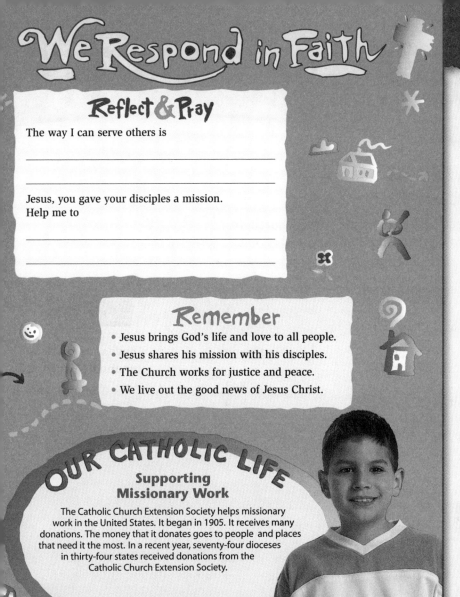

Our Catholic Life Read aloud the paragraph. Help children recognize that they can support missionary work in our own country. Stress that they can save and collect funds to help people right here in the United States. Consider sponsoring a collection for the Catholic Church Extension Society. Remind children to pray that more people will follow Jesus in mission work in the United States and around the world.

HOME CONNECTION

Sharing Faith with My Family

Make sure to send home the family page (text page 194).

Encourage the children to design, with their family's help, a trading card, "Helping the Kingdom Grow." Each week the family will focus on a different family member.

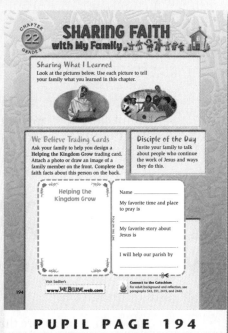

PUPIL PAGE 194

For additional information and activities, encourage families to visit Sadlier's

www.WeBelieveweb.com

Plan Ahead for Chapter 23

Prayer Space: a cross and a fish-symbol, pictures of people who practice different religions, small globe or map of the world

Materials: copies of Reproducible Master 23, colored pencils or crayons, markers, two strips of paper per child

Overview

In Chapter 22 the children learned about the mission of the Church. In this chapter the children will learn that the Church respects all people in the world.

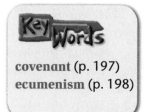

Key Words

covenant (p. 197)
ecumenism (p. 198)

Catechist Background

Who do I know that professes a religious belief that is different from my own?

In our world today, more than ever before, we live and work with people who hold beliefs that are different from our own. This pluralism presents wonderful opportunities and challenges. We honor and respect the beliefs of others. Many non-Christians witness to a deep religious faith and share with us many beliefs about God.

We share a particular closeness with the Jews, who have been called our elder brothers and sisters in faith. Jesus and Mary were faithful Jews, as were most of the early followers of Christ. Our faith has its foundations in the covenant that God made with the Jews. St. Paul reminds us that God's covenant is irrevocable. (See Romans 11:29.)

The people of Islam also share with us a belief in the One God, whom they call *Allah*. Following the teachings of the Prophet Muhammad, they hold Jesus and Mary in high regard and respect the prophets of the Old Testament. "The Church considers all goodness and truth found in these religions as 'a preparation for the Gospel and given by him who enlightens all men that they may at length have life'" (*Lumen gentium* 16; CCC 843). We honor and respect the people of all religious traditions because we share with them a commitment to celebrate the sacred aspects of our lives.

One of the sad facts of our time is that there are divisions, even among Christians. "The desire to recover the unity of all Christians is a gift of Christ and a call of the Holy Spirit" (CCC 820; see *Unitatis redintegratio* 1). We respect those of other Christian traditions and look for opportunities to work together. We pray for the day when we will live the unity that Jesus desires for us.

How can I promote greater religious understanding among people in my life?

Lesson Planning Guide

Lesson Steps	Presentation	Materials

① WE GATHER

Lesson Steps	Presentation	Materials
page 195 **Prayer** **Focus on Life**	• Pray general intercessions from the Good Friday liturgy. • Discuss interesting people the children have met or places they have visited.	For the prayer space: a cross and a fish-symbol; pictures of people who practice different religions; small globe or map of the world.

② WE BELIEVE

Lesson Steps	Presentation	Materials
page 196 *People around the world have different beliefs about God.*	• Present the brief summaries of the beliefs of Jews, Muslims, and Native Americans. Use the pictures and talk about respect for others.	
page 197 *The Jewish faith is important to Christians.*	• Read about and discuss the Jewish faith. Write a prayer in the scroll.	• copies of Reproducible Master 23, guide page 195C • colored pencils or crayons
page 198 *Christ calls his followers to be united.*	• Discuss beliefs shared by all Christians. • Read and discuss *As Catholics.* List ways to show we are Christians.	
pages 198–199 *The Church works for Christian unity.*	• Discuss ways to know and live our faith. • Discuss ways to work for Christian unity.	

③ WE RESPOND

Lesson Steps	Presentation	Materials
page 199	Draw or write something to encourage unity.	• crayons, markers, or colored pencils
page 200 **Review**	• Complete questions 1–5. Work on *Assessment Activity.*	• two strips of paper per child • Chapter 23 Test in Assessment Book, pp. 45–46 • Chapter 23 Test in Test Generator • Review & Resource Book, pp. 52–54
page 201 **We Respond in Faith**	• Review *Remember* and *Key Words.* • Complete the *Reflect & Pray* activity. • Read and discuss *Our Catholic Life.* • Discuss **Sharing Faith with My Family**.	• Family Book, pp. 65–67

For additional ideas, activities, and opportunities: Visit Sadlier's **www.WeBelieveweb.com**

Name _____

Christians and Jews sometimes pray special prayers called blessings. This blessing is taken from words in the Old Testament (Numbers 6:24–26). We often pray it at the end of Mass. Decorate the border and then share this blessing prayer with your family and friends. (The **R.** means "Response.")

May the Lord bless you and keep you.

R. Amen.

May his face shine upon you,
and be gracious to you.

R. Amen.

May he look upon you with kindness,
and give you his peace.

R. Amen.

May almighty God bless you,
the Father, and the Son, ✝
and the Holy Spirit.

R. Amen.

Connections

To Community

We are to respect those who do not share our faith in Jesus. Point out that people around the world experience prejudice and cruelty from others who disagree with their religious beliefs. Tell the children that even though we are called to tell others about Jesus, we must do so with great love and humility. Encourage the children to think of ways that they can show respect and care for all people, regardless of their religion, age, economic status, or nationality.

To Liturgy

The *We Gather* for this chapter takes two prayers from the liturgy of Good Friday. In that liturgy, we pray: *for the unity of Christians, for the Jewish people, for those who do not believe in Christ, for those who do not believe in God,* and *for those in special need.* (The Roman Missal) You might want to plan a five-day "week of prayer." Each day plan to pray for one of the intentions above. Make up your own prayers or use the ones given in the Sacramentary.

FAITH and MEDIA

▶ In connection with the mosaic art frame on page 199, you might remind the class that because mosaics, like murals and stained-glass windows, were often designed to help people understand their faith, they are a form of media. You might go online or bring in art books to show the class some early Christian and medieval mosaics such as those in the Basilica of Santa Maria Maggiore in Rome, in the Mausoleum of Galla Placidia and the Basilica of San Vitale in the Italian city of Ravenna, and in the cathedrals of Monreale and Cefalù and the Palatine Chapel in Palermo, in Sicily. To see examples of modern mosaics, you might also visit the Web site of the National Shrine of the Immaculate Conception in Washington, DC.

Meeting Individual Needs

Children with Developmental Needs

Be sure to provide opportunities for children with developmental needs to participate in role-playing exercises. Help their partners in the exercises to review the content of whatever story is being role-played so that the children with developmental delays understand the story's message and are able to demonstrate it to the class. Be sure to establish an environment of encouragement and acceptance within your class.

ADDITIONAL RESOURCES

Book   *10 More Good Reasons to Be a Catholic,* Jim Auer, Liguori Publications, 1999. This book shows children the special meaning of being a Catholic.

Video   *How Do You Spell God?,* Ralph Harmon, HBO Home Video, 1996. This tape provides a unique perspective on questions every child asks about God, faith, and their place in the world (32 minutes).

To find more ideas for books, videos, and other learning material, visit Sadlier's

www.WeBelieveweb.com

Focus on Life

Chapter Story

This is a traditional Jewish folktale. Listen carefully. Does it remind you of a story Jesus told?

Once a very generous father gave his son a great deal of money. After getting it, the son ran away from home. The father was left brokenhearted.

Many years passed, and the runaway son became extremely rich. Then he married and had a son. He was very strict with the boy. One wintry evening an old beggar knocked at the rich man's door. The young boy answered. The freezing beggar asked for a blanket. Quickly, the boy ran upstairs to get a blanket and a pair of scissors. By the time he returned, his angry father was standing in the doorway. "Where are you going with that blanket and those scissors?" he roared. For a brief moment the young boy looked at his father and then at the old beggar. "Father, I was going to cut the blanket in two. I will give one half to the beggar. The other half I was going to save for you when you are old."

▶ *What do you think the father said to his son? What does the story remind us to do?*

The Church Respects All People

WE GATHER

✝ **Leader:** Let us sit quietly.
Thank God for his many blessings.
Now let us offer our prayers to him.

Reader: Let us pray
for all our brothers and sisters
who share our faith in Jesus Christ,
that God may gather and keep together
in one Church
all those who seek the truth
with sincerity.
We pray to the Lord.

All: Lord hear our prayer.

Reader: Let us pray
for the Jewish people,
the first to hear the word of God,
that they may continue to grow
in the love of his name
and in faithfulness to his covenant.
We pray to the Lord.

All: Lord hear our prayer.

Leader: Almighty and eternal God,
enable those who do not
acknowledge Christ
to find the truth as they walk before you
in sincerity of heart.
We ask this through Christ our Lord.

All: Amen.

 What interesting things have you learned about people and places in other countries? Talk about these things together.

195

PREPARING TO PRAY

The children will pray intercessory prayers for unity and respect for all people from the Good Friday liturgy.

• Tell the children you will be prayer leader.

• Choose two children to be the readers. Give them a few moments to review their parts.

• Point out the photo on this page. The Jewish boy wears a *yarmulke*. The Native American boy wears a necklace of beads. The Muslim girl wears a *hijab* or headscarf.

The Prayer Space

• Provide a cross and a fish-symbol to represent the Christian faith.

• Display pictures of people who practice different religions.

• Place a small globe or map of the world on the prayer table.

📖 **This Week's Liturgy**
Visit **www.webelieveweb.com** for this week's liturgical readings and other seasonal material.

Lesson Plan

WE GATHER   ___ minutes

✝ Pray

• Gather in the prayer space. Point out the cross and the fish as signs of Jesus and of our faith.

• Explain that we will pray the same prayers Catholics pray during the Good Friday liturgy.

• Lead by praying the Sign of the Cross and the opening paragraph.

• Have the readers pray the intercessions.

• Remind the children that all Christians are our brothers and sisters in faith, and that we have a special connection to the Jewish people.

☀ Focus on Life

• Have the children respond to the question about differences. In this lesson they will learn about faiths that are practiced around the world.

• Read the *Chapter Story* on page 195E. Explain that every culture and religion has its own stories and wise sayings.

Home Connection Update

Have the children share experiences of using the Chapter 22 family page. *What did the children and their families learn about the works of people who follow Jesus?*

Catechist Goal

• To highlight the Church's respect for all people and to emphasize our call to Christian unity.

Our Faith Response

• To name ways in which we can show respect for people of different faiths and to identify ways to work for Christian unity

 covenant   ecumenism

Lesson Materials

• Reproducible Master 23

• colored pencils or crayons, markers

• two strips of paper per child

Teaching Tip

Classroom Visitors

A good way to interest third graders in different religions or churches is to invite visitors representing these groups to the classroom. Ask the visitors to prepare a very short talk on what they believe or how they pray. If possible, photograph each visitor with the children. Have the class write a thank-you note to the guest.

WE BELIEVE
People around the world have different beliefs about God.

Christians are people of faith who believe in and follow Jesus Christ. Not everyone in the world believes in Jesus as Christians do. This does not mean that they are not people of faith. They believe in God and worship God in different ways. They live their faith at home, in school, and in their communities.

Jews are people of faith who keep God's law and follow the Ten Commandments. They often call God Yahweh and Lord. They celebrate many feasts and holidays.

Christians have a special connection to the Jewish people. Many Christian beliefs and practices come from the Jewish faith.

Muslims are people of faith who follow the teachings of Muhammad. They call God Allah. They pray and worship God in unique ways. Muslims have some of the same beliefs as Jews and Christians.

Many native tribes worship God by honoring and respecting his creation. They call God the Great Spirit.

There are many other people of faith. They, too, follow a set of beliefs and show their faith in different ways.

Look at the pictures on these pages. Are any of these faiths practiced in your town or city? Talk about ways you can show respect for people of all faith.

Native American boy at powwow

Buddist woman offering incense

Hindu festival

196

Lesson Plan

WE BELIEVE   ___ minutes

Have a volunteer read aloud the *We Believe* statement and paragraphs. Stress that people worship God in different ways. Point out that Christians and Jews share a heritage of faith. Tell the children that Muslims are devoted to their own holy book, the Koran, and the teaching of the prophet Muhammad.

Look at the on-page photos, discuss the question and ways to show respect.

Read aloud the *We Believe* statement on page 197. Have the children work with partners and read and highlight the *We Believe* text. Emphasize the following points:

• God made a covenant with Moses and his people. God said that he would be their God and protect them if they would follow his laws and worship him as the one true God.

• The people did not always keep the covenant. God continued to love his people and sent prophets to remind them of their promise. John the Baptist was a prophet who prepared the people for the coming of the Messiah.

Write prayers for the Jewish people.

The Jewish faith is important to Christians.

Reading the Old Testament can help us to understand Jewish history and beliefs. This is important because they are part of our history, too.

We learn from the Old Testament about God's covenant with Moses. A **covenant** is an agreement between God and his people.

In this covenant with Moses and the people, God promised to be their God. He would give his people a land all their own. The people promised to be God's people and to believe in him. They promised to worship only the one true God. They agreed to live by God's law and to follow the Ten Commandments.

God continued to love his people. He spoke to them through the prophets. The prophets reminded the people of their promises to God.

John the Baptist was one of these prophets. He prepared the people for the coming of the Messiah. The Messiah would be sent by God to bring mercy, peace, and justice.

Some Jews believed that Jesus was this Messiah. They followed him and became his disciples. After Jesus' death and Resurrection, the number of Jesus' disciples grew. Those who followed Jesus and his teachings became known as Christians.

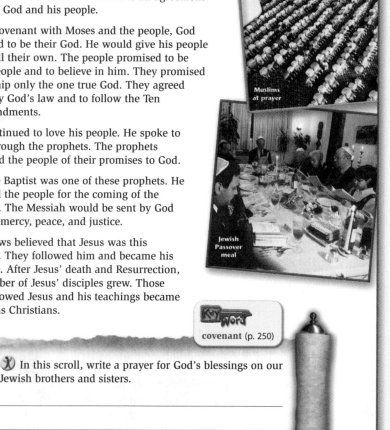

Muslims at prayer

Jewish Passover meal

Key Word

covenant (p. 250)

In this scroll, write a prayer for God's blessings on our Jewish brothers and sisters.

_____

_____

_____

197

ACTIVITY BANK

Curriculum Connection

Drama

Activity Materials: an oblong piece of fake fur or some other rough, brown fabric to drape over a child's clothing as a "costume"; rubber or plastic insects.

John the Baptist was chosen by God to prepare the people for the coming of Jesus Christ. John lived in the desert, dressed in camel skins, and ate locusts and wild honey. He lived simply and dedicated his life to God. Because he was a holy person and a prophet, people listened to his message. Have children take turns acting out John the Baptist as he proclaims his message. Ask volunteers to be members of the crowds around him. Encourage the children portraying crowd members either to agree with John about the Messiah or to turn away and refuse to believe. (The teachings of John the Baptist can be found in Luke 3: 1–20.)

Distribute copies of Reproducible Master 23. Ask the children to plan a time to pray this blessing with their families.

Quick Check

✔ *Why is the Jewish faith important to Christians?* (The Jews followed God's commandments and trusted in God's promise to send a Messiah)

✔ *How should we treat people of different faiths?* (with respect and love)

Teaching Note

Exploring the Bible

All Christians believe that the Holy Spirit inspires the Bible. Help your third graders to become familiar with the Bible. Encourage the children to read stories about Jesus in the New Testament, and to find prayers in the Old Testament such as Psalm 23. Remind the children that reading the Bible is an activity all Christians share.

As Catholics...

Christian Unity

Have a volunteer read aloud the text. From the parish bulletin, share a list of activities that promote ecumenism within the community. Help the children to understand that it takes involvement from members of each faith community for unity to occur. Have your children encourage their families to take part in these activities.

Christ calls his followers to be united.

At the Last Supper, Jesus prayed that his followers would always be one community. He prayed, "I pray not only for them, but also for those who will believe in me through their word, so that they may all be one . . ." (John 17:20–21)

Christians believe in and follow Jesus. Catholics are Christians. As Catholics we follow the teachings and example of Jesus Christ. We belong to the Catholic Church.

There are Orthodox Christians and Episcopal Christians. Other Christians may be Lutheran, Methodist, Presbyterian, and Baptist.

All Christians have some important things in common. All Christians are baptized and share some very important beliefs.

• God is Father, Son, and Holy Spirit.

• Jesus is both divine and human.

• Jesus died for our sins and rose again from the dead.

• The Bible was inspired by the Holy Spirit.

Today the Catholic Church is working with other Christians to bring together all baptized people. This work toward Christian unity is called **ecumenism**.

In groups list some things we can do to show that we are Christians. Share your ideas.

The Church works for Christian unity.

How can each one of us work for Christian unity? We first need to know our faith and be the best Catholics we can be. Other Christians can learn about the Catholic Church by who we are and what we do.

As Catholics...

Each year in January the Church celebrates a week of prayer for Christian Unity. We pray that all Christians may be one. Prayer services and discussion groups are held. Together Christians try to grow in love and understanding. As Catholics every week at Mass we pray that all Christians will be one.

Find out how your parish works with other Christian churches in your neighborhood.

ecumenism (p. 251)

198

Lesson Plan

WE BELIEVE (continued)

Read aloud the *We Believe* statement on page 198 and the *We Believe* paragraphs. Ask: *What did Jesus pray for at the Last Supper?* (that his followers would all be one.) *Who are Christians?* (people who believe in and follow Jesus) *Are Catholics Christians?* (Yes.) *Name some important beliefs all Christians have in common.* (God is Father, Son, and Holy Spirit; Jesus is both divine and human; Jesus died and rose again; the Bible is the inspired word of God.) *What is ecumenism?* (Ecumenism is Christians working toward unity.)

Draw attention to the *Key Word*. Write the phonetic spelling on the board (e-q-me-niz-m). Check that everyone understands the word.

List and share ways to show we are Christians.

Read aloud the *We Believe* statement at the bottom of the page. Read aloud the *We Believe* text. Stress that we show our unity by treating one another with respect. By receiving the sacraments we grow stronger in our faith. Before sharing our faith with others we need to understand our faith. We can help achieve Christian unity by praying for one another.

We try to treat people the way Jesus did. We receive the sacraments. Receiving the sacraments is an important part of being Catholic. The sacraments strengthen our faith. The sacraments help us grow closer to God and to one another.

We also need to know our faith so we can share it with others. We cannot tell other people what it means to be a Catholic if we do not know. We read the Bible and ask God to help us to understand his word. We learn the history of our Church. We also learn what the Church teaches about important topics. This helps us to follow the Church's teachings.

WE RESPOND

What is something you can do to show you are Christian?

✖ Draw or write something that will encourage all Christians to work together for unity.

199

ACTIVITY BANK

Catholic Social Teaching

Solidarity of the Human Family
Activity Materials: list of solidarity projects

The principle of human solidarity lies at the heart of the Church's social teaching. Young people need to be given frequent opportunities to understand and practice this primary demand of Christian living. Present the class with a list of specific solidarity or friendship projects and have them choose what they will do. For example, invite third graders from another Christian school to join you and the children on a visit to a nursing home where they will entertain residents by singing together.

WE RESPOND ___ minutes

Note that the frame on the page is a *mosaic*. It shows closely set stones or tiles that form a design. For centuries, pictures in the form of mosaics have decorated churches. They have been used to help Christians understand their faith.

✖ **Draw** or write ways to encourage Christian unity.

CHAPTER TEST

Chapter 23 Test is provided in the Grade 3 Assessment Book.

Sadlier
WE BELIEVE
Assessment Book

Reproducible Masters   Grade 3

Match the words in Column A to the correct descriptions in Column B.

A	B
1. Muslims	__2__ call God *Yahweh* and *Lord*
2. Jews	__3__ an agreement between God and his people
3. covenant	__4__ believe in and follow the teachings of Jesus Christ
4. Christians	__1__ call God *Allah*

Answer the questions.

5. What is ecumenism? Why is it important?

See pages 198–199.

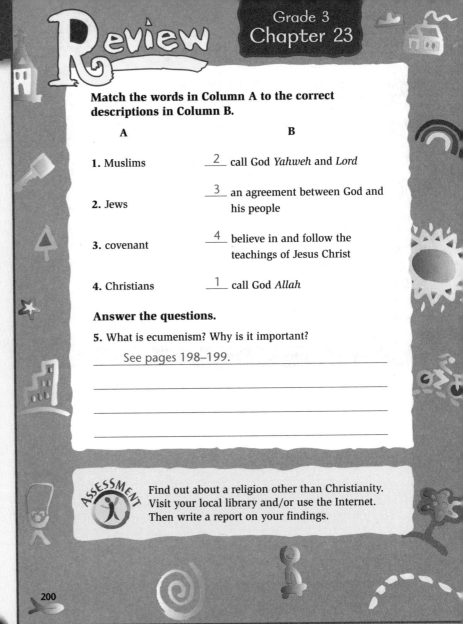

ASSESSMENT

Find out about a religion other than Christianity. Visit your local library and/or use the Internet. Then write a report on your findings.

200

Lesson Plan

Review   ___ minutes

Chapter Review Have the children complete questions 1–4. Discuss responses to the twofold question 5, then have the children write their answers in their texts. Invite them to share answers.

Assessment Activity Have a volunteer read aloud the directions. Allow children time and resources to find the information and assist them in their search. Invite the children to share their findings.

We Respond in Faith   ___ minutes

Reflect & Pray Discuss different ways we can show respect to other people. Brainstorm ideas with which to complete the statement and the prayer. When the children have finished, ask them to pray silently the prayer they wrote to Jesus.

 **Key Words** Write the *Key Words* on the board. Ask the children to write definitions of the words on a slip of paper. Collect the definitions and review them to ensure that they know the meaning of the *Key Words*. If there is any confusion, discuss the words with the class and reinforce their understanding of each word's meaning.

Reflect & Pray

It is not always easy to respect people who believe and worship differently than we do.

I can be more respectful by

_____

_____

Complete this prayer:

Jesus, you showed us how to treat others.

This week, help me to _____

_____

Key Words

covenant (p. 250)
ecumenism (p. 251)

Remember

- People around the world have different beliefs about God.
- The Jewish faith is important to Christians.
- Christ calls his followers to be united.
- The Church works for Christian unity.

Our Catholic Life

Houses of Worship

Most people gather to pray together in houses of worship. Some of these places have special names. Hindus, Buddhists, and Jews gather to worship in buildings called *temples*. Jews also gather for prayer and study in buildings called *synagogues*. The buildings that Muslims worship in are called *mosques*. Christians, including Catholics, have several names for their houses of worship—*church*, *chapel*, and *cathedral* are a few of them. We respect the rights of all people to worship. So we respect their holy places, too.

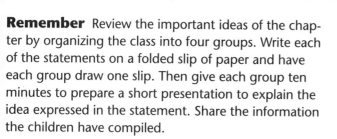

HOME CONNECTION

Sharing Faith with My Family

Make sure to send home the family page (pupil page 202).

Encourage the children to talk with family members about respecting other faiths. Remind them to ask their families' help in making this week's Helping the Kingdom Grow card.

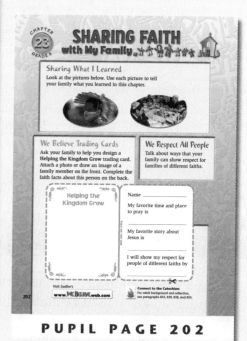

PUPIL PAGE 202

For additional information and activities, encourage families to visit Sadlier's

www.WeBelieve.web.com

Remember Review the important ideas of the chapter by organizing the class into four groups. Write each of the statements on a folded slip of paper and have each group draw one slip. Then give each group ten minutes to prepare a short presentation to explain the idea expressed in the statement. Share the information the children have compiled.

Our Catholic Life Read aloud the text. Have the children discuss the different places where people worship. Ask the children to share any experiences they might have had visiting places of worship, for example, a temple or synagogue, a mosque, a chapel, or a cathedral.

Plan Ahead for Chapter 24

Prayer Space: a small globe or world map, a parish bulletin or Catholic magazine

Materials: markers, crayons, or colored pencils, parish Baptismal Register (if possible), copies of Reproducible Master 24, Grade 3 CD

Chapter 24 The Church Is Worldwide

Overview

In Chapter 23 the children learned that the Church respects all people of every faith and is working toward unity among all Christians. In this chapter, the children will learn that Catholics all around the world share the same faith and celebrate that faith in different ways.

Doctrinal Content	For Adult Reading and Reflection *Catechism of the Catholic Church*
The children will learn:	Paragraph
• The Catholic Church is all over the world.	835
• Catholics share the same faith.	1203
• Catholics celebrate their faith in different ways.	1204
• We are the light of the world.	2105

Rite (p. 205)

Catechist Background

What expressions of faith are part of my family tradition?

One of the gifts of Catholicism is the great diversity of expressions of the one faith we share. From its beginnings, Christianity has been a Church on the move, spreading from the Middle East and Africa to all parts of Europe, Asia, and the Americas. Now, more than ever, the Church is global.

As the Church has spread throughout the world, we have come to express a common faith within a variety of cultures and languages. "Christian life is nourished by various forms of popular piety, rooted in the different cultures" (CCC 1679). These cultural expressions used in the liturgy bring a variety of local traditions that celebrate local saints and holy days in ways that are unique to the culture of the people who celebrate them. We as a Church celebrate unity even in our diversity.

Within the Catholic Church, there are a variety of Rites, or expressions of the Catholic faith. In the United States most Catholics belong to the Roman, or Latin, Rite. However, other expressions of the Catholic faith, the Eastern Churches, include the Byzantine Rite, the Maronite Rite, and others. Together with these, we form a single communion of faith, expressed in the Nicene Creed, the seven sacraments, and union with the bishops and the pope.

What can I do to appreciate the variety of expressions of the Catholic faith?

Lesson Planning Guide

Lesson Steps	Presentation	Materials

WE GATHER

page 203 ✚ **Prayer** ☀ **Focus on Life**	• Listen to Scripture. 🎵 Respond in song. • Discuss what the children know about other countries.	For the prayer space: small globe or world map; parish bulletin or Catholic magazine 🎵 "We Are the Church," Christopher Walker, #19, Grade 3 CD

② WE BELIEVE

pages 204–205 *The Catholic Church is all over the world.*	• Read and discuss the Church as world-wide and its many different customs and traditions. 🏃 Discuss worship with Catholics in another part of the world.	• parish Baptismal Register, if possible
page 205 *Catholics share the same faith.*	• Read and discuss the Latin and Eastern Rites of the Catholic Church. • Read and discuss *As Catholics*. 🏃 Write one way Catholics practice their faith.	
page 206 *Catholics celebrate their faith in different ways.*	• Read and discuss the different ways of celebrating the Church's liturgy. 🏃 Act out celebration of faith in the activity.	
pages 206–207 *We are the light of the world.*	• Read and discuss Catholics as the light of the world.	

③ WE RESPOND

page 207	🏃 Reflect upon the questions and draw in response.	• markers, crayons, or colored pencils • copies of Reproducible Master 24 🎵 "Make Us a Sign" Bernadette Farrell, #20, Grade 3 CD (optional)
page 208 **Review**	• Complete questions 1–5. 🏃 Work on *Assessment Activity*.	• Chapter 24 Test in Assessment Book, pp. 47–48 • Chapter 24 Test in Test Generator • Review & Resource Book, pp. 55–57
page 209 **We Respond in Faith**	• Complete the *Reflect & Pray* activity. • Review *Remember* and *Key Words*. • Read and discuss *Our Catholic Life*. • Discuss Sharing Faith with My Family.	• Family Book, pp. 68–70

For additional ideas, activities, and opportunities: Visit Sadlier's **www.WeBelieve.web.com**

203B

Name _____

God gives each of us talents or gifts that enable us
to do his work and be a good example to others.
Think about your family and friends' talents and
then think about your own. Think of a talent, gift,
or ability you have. Possibly you can run fast, write
well, listen to others, or are friendly and kind.
Complete the gift boxes below.

Others' Talents or Gifts

_____
_____
_____

Ways to Use This Talent
to Do God's Work

_____
_____
_____

My Talents or Gifts

_____
_____
_____

Ways to Use This Talent
to Do God's Work

_____
_____
_____

Connections

To Parish

As you teach this lesson, look for opportunities to help children recognize the things we have in common as Catholics. Though families within the parish may be diverse, we are all Catholics who love and follow Jesus. Point out the various countries of origin represented in the parish, and note how wonderful it is that the Church is made up of such a rainbow of people. Remind the children that, as Catholics, we share the same beliefs, celebrate the seven sacraments, and are united as one Church.

To Stewardship

Throughout the chapter, the message is that we are all members of one Catholic Church and that the Church is worldwide. Emphasize that we are trying to make our world a better place for everyone. Consider inviting a parishioner who is involved with mission projects at the parish. Have this person explain what the parish does to help different missionaries and mission projects around the world. Ask this person to suggest some specific ways that the children could give of their time, talent, or treasure to help parish mission work.

FAITH and MEDIA

▶ After the children have read the *Our Catholic Life* text "One Faith, Many Languages," you might go online to visit the Web site of Vatican Radio. There you will see a list of the languages in which the Mass is broadcast to people around the world. On different days throughout any given month the Mass and other liturgies are broadcast in Italian, in English, in Russian, in Chinese, and in various languages used in the Eastern Rites. The Mass is also broadcast every morning in Latin, the official language of the Church. In addition, Vatican Radio offers newscasts, live broadcasts of papal events, and various other programs in forty different languages via radio, satellite, and the Internet.

Meeting Individual Needs

Children with Auditory Needs

Children with auditory needs can benefit from having the spoken word recorded on tape for them to listen to closely at their own volume and pace. As you teach this week's lesson, consider recording the opening prayer on tape. Provide the child with headphones, a tape player, and time to review the recording.

ADDITIONAL RESOURCES

Books

God Loves Us All, Lawrence G. Lovasick, Catholic Book Publishing, 1990. This book emphasizes God's love for all people of the earth.

Eastern Catholics in the United States of America, United States Catholic Conference of Bishops, 1999. This adult resource gives an overview of Roman and Eastern Churches.

To find more ideas for books, videos, and other learning material, visit Sadlier's

www.WeBelieveweb.com

Focus on Life

Chapter Story

Tony Belmont was a very good singer. He liked to sing when he was by himself. He liked to sing for his family. He liked to sing with the parish during Mass on Sunday.

One day Tony was waiting for soccer practice to begin. He started to sing. Some of his teammates started to laugh at him. Tony stopped singing right away.

After that happened, Tony did not sing at all. His family wondered what was wrong. They never heard Tony sing again, either at home or at church.

Mrs. Durcan, Tony's neighbor, was very sick. Tony's dad was going to visit her. She had asked Mr. Belmont to bring Tony. She thought hearing Tony sing would help her feel better.

At first, Tony told his dad that he didn't want to go. He said, "And Mrs. Durcan can just forget about asking me to sing." He told his dad what had happened at soccer practice.

Tony's dad said, "Tony, they should not have laughed at you like that. Most people like to hear you sing. It cheers them up. Now, put on your jacket and let's go see Mrs. Durcan."

That afternoon Tony sang for Mrs. Durcan. His dad sang some songs with him and Mrs. Durcan sang, too. Tony helped his neighbor feel better that day. And Tony felt better, too!

On the way home, Tony's dad said, "You know, God gives us our gifts and talents to share with others. I hope you always appreciate and share your gifts. And I know you will never laugh at anyone else when they share theirs."

▶ *How did people react to Tony's talent for singing?*

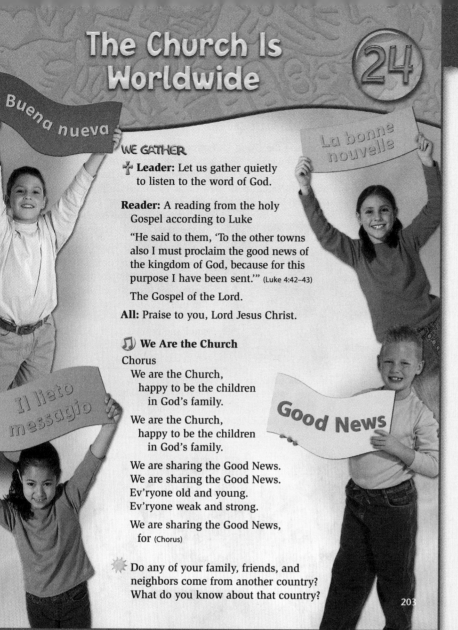

The Church Is Worldwide

24

Buena nueva

La bonne nouvelle

Il lieto messaggio

Good News

WE GATHER

✝ **Leader:** Let us gather quietly to listen to the word of God.

Reader: A reading from the holy Gospel according to Luke

"He said to them, 'To the other towns also I must proclaim the good news of the kingdom of God, because for this purpose I have been sent.'" (Luke 4:42–43)

The Gospel of the Lord.

All: Praise to you, Lord Jesus Christ.

♪ We Are the Church

Chorus
We are the Church,
  happy to be the children
  in God's family.

We are the Church,
  happy to be the children
  in God's family.

We are sharing the Good News.
We are sharing the Good News.
Ev'ryone old and young.
Ev'ryone weak and strong.

We are sharing the Good News,
  for (Chorus)

☀ Do any of your family, friends, and neighbors come from another country? What do you know about that country?

203

PREPARING TO PRAY

The children will listen to Jesus' words about his mission to bring the good news and be light to the world. They will respond in song.

• Invite volunteers to place the items in the prayer space at the appointed time.

• Explain to the children that you will be the prayer leader.

• Choose a volunteer to read the Scripture.

• Practice song "We Are the Church," #19 on the Grade 3 CD.

The Prayer Space
• Gather the following items: a small globe or world map, a parish bulletin or Catholic magazine

This Week's Liturgy
Visit **www.webelieveweb.com** for this week's liturgical readings and other seasonal material.

Lesson Plan

WE GATHER
_____ minutes

✝ Pray
• Explain the signs. "Good news" is written in four languages: Spanish (upper left), Italian (bottom left), French (upper right), and English.

• Begin the opening prayer.

• Have the reader proclaim the Scripture.

• Invite volunteers to place the items in the prayer space.

• Sing the song.

• Remind the children that the members of our Church family live all around the world.

☀ Focus on Life
Discuss the questions about other countries. Tell the children that in this lesson they will learn that the Church is all over the world.

Home Connection Update
Invite the children to talk about the Chapter 23 family page. *What did you and your family do with the trading cards?*

Catechist Goal

• To introduce that the Catholic Church is worldwide

Our Faith Response

• To appreciate the different ways of expressing our Catholic faith

 **Rite**

Lesson Materials

• markers, crayons, or colored pencils
• parish Baptismal Register, if possible
• Reproducible Master 24
• Grade 3 CD

As Catholics...

The Baptismal Register

Read aloud the text. Encourage the children to share their feelings about having their names recorded in the register. Ask: *Does it strengthen your sense of belonging to the Church family?* Remind the children that Baptism unites us with the family of believers around the world. If possible, ask your pastor if you may show the children the parish's *Baptismal Register.*

 WE BELIEVE

The Catholic Church is all over the world.

The Catholic Church is made up of people from all over the world. They have different customs. Customs are the way a group of people live, dress, and celebrate. The customs and history of each part of the world add beauty and wonder to the Church.

All around the world Catholics use their local customs to praise and worship God. In Africa drums and tribal dances are part of the celebration of the Mass. In Asia the Catholic Church celebrates with special traditions. For example, in Korea and in the Philippines musical instruments and native costumes add to the celebration of the Mass.

Many Catholics in the United States follow the customs of their native countries. For example, many Mexican Americans keep the custom of using luminarias. *Luminarias*, also called *faroles*, are paper sacks filled with sand and lighted candles. Before evening Masses luminarias are placed on paths leading to the church.

The Catholic Church is a wonderful mix of people with different languages, music, and customs. We are united by our faith in Jesus and our membership in the Church. We can all grow and learn from the traditions of one another.

Immaculate Conception Church

204

Lesson Plan

WE BELIEVE ___ minutes

Read aloud the *We Believe* statement. Have the children form small groups and read the first four *We Believe* paragraphs together. Tell them to write four main points presented in the text and have the groups compare points. Emphasize the following:

• The Church is made up of people from all over the world.
• People of the Church use their customs to praise and worship God.
• Many Catholics in the United States follow customs of their native countries.
• We can all grow and learn from the traditions of one another.

Ask children to share where they would like to travel to worship with other Catholics.

Read aloud the *We Believe* statement on page 205. Have volunteers read aloud the *We Believe* paragraphs. Stress that Catholics sometimes celebrate their faith in different ways. Point out that each Rite, Latin and Eastern, has a special way of celebrating and worshiping God. The Rites share in the Apostles' Creed, the sacraments, and are united with their bishops under the leadership of the pope.

Note the photos. Ask: *What differences do you see in the two photos on these pages? What is similar about these photos? Can you find the priest in the photo?* (The priest of the Roman Rite is wearing a Roman collar. The priest of the Eastern Rite is vested for liturgy.)

If you could worship with Catholics in any part of the world, where would you choose to go? Why?

Catholics share the same faith.

Catholics in different parts of the world sometimes celebrate their Catholic faith in different ways. A **Rite** is a special way that Catholics celebrate, live, and pray to God.

Most Catholics in the United States follow the Latin, or Roman, Rite. Other Catholics follow one of the Eastern Rites.

Catholics of the Eastern Rites and Latin Rite make up the whole Catholic Church. We are all joined together in three important ways.

- We all share the same beliefs. We state these beliefs in creeds such as the Apostles' Creed.

- We all celebrate the seven sacraments.

- With our bishops we are all united with the pope as one Church.

Catholics everywhere live as disciples of Jesus in their families, schools, and communities.

 Think about Catholics in your neighborhood or city. Write one way they practice their faith.

_____

_____

As Catholics...

All Catholics are officially listed as members of the Catholic Church. In the parish where you were baptized, your name is written down in a special book called the *Baptismal Register*. Your name will always be there. As you celebrate other sacraments, they are also recorded in the Baptismal Register.

Find out the names of the parishes where your family members were baptized.

Key Word
Rite (p. 253)

ACTIVITY BANK

Multiple Intelligences

Logical-Mathematical

Activity Materials: chart paper

Ask the children to make a chart illustrating the similarities and differences of Catholic worship around the world. At the top of the chart, have them write "One Faith" to emphasize that, regardless of our differences, we are united in faith. Have the children make two columns, one labeled *Similarities* and the other, *Differences*. Encourage them to list as many items as possible under each heading. For example, under *Similarities* they could list "We all say the Apostles' Creed." Under the *Differences* column they could list "We speak different languages." (Children could also list specific languages.) Invite them to share their charts.

Saint Michael's Russian Catholic Church

205

 Do the activity about the ways Catholics practice their faith.

Quick Check

✔ *What is a Rite?* (a special way that Catholics celebrate, live, and pray to God)

✔ *How are Catholics of the Eastern Rites and the Latin Rite joined together?* (share same beliefs, sacraments. and are united with the pope)

Teaching Tips

Knowledge Resources

In this lesson, children are asked to think about different ways in which the liturgy is celebrated. To make these comparisons, have the children tap into various resources in print, the Internet (under adult supervision), and visitors to the class. By using reliable sources, the children can come to appreciate the mosaic of worship that is found in the Church worldwide.

Distinguish Between Fact and Opinion

When a child makes a statement in class, it may be based on fact or on opinion. Determining whether the statement is one or the other is a necessary learning process. Sometimes it is a matter that can be checked out easily from a reliable source. At other times, it can be a painful process of sorting through prior misinformation learned on the playground, at home, or from the media.

Catholics celebrate their faith in different ways.

Catholics celebrate and live out their faith in many ways. For example, all Catholics participate in the liturgy, the official public prayer of the Church.

However, the different Rites have different ways of celebrating. In the liturgy, the wording of some of the prayers is not always the same. The things the priest and people do are a little different, too.

The pictures on these pages show ways the Eastern Rites and the Latin Rite celebrate their Catholic faith. Talk about what the people in these pictures are doing. What is familiar to you? What questions might you have for the people in these pictures?

Talk about ways your parish celebrates its faith. Then act one way out.

Receiving the Eucharist

The altar at Curé of Ars Church

206

We are the light of the world.

As Catholics, we are united as one community. We are joined with Catholics all around the world. We pray and grow in holiness. No matter how we celebrate, we are all disciples of Jesus. We follow the beliefs and teachings handed down from the apostles. Together we try to live, pray, and work as Jesus taught.

Jesus told his disciples, "You are the light of the world. Your light must shine before others, that they may see your good deeds and glorify your heavenly Father." (Matthew 5:14, 16)

Lesson Plan

WE BELIEVE (continued)

Read aloud the *We Believe* statement. Have volunteers read aloud the *We Believe* paragraphs. Ask: *In what do all Catholics everywhere participate?* (in the liturgy or public prayer of the Church)

• *How do the Rites differ?* (in the wording of the prayers and in what the priests and people do)

• *What do the pictures tell us about the Eastern and Latin Rites?* (Answers will vary.)

Talk about and have children act out ways to celebrate faith.

Have a volunteer read aloud the *We Believe* statement in the second column on page 206. Ask volunteers to read aloud the *We Believe* paragraphs. Point out that Catholics share the same faith and we all follow Jesus. Explain that Jesus told his first disciples they were the light of the world. We are, too! We can be the light of the world by using our talents for the good of others.

Read the *Chapter Story* on guide page 203E. Discuss Tony's gift. Ask the children to think about their own gifts and the gifts of others. Then distribute Reproducible Master 24. Encourage the children to work independently to complete the charts.

Jesus calls each of us to be a light for all the world to see. When we share our gifts and talents for the good of others, we are a light in the world. When we follow Jesus' example, others can see the goodness of God. They can see the power of God's love in the world.

Celebrating the sacrament of Matrimony at Saint Michael's Russian Catholic Church

Receiving the Eucharist

WE RESPOND

Think about your gifts and talents. They could be things that you enjoy doing or things that you do well. How can you use your gifts and talents for the good of others? Draw one way you can shine for all the world to see.

207

ACTIVITY BANK

Curriculum Connection
Social Studies

Activity materials: large inexpensive map of the world, stars or colored stickers

Place the map in a convenient space. Encourage the children to place a star or sticker on a country where they know Catholics live. Some of the children might wish to mark the place from which their ancestors came. The world will soon fill up with stickers as Catholics are found everywhere. Some countries have few and others have many. This visual will give the children a concrete idea of the vastness of the Church.

WE RESPOND   ___ minutes

Connect to Life Have the children use the *We Respond* question to think about things they do well that can benefit others.

Ask the children to draw one way to shine for all the world to see. Ask volunteers to share their drawings.

Close the lesson by listening to "Make Us a Sign," #20 on the Grade 3 CD. (option)

Grade 3
Chapter 24

CHAPTER TEST

Chapter 24 Test is provided in the
Grade 3 Assessment Book.

**Circle T if the sentence is true. Circle F if the
sentence is false.**

1. Catholics live all over the world.

    (T)   F

2. A Rite is a special way that Catholics celebrate, live, and
   pray to God.

    (T)   F

3. Only some Catholics celebrate seven sacraments.

    T   (F)

4. All Catholics are united with their bishops and the pope.

    (T)   F

Answer the question.

5. You are a light in the world. What does this mean?

    See pages 206–207.
    _____

    _____

    _____

This week, find out about the Catholic Church in
another part of the world. Draw a picture or write
a paragraph about the language, music, a saint, or
a special custom found in that part of the world.

208

Lesson Plan

                              __ minutes

                              __ minutes

Chapter Review Explain to the children that they
are now going to review what they have learned. Have
them complete questions 1–4. Tell the children to
complete question 5 in their texts. Ask volunteers to
share answers.

Assessment Activity Invite a volunteer to read
aloud the directions. Allow the children to consult any
helpful resources that may be found in the classroom
or library, including Catholic Web sites. Invite the children to share what they learn with the class.

Reflect & Pray Have the children complete the sentence. If any need assistance, guide them and remind
them of the work they completed in this chapter.
Encourage the children to conclude the prayer and to
pray it silently.

Key Words Write the *Key Word (Rite)* on
the board. Ask the children to share with their neighbor what this word means. Then check for understand-
ings.

Reflect & Pray

I celebrate, live, and pray my faith by

_____

_____

Finish this prayer.

Heavenly Father, we are united by our belief in Jesus Christ, your Son. Help all members of your Church to

_____

_____

Key Word

Rite (p. 253)

Remember

- The Catholic Church is all over the world.
- Catholics share the same faith.
- Catholics celebrate their faith in different ways.
- We are the light of the world.

OUR CATHOLIC LIFE

One Faith, Many Languages

The Catholic Church shows respect for the languages of its members. The Mass and the sacraments are celebrated in many languages, such as English, French, Spanish, Polish, Armenian, Greek, Ukrainian, Albanian, Romanian, Syrian, Coptic, and Ethiopian. They are also celebrated in many Native American languages.

HOME CONNECTION

Sharing Faith with My Family

Make sure to send home the family page (text page 210).

Encourage the children to ask family members to help them design a "Helping the Kingdom Grow" card. Remind them to lead their families in praying the Family Prayer.

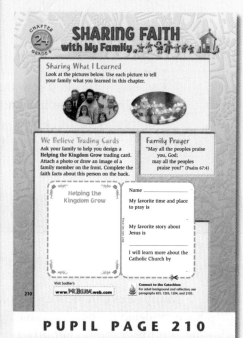

PUPIL PAGE 210

For additional information and activities, encourage families to visit Sadlier's

www.WE BELIEVE.web.com

Remember Form four groups. Review the important ideas of the chapter by discussing the chapter's statements. Go over the sentences one at a time and ask each group to choose one statement. Have each group prepare an explanation of its statement. After allowing a few minutes for small-group discussion, ask each group to share its work with the class. Clarify any misconceptions or misunderstandings.

Our Catholic Life Read aloud the text. Discuss why it is important to respect the different languages of the members of the Catholic Church. Affirm that speaking more than one language is a gift and talent that can be shared with others.

Plan Ahead for Chapter 25

Prayer Space: a picture or statue of Mary, a rosary, a book about the saints

Materials: Grade 3 CD, copies of Reproducible Master 25, crayons or markers, chart paper, globe

Overview

In Chapter 24 the children learned that Catholics worldwide celebrate their faith in different ways. In this chapter the children will learn about Mary and the saints as models of holiness.

Doctrinal Content	For Adult Reading and Reflection *Catechism of the Catholic Church*
The children will learn:	Paragraph
• We belong to the communion of saints.	957
• Mary is the greatest of all the saints.	972
• The Church remembers and honors Mary.	971
• God calls us to be saints.	2013

Key Words

saints (p. 213)
communion of saints (p. 213)
Immaculate Conception (p. 213)
Assumption (p. 213)

Catechist Background

Who have been models of holiness for me?

Many of us can identify people in our lives who have modeled for us what is means to be holy. For me, it is my grandmother. Always the first awake, she could be found praying her novena in the kitchen while the meals of the day were already cooking on the stove. She didn't convert nations, but she did witness Christ's faithfulness by her devotion to the family God gave to her.

One of the great gifts of our Catholic Tradition is that we share a relationship with all the faithful people of God that extends across time and space, the communion of saints. All those who are baptized are part of this communion. "We believe in the communion of all the faithful of Christ, those who are pilgrims on earth, the dead who are being purified, and the blessed in heaven, all together forming one Church; and we believe that in this communion, the merciful love of God and his saints is always [attentive] to our prayers" (Paul VI, *Credo of the People of God,* 30; see CCC 962).

The Church also celebrates the call to holiness by naming certain exemplary people as saints. As Catholics, we believe that Mary, the Mother of God, is the greatest of all the saints. She was the first disciple of Jesus, chosen by God to bring Jesus to birth on the earth. She was born without stain of original sin (the Immaculate Conception). We believe that God did not permit death to decay Mary's body; rather, at her death, God took her body and soul to heaven (the Assumption).

Mary is our model of what it means to be a follower of Jesus. She is both Mother of the Church and our Mother. Our prayer and devotion to Mary helps us to be faithful to Jesus.

How do I try to follow the example of the saints in my life?

Lesson Planning Guide

Lesson Steps	Presentation	Materials

 WE GATHER

Lesson Steps	Presentation	Materials
page 211 ✝ Prayer ☀ Focus on Life	🎵 Pray in song. • Identify ways we remember and honor special people.	For the prayer space: picture or statue of Mary, rosary, and a book about the saints 🎵 "Sing a Song to the Saints," Jack Louden, #21, Grade 3 CD

② WE BELIEVE

Lesson Steps	Presentation	Materials
page 212 *We belong to the communion of saints.*	• Read and discuss the text about saints and the communion of saints.	
page 213 *Mary is the greatest of all the saints.*	• Read and discuss *As Catholics.* • Read about and discuss the Immaculate Conception and the Assumption of Mary. 🧍 Talk about following Mary's example and pray the Hail Mary.	• copies of Reproducible Master 25 (option) • crayons or markers
pages 214–215 *The Church remembers and honors Mary.*	• Discuss ways to honor Mary. • Read and discuss the mysteries of the rosary. 🧍 Discuss and plan to pray the rosary.	
page 215 *God calls us to be saints.*	• Read and discuss saints' lives and their examples of holiness in the text.	• a rosary for each child

③ WE RESPOND

Lesson Steps	Presentation	Materials
page 215	🧍 Make a list of "Saints of Our Time."	
page 216 **Review**	• Complete questions 1–5. 🧍 Work on *Assessment Activity.*	• chart paper • Chapter 25 Test in Assessment Book, pp. 49–50 • Chapter 25 Test in Test Generator • Review & Resource Book, pp. 58–60
page 217 **We Respond in Faith**	• Complete the *Reflect & Pray* activity. • Review *Remember* and *Key Words.* • Read and discuss *Our Catholic Life.* • Discuss Sharing Faith with My Family.	• Family Book, pp. 71–73

For additional ideas, activities, and opportunities: Visit Sadlier's www.WeBelieveweb.com

211B

Name _____

Images of Mary holding the child Jesus are found on stained-glass windows in many churches. Color the stained-glass window of Mary and Jesus.

Connections

To Catholic Social Teaching

The Call to Family, Community, and Participation
The important of becoming a community of saints and being holy is stressed in this chapter. Emphasize that the Catholic Church teaches human beings how to grow and achieve fulfillment in community. Invite one or more representatives of community service organizations from the local Catholic Charities Office to come to speak briefly to the class about the needs of their organizations. With the guest speaker, help the children discover how they could participate in this work.

To Family

Explore with the children the many saints' names that are used within their extended families. Ask them to find out about the saints' names their ancestors may have used. Note that these may be given names, baptismal, or Confirmation names. Have each child draw a family tree with all the saints represented as branches. Display these near the prayer table.

FAITH and MEDIA

▶ After the children have learned to honor Mary by praying the rosary (*We Believe*), you might go online to visit the Mary Page, a Web site maintained by the Marian Library at the University of Dayton, in Ohio. There you will find an excellent compilation of prayers to Mary, including the Hail Mary in many different languages and a variety of litanies. Elsewhere on the site, on the Meditations page, you will find a link to "The Rosary in Image and Text," a series of illustrated meditations on the rosary based on the *Catechism of the Catholic Church*. Among its many other riches, the site also offers over fifty artists' images of Mary and an archive of hymns to Mary.

Meeting Individual Needs

English Language Learners

In this lesson the children are asked to share what they know about saints. For this activity, you may wish to partner English language learners with English-proficient children. Ask the English-speaking children to act as secretaries to allow the ESL children to brainstorm and express ideas.

ADDITIONAL RESOURCES

Book   *Journeys with Mary; Apparitions of Our Lady,* Zerlina De Santis, Pauline Books and Media, 2001. Nine apparitions of Mary show how she continues to watch over us and lead us to God.

Video   *We Pray with Mary,* Ikonographics, St. Anthony Messenger Press, 2000. Children learn favorite Marian prayers and feasts from different cultures throughout the world. (18 minutes)

To find more ideas for books, videos, and other learning material, visit Sadlier's

www.WeBelieveweb.com

Focus on Life

Chapter Story

My name is Rita. I grew up in the big city of New York. We lived in a small apartment building with five floors. We lived on the third floor and my grandmother—we called her Nonna—lived on the first floor. Every Saturday, Nonna would go to the markets on Broadway and buy fresh vegetables for Sunday's big dinner. As usual, I tagged along to carry the groceries.

Nonna poked, pinched, or squeezed every item she bought. If she did not think the eggplant was ripe enough, she would smack her lips in disgust, and ask the grocer where the ripe ones were. He would fumble around the vegetable bin and pull out the freshest one for her. She would pay for it, and we would slip away to the next store.

When we finished shopping, I knew that Nonna would buy me a soda or some candy because I had helped her. But, before I would get my treat, Nonna always made her most important stop—a visit to "Momma," her name for Our Lady.

Quiet as mice, we would go hand in hand into the big Church of Our Lady of Pompeii. Nonna would go directly to the statue of Mary. Together we would light a candle. Then we would pray a moment. A certain smile would come over Nonna's wrinkled face. "Now, we can go for your treat."

▶ *What did this little girl do with her grandmother? How do you honor Mary?*

We Are God's Holy People

25

WE GATHER

✝ **Leader:** Let us sing a song to the saints.

🎵 **Sing a Song to the Saints**

Chorus:
Sing a song to the saints,
   the saints of God the most
   high.
Sing a song to the saints,
   with names like yours
   and mine.

Saint Francis, pray for us.
Saint Cecilia, pray for us.
Saint Peter, pray for us.
Saint Mary Magdalen,
   pray for us.
Sing a song to the saints.

Saint George, pray for us.
Blessed Mary, pray for us.
Saint Thomas, pray for us.
Saint Anastasia, pray for us.
Sing a song to the saints.

Saint Benedict, pray for us.
Saint Margaret, pray for us.
Saint Joseph, pray for us.
Saint Elizabeth, pray for us.
Sing a song to the saints.

☀ What are some ways we remember and honor special people who have lived before us?

Saint Peter

Saint Elizabeth of Hungary

Saint Mary Magdalen

Saint Francis

211

PREPARING TO PRAY

The children will sing a song in honor of the saints as their opening prayer.

• Play the CD to teach the song, "Sing a Song to the Saints," #21 on the Grade 3 CD. Emphasize that singing is a way of praying.

• Tell the children that you will be the prayer leader.

The Prayer Space

• Gather the following items: a picture or statue of Mary, a rosary, a book about the saints.

📖 **This Week's Liturgy**
Visit **www.webelieveweb.com** for this week's liturgical readings and other seasonal material.

Lesson Plan

WE GATHER

___ minutes

✝ **Pray**

• Pray the Sign of the Cross and opening prayer.

• Sing the song.

• Encourage the children to add more saints' names to the song's list of saints.

• Note that the children in the photos are dressed as saints. Ask the children to choose saints they would like to "be" for a day. Sing the song as a prayer on that day, using the names of the saints the group named.

☀ **Focus on Life**

• Discuss ways we honor people. In this lesson we will learn how we honor Mary and the saints.

Home Connection Update

Invite the children to share some things about the Chapter 24 family page. *Did the family do any of the activities or use the page in any way?*

Catechist Goal

• To present the communion of saints and the reasons we honor Mary and the saints

Our Faith Response

• To grow in holiness by honoring the saints and following their examples

 **saints**

communion of saints

Immaculate Conception

Assumption

Lesson Materials

• Grade 3 CD
• copies of Reproducible Master 25
• crayons or markers
• globe   • chart paper

As Catholics...

Being Canonized a Saint

Read the text to the children. Define what *canonized saint* means. Ask the children to name their parish saint and share facts about him or her. Remind them that each canonized saint has a special feast day.

WE BELIEVE

We belong to the communion of saints.

God is holy. He shares his holiness with us when we are baptized. The word *saint* means "one who is holy." God calls all of us to be saints. **Saints** are followers of Christ who lived lives of holiness on earth and now share in eternal life with God in heaven.

The saints are examples of holiness. We learn from them how to love God and care for others. Their lives show us how to be true disciples of Jesus.

The Church honors all the saints in heaven in a special way on November 1. We call this day the feast of All Saints. On this day we remember the holy people who have gone before us. We ask them to pray for us always.

Raphael (1483–1570),
The Madonna of the Chair

Edith Catlin Phelps (1875–1961),
Wayside Madonna

212

The union of the baptized members of the Church on earth with those who are in heaven and in purgatory is called the **communion of saints**. Through Baptism we are united to Christ and one another. We are united with all members of the Church who are alive on earth, and all who have died and are in heaven or purgatory.

Saints come from all over the world. Who are some saints you know about?

_____

_____

_____

Tell about them.

Lesson Plan

WE BELIEVE   ___ minutes

Ask a volunteer to read the *We Believe* statement. Have volunteers read aloud the first three *We Believe* paragraphs. Stress that Baptism begins our lives of holiness that come from God. Point out that we learn from the lives of saints how to love God and care for others.

Have a volunteer read aloud the fourth *We Believe* paragraph. Write on the board *November 1*. Explain: *This date is a very special one in the Church because it is the feast of All Saints. On this day we remember all the holy people who have lived before us.*

Write and tell about saints we know.

Read aloud the *We Believe* statement on page 213. Have the children form three groups and read the *We Believe* text together. On the board write *Immaculate Conception* and *Assumption*. Ask:

• *Why did God treat Mary in a very special way?* (God chose her to be the mother of his Son.)

Explain that we have two special beliefs about Mary. Point to *Immaculate Conception* and explain: *This is the belief that Mary was free from original sin from the very first moment of her life.* Point to *Assumption* and explain: *This is the belief that when Mary's work on earth was done, God brought her body and soul to live forever with the risen Christ.*

212

Mary is the greatest of all the saints.

Mary was blessed by God. She was free from original sin from the very first moment of her life. This belief is called the **Immaculate Conception**.

Mary was chosen by God and asked to be the mother of his Son. Mary said, "May it be done to me according to your word" (Luke 1:38). Mary trusted God completely.

Mary loved and cared for Jesus. She listened to his teachings and saw the ways he treated others. She believed in him when others did not. She stayed at the cross as he was dying. She was with the disciples when the Holy Spirit first came to them.

When Mary's work on earth was done, God brought her body and soul to live forever with the risen Christ. This belief is called the **Assumption**.

Mary was Jesus' mother. She is the mother of the Church, too. Jesus loved and honored his mother. The Church loves and honors Mary as well. When we remember Mary, we remember Jesus. We remember that God sent his Son to us.

Mary is an example for all of Jesus' disciples. Mary is the greatest of all the saints. We pray special prayers to honor Mary. The Hail Mary is one of these prayers. In the Hail Mary we praise Mary and ask her to pray for us.

Talk about ways we can follow Mary's example. Then pray together the Hail Mary found on page 241.

Father John Giuliani,
Hopi Virgin and Child II

Key Words

saints (p.253)

communion of saints (p.250)

Immaculate Conception (p.251)

Assumption (p.250)

As Catholics...

A *canonized* saint is a person who has been officially named a saint by the Church. The life of this person has been examined by Church leaders. They have decided that the person has lived a life of faith and holiness.

When someone is canonized a saint, his or her name is entered into the worldwide list of saints recognized by the Catholic Church. Each canonized saint has a special feast day.

Is your parish named after a saint? What do you know about him or her?

ACTIVITY BANK

Multicultural Connection

Holy Days Around the World: Giant Kite Festival

Activity Materials: photographs of the celebration (a number of Web sites have pictures of the Giant Kite Festival), sheets of square paper in the shape of a kite, colorful streamers, glue, crayons or markers

The people of Santiago Sacatepequez, Guatemala, have a colorful way of celebrating All Saints' Day. They make very large, multicolored kites called *barriletes*. People write messages to God and to the saints. They tie the messages to the tails of the kites. People come from all over the country and even the world on November 1st to see the celebrators fly their kites. Invite the children to use the supplies to make and decorate their own *barriletes*. Don't let them forget the messages, but remind them that God always hears the prayers we pray in our hearts.

213

 Invite the children to talk about ways to follow Mary's example. Pray the Hail Mary together. Distribute Reproducible Master 25. Allow the children to honor Mary by coloring the picture either now or at home.

Quick Check

Who are saints? (followers of Christ who lived lives of holiness on earth and share eternal life with God in heaven)

In what way did Mary live her life? (She loved and obeyed God. She did not commit sin. She lived a life of holiness.)

The Church remembers and honors Mary.

Catholics all over the world honor Mary. We remember how God blessed her. We remember Mary when we celebrate Mass on her feast days.

Another way to honor Mary is by praying the rosary. The rosary combines many prayers. When we pray the rosary, we recall special times in the lives of Mary and Jesus. The mysteries of the rosary recall these special times. We remember a different mystery at the beginning of each decade, or set of ten small beads.

We use rosary beads like this one to say the rosary. Read these directions.

1. Start at the crucifix with the *Sign of the Cross*.
2. Then pray the *Apostles' Creed*.
3. Pray an *Our Father* at every large bead.
4. Pray a *Hail Mary* at every small bead.
5. Pray a *Glory to the Father* after each set of small beads.
6. Pray the *Hail, Holy Queen* to end the rosary.

With a partner discuss why the rosary is a special prayer. Plan when you can pray the rosary.

214

Joyful Mysteries
The Annunciation
The Visitation
The Nativity
The Presentation
The Finding of the Child Jesus in the Temple

Sorrowful Mysteries
The Agony in the Garden
The Scourging at the Pillar
The Crowning with Thorns
The Carrying of the Cross
The Crucifixion

Glorious Mysteries
The Resurrection
The Ascension
The Coming of the Holy Spirit upon the Apostles
The Assumption of Mary
The Coronation of Mary

Mysteries of Light
Jesus' Baptism in the Jordan
The Miracle at the Wedding at Cana
Jesus Announces the Kingdom of God
The Transfiguration
The Institution of the Eucharist

Teaching Tip
Reading Skills

Third graders are making the transition from learning to read to reading to learn. Help them to become more confident in their reading skills by providing opportunities to read in unison or to share a reading with you (or with other advanced readers).

Lesson Plan

WE BELIEVE (continued)

Read aloud the *Chapter Story* on page 211E. Discuss the way Rita and her grandmother honored Mary.

Have a volunteer read aloud the *We Believe* statement. Ask volunteers to read aloud the *We Believe* paragraph. Ask: *In what way does the Church honor Mary?* (by celebrating Mass on her feast days) *What special prayer honors Mary?* (the rosary) *What do the mysteries of the rosary recall?* (events in the lives of Jesus and Mary)

Direct the children's attention to the rosary. Tell them that each group of ten beads is called a *decade*. Explain that they will learn to pray the rosary.

Explain: *The Joyful Mysteries refer to happy moments in Jesus and Mary's lives. The Sorrowful Mysteries help us to remember the suffering and death of Jesus. The Glorious Mysteries recall Jesus' resurrection and the wonderful things that happened after this event. The Mysteries of Light recall the miracles of Jesus, his mission on earth, and the institution of the Eucharist.*

Using the directions, guide the group in praying a decade of the rosary (or half a decade) as time permits. The Hail, Holy Queen is on page 247 in the text.

Form the group into partners. Discuss why the rosary is important. Help each other plan time to pray the rosary.

We can also honor Mary by praying a litany. In a litany for Mary, we call on her by using some of her many titles. After the leader prays each title, we repeat a response.

God calls us to be saints.

The saints answered God's call to lead holy lives. Men, women, and children from every part of the world have become saints. Here are some examples:

Saint Louise de Marillac

• Saint Louise de Marillac was a wife and mother. After her husband died, she began the Daughters of Charity. They served the needs of people who were poor.

• Saint Charles Lwanga lived in Uganda, Africa. He was baptized as an adult. He helped many people in Africa, including those who served in the king's court, to become Christians.

• Saint Joan of Arc was a soldier in France. She tried her best to obey God's will.

• Saint Andrew Nam-Thuong was a mayor of a Vietnamese village. He taught others about the faith.

Saint Andrew Nam-Thuong

• Saint Dominic Savio was a boy who prayed to God everyday. Dominic saw God in the happenings of everyday life. He was always ready to help out a classmate.

God calls you to become a saint, too. How can you become a saint? You can know and live your faith every day. You can learn as much as possible about Jesus and the way he treated others. You can also find out more about the lives of the saints.

God helps each of us to be holy. We are strengthened by prayer. We receive grace from the sacraments. We also get support from our family and our parish. Together we can follow Jesus and grow in holiness.

WE RESPOND

With a partner list people who could be on a "Saints of Our Time" Web site. Give some reasons why they might be included.

_____

_____

_____

_____

_____

215

ACTIVITY BANK

Faith and Media
Saints
Activity Materials: Internet
Form the children into three groups. Assign to each group one of the following saints: Charles Lwanga, Andrew Nam-Thuong, and Joan of Arc. Using Catholic Web sites, have children research these saints and do a report that they will present to the class.

Curriculum Connection
Reading Skills
Activity Materials: Bible, tape recorder, list of questions
Tape a gospel story. Invite the children to take turns listening to the tape and reading along in the Bible. Prepare some simple comprehension questions for the story that you choose to use. Have the children answer the questions to make sure they have understood the main ideas. Afterwards, make dioramas.

Read aloud the *We Believe* statement. Have volunteers read the *We Believe* paragraph and each of the saints profiled. On the globe locate where each saint lived and worked. For example, Saint Louise de Marillac lived and worked in France, while Saint Dominic Savio lived in Italy.

Have volunteers read aloud the remaining *We Believe* paragraphs. Emphasize the following points:

• Saints are examples to us because they teach us ways to be holy.

• Living holy lives will lead people to eternal life with God.

• God calls everyone to become a saint by living their faith every day.

• Following Jesus will help us grow in holiness.

WE RESPOND   ___ minutes

Connect to Life Have the children reflect on present-day people who could be saints.

Invite the children to explain why they have chosen particular people.

215

CHAPTER TEST

Chapter 25 Test is provided in the Grade 3 Assessment Book.

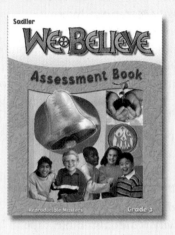

Use these terms to complete the sentences.

saints	communion of saints
Immaculate Conception	Assumption

1. The union of all the baptized members of the Church on earth with those who are in heaven and in purgatory is the

   _____communion of saints_____ .

2. The _____Assumption_____ is the belief that, when Mary's work on earth was done, God brought her body and soul to live forever with the risen Christ.

3. The _____Immaculate Conception_____ is the belief that Mary was free from original sin from the very first moment of her life.

4. Those who lived a life of holiness and now share in

   eternal life with God are _____saints_____ .

Answer the question.

5. How can you become a saint?

   _____See page 215._____

   _____

 Interview a family member or friend. Ask him or her to name a favorite saint and to tell why. As a class, make a chart to show which saints are favorites and why.

216

Lesson Plan

 ___ minutes

Chapter Review Explain to the children that they are now going to review what they have learned. Then have the children complete questions 1–4. Brainstorm answers to question 5. Then have the children write their answers to question 5 in their textbooks. Ask volunteers to share responses.

Assessment Activity Have a volunteer read aloud the directions for the activity. Encourage the children to share the favorite saint of a family member or friend. As a class, then make the chart of favorite saints. Invite the children to share their interview stories.

We Respond in Faith ___ minutes

Reflect & Pray Ask the children to recall the different titles used for Mary. (Here are a few from the Litany of the Blessed Virgin Mary: Holy Mother of God, Mother of the Church, Health of the sick, Comfort of the troubled, Help of Christians, Queen of all saints, Queen of peace). Write the titles on the board. Ask the children to choose a title and write a prayer using the title for Mary they have chosen. Revisit the prayer space, sharing each child's prayer to Mary.

 **Key Words** To review the *Key Words*, write them on the board. Invite the children to design an acrostic poem using one of the key words as the main word or phrase.

We Respond in Faith

Reflect & Pray

Catholics have many titles for Mary. Each title tells us something special about her. Which title do you think of when you remember Mary?

Write a prayer using this title of Mary.

_____

_____

_____

_____

Key Words

saints (p. 253)
communion of saints (p. 250)
Immaculate Conception (p. 251)
Assumption (p. 250)

Remember

- We belong to the communion of saints.
- Mary is the greatest of all the saints.
- The Church remembers and honors Mary.
- God calls us to be saints.

OUR CATHOLIC LIFE

Praying for the Dead

As members of the communion of saints, we pray for all those who have died. We do this at every Mass.

The Church sets aside a special day each year for remembering the dead. This day is November 2, All Souls' Day. On this day we pray for all those who have died, especially during the past year. We pray that they may enjoy eternal life with God forever.

HOME CONNECTION

Sharing Faith with My Family

Make sure to send home the family page (text page 218).

Encourage the children to look for names of saints in their neighborhoods.

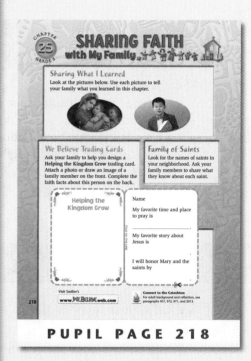

PUPIL PAGE 218

For additional information and activities, encourage families to visit Sadlier's

www.WeBelieveweb.com

Remember Review the important ideas of the chapter by discussing the four statements. Have the class form into four groups. Assign one statement to each group. Have each group discuss what the sentence means.

Our Catholic Life Read the text aloud. Ask: *Why do we pray for those who have died?* (that they may enjoy eternal life with God forever) Print on the board: *November 2, All Souls' Day.* Invite the children to share their own experiences of praying for those who have died in their family or community.

Plan Ahead for Chapter 26

Prayer Space: container of potting soil, packet of seeds or growing plant, illustrated Bible

Lesson Materials: copies of Reproducible Master 26 (option), markers or crayons

Overview

In Chapter 25 the children learned about Mary, the Mother of God, and the saints of the Church. In this chapter, the children will learn what Jesus taught his followers about the Kingdom of God, and that it continues to grow today.

Doctrinal Content	For Adult Reading and Reflection *Catechism of the Catholic Church*
The children will learn:	Paragraph
• Jesus used parables to teach about the Kingdom of God.	546
• Jesus taught that the Kingdom of God will grow.	541
• Jesus' miracles were signs of the Kingdom of God.	548
• The Kingdom of God grows.	2818

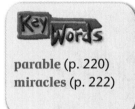

Key Words

parable (p. 220)
miracles (p. 222)

Catechist Background

What is your favorite parable of Jesus?

We all enjoy a good story. Think about the way you can hold your children entranced by sharing a well-written book. Jesus knew about the power of stories. Think about ways you use stories to teach. The best stories teach on many levels. Jesus' parables are like that. Through them he taught both the simple and the most sophisticated.

But, Jesus' parables were more than good stories. Together with the miracles he performed, Jesus used the parables to witness to the Kingdom of God that he came to proclaim. "Through his parables he invites people to the feast of the kingdom, but he also asks for a radical choice: to gain the kingdom, one must give everything. Words are not enough; deeds are required" (*CCC* 546).

Jesus' miracles also tell us about the Kingdom of God. Miracles witness to a special in-breaking of God's power. Jesus was able to heal the sick and to forgive sins. He had power over nature, calming the wind, walking on water, changing water to wine. These things show the possibilities of what can happen if people allow God to be fully present and active in their lives. Jesus' miracles helped people to believe that he was, indeed, the Son of God.

By word and deed, Jesus taught us that the Kingdom of God was already here, and yet it is not yet fully realized. We are called to participate in its growth. We are called to be like salt, like yeast, like light. In each of these, a little can be made to go a long way, to have great effects. As disciples of Jesus, we are called to be witnesses to the power of God's love in little ways, confident that God's can use our actions to great effect.

How can I be salt, yeast, and light for the people and situations of my life?

Lesson Planning Guide

Lesson Steps	Presentation	Materials

1 WE GATHER

page 219 ✝ Prayer ☀ Focus on Life	• Listen to Scripture. • Pray the Our Father with movements. • Discuss favorite stories.	For the prayer space: container of potting soil, packet of seeds or a plant, illustrated Bible

2 WE BELIEVE

page 220 *Jesus used parables to teach about the Kingdom of God.* 📖 *Luke 13:18–19*	• Read and discuss parables and the Kingdom of God in the text. 🤸 Identify signs of God's love.	
page 221 *Jesus taught that the Kingdom of God will grow.*	• Read and discuss growth of the Kingdom of God. 🤸 Write and share parables. • Read and discuss *As Catholics*.	• copies of Reproducible Master 26 (option)
pages 222–223 *Jesus' miracles were signs of the Kingdom of God.* 📖 *Matthew 14:22–33*	• Read and discuss Jesus' miracles, particularly his calming of the storm. 🤸 Write ways to show faith.	
page 223 *The Kingdom of God grows.*	• Read and discuss the Church and ways we can give witness to the Kingdom of God.	• markers or crayons

3 WE RESPOND

page 223	🤸 Choose and discuss time capsule items.	
page 224 **Review**	• Complete questions 1–5. 🤸 Work on *Assessment Activity*.	• pencils and drawing materials • Chapter 26 Test in Assessment Book, pp. 51–52 • Chapter 26 Test in Test Generator • Review & Resource Book, pp. 61–63
page 225 **We Respond in Faith**	• Complete the *Reflect & Pray* activity. • Review *Remember* statements and *Key Words*. • Invite reflections in *Our Catholic Life*. • Discuss **Sharing Faith with My Family**.	• Family Book, pp. 74–76

For additional ideas, activities, and opportunities: Visit Sadlier's **www.WeBelieveweb.com**

Name _____

Choose six readers or divide the group into six small
groups. Give each reader or group a verse to read aloud.
You may want to choose actors (Sower, Seeds, Birds, Thorns)
to act out each verse as it is read.

Reader 1

Do you want to hear a story
Jesus told so long ago?
Then listen very carefully
And his teachings you will know.

Reader 2

A sower went to sow his seed.
"I'll have a good crop," he said.
But the seed fell on the pathway,
While the birds flew 'round his head.

Reader 3

"Go away, you birds!" the
     sower cried.
But it was far too late.
The birds had spied a tasty meal.
They flew down, stopped, and ate.

Reader 4

The sower tried again and spread
His seeds on rocky ground.
The seeds cried, "Water!" Then
     they died,
For no water could be found.

Reader 5

Then the sower's seeds fell
     on thorny ground.
They grew, but the thorns
     grew faster.
Soon the seeds were
     choked to death—
Another seed disaster!

Reader 6

At last the seeds fell on
     good rich soil.
They grew and grew and grew!
These are the seeds that Jesus says
Are just like me and you!

All:

Our good soil is the word of God.
Like seeds, we grow each day.
Our love and joy bear special fruit
As we follow the Jesus way!

Connections

To Evangelization

Children learn in this chapter that the Church encourages all of us to be witnesses to Jesus Christ. One way that we can act as witnesses is through evangelization—telling others about the good news of Christ. When we share the gospel with others, we act as God's messengers and we represent Jesus. Encourage the children to think about the ways they can be witnesses to Jesus by telling people about him. Remind them that, as we witness to others, we must do so with love and gentleness.

To Scripture

In this chapter children will read Jesus' words in Matthew 13:31. Explain to the children that, when we hear or read the word of God, it is like a seed of faith that is planted in our hearts. For the seed of faith to grow, we must provide the good soil of love of God and one another. As you teach this chapter, look for opportunities to illustrate this seed metaphor by planting ideas in their hearts and rejoicing with them when they bring forth the green shoots of inspired actions.

FAITH and MEDIA

▶ In his message for the 36th World Communications Day, May 12, 2002, Pope John Paul II spoke on the theme of "Internet: A New Forum for Proclaiming the Gospel." His words about using this most modern of media to help the Kingdom of God to grow are well worth pondering: "For the Church the new world of cyberspace is a summons to the great adventure of using its potential to proclaim the Gospel message. . . . The Internet can offer magnificent opportunities for evangelization. . . . Above all, by providing information and stirring interest it makes possible an initial encounter with the Christian message, especially among the young who increasingly turn to the world of cyberspace as a window on the world" (numbers 2, 3).

Meeting Individual Needs

Children with Visual Needs

Children who have visual needs respond quite well to audio recordings. Obtain some parables of Jesus on CD or cassette. Set up the classroom so that all the children can listen to the parables. For the visually impaired child, you may wish to provide a prerecorded reading of the chapter for the child to take home.

ADDITIONAL RESOURCES

Video *Parables for Kids, Volume 2,* Pauline Books and Media, 2001. These four-minute parables include The Talents, The Lost Coin, The Good Shepherd, and others. (22 minutes)

To find more ideas for books, videos, and other learning material, visit Sadlier's

www.WeBelieve.web.com

Chapter Story

The Ant and the Grasshopper

One sunny day a grasshopper watched an ant carrying a large kernel of corn. The grasshopper asked, "Why are you working so hard? We've got plenty of food! What are you worried about?"

The ant replied, "We ants are storing food for the winter." The ant went back to work. But the grasshopper went right on playing.

Then winter came. The grasshopper was very cold and hungry. He had not eaten in a very long time. Then he remembered what the ant had said to him that sunny summer day.

The Lion and the Mouse

One day when a lion was sleeping, a mouse began to run back and forth on the lion's back. This woke the lion up. He grabbed the mouse to eat him. But the mouse begged the lion to let him go. He told the lion, "If you let me go, I will help you someday."

The large king of the jungle thought, "How can a mouse help me?" But he let the mouse go.

A few months passed. Some hunters trapped the lion and tied him to a wagon. The mouse immediately went to help the lion. He gnawed and chewed at the ropes until the lion could break free.

▶ *What can each story teach us?*

The Kingdom of God Continues to Grow

26

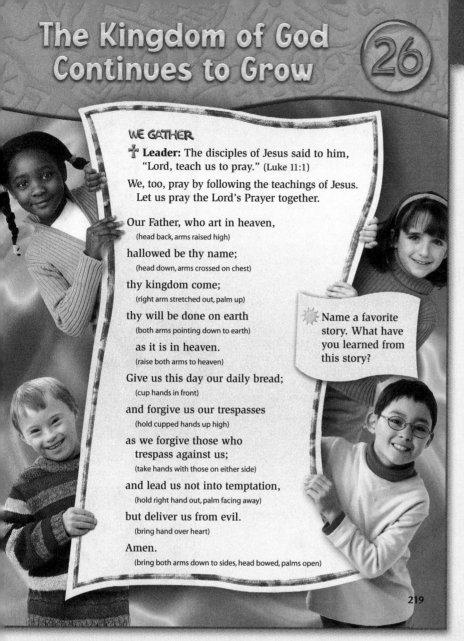

WE GATHER

✝ **Leader:** The disciples of Jesus said to him, "Lord, teach us to pray." (Luke 11:1)

We, too, pray by following the teachings of Jesus. Let us pray the Lord's Prayer together.

Our Father, who art in heaven,
(head back, arms raised high)

hallowed be thy name;
(head down, arms crossed on chest)

thy kingdom come;
(right arm stretched out, palm up)

thy will be done on earth
(both arms pointing down to earth)

as it is in heaven.
(raise both arms to heaven)

Give us this day our daily bread;
(cup hands in front)

and forgive us our trespasses
(hold cupped hands up high)

as we forgive those who trespass against us;
(take hands with those on either side)

and lead us not into temptation,
(hold right hand out, palm facing away)

but deliver us from evil.
(bring hand over heart)

Amen.
(bring both arms down to sides, head bowed, palms open)

 Name a favorite story. What have you learned from this story?

219

PREPARING TO PRAY

The children will pray the Our Father with accompanying movements.

• Explain to the children that you will lead them in praying the Lord's Prayer and show them movements that go with each line of the prayer.

• Read through the list of movements and have the children practice them.

The Prayer Space
• Place a container of potting soil, a packet of seeds or a growing plant to represent ourselves growing in God's love.

• Display a page from an illustrated Bible that shows Jesus performing a miracle.

📖 **This Week's Liturgy**
Visit **www.webelieveweb.com** for this week's liturgical readings and other seasonal material.

Lesson Plan

WE GATHER ___ minutes

✝ Pray

• Place your book so that your hands are free. Read the part of the leader.

• Pray the Our Father with its accompanying movements.

• Explain that we can express our praise to God through our bodies in prayer.

🌟 Focus on Life

Share the *Chapter Story* on guide page 219E. Discuss the question about stories. Tell the children that in this lesson they will learn how Jesus used stories called *parables* to teach people about the Kingdom of God.

Home Connection Update

Invite the children to talk about the ways they used the Chapter 25 family page. *Did you find any saints' names used in your neighborhood?*

Catechist Goal

• To introduce Jesus' teachings about the Kingdom of God

Our Faith Response

• To appreciate the signs of God's Kingdom in the world today

 **Key Words** **parable**   **miracles**

Lesson Materials

• Reproducible Master 26 (option)

• markers or crayons

As Catholics...

Catholic Action

Ask the children to compare Saint Elizabeth's earthly kingdom to God's Kingdom. Ask them what they think today's world leaders could learn from Saint Elizabeth's example. Remind the children that God wants all leaders to treat people kindly and to govern with love, compassion, and justice. Encourage children to pray for world leaders to rule with God's mercy and truth.

WE BELIEVE
Jesus used parables to teach about the Kingdom of God.

Jesus wanted to teach the people about God's Kingdom. The people of Jesus' time had heard about the Kingdom of God. Many of them thought God's Kingdom was about power and money. They thought it was like an earthly kingdom.

The kingdom that Jesus taught about was not the kingdom the people expected. Jesus wanted everyone to know that the Kingdom of God is the power of God's love active in the world. To help them understand this, Jesus told the people parables. A **parable** is a short story that uses things from everyday life. Parables are stories with a message.

📖 Luke 13:18–19

Jesus described the Kingdom of God with this parable. He said, "What is the kingdom of God like? To what can I compare it? It is like a mustard seed that a person took and planted in the garden. When it was fully grown, it became a large bush and 'the birds of the sky dwelt in its branches.'" (Luke 13:18–19)

Jesus was telling his disciples that, although small, the kingdom would grow. As more people respond to God's love, the Kingdom of God will grow. When we believe in and follow Jesus Christ, we respond to God's love and the kingdom grows.

✖ Name some signs of God's love active in our world today.

_____

_____

Key Word parable (p. 252)

220

Lesson Plan

WE BELIEVE ___ minutes

Read together the *We Believe* statement and the paragraphs. Stress that God's Kingdom is still growing because more people follow Jesus and believe in his message.

Have a volunteer read aloud the *We Believe* statement. Read aloud the *We Believe* paragraphs. Write the word *parable* on the board. Explain that a parable is a short story that uses things from everyday life to help people understand important messages.

📖 **Have** a volunteer read aloud the parable of the mustard seed. Ask another volunteer to read the meaning of the parable in the next paragraph.

✖ **Ask** the children to name and write some signs of God's love active in our world today.

Read the *We Believe* statement on page 221. Ask volunteers to read the two paragraphs in the box.

Draw a simple time-line on the board: JESUS' GOOD NEWS → THE DISCIPLES → US! → OUR WORDS AND ACTIONS → OUR PRAYERS = GOD'S LOVE WILL RULE!

Jesus taught that the Kingdom of God will grow.

Jesus taught his disciples that the Kingdom of God is a kingdom of love. God's love was already active among them. Through Jesus' words and actions, the kingdom had begun. The kingdom would grow as more people followed Jesus and believed his message.

The kingdom begins with the good news of Jesus Christ. It continues when we, his disciples, respond to God's love. We show by our words and actions that God's love is active in our lives and in the world. We pray for the time when God's love will rule the world. We pray for the coming of God's Kingdom in its fullness.

As Catholics...

Saint Elizabeth of Hungary is an example of someone who believed in Jesus and worked to spread God's Kingdom. In the thirteenth century, Elizabeth was a princess in the country of Hungary. She was married and had three children. She lived in a castle and had more things than she would ever need. Yet she spent her life helping those who were sick and poor. She built a hospital and gave food to those who were hungry.

After her husband died, Elizabeth used all of her money to build shelters for those who were homeless, sick, and elderly. Through Elizabeth's words and actions, many people experienced God's love active in the world.

Find out when the Church celebrates the feast day of Saint Elizabeth of Hungary.

Make up a new parable that describes the Kingdom of God. Use things that are familiar to people today. Share your parable by writing or drawing it. Then act it out.

221

ACTIVITY BANK

Multiple Intelligences
Bodily-Kinesthetic
Activity Materials: a book of children's prayers; recordings of Christian music

Remind the children of the movements they used to pray the Lord's Prayer. Tell them that we can use the movements of our bodies to communicate and to bring the words of a prayer, song, or story to life. Ask children to choose a Bible story, a prayer, or a song that expresses something about God's Kingdom. Invite them to make up movements to accompany their choice. Write the chosen text on an overhead projector for the class to see. Then ask the children to demonstrate the movements they made up for the class.

Distribute copies of Reproducible Master 26 (option). It is a rhymed version of the parable of the sower and the seed (Matthew 13:3–8; 18–23). You may want to have the children read it aloud in groups, or choose individual readers to read while others act it out.

Brainstorm ideas for the activity. Ask children to join in small groups to write, draw, and act out their parables.

Quick Check

✔ *What did Jesus want people to know about the Kingdom of God?* (It is the power of God's love active in the world.)

✔ *How will the Kingdom of God grow?* (It will grow as people respond to God's love.)

Jesus' miracles were signs of the Kingdom of God.

Jesus did amazing things that only God could do. He calmed the stormy seas, made the blind to see, walked on water, and even changed water into wine. These amazing events were beyond human power. They were **miracles**.

Key Word

miracles (p. 252)

Jesus' miracles showed that he was divine. They were special signs that God's Kingdom was present in him. His miracles helped people to believe that he was the Son of God.

📖 Matthew 14:22–33

One day Jesus' disciples were out in a boat on the sea. Jesus went up to a mountain to pray alone. As night approached "the boat, already a few miles offshore, was being tossed about by the waves, for the wind was against it. During the fourth watch of the night, he came toward them, walking on the sea. When the disciples saw him walking on the sea they were terrified. 'It is a ghost,' they said, and they cried out in fear. At once [Jesus] spoke to them, 'Take courage, it is I; do not be afraid.' Peter said to him in reply, 'Lord, if it is you, command me to come to you on the water.' He said, 'Come.' Peter got out of the boat and began to walk on the water toward Jesus. But when he saw how [strong] the wind was he became frightened; and, beginning to sink, he cried out, 'Lord, save me!' Immediately Jesus stretched out his hand and caught him." (Matthew 14:24–31)

Christ Walking on the Water (Armenian miniature, twelfth-thirteenth century)

After Jesus and Peter got into the boat the wind stopped. The disciples who were in the boat said, "Truly, you are the Son of God." (Matthew 14:33)

Jesus' walking on water strengthened the faith of his disciples. The first disciples knew Jesus, saw his miracles, and believed.

222

Lesson Plan

WE BELIEVE (continued)

Choose volunteers to read aloud the *We Believe* statement and the first two *We Believe* paragraphs. Write the word *miracles* on the board. Explain that miracles are amazing events that are beyond human power.

📖 **Read** aloud and dramatically the parable so that the children can vividly imagine the event. Have volunteers read the parts of the narrator, Jesus, and Peter.

Ask: *How would you feel if you were Peter as he sat in a boat and suddenly saw Jesus walking on the sea? Would you feel very surprised or afraid?* Ask volunteers to take turns pretending that they are witnessing the miracle on the water. Tell them to describe how they reacted to what they were seeing.

Read aloud the next *We Believe* paragraphs. Emphasize the following points:

• Jesus did amazing things that only God could do. These amazing things are called miracles.

• The first disciples told others about Jesus and the amazing things that he did.

• As the first disciples showed their faith in Jesus, others believed in him, too.

🎭 **Brainstorm** ways to show faith in Jesus. Ask the children to choose one way and write it in their texts.

Ask a volunteer to read aloud the *We Believe* statement and the following paragraphs. Have the children highlight the bulleted list of ways we can be witnesses.

They told others about Jesus and tried to live as he taught them. By their words and actions, the disciples were witnesses to Jesus.

Witnesses speak and act based upon what they know and believe. We are called to show our faith in Jesus and to be his witnesses.

(X) Write one way you can show others that you have faith in Jesus.

_____

_____

The Kingdom of God grows.

For the past two thousand years, members of the Church have helped one another to be witnesses to Jesus Christ. We can be witnesses by:

- treating people with kindness and respect
- living peacefully with one another
- being fair with all those we meet
- doing what is right even when it is hard
- being faithful members of the Church
- working together for justice and peace.

In the Lord's Prayer we pray for the final coming of God's Kingdom that will take place when Jesus returns in glory. Jesus' coming at the end of time will be a joyful event. It will bring about the fullness of God's Kingdom.

The Church does not pray only for the coming of God's Kingdom. We also ask God the Father to help us to spread the kingdom in our families, schools, and neighborhoods. Everyone in the Church works together so that God's love may be active and present throughout the world.

WE RESPOND

What would you put in a time capsule to show how the Church has spread God's Kingdom? Why?

223

ACTIVITY BANK

Community

Witnessing and Respecting
Activity Materials: construction paper, magazines

Remind the children that to be witnesses to Jesus we must respect one another. Respecting others involves appreciating people's unique personalities and gifts. Have the children sign affirmation cards for their classmates. Write each class member's name on a card and pass the cards around the room. Ask the children to write something that they appreciate or like about their classmate. Make sure everyone has signed each other's card. When they are finished and have received their own cards back, allow them time to read what was written about them. Then invite them to decorate the front of the card with images that express their unique interests.

Take a moment to pray or review the Lord's Prayer. Stop at "thy kingdom come, thy will be done on earth, as it is in heaven." Ask: *What does this mean?* Ask volunteers to read the last two paragraphs on page 223 to find out.

WE RESPOND ___ minutes

Connect to Life Explain the purpose of a time capsule (to save important objects and documents for people in the future to find).

(X) **Have** the children discuss what they would want to put into the time capsule. Share ideas.

CHAPTER TEST

Chapter 26 Test is provided in the Grade 3 Assessment Book.

Review

Use the words in the box to complete the sentences.

miracles	kingdom	parable
witnesses	mustard seed	

1. A _____parable_____ is a short story that uses things from everyday life.

2. Jesus said that the Kingdom of God is like a _____mustard seed_____.

3. _____Miracles_____ are amazing events that are beyond human power.

4. The Church encourages us to be _____witnesses_____ to Jesus Christ.

Answer the question.

5. How can I witness to God's Kingdom today?

See page 223.

With your family, find a story in your parish bulletin, diocesan newspaper, or on the Internet that shows Catholics helping to spread God's Kingdom. Write a short report or draw a picture about the story. Tell what people can learn from this story.

224

Lesson Plan

___ minutes

Chapter Review Review what the children have learned about God's Kingdom. Have them complete questions 1–4. Have them brainstorm answers to question 5 and write their answers in their texts.

Assessment Activity Read aloud the directions. Assist them with their search in class.

Sharing Faith in Class and at Home At this time you may want to work on pages 237–238 of Chapter 28. Refer to the *Lesson Planning Guide* on page 233B before you present these pages.

___ minutes

Reflect & Pray Allow the children time to think about their responses. Remind them that the good soil refers to people who believe God's good news. Then ask the children to think of ways that they would like Jesus to help them be witnesses to him. Encourage children to pray often for the courage to act and speak about God's Kingdom.

Key Words Review the words *parable* and *miracles*. Make a word web on the board for each word. Then invite the children to suggest other words that relate to each *Key Word* and write them in the web. Ask the children how the related terms added to their overall understanding of each *Key Word*.

We Respond in Faith

Reflect & Pray

If I am to spread God's Kingdom, I must be like the good, rich soil. Each day, no matter how hard it is, I will try to witness to God's Kingdom by

_____

_____

Jesus, help me to

_____

_____

Key Words

parable (p. 252)
miracles (p. 252)

Remember

- Jesus used parables to teach about the Kingdom of God.
- Jesus taught that the Kingdom of God will grow.
- Jesus' miracles were signs of the Kingdom of God.
- The Kingdom of God grows.

OUR CATHOLIC LIFE

Tell your story here.

Place your photo here.

225

HOME CONNECTION

Sharing Faith with My Family

Make sure to send home the family page (text page 226).

Encourage the children to pray for and with their families.

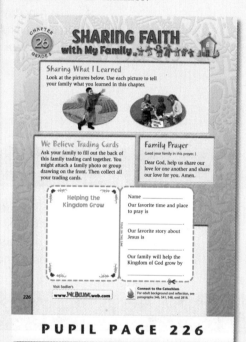

PUPIL PAGE 226

For additional information and activities, encourage families to visit Sadlier's

www.WeBelieveweb.com

Remember Ask a volunteer to read aloud the statements. Then write the headings *Who, What, When, Where,* and *Why* on the board. Ask the children to write down questions that begin with one of the headings and relate to the sentences. For example, *Why did Jesus use parables to teach about God's Kingdom? Who can do miracles? What helps God's Kingdom to grow?* Share their questions and invite volunteers to give answers.

Our Catholic Life Ask the children to reflect on what they learned this year about their Catholic faith. Encourage them to write about ways they can apply what they learned to help them grow as Catholics. Have them recall ways they served their community and showed others Jesus' love. Allow sufficient time for the children to write their responses.

Easter

The fifty days from Easter Sunday to Pentecost are celebrated in joyful exultation as one feast day...These above all others are the days for the singing of the Alleluia.

(Norms Governing Liturgical Calendars, 22)

Overview

In this chapter the the children will learn that in the Easter Season we celebrate the Resurrection of Jesus. They will learn that the Easter seaon goes on for fifty days, until Pentecost Sunday.

For Adult Reading and Reflection
You may want to refer to paragraphs 1169 and 638 of the *Catechism of the Catholic Church*.

Catechist Background

How do you hope to experience new life in this Easter season?

During the fifty days of the Easter season, the Church celebrates the resurrection as "the confirmation of all Christ's works and teachings" and the "definitive proof of his divine authority" (CCC 651). We sing "Alleluia!" because Christ has liberated us from sin by his death and, by his Resurrection, has opened the way to a new life.

In his appearances to his disciples, the risen Jesus demonstrates that his humanity is no longer bound by earth's limitations. However, his glorious body retains the traces of his suffering and death. Thomas can be reassured by touching Christ's wounds. We (those who have not seen yet have believed) rejoice in the certainty that "the trumpet will sound, the dead will be raised incorruptible, and we shall be changed" (1 Corinthians 15:52).

Christ's Resurrection is the promise of our own future resurrection.

Easter is therefore celebrated as the "Feast of feasts" and "Solemnity of solemnities" (CCC 1169). The Church triumphantly sings:

"Dying you destroyed our death, rising you restored our life. Lord Jesus, come in glory."
(*Memorial Acclamation*)

What evidence of Christ's new life will you, b your witness, provide?

Lesson Planning Guide

Lesson Steps	Presentation	Materials
① WE GATHER		
page 227 **Introduce the Season**	• Read the *Chapter Story*. • Introduce the Easter season. • Proclaim the words on the banner.	• brightly colored chalk
page 228	• Name three beliefs about God.	
② WE BELIEVE		
pages 228–229 *In the Easter season we celebrate the Resurrection of Jesus.* 📖 *John 20:19–29*	• Read and discuss the Resurrection of Jesus. • Present the Scripture account as a play.	• large stick-on name tags • curtain or drapery • white tunic
③ WE RESPOND		
page 230	🏃 Brainstorm ways to share faith in Jesus Christ and complete activity. 🎵 Sing the song.	🎵 "Glory and Praise to Our God," Dan Schutte, #22, Grade 3 CD
page 231 **We Respond in Prayer**	• Pray an Easter season litany.	• prayer space items: large white candle, fresh flowers, butterfly cut-out, an Easter egg, a cross, small paper or fabric flowers, white or gold cloth • rhythm instruments
Guide pages 232A–232B **We Respond in Faith**	• Explain the individual Easter season project. • Explain the group Easter season project. • Discuss the Sharing Faith with My Family page.	• Reproducible Master 27 • supplies for Easter egg decorating • books or Internet sources for painting and decorating eggs • Family Book, pp. 77–78

For additional ideas, activities, and opportunities: Visit Sadlier's 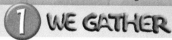 **www.WeBelieveweb.com**

Focus on Life

Chapter Story

Alexis was born deaf. Until she was ten years old, she spoke to her family and friends in sign language. But then, something unbelievable happened. Her parents heard on the news about a device that could be surgically implanted so that deaf people could hear sounds. Alexis's parents had no doubts. They wanted Alexis to have the operation

Although some deaf people do not want to change their nonhearing condition, Alexis wanted to hear the sound of her parents' voices, the phone ringing, the birds singing. She knew that, after the surgery, it would take her a long time to learn how to speak. But all the hard work would be worth it. She couldn't wait to hear what her favorite band actually sounded like!

After the operation, the first sound Alexis heard was her father's voice. She laughed and signed, "I can hear you!" Then she hugged him and her mother and even the doctor, who was grinning from ear to ear. In her heart, Alexis prayed, "Thank you, God! Thank you!"

The first time she heard bees buzzing, birds chirping, and leaves rustling in the breeze, Alexis was astounded. But when she heard the waves splashing on the shore, she felt like a big balloon that would just burst from happiness. She ran along the shore, waving her arms and imitating the sound of those booming waves.

Alexis knew that her life was forever changed!

▶ *What do you know about Alexis from this story? What kind of person is she?*

Easter

Advent　Christmas　Ordinary Time　Lent　Three Days　Easter　Ordinary Time

"Blessed are those who have not seen and have believed." (John 20:29)

227

Catechist Goal

• To introduce the Easter season as the time we celebrate the Resurrection of Jesus

Our Faith Response

• To thank God for new life in Christ

ADDITIONAL RESOURCES

Videos *Following Jesus Through the Church Year: Resurrection Road,* Twenty-Third Publications, 1991. Krispin meets the followers of Jesus who have seen him alive. (10 minutes)

The Story of Jesus for Children, Inspirational Films, 1979 This is an excellent drama of Jesus' life and works through the eyes of children. Use the Resurrection segment. (22-minute segment of 62-minute tape)

To find more ideas for books, videos, and other learning material, visit Sadlier's

www.WE BELIEVE web.com

Lesson Plan

Introduce the Season ___ minutes

• **Pray** the Sign of the Cross and "Yes, Lord, we do believe!"

• **Ask** volunteers to demonstrate how they felt and acted when they experienced great joy or new life. Invite a few the children to tell why they were so joyful. Explain that we will share a story about a girl who has a wonderful reason to celebrate a new life.

• **Read** or tell the *Chaper Story* on page 227C. Discuss Alexis's new life that began when she was ten years old. Ask: *What kind of person is Alexis?* (courageous, trusting, loving, curious, enthusiastic, life-loving). Note that doing something new is not always easy. Point out that the surgery was brand new, and her parents could not be sure that everything would go well. Yet they and Alexis believed that God would be with them no matter what.

• **Print** the words *Easter Season* on the board in a bright color chalk. Ask: *What do you think of when you see those words?* Brainstorm within a two-minute time limit. List on the board. Then stop and summarize the list by emphasizing that the Easter season is the time when we celebrate the Resurrection of Jesus.

• **Invite** the children to look at the photo. Ask: *Why do you think these children look so happy?*

• **Proclaim** together the words on the banner.

Lesson Materials

- large stick-on name tags
- curtain or drapery
- white tunic
- Grade 3 CD
- rhythm instruments
- Reproducible Master 27
- supplies for Easter egg decorating
- books or Internet sources for painting and decorating eggs

Teaching Tip

Making Mobiles

The children will learn cooperation in the small group process of making mobiles. Guide them in crossing the two dowels or unbent coat hangers. Then tape the two together in the center. Have them attach a piece of wire to the center and form the other end into a hook for hanging. Working together will also be necessary when hanging and balancing the paper shapes from the cross beams.

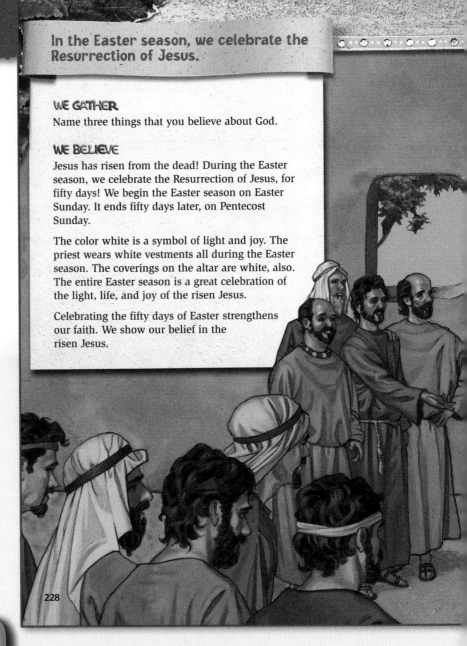

In the Easter season, we celebrate the Resurrection of Jesus.

WE GATHER

Name three things that you believe about God.

WE BELIEVE

Jesus has risen from the dead! During the Easter season, we celebrate the Resurrection of Jesus, for fifty days! We begin the Easter season on Easter Sunday. It ends fifty days later, on Pentecost Sunday.

The color white is a symbol of light and joy. The priest wears white vestments all during the Easter season. The coverings on the altar are white, also. The entire Easter season is a great celebration of the light, life, and joy of the risen Jesus.

Celebrating the fifty days of Easter strengthens our faith. We show our belief in the risen Jesus.

228

Lesson Plan

WE GATHER ___ minutes

Focus on Life Call attention to the *We Gather* on text page 228. Invite the children to write their responses. Then collect and redistribute the papers. Have the children share what their classmates what they have written. Make a list on the board. If any misconceptions arise, gently correct the statement before adding it to the list.

WE BELIEVE ___ minutes

• **Ask** a volunteer to read aloud the *We Believe* statement at the top of page 228. Ask: *What is the most important thing we celebrate in this season?* (Jesus has risen from the dead!) Have the children read silently the first three paragraphs of *We Believe* to find out how long

Easter lasts (from Easter to Pentecost, fifty days), what color is associated with the season and why (white, color of light and joy), and what we do in this season (show our faith in the risen Lord).

• **Gather** the children in a circle and read aloud from John 20:19–29 the story of the risen Jesus and his apostle Thomas. Have two the children supply the voices of Jesus and Thomas. Ask:

- *What did Thomas say when the other disciples told him about Jesus?* (He did not believe and wanted to touch Jesus with his own hands.)

- *What did Jesus tell Thomas?* (Put your hand into my side and believe; blessed are those who have not seen yet have believed.)

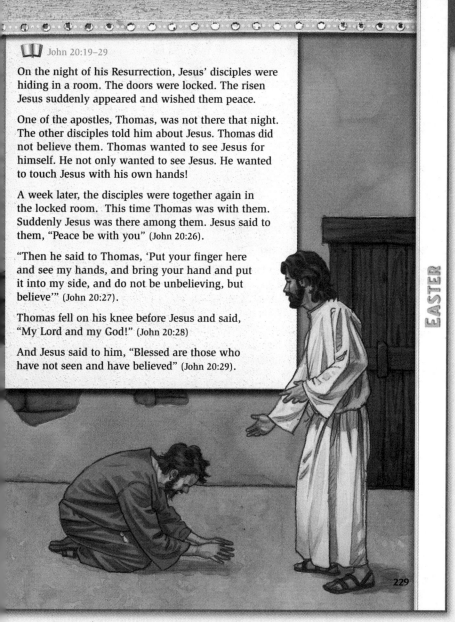

📖 John 20:19–29

On the night of his Resurrection, Jesus' disciples were hiding in a room. The doors were locked. The risen Jesus suddenly appeared and wished them peace.

One of the apostles, Thomas, was not there that night. The other disciples told him about Jesus. Thomas did not believe them. Thomas wanted to see Jesus for himself. He not only wanted to see Jesus. He wanted to touch Jesus with his own hands!

A week later, the disciples were together again in the locked room. This time Thomas was with them. Suddenly Jesus was there among them. Jesus said to them, "Peace be with you" (John 20:26).

"Then he said to Thomas, 'Put your finger here and see my hands, and bring your hand and put it into my side, and do not be unbelieving, but believe'" (John 20:27).

Thomas fell on his knee before Jesus and said, "My Lord and my God!" (John 20:28)

And Jesus said to him, "Blessed are those who have not seen and have believed" (John 20:29).

EASTER

229

ACTIVITY BANK

Make Easter Mobiles

Activity Materials: dowels or coat hangers, construction paper, scissors and markers, string or wire, heavy tape

Form three or more small groups and distribute the mobile-making materials. Ask one the child in each group to serve as the "labor leader." He or she will divide the work among group members. Some of the children will assemble the mobile frame and hanger. Others will begin making the paper cut-outs of Christian symbols (fish, butterfly, egg, lily, cross, candle, baptismal font, dove, empty tomb). Then all can work together to hang the symbols in balance on the frame. Display the completed mobiles around the room.

Saints of the Easter Season

Share these Easter season saints: Saint Bernadette of Lourdes (April 16); Saint George, a Roman martyr (April 23); Saint Catherine of Siena, peacemaker and advisor to popes (April 29); and Saints Philip and James, apostles (May 3).

• **Ask** the entire group to repeat the prayer of the apostle Thomas "My Lord and my God!"

• **Distribute** markers and name tags, as well as the white tunic for Jesus. Have the children make name tags for apostles and disciples (Thomas, Peter, John, and so on; Mary, Martha, Mary Magdalene, and so on). Ask three of the children to alternate as narrators while the others act out the story of the apostle Thomas. For the locked door, have two volunteers hold up the drapery through which Jesus will appear.

Quick Check

✔ *What do we celebrate in the Easter Season?* (the Resurrection of Jesus)

✔ *What do we believe Jesus brings us?* (new life, now and forever)

CONNECTION

To Liturgy

The Easter Season culminates in the joyful feast of Pentecost. Red is the liturgical color of the day. It represents the tongues of fire representing the descent of the Holy Spirit. Encourage the children to wear red on Pentecost. In honor of the Holy Spirit's coming "like a strong driving wind" (Acts 2:2), they might also fly balloons, kites, or windsocks at Pentecost. Red paper flowers, flames, and crepe-paper streamers might be used to decorate the classroom.

To Stewardship

The celebration of Earth Day occurs during the Easter season, on April 22. Share with the children that this day was established in 1970, after we had seen a photo of our planet Earth taken from space. The beauty of this "big blue marble" convinced Americans that God's creation must be protected from pollution. Check the Internet for Earth Day projects.

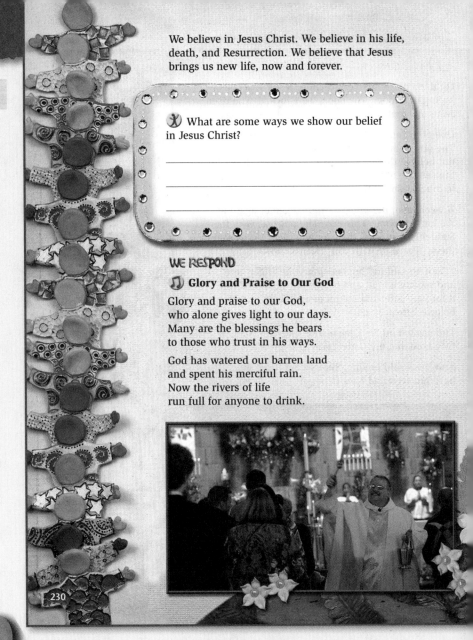

We believe in Jesus Christ. We believe in his life, death, and Resurrection. We believe that Jesus brings us new life, now and forever.

What are some ways we show our belief in Jesus Christ?

_____

_____

_____

WE RESPOND

♪ **Glory and Praise to Our God**

Glory and praise to our God,
who alone gives light to our days.
Many are the blessings he bears
to those who trust in his ways.

God has watered our barren land
and spent his merciful rain.
Now the rivers of life
run full for anyone to drink.

230

Lesson Plan

WE RESPOND   ___ minutes

Connect to Life Tell the children that the song on this page will help us give praise to God. Play the "Glory and Praise to Our God" from the Grade 3 CD. Then play it a second time for the the children to sing along.

• **Ask** the children to read the first paragraph together in one voice, as an Easter choral proclamation.

Brainstorm responess to the activity question. (We can share a smile, offer help, tell a story, do an errand, say a prayer for someone.) Write them on the board. Say: *Now choose three you would like to do and write them on the lines.*

• **Conclude** by saying: *Now quietly tell Jesus what you will do to show your faith in him.*

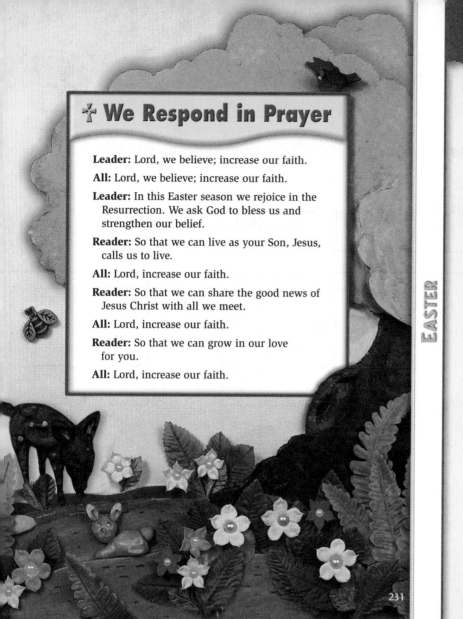

✝ We Respond in Prayer

Leader: Lord, we believe; increase our faith.

All: Lord, we believe; increase our faith.

Leader: In this Easter season we rejoice in the Resurrection. We ask God to bless us and strengthen our belief.

Reader: So that we can live as your Son, Jesus, calls us to live.

All: Lord, increase our faith.

Reader: So that we can share the good news of Jesus Christ with all we meet.

All: Lord, increase our faith.

Reader: So that we can grow in our love for you.

All: Lord, increase our faith.

231

EASTER

PREPARING TO PRAY

The children will pray an Easter season litany.

• Invite the children to learn the response by heart so that they will be able to be attentive to the words of the leader and readers.

The Prayer Space

• In the prayer space, place a large white candle, fresh flowers, a butterfly cut-out, an Easter egg, and a cross. You may also want to have the children decorate using the mobiles that they made this week. Also have ready small paper or fabric flowers and white or gold cloth to drape over the cross.

 This Week's Liturgy
Visit **www.webelieveweb.com** for this week's liturgical readings and other seasonal material.

✝ We Respond in Prayer ___ minutes

• **Gather** in the prayer space and have volunteers arrange the symbolic items on the white-covered table. Ask others to decorate the space with the paper or fabric flowers and to drape the cross with the cloth. Brighten the space with lamps.

Invite the children to close their eyes and breathe deeply. Ask them to imagine what the face of Jesus may have looked like when he rose from the dead. Then have them pray within their hearts: Joy of Jesus, live in me.

• **Serve** as the prayer leader and invite three the children to alternate as readers. Explain that we, like the apostle Thomas, are going to pray that the Lord will increase our faith.

• **Pray** the Sign of the Cross and the prayer. You may want to conclude with the song "Glory and Praise to Our God." You may want to have the children accompany themselves with bells or other rhythm instruments at this time.

231

Name _____

Solve this Easter season crossword puzzle.

Across

1. The number of days this season lasts

5. The risen Jesus is our _____ .

7. We believe and so we say, "_____ Lord and my God!"

8. The season when we celebrate Jesus' rising from the dead

9. The Sunday when this season ends

11. Jesus said, "Blessed are those who have not _____ and have believed."

Down

2. The apostle who would not believe unless he saw and touched Jesus was _____ .

3. Jesus' rising from the dead is called the _____ .

4. The color of the priest's vestments in this season

6. What we do in the season of Jesus' rising

10. Jesus brings us _____ life.

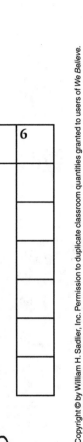

We Respond in Faith

Individual Project

Distribute Reproducible Master 27 and invite the children to complete the seasonal crossword puzzle. Then have them exchange papers and check each other's work. Challenge them to use each word to retell the events of the first Easter season.

Answers: **Across:** fifty, Savior, my, Easter, Pentecost, seen; **Down:** Thomas, Resurrection, white, rejoice, new

Group Project

Explain to the children that the ancient art of *pysanka* or decorating Easter eggs can be practiced as a form of prayer. While carefully and patiently drawing designs, the decorator meditates on the meaning of Christian symbols like the fish for Jesus or a butterfly for Resurrection. With the help of parent or older the child mentors, involve the third graders in the process of making "prayer eggs." Each colored egg should be adorned with one or more Easter symbols as the artist quietly considers its meaning. While working, the children may also pray for the person to whom they will present the egg as a gift. You can find directions for egg decorating on many Internet sites and in books at your local library.

HOME CONNECTION

Sharing Faith with My Family

Make sure to send home the family page (pupil page 232).

Encourage the the children to involve their families in the Easter egg game on Easter Sunday. Remind them to write a joyful Easter prayer with their families.

For additional information and activities, encourage families to visit Sadlier's

www.WeBelieveweb.com

PUPIL PAGE 232

Chapter 28 Sharing Faith in Class and at Home

Sharing Faith

"The family home is rightly called 'the domestic church,' a community of grace and prayer, a school of human virtue and of Christian charity."

Catechism of the Catholic Church, 1666

Overview

This chapter will focus on three major concepts of the Grade 3 program: that we help the Church grow by sharing our love for Jesus; that a sacrament is a special sign given to us by Jesus; that we share our belief in Jesus through our words and actions.

For Adult Reading and Reflection
You may want to refer to paragraphs 1655–56, 2205, 2208, and 2233 of the *Catechism of the Catholic Church*.

Catechist Background

Who is someone you admire?

People inspire us for different reasons. We may like the way a movie star looks or the way a football player throws the ball. We may wish we could sing like a diva or be as rich as a millionaire. Such people are considered role models because they generate a desire to replicate what they do or have.

There are other people we *admire*. We do not want to be like them because of what they look like or what they possess. We respect them because of their traits of love, compassion, integrity, or generosity. As role models they inspire us to imitate their behavior and attitudes.

Parents need good role models as much as their children. All too often news stories and pop entertainment focus the spotlight on parents who are

negligent, self-absorbed, or incompetent. It can lead to stereotyping parents unfairly and a tendency to seek out the worst in family life.

The Church views the family in a different, more positive light. As "domestic church" the family is the locus for Christian formation. It shares in the mission of the larger Church and has much to contribute to spreading the word of God to others. When, as catechists, we provide resources, encouragement, affirmation, and inspiration to parents, we help to strengthen the domestic church.

What examples of Christian charity do you see in family life today?

Planning Guide

Focus	Presentation in Class	Presentation At Home
Part 1		
pages 233–234 *Catholics carry out Jesus' work in the world by sharing his good news with others.* **For preview:** before Chapter 4, page 43 **For review:** after Chapter 5, pages 56–57	• Read the story together. You may want to choose students to read the parts of Theo, Uncle Jack, and Narrator. Then discuss *Talk About It*. • Discuss *Because We Believe*. • Make plans for a Good News-paper. Brainstorm ideas. Have students work in pairs. • Send home page 234 and the Family Blessing found on page 238A.	• Talk about ways families share good news among themselves and with others. • Discuss the questions in *With Your Family*. • Discuss ways your parish shares the good news of Jesus with your community. • Discuss the photo and pray the prayer.
Part 2		
pages 235–236 *We can be signs of God's love by what we say and do.* **For preview:** before Chapter 15, page 131 **For review:** after Chapter 19, pages 168–169	• Discuss the pictures and ask the children to circle the signs of God's love. Discuss the questions in *Talk About It*. • Read and discuss *Because We Believe*. • Work in small groups and discuss the topics listed in *With Your Class*. You may want to chart ideas and choose to act on one or two. • Send home page 236.	• Discuss the signs of God's love you see around you, especially in your family. • Discuss the questions in *With Your Family*. • Discuss any special challenge or responsibility you face as a family, and how each member can help. • Pray the verses from Psalm 86.
Part 3		
pages 237–238 *We can be witnesses by sharing our belief in Jesus through our words and actions.* **For preview:** before Chapter 26, page 219 **For review:** after Chapter 26, pages 224–225	• Read and discuss the story. Consider why we "look up to" various people. • Read and discuss *Because We Believe*. • Recall favorite saints and saints familiar to the group. Two or three children may wish to work together to write about a particular saint. • Send home page 238 and the *We Believe* Family Survey on page 233C.	• Discuss what witnessing to faith in Jesus Christ means. • Find pictures and stories of people who are witnesses to Jesus Christ in word and action. You may want to display these at home. • List ways your family can witness to Jesus. • Pray the Hail Mary together.

For additional ideas, activities, and opportunities: Visit Sadlier's **www.WeBelieveweb.com**

We Believe Family
SURVEY

Your child brought home three different kinds of family pages this year. Through these pages you shared faith together!

What was your child most enthusiastic about sharing with your family?

_____

_____

_____

What activities sparked spirited family discussion?

_____

_____

_____

What part of these SHARING FAITH pages did your family enjoy the most?

_____

_____

_____

What activities did they like most?

_____

_____

_____

Does your family have any special prayers or activities that you would like to share with other _We Believe_ families? If so, tell us about them.

_____

_____

_____

Is there anything else you'd like to share?

_____

_____

_____

We'd like to hear from you!

Send us this survey at: _We Believe_ Family Survey
c/o Sadlier, 9 Pine Street, New York, NY 10005
or at:

www.WeBelieveweb.com

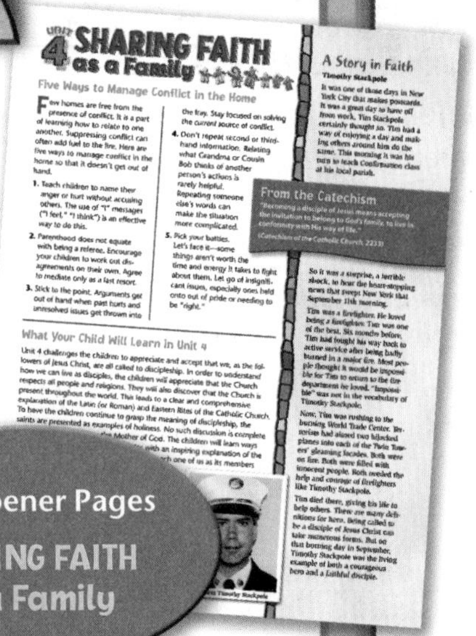

Unit Opener Pages

SHARING FAITH
as a Family

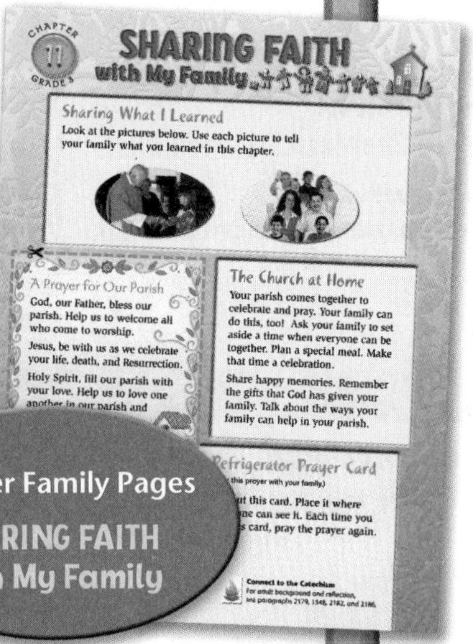

Chapter Family Pages

SHARING FAITH
with My Family

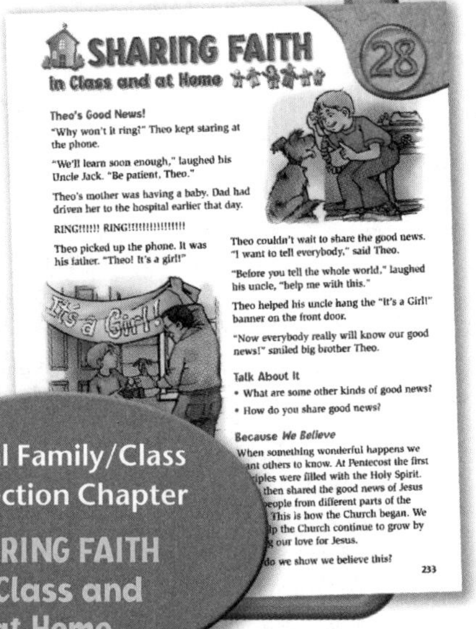

Special Family/Class Connection Chapter

SHARING FAITH
in Class and
at Home

SHARING FAITH
in Class and at Home

Theo's Good News!

"Why won't it ring?" Theo kept staring at the phone.

"We'll learn soon enough," laughed his Uncle Jack. "Be patient, Theo."

Theo's mother was having a baby. Dad had driven her to the hospital earlier that day.

RING!!!!!! RING!!!!!!!!!!!!!!!

Theo picked up the phone. It was his father. "Theo! It's a girl!"

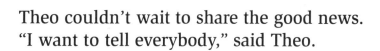

"Do not be afraid; for behold, I proclaim to you good news of great joy."
Luke 2:10

Theo couldn't wait to share the good news. "I want to tell everybody," said Theo.

"Before you tell the whole world," laughed his uncle, "help me with this."

Theo helped his uncle hang the "It's a Girl!" banner on the front door.

"Now everybody really will know our good news!" smiled big brother Theo.

Talk About It

• What are some other kinds of good news?

• How do you share good news?

Because *We Believe*

When something wonderful happens we want others to know. At Pentecost the first disciples were filled with the Holy Spirit. They then shared the good news of Jesus with people from different parts of the world. This is how the Church began. We can help the Church continue to grow by sharing our love for Jesus.

How do we show we believe this?

233

We can carry out Jesus' work in the world by sharing his good news with others.

With Your Class

Work with your classmates to make a "*Good News*-paper."

• Give your paper a name.

• Write a story about Jesus' good news.

"The Christian family has an evangelizing and missionary task."

(Catechism of the Catholic Church, 2205)

With Your Family

Read page 233 together. Talk about ways we share good news with others.

Take a look at your family. What "good news" do you see?

• What is something our family does well together?

• How did someone in our family help me today?

• How has our family helped others?

Pray Together

Loving Jesus,

Our family and parish have been blessed with your good news.

Amen.

NOW WHAT?
Bring this page back to class ☐   Keep this page at home ☐

SHARING FAITH
in Class and at Home

Look at the pictures. Circle the signs of God's love.

Talk About It

Look at what you circled. Why are these signs of God's love?

Because *We Believe*

A sacrament is a special sign given to us by Jesus. Through the sacraments we receive and share in God's own life and love. The Church celebrates seven sacraments. The seven sacraments are Baptism, Confirmation, Eucharist, Reconciliation, Anointing of the Sick, Matrimony, and Holy Orders.

How do we show we believe this?

Christ the King PARISH Clothing Drive

"For you are great and do wondrous deeds; and you alone are God."

Psalm 86:10

235

We can be signs of God's love by what we say and do.

With Your Class

Work in small groups and discuss:

- things you can do to make new classmates feel welcome

- ideas for making your classroom a more forgiving place

- ways that your class can reach out to people in need in your community.

With Your Family

Read page 235 together. Talk about the signs of God's love that are around us. Answer these questions.

- How does your family offer forgiveness to one another?

- How does your family show love for one another?

- How does your family help people outside of your home?

"The family should live in such a way that its members learn to care and take responsibility for the young, the old, the sick, the handicapped, and the poor."

(Catechism of the Catholic Church, 2208)

Pray Together

**"Teach me, LORD, your way that I may walk in your truth. . . .
I will praise you with all my heart,
glorify your name forever,
Lord my God.
Your love for me is great."**

Psalm 86:11–13

NOW WHAT?
Bring this page back to class ☐   Keep this page at home ☐

SHARING FAITH
in Class and at Home

A Good Example

Ben and Will could not believe their luck. Ben's mom had gotten tickets for the soccer game. Ben wanted to be just like Michael Wilson, the star soccer player.

Suddenly Michael Wilson was right in front of Ben and Will! The crowd moved toward the soccer star. Then a small frightened voice called, "Help!" The crowd was pushing a young child! In a split second, Michael Wilson raced to the child's side. He quickly picked her up until her parents were able to get to her.

Ben now knew another reason why he wanted to be just like Michael Wilson.

What Do You Think?

• How is Michael Wilson a good example?

• Why did Ben want to be like Michael?

Because *We Believe*

Saints are examples, too. They are followers of Jesus who lived lives of holiness on earth and now share eternal life with God. Saints show us how to be disciples of Jesus.

Disciples of Jesus Christ are *witnesses* to their faith. We are witnesses when we treat others with kindness and respect. We are witnesses when we live peacefully and fairly with others. We are witnesses when we do what is right even when it is hard.

How do we show we believe this?

"For those who are led by the Spirit of God are children of God."

Romans 8:14

All of us can be witnesses by sharing our belief in Jesus through our words and actions.

With Your Class

Saints show us how to be disciples of Jesus. Name a saint whom you admire.

- How does his or her life serve as a witness to the faith?

- How do you want to be like him or her?

A march for peace

"**Becoming a disciple of Jesus means accepting the invitation to belong to _God's family_, to live in conformity with His way of life.**"

(Catechism of the Catholic Church, 2233)

With Your Family

Read page 237. Talk about what it means to be a witness to faith in Jesus Christ.

Use newspapers, magazines, or the Internet to find pictures and stories of people who are witnesses to faith in Jesus through their words and actions. Share these stories with your family. List ways that your family can be witnesses to faith in Jesus.

Pray Together

**Mary is our greatest example of witness.
Pray the Hail Mary together.**

NOW WHAT?
Bring this page back to class ☐   Keep this page at home ☐

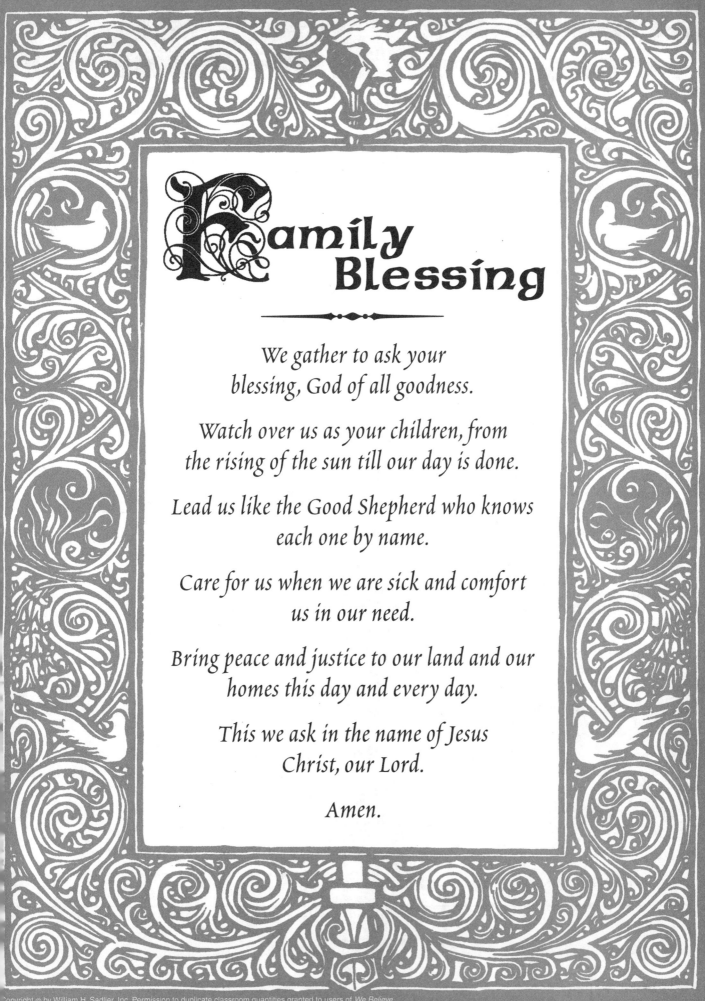

Family Blessing

We gather to ask your
blessing, God of all goodness.

Watch over us as your children, from
the rising of the sun till our day is done.

Lead us like the Good Shepherd who knows
each one by name.

Care for us when we are sick and comfort
us in our need.

Bring peace and justice to our land and our
homes this day and every day.

This we ask in the name of Jesus
Christ, our Lord.

Amen.

ASSESSMENT

In the *We Believe* program each core chapter ends with a review of the content presented, and with activities that encourage the children to reflect and act on their faith. The review is presented in two formats, standard and alternative.

Each unit is also followed by both standard and alternative assessment. The standard test measures basic knowledge and vocabulary assimilation. The alternative assessment allows the children another option—often utilizing another learning style—to express their understanding of the concepts presented.

Using both forms of assessment, perhaps at different times, attends to the various ways children's learning can be measured. You can also see the Grade 3 *We Believe* Assessment Book for:

• standard assessment for each chapter

• alternative assessment for each chapter

• standard assessment for each unit

• alternative assessment for each unit

• a semester assessment which covers material presented in Units 1 and 2

• a final assessment which covers material presented in Units 1, 2, 3, and 4.

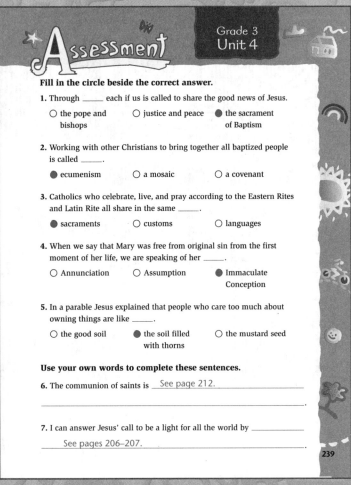

Assessment — Grade 3 Unit 4

Fill in the circle beside the correct answer.

1. Through _____ each if us is called to share the good news of Jesus.
   ○ the pope and bishops   ○ justice and peace   ● the sacrament of Baptism

2. Working with other Christians to bring together all baptized people is called _____.
   ● ecumenism   ○ a mosaic   ○ a covenant

3. Catholics who celebrate, live, and pray according to the Eastern Rites and Latin Rite all share in the same _____.
   ● sacraments   ○ customs   ○ languages

4. When we say that Mary was free from original sin from the first moment of her life, we are speaking of her _____.
   ○ Annunciation   ○ Assumption   ● Immaculate Conception

5. In a parable Jesus explained that people who care too much about owning things are like _____.
   ○ the good soil   ● the soil filled with thorns   ○ the mustard seed

Use your own words to complete these sentences.

6. The communion of saints is _See page 212._
   _____.

7. I can answer Jesus' call to be a light for all the world by _____
   See pages 206–207. _____.

239

 ALTERNATIVE ASSESSMENT

Using the clues in ( ) for help, unscramble the letters to make words. Write the letters in the spaces and circles below.

1. (event in Mary's life) SNAOSIUTMP
   Ⓐ S S U Ⓜ P T Ⓘ O N

2. (agreement) TNANCEOV
   Ⓒ O V Ⓔ N A N T

3. (people who lived holy lives) STSANI
   Ⓢ A I N S

4. (story) BLAPARE
   P A Ⓡ A B Ⓛ E

Now write the circled letters here.
Ⓐ Ⓜ Ⓘ Ⓒ Ⓔ Ⓢ Ⓡ Ⓛ

Unscramble the circled letters to find the word that finishes this sentence:

Amazing events beyond human power are called
M I R A C L E S.

Now use each of the five unscrambled words in a sentence.

240

Prayers and Practices

Sign of the Cross

In the name of the Father, and of the Son, and of the Holy Spirit. Amen.

Our Father

Our Father, who art in heaven,
hallowed be thy name;
thy kingdom come;
thy will be done on earth
    as it is in heaven.
Give us this day our daily bread;
and forgive us our trespasses
as we forgive those
    who trespass against us;
and lead us not into temptation,
but deliver us from evil. Amen.

Glory to the Father

Glory to the Father, and to the Son,
    and to the Holy Spirit:
as it was in the beginning,
    is now, and will be forever. Amen.

Hail Mary

Hail Mary, full of grace,
the Lord is with you!
Blessed are you among women,
and blessed is the fruit
    of your womb, Jesus.
Holy Mary, Mother of God,
pray for us sinners,
now and at the hour of our death.
Amen.

Act of Contrition

My God,
I am sorry for my sins with all my heart.
In choosing to do wrong
and failing to do good,
I have sinned against you
whom I should love above all things.
I firmly intend, with your help,
to do penance,
to sin no more,
and to avoid whatever leads me to sin.
Our Savior Jesus Christ
suffered and died for us.
In his name, my God, have mercy.

• contrition •

• confession •

• penance •

• absolution •

Morning Offering

My God, I offer you this day
all that I think and do and say,
uniting it with what was done
on earth, by Jesus Christ, your Son.

Evening Prayer

Dear God, before I sleep
I want to thank you for this day
so full of your kindness and your joy.
I close my eyes to rest
safe in your loving care.

Grace Before Meals

Bless ✝ us, O Lord,
   and these your gifts,
which we are about to receive
   from your goodness.
Through Christ our Lord. Amen.

Grace After Meals

We give you thanks, almighty God,
for these and all your gifts
which we have received through
Christ our Lord. Amen.

Stations of the Cross

In the stations we follow in the footsteps of Jesus during his passion and death on the cross.

Jesus is condemned to die.

Jesus takes up his cross.

Jesus falls the first time.

Jesus meets his mother.

Simon helps Jesus carry his cross.

Veronica wipes the face of Jesus.

Jesus falls the second time.

Jesus meets the women of Jerusalem.

Jesus falls the third time.

Jesus is stripped of his garments.

Jesus is nailed to the cross.

Jesus dies on the cross.

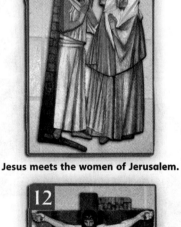

Jesus is taken down from the cross.

Jesus is laid in the tomb.

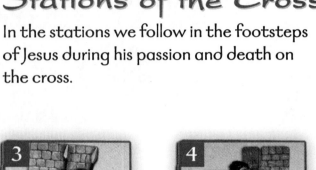

244

Apostles' Creed

I believe in God, the Father almighty,
    creator of heaven and earth.

I believe in Jesus Christ,
    his only Son, our Lord.
He was conceived by the power
    of the Holy Spirit
    and born of the Virgin Mary.
He suffered under Pontius Pilate,
    was crucified, died, and was buried.
He descended to the dead.
On the third day he rose again.
He ascended into heaven,
    and is seated at the right hand
        of the Father.
He will come again to judge
    the living and the dead.

I believe in the Holy Spirit,
    the holy catholic Church,
    the communion of saints,
    the forgiveness of sins,
    the resurrection of the body,
    and the life everlasting.
Amen.

245

The Rosary

A rosary is made up of groups of beads arranged in a circle. It begins with a cross followed by one large bead and three small ones. The next large bead (just before the medal) begins the first "decade." Each decade consists of one large bead followed by ten smaller beads.

Begin the rosary with the Sign of the Cross. Recite the Apostles' Creed. Then pray one Our Father, three Hail Marys, and one Glory to the Father.

To pray each decade, say an Our Father on the large bead and a Hail Mary on each of the ten smaller beads. Close each decade by praying the Glory to the Father. Pray the Hail, Holy Queen as the last prayer of the rosary.

The mysteries of the rosary are special events in the lives of Jesus and Mary. As you pray each decade, think of the appropriate Joyful Mystery, Sorrowful Mystery, Glorious Mystery, or Mystery of Light.

The Five Joyful Mysteries

1. The Annunciation
2. The Visitation
3. The Birth of Jesus
4. The Presentation of Jesus in the Temple
5. The Finding of Jesus in the Temple

The Five Sorrowful Mysteries

1. The Agony in the Garden
2. The Scourging at the Pillar
3. The Crowning with Thorns
4. The Carrying of the Cross
5. The Crucifixion and Death of Jesus

The Five Glorious Mysteries

1. The Resurrection
2. The Ascension
3. The Coming of the Holy Spirit upon the Apostles
4. The Assumption of Mary into Heaven
5. The Coronation of Mary in Heaven

The Five Mysteries of Light

1. Jesus' Baptism in the Jordan
2. The Miracle at the Wedding at Cana
3. Jesus Announces the Kingdom of God
4. The Transfiguration
5. The Institution of the Eucharist

Hail, Holy Queen

Hail, holy Queen, mother of mercy,
hail, our life, our sweetness, and our hope.
To you we cry, the children of Eve;
to you we send up our sighs,
mourning and weeping in this land of exile.
Turn, then, most gracious advocate,
your eyes of mercy toward us;
lead us home at last and show us
the blessed fruit of your womb, Jesus:
O clement, O loving, O sweet Virgin Mary.

Prayer for My Vocation

Dear God,
You have a great and loving plan
for our world and for me.
I wish to share in that plan fully,
faithfully, and joyfully.

Help me to understand what it
is you wish me to do with my life.
Help me to be attentive to the signs
that you give me about preparing for
the future.

And once I have heard and understood
your call, give me the strength
and the grace to follow it
with generosity and love.
Amen.

Holy Water

A holy water font containing blessed
water is placed near the door of the
church. When we enter the church, we put
our fingers into the holy water and then
make the sign of the cross. The water
reminds us of our Baptism, and the prayer
we say expresses our belief in the Blessed
Trinity. Many Catholic families also have
holy water in their homes.

Holy Places

We treat places of prayer (churches,
synagogues, temples, and mosques) with
reverence. In our Catholic churches, we
genuflect toward the tabernacle as we
enter our pew. Genuflecting (touching
our right knee to the floor) is a sign of our
reverence for Jesus Christ, who is really
present in the Blessed Sacrament.

Visits to the Blessed Sacrament

Before Mass on Sundays or at other special times, take a few minutes to visit Jesus, present in the Blessed Sacrament. After you have taken your place in church, kneel or sit quietly. Be very still. Talk to Jesus about your needs and your hopes. Thank Jesus for his great love. Remember to pray for your family and your parish, especially anyone who is sick or in need.

Prayer Before the Blessed Sacrament

Jesus,
you are God-with-us,
especially in this sacrament
of the Eucharist.
You love me as I am
and help me grow.

Come and be with me
in all my joys and sorrows.
Help me share your peace and love
with everyone I meet.
I ask in your name. Amen.

The Seven Sacraments

The Sacraments of Christian Initiation
Baptism

Confirmation

Eucharist

The Sacraments of Healing
Penance and Reconciliation

Anointing of the Sick

The Sacraments at the Service of Communion
Holy Orders

Matrimony

The Ten Commandments

1. I am the LORD your God: you shall not have strange gods before me.

2. You shall not take the name of the LORD your God in vain.

3. Remember to keep holy the LORD's Day.

4. Honor your father and your mother.

5. You shall not kill.

6. You shall not commit adultery.

7. You shall not steal.

8. You shall not bear false witness against your neighbor.

9. You shall not covet your neighbor's wife.

10. You shall not covet your neighbor's goods.

Glossary

Acts of the Apostles (page 52)
book in the Bible that tells the story of the work of the apostles in the early Church

apostle (page 23)
one who is sent

Apostles' Creed (page 85)
Christian statement of beliefs based on the teachings of Jesus Christ and the faith of the apostles

Ascension (page 44)
Jesus' returning to the Father in heaven

assembly (page 142)
people gathered to worship in the name of Jesus Christ

Assumption (page 213)
the belief that, when Mary's work on earth was done, God brought her body and soul to live forever with the risen Christ

Bible (page 28)
collection of books about God's love for us and our call to live as God's people

bishops (page 77)
the successors of the apostles who lead the Church

Blessed Trinity (page 20)
the three Persons in one God: God the Father, God the Son, and God the Holy Spirit

Christians (page 46)
baptized people, followers of Jesus Christ

Church (page 46)
community of people who are baptized and follow Jesus Christ

communion of saints (page 212)
the union of the baptized members of the Church on earth with those who are in heaven and in purgatory

Concluding Rite (page 151)
the last part of the Mass that reminds us to continue praising and serving God each day

conscience (page 158)
God's gift that helps us know right from wrong

covenant (page 197)
an agreement between God and his people

crucified (page 30)
nailed to a cross

deacon (page 101)
a man who is not a priest but has received the sacrament of Holy Orders and serves the Church by preaching, baptizing, and assisting the bishop and priests

dioceses (page 77)
local areas of the Church led by bishops

disciples (page 22)
those who follow Jesus

ecumenism (page 198)
work toward Christian unity

eternal life (page 166)
living forever with God in the happiness
of heaven

Eucharist (page 140)
the sacrament of Jesus' Body and Blood

faith (page 30)
a gift from God that helps us to believe and
trust in him

funeral Mass (page 167)
a special Mass at which we thank God for
the life of a person who has died

gospel (page 53)
good news that we are saved by Jesus
Christ, the Son of God

grace (page 132)
our share in God's life and love

heaven (page 38)
life with God forever

Immaculate Conception (page 213)
the belief that Mary was free from original
sin from the very first moment of her life

Incarnation (page 20)
the truth that God the Son became man

Introductory Rites (page 148)
the first part of the Mass in which we become
one as we prepare to listen to God's word and
to celebrate the Eucharist

justice (page 87)
treating everyone fairly and with respect

Kingdom of God (page 28)
the power of God's love active in
the world

last judgment (page 38)
Jesus Christ coming at the end of time to
judge all people

laypeople (page 108)
baptized members of the Church who share
in the mission to bring the good news of
Christ to the world

liturgy (page 93)
the official public prayer of the Church

Liturgy of the Eucharist (page 150)
the part of the Mass when the bread and wine become the Body and Blood of Christ, which we receive in Holy Communion

Liturgy of the Word (page 148)
the part of the Mass when we listen and respond to God's word

marks of the Church (page 78)
four characteristics that describe the Church: The Church is one, holy, catholic, and apostolic.

martyrs (page 54)
people who die for their faith

Mass (page 141)
celebration of the Eucharist

miracles (page 222)
amazing events that are beyond human power

mission (page 44)
special job

oil of the sick (page 165)
holy oil that has been blessed by a bishop for use in the Anointing of the Sick

original sin (page 133)
the first sin committed by the first human beings

parable (page 220)
a short story that uses things from everyday life

parish (page 100)
community of believers who worship and work together

Passover (page 140)
the Jewish feast celebrating freedom from slavery in Egypt

pastor (page 101)
the priest who leads the parish in worship, prayer, and teaching

Pentecost (page 45)
the day the Holy Spirit came upon the apostles

pilgrimages (page 95)
prayer-journeys to holy places

pope (page 77)
the bishop of Rome, who leads the whole Catholic Church

prayer (page 92)
listening and talking to God

prophet (page 22)
someone called by God to speak to the people

public ministry (page 22)
Jesus' work among the people

repent (page 22)
to turn away from sin and to ask God for help to live a good life

Resurrection (page 31)
Jesus' being raised from the dead

Rite (page 205)
a special way that Catholics celebrate, live, and pray to God

sacrament (page 132)
special sign given to us by Jesus through which we share in God's life and love

sacraments of Christian initiation (page 133)
the sacraments of Baptism, Confirmation, and Eucharist

sacrifice (page 141)
a gift offered to God by a priest in the name of all the people

saints (page 212)
followers of Christ who lived lives of holiness on earth and now share in eternal life with God in heaven

second coming (page 37)
Jesus' coming at the end of time

sin (page 156)
a thought, word, or action that is against God's law

synagogue (page 92)
the gathering place where Jewish people pray and learn about God

vocation (page 108)
God's call to serve him in a certain way

vows (page 110)
promises to God

Index

The following is a list of topics that appear in the pupil's text.
Boldface indicates an entire chapter or section.

Catechist Development

Sadlier is committed to supporting you, the catechist, in your faith and in your ministry. The Sadlier *We Believe* program includes twenty-one Catechist Development articles. Each article provides you with on-going development and helps you to become more aware of the elements of effective catechesis. The opening article precedes the Introductory Chapter and the other articles are found in the final section of your guide.

Each article addresses a specific topic and is written by a nationally recognized expert in that field. The *Resources* section follows each article and offers print and video suggestions to enable you to delve further into the topic. The *Ways to Implement* offers some practical ideas to bring the topic to life in your class. Finally, the *Catechist Corner* features an idea from a catechist and the successful implementation of that idea.

Here are the twenty-one topics, their authors, and the pages on which you can find the articles in your Sadlier *We Believe* Catechist Guide:

Topics and Authors

For additional ideas, activities, and opportunities: Visit Sadlier's **www.WeBelieveweb.com**

257

Catechesis Today and the Catechist

by Carole Eipers, D. Min.

Carole Eipers is the Director of Catechetics for William H. Sadlier, Inc. She has served in parish ministries for over 20 years. Carole was Director of the Chicago Office for Catechesis. She was the President of the National Conference of Catechetical Leadership, and has taught at the Mundelein Seminary, Loyola Chicago, and Loyola New Orleans.

"What's your hurry?" This question may sound quaint, like the memory of a saying on an antique needlepoint. We are more likely in today's world to be told to get going, to hustle, to speed it up. Instant coffee, microwaveable food, half-hour pizza delivery time and instantaneous communications underline the importance of quickness. How *quickly* something can be done seems more important than the *quality* of what is done.

Faith grows slowly. The *General Directory for Catechesis* reminds us that catechesis "is also a gradual activity." (88) How can a catechist honor the slowness necessary for catechesis in a world that is defined by speed?

First, we need to recognize what it is that we are doing in catechesis. "The definitive aim of catechesis is to put people not only in touch, but also in communion and intimacy, with Jesus Christ." (*Catechesi Tradendae* 5) Catechesis is gradual because it is today, as it has always been, a process of developing our relationship with Jesus Christ, through him with the Father and Holy Spirit, and with the community of faith, the Church.

Second, we have to keep a perspective that embraces all of the dimensions of faith and the tasks these dimensions dictate: knowledge of the faith, liturgical education, moral formation, prayer, community life and missionary initiation. (*General Directory for Catechesis*, 85–87) Each of these dimensions of catechesis takes time—for our own faith and for the faith of the children we catechize.

"Why did God make you?" a catechism of the 1950s asked. It answered: "God made us to know, love, and serve him in this life and to be happy with him in the next." That is what catechesis is still about today. Faith is worth the time it takes, for it brings us to eternity. What's your hurry?

Resources

Congregation for the Clergy, *General Directory for Catechesis*. Vatican City: Libreria Editrice Vaticana, 1997.

John Paul II, *On Catechesis in Our Time*. Vatican City: Libreria Editrice Vaticana, 1979.

Ways to Implement Catechesis Today

- The saying "You can't give what you don't have" is certainly true of catechesis. Preparing your lessons carefully means reviewing, learning, and revitalizing the faith we want to share within ourselves first. In preparing well, we reflect on the children we catechize, their lives and needs so we can more effectively relate the message of faith to them. Knowing that faith is God's gift and the Spirit's work, our preparation necessarily includes prayer.

- Catechesis does not happen solely in our lessons. The children are also formed by their families and the parish community. Meet with the children's primary religious educators, their parents/guardians. Share expectations and support. Offer resources to assist them in fulfilling their responsibilities as first teachers of the faith. Identify ways you will have the children get to know the people of the parish.

- In order to connect Jesus and his message with the child's life, we have to know what that child is experiencing. Greet each child as he or she enters, and try to sense his or her feelings and moods. Faith's never-changing assurance of God's love has to speak to all the children as they are this day. It speaks that assurance through you.

- As the day's lesson progresses, listen to the children. Are they engaged? interested? evidencing understanding? If not, how can the discussion or activity be altered to be more helpful to their growth in faith? Let them ask, share, answer, so that the faith becomes their own.

- Faith calls for a response. At the end of each lesson send the children forth on their mission. For young children, it may be a word whispered to them that they will try to live. Older children could be asked to do one simple thing that flows from the lesson.

For additional ideas, activities, and opportunities, visit Sadlier's

www.WeBelieveweb.com

Catechist Corner

With thanks to:

Catherine Walsh
Grade 4 Catechist
Our Lady of Perpetual Help Parish
Brooklyn, New York

Under Catherine's direction, the children in her group have the opportunity to take a "time out" in a special quiet place that is away from the group activities. Catherine designates an area in her room, consisting of a small rug and comfortable pillows. By taking a "time out," the children are free to read books to learn about Jesus, listen to music on the *We Believe* CDs, promote peace by settling differences that they may have with others. They can also take a "time out" to reflect on the day's lesson or have a few quiet moments of prayer. All of which in turn helps in their faith formation.

Notes

Connecting to the Family

by Kathy Hendricks

Kathy Hendricks is a speaker and writer specializing in topics related to religious education, spirituality, and family life. She has over 25 years' experience as a pastoral minister, teacher, and catechetical leader. Kathy is married and has two grown children.

Faith begins in the home. The family is the first school of Christian love, the place where faith is seeded, where it grows and matures. Here are six ways this happens in the midst of everyday life.

Storytelling Families tell stories—about who they are, where they come from, and what they hold dear. These stories are about ways to live and behave towards one another, about life and death, forgiveness and healing. They are stories about love. Storytelling occurs around the dinner table and in the car, at funerals and weddings, when persons, new or familiar, come to visit or stay. Family stories are essentially connected to the larger story of faith.

Celebration Welcoming new family members, sharing meals, forgiving one another are all ways in which families celebrate the presence of God in their lives. Cherished rituals and symbols express love, care, and healing in ways that go beyond what words can convey.

Prayer As they gather around a table or prepare to go to bed at night, families share and teach prayer within the framework of daily life. The rhythmic nature of prayer is woven into the fabric of each day and throughout the seasons of the year.

Morality When families set rules and provide guidelines for behavior, they promote an understanding of Christian morality as a code of conduct that puts family members in strong relationship with God and with one another.

Community Taking one's place in the family provides the first experience of what it means to belong to something bigger than oneself. It means belonging to a community of people who love and care for one another.

Outreach Families' love often spills beyond itself and into the larger community through acts of charity and justice. Whether hosting a foreign exchange student or fixing a Thanksgiving basket for someone in need, families can demonstrate the Church's mission of bringing the good news of Jesus Christ to others.

Resources

A Family Perspective in Church and Society—Tenth Anniversary Edition. Washington, D.C.: United States Catholic Conference, Inc., 1998.

Curran, Dolores. *Traits of a Healthy Family.* New York: Ballantine Books, 1983.

Ways to Implement Connecting to the Family

• Invite the children to draw a picture and tell a story about a favorite family celebration. What did they do (ritual)? What special food or treasured family artifacts (symbol) did they use?

• Send home simple prayer ideas that families can use together. These might come from *We Believe*, other resources, or from the children themselves. Younger children can write simple prayers and take them home. Older children might compose a class prayer for use as grace before or after meals or at another family gathering.

• Create a class mural about families. Have each child color a part of the mural, including a picture of who lives in his or her family and what is special or unique about the household.

• Emphasize images of God who loves us the way loving parents and guardians care for their children.

• Compile a list of rules that the children might want to live by when they are at home. Compare the rules to the ways that we are asked to behave as Christians.

• Be sensitive to various family situations. Use language that keeps in mind children who come from single-parent homes, from blended families, or from homes where a guardian is the primary caregiver.

For additional ideas, activities, and opportunities, visit Sadlier's

www.WeBelieveweb.com

Catechist Corner

With thanks to:
Debby Welch
St. Margaret of Scotland Parish
Green Tree, PA

Debby uses a fun game that involves the children and their family with the parish. Each week, the children are encouraged to lead their families as disciples of Jesus Christ. At the end of the week, Debby invites each child to stand up and tell what his or her family has done to help someone in need. The name of the child and the family's good deed is written on the chalkboard. All the children and their families are congratulated. Then Debby asks her group to decide on the family who will receive a torch. This unlit torch is made by the children from construction paper, plastic cups and dial rods. The "Good News" torch is sent home with the child to the family with a thank-you card signed by the entire class. Debby makes sure that all families get a chance to "win." The children love the game, and families have offered positive feedback.

Notes

T27

Creating an Environment for Catechesis

by Eleanor Ann Brownell, D. Min.

Eleanor Ann Brownell, D. Min. and Vice President for Religion at William H. Sadlier, Inc., has served in Catholic school and parish ministries for over forty years. She is recognized nationally and internationally for her enthusiastic seminars and workshops in Catholic education and leadership. Eleanor has a profound influence on Catholic religious education.

As a catechist, creating an environment that promotes the catechesis of your students is an important goal. A welcoming environment that promotes love and understanding is essential to enrich the children on their faith journey.

Create an environment for catechesis *within* you. The beginning to successful catechesis begins with you. The manner and spirit in which you present the stories and truths of our faith will do more to create a welcoming environment than any physical object that you place in a room.

Think for moment. How do you communicate with others? What is your personal learning style? How does this influence your teaching style? What are your strengths? What are your weaknesses? What are some ways that you can foster love and learning in your students? Solicit the opinions of your colleagues in faith. Make a plan. How would you like to guide your group on their faith journey?

Creating an environment for catechesis *around* you. There are many wonderful things you can do to physically create a welcoming environment for catechesis, such as a prayer space, learning centers, colorful posters on the walls, etc. Greeting the children personally as they enter the room, is one way to help everyone feel welcomed.

Using the *We Believe* process of "We Gather," "We Believe," and "We Respond" offers excellent opportunities of creating an environment for catechesis around you. For example, the questions found in the "We Gather" allow the children to share their life experiences. This feature is an excellent teaching tool that gives you, the catechist, an opportunity to show respect for the children's stories and opinions, while learning about their experiences.

Creating an environment for catechesis begins with you. Be open. Be honest. Be an example to the children of how a follower of Jesus listens and shares.

Resources

Coles, Robert. *The Spiritual Life of Children.* Boston: Houghton-Mifflin, 1990.

Mongoven, Anne Marie. *The Prophetic Spirit of Catechesis.* Mahwah: Paulist Press, 2000.

Ways to Implement Creating an Environment for Catechesis

- Share your own ideas and stories with the children. As they get to know you, they will be more willing to participate in the class or group.

- Invite the children to make a group or class list of words that "help" or "heal," and encourage them to avoid using words that "hurt." Set an example by being encouraging, complimentary, and optimistic. Avoid critical or judgmental responses.

- Get to know your children. Try to have casual conversations individually and as a group, as often as possible. Meet the children's parents or guardians. Encourage interactive communication between the home and the parish or school.

- You might want to have music playing as the children settle for the "We Gather" discussion or activity. The *We Believe* CDs are excellent resources.

- Build community in your class or group by encouraging everyone to participate. Include fun activities in your lessons. Share a laugh with your class or group. Bring your children together by showing how much you enjoy being with them.

- Personalize your room however possible. Display photographs of the children, class work, artwork, etc. Children who see their names in the room get a feeling of belonging.

For additional ideas, activities, and opportunities, visit Sadlier's

www.We Believe web.com

Catechist Corner

With thanks to:

Zee Ann Poerio
Third Grade Teacher
St. Louise de Marillac School
Pittsburgh, PA

Zee Ann Poerio asks her students, "What would Jesus want us to do?" to create an environment for catechesis. At the beginning of the year, Zee Ann has her students work together to make a list of classroom rules. She writes their rules on a large poster board. Then, she tells her students that they only need to remember one thing and tears up the rules. She writes on the board, *What would Jesus want us to do?* Zee Ann tells her children to ask themselves that question whenever they are making a choice. If ever there is a problem in the class during the year, she asks her students, "Is that something Jesus would want us to do?" This one question helps everyone learn to make the right choices.

Notes

T29

Using Storytelling with Children

by Julie Brunet

Julie Brunet is an author and national creative consultant for William H. Sadlier, Inc. Julie received her B.A. in religious studies from Loyola University in New Orleans and a B.A. in elementary education from the University of Southwestern Louisiana in Lafayette, LA.

Jesus was a master teacher. He knew how very important the experiences of his listeners were. Jesus taught by using parables—stories that touched on the daily life experiences of his listeners—so that they could understand the meaning behind the stories.

Storytelling is an integral aspect of educating children in the truths of our faith. Used to teach values as well as to entertain, stories can be a great way for children to learn about the world around them. Not only is information communicated easily and effectively through a story, but children themselves benefit as well. They can explore their own ideas and feelings. They can express themselves so that others get to know them better even as they get to know themselves. Socialization skills are practiced, and language abilities are developed. A child's cultural heritage can be explored and shared as well.

How can stories be included effectively in the classroom? They can be used to begin, develop, reinforce, or conclude a lesson. Stories can provide information, emphasize lesson themes, and help children make connections and discover insights into what they are learning.

One of the most important aspects of storytelling is the relationship between the teller and the listener. Select stories that will be interesting for the children. The stories should be interesting and varied. Familiarize yourself with the story beforehand so that you can tell it confidently and enthusiastically.

Develop your own storytelling style by using your voice and gestures to make the story come alive. Involve the children directly to make them partners in the experience. Adapt details to personalize the story for your listeners, and invite

(continued on next page)

Resources

Cooper, Patsy. *When Stories Come to School: Telling, Writing & Performing Stories in the Early Childhood Classroom.* New York: Teachers and Writers Collaborative, 2000.

MacDonald, Margaret Read. *The Storyteller's Start-up Book.* Little Rock, Arkansas: August House Publishers, Inc., 1993.

Storytelling, Learning and Sharing, with Sandy Jenkins, 45 minutes, Coyote Creek Productions, 1995. (VHS format)

them to repeat a response, a sound, or an action as you tell the story. Being open to the unexpected can enhance your listeners' experience of the story as well as your own.

Ways to Implement Using Storytelling with Children

- Choose stories that appeal to the group.

- Be familiar with the story.

- Establish eye contact with the listeners.

- Use music and poetry to embellish the story.

- Have the children repeat phrases or patterns from the story.

- Provide props for the children to manipulate as the story unfolds.

- Have the children represent characters in the story, acting out the story as it is told.

- Ask thought-provoking questions throughout the story to encourage the children to become active participants.

- Have the children make up the ending of the story or retell the story with a new ending.

- Have the children make up a story as a group.

- Provide puppets for the children to use to act out the story as it is told.

- Provide flannel-board characters for the children to use to retell the story.

For additional ideas, activities, and opportunities, visit Sadlier's

www.WeBelieve.web.com

Catechist Corner

With thanks to:
Veronica Clark
Third Grade Teacher
St. Margaret of Scotland Parish
Green Tree, PA

Veronica uses drawing as a storytelling tool with her third grade class. For example, when the children learn about a story from Scripture, they are asked to illustrate a part of the story at home or in the classroom. The next time that the children come together, Veronica asks them to retell the story using the pictures they drew. The children's pictures are compiled into one book. This book of drawings is then shared with another class.

Notes

Catechist Development

Nurturing Prayer in Children

by John Stack

The late John Stack was a vital member of the sales team at William H. Sadlier, Inc. for over nineteen years. In addition, John served as a Catholic schoolteacher and a catechist in the Diocese of Pittsburgh, PA and Wheeling-Charleston, WV for over thirty years. His talks and workshops will be remembered fondly by the thousands of people who were inspired by his unique gifts and his extraordinary witness for Christ.

The followers of Jesus made a request of him: "Lord, teach us to pray."(Luke 11:1) I firmly believe that, to this day, the greatest gift that we as catechists can share with the children is to develop a lifelong, personal relationship with God through the power of prayer.

We know that prayer is conversation with God, but sometimes we overlook the fact that this conversation is part of a *relationship* and is a *dialogue*, not a monologue. Prayer comes from who we are and is necessary to our relationship with God. Help to nurture the children's relationship with God by encouraging them to "talk" to God everyday. Let them know that they can talk to God about anything at anytime anywhere.

The Scriptures show us the way Jesus wants us to pray when he taught us the Lord's Prayer. Children learn by example. Encourage the children to pray using Jesus as a model. Jesus turned to his Father in prayer before important moments in his life. Children need to know that they can turn to God in the decisive moments of their lives. As Jesus drew apart from his followers to pray in solitude, children need to learn to set aside time regularly to be alone with God as well. Children can also learn to pray in faith as Jesus did. They can learn from his example to rely on God in everything and to ask for what they need.

Remind the children that they can pray in thanksgiving and praise, to bless, to ask for help (petition), and pray for others and themselves (intercession). Help the children to learn the cycle of the liturgical year and its great feasts. These provide the basic rhythms of the Catholic life of prayer. Invite the children to learn to focus their attention on Jesus for brief periods of time in order to lay the groundwork for meditation and contemplation later on in their lives.

Whenever possible include prayer for the children's families as part of your own personal prayer as well as classroom or group prayer. Encourage families to participate in prayer whenever possible at home, at school, and in the parish.

Resources

Cronin, Gaynell Bordes. *Friend Jesus: Prayers for Children (Guiding Children into Daily Prayer)*. Cincinnati: St. Anthony's Messenger Press, 1999.

Gargiulo, Barbara. *How Do I Talk to God?* Allen, TX: Thomas More Publishing Co., 1998.

Ways to Implement Nurturing Prayer in Children

- At the beginning of the year gather the building blocks for your prayer space: the Bible, a crucifix, various colored cloths (green, purple, red, and white) to reflect the liturgical year, natural elements of the seasons, and pictures or statues of the saints whose feast days are celebrated in a particular month.

- Gather information to personalize the class or group prayer experience. A "Good News" center is a great way to collect information about the children's life stories. Ask for their birthdays, their baptismal dates, the names of their pets, and family members' birthdays. From this information, you can personalize the prayer space throughout the year. You will have the names of the children who are celebrating birthdays each week. For the feast of Saint Francis of Assisi on October 4, you can display the names of the children's pets. On the Baptism of the Lord, showcase the children's names and their baptismal dates.

- Develop the children's global awareness of the necessity of prayer. Using an inflatable globe and a box of adhesive bandages, encourage the children to place a bandage on the part of the world where the people who most need comfort and prayer live.

- Make a visit to the church. Stand by the ambo and pray for everyone who proclaims the word of God. Or perhaps you can walk to the rectory and pray for strong leadership to guide your parish and to pray for vocations.

- Build into each lesson a few moments for the children to meditate. Meditation engages thought, imagination, and emotion as well as strengthens the will to follow Jesus.

For additional ideas, activities, and opportunities, visit Sadlier's

www.WeBelieveweb.com

Catechist Corner

With thanks to:
Rosemary Hart
Teacher and Catechist
Saint Margaret Mary Church
Lomita, California

Rosemary uses a prayer collection to expand her students' knowledge, appreciation, and love of prayer. She asks each catechist in her parish to submit his or her favorite prayer and a brief explanation, describing how the prayer became known to the catechist. Then, Rosemary compiles the catechists' favorite prayers and explanations into a prayer collection for her students. During the year, she shares these prayers with the class. As the students become acquainted with the prayers, she asks everyone to share the prayers with their families. As an end-of-the-year project, Rosemary asks her students to submit their own favorite prayers for another collection of prayers. This collection is made available for each student to share with his or her family.

Notes

Teaching to Multiple Intelligences

by Brother Robert R. Bimonte, FSC

Brother Robert is currently the Executive Director of the NCEA Elementary Department. He holds graduate degrees in education, psychology, and theology, and conducts workshops for schools, dioceses, and religious communities throughout the country.

The Theory of Multiple Intelligences was developed in 1983 by Dr. Howard Gardner, a professor of education at Harvard University. The theory confirms what teachers have always known—all children learn differently. Through Gardner's research, multiple-intelligence theory has expanded our understanding of intelligence. It has helped us to see that children can be "smart" in a variety of ways.

Dr. Gardner proposed that there are eight types of intelligence or learning styles. They are:

- Musical intelligence (music "smart")
- Linguistic intelligence (word "smart")
- Logical-Mathematical intelligence (reasoning/number "smart")
- Spatial intelligence (picture "smart")
- Bodily-Kinesthetic intelligence (physically "smart")
- Naturalist intelligence (nature "smart")
- Interpersonal intelligence (people "smart")
- Intrapersonal intelligence (self "smart")

Dr. Gardner emphasizes that everyone possesses all eight intelligences to one degree or another. Among the first six, we each have a dominant one, but usually have a repertoire of two or more in which we are comfortable. Between Interpersonal intelligence and Intrapersonal intelligence, Dr. Gardner indicates that individuals have a preference.

Lessons that incorporate multiple intelligences must become a regular part of our teaching methodology. Giving children the option of drawing a picture, making a chart, or acting out a skit taps into several intelligences. Simultaneously, using the multiple-intelligence theory in the classroom or parish setting allows children to express themselves in the way that is most natural for them as well as the manner in which they learn best. There is no question that the best learning takes place when children are actively involved and emotionally engaged in the learning process.

Resources

Armstrong, Thomas. *Multiple Intelligences in the Classroom.* Virginia: ASCD, 1994.

Gardner, Howard. *Intelligence Reframed: Multiple Intelligences for the 21st Century.* New York: Basic Books, 2000.

Ways to Implement Teaching to Multiple Intelligences

- For children with Musical intelligence, include hymns that are connected to the main theological point of the lessons. Encourage them to use music and song to respond to material.

- For children with Linguistic intelligence, include dramatic readings of Scripture, poems and prayers written by saints, and creative writing to connect to the lessons.

- For children with Logical-Mathematical intelligence, include problem-solving activities, timelines, and graphs that relate to the lesson. Introduce the children to ancient units of measure, such as the ephah and the omer.

- For children with Spatial intelligence, include maps of the Bible and other holy places that relate to the lesson. Use art to teach concepts.

- For children with Bodily-Kinesthetic intelligence, include gestures and movements when praying and singing. Engage the children in social service activities that involve physical activity such as walkathons, painting, sorting food/clothes, etc.

- For children with Naturalist intelligence, include information about plants and animals in biblical times that relate to the lessons. Encourage them to care for the environment by planting or tending to a class/parish garden.

- For children with Interpersonal intelligence, include group activities and discussions that relate to the lesson.

- For children with Intrapersonal intelligence, include opportunities for them to spend time working on their own. Encourage the children to keep a journal with reflections on the material.

For additional ideas, activities, and opportunities, visit Sadlier's

www.WeBelieveweb.com

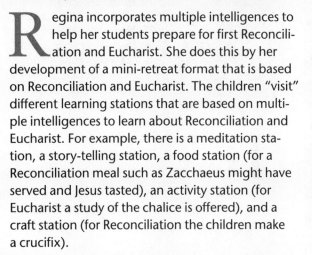

Catechist Corner

With thanks to:
Regina Doherty, CRE
Catechist (2nd grade)
Immaculate Conception Parish
Stony Point, New York

Regina incorporates multiple intelligences to help her students prepare for first Reconciliation and Eucharist. She does this by her development of a mini-retreat format that is based on Reconciliation and Eucharist. The children "visit" different learning stations that are based on multiple intelligences to learn about Reconciliation and Eucharist. For example, there is a meditation station, a story-telling station, a food station (for a Reconciliation meal such as Zacchaeus might have served and Jesus tasted), an activity station (for Eucharist a study of the chalice is offered), and a craft station (for Reconciliation the children make a crucifix).

Notes

Meeting Individual Needs

by Kirk Gaddy

Kirk Gaddy is principal of St. Katharine School in Baltimore, Maryland. A past president of the Elementary School Principals Association as well as a professionally certified catechist, Mr. Gaddy has served the Archdiocese of Baltimore on the Collaborative Council of the Division of Catholic Schools and on the Board of Directors of the Office of African American Catholic Ministries.

The purpose of catechesis is to form disciples of Jesus Christ. This formation is a process "undertaken to reach the maturity of the faith 'given as Christ allotted it' (*Eph 4:7*) and according to the possibilities and the needs of everyone." (*GDC* 143)

Each student we catechize has unique possibilities and needs. To be an effective catechist, one must get to know each student in order to recognize his/her individual strengths and weaknesses. By being aware of the individual student's developmental stage, reasoning abilities, comprehension level, and social skills, the catechist can effectively build on the student's existing strengths and help with weaknesses.

Catechists need to observe students to determine how well each student is learning. Regular assessments can enable the catechist to identify teaching strategies that prove effective for each learner. Assessment can also help the catechist to note the faith concepts that an individual student may need reinforced. No matter what his or her abilities are catechists should have positive expectations for each student.

If catechists teach as Jesus did, students will know they are understood, accepted, and supported. They will feel welcomed and included in each lesson, as well as called to learn and grow in their knowledge and practice of the faith.

Each student, made in the image and likeness of God, is an equally important member of the school or parish community. It is the catechist who takes the lead in ensuring an atmosphere of acceptance toward each student. Through this modeling behavior, students, too develop an attitude of acceptance of all, thus helping to build the kingdom of God on earth.

Resources

Levine, Mel D. *A Mind at a Time: America's Top Learning Expert Shows How Every Child Can Succeed.* New York: Simon & Schuster, 2002.

Vail, Priscilla L. *Smart Kids with School Problems: Things to Know & Ways to Help.* New York: Penguin, 1988.

Ways to Implement Meeting Individual Needs

Catechists can effectively meet the various learning needs of each student by doing the following:

- Meet basic needs for physical comfort with appropriate furniture and equipment, ventilation, and opportunities for movement.

- Know and review regularly the developmental stages of the children to target their specific needs.

- Identify the strengths of the students and invite them to use their unique gifts.

- Use cooperative learning with partners or groups selected to balance needs and talents.

- Offer opportunities for success in a safe and caring atmosphere that fosters self-esteem.

- Provide clear expectations, concise directions, and explicit time frames for assignments and activities.

- Be flexible with class or group procedures to accommodate particular student needs or situations.

- Employ a variety of teaching techniques and learning experiences. Use visual, auditory, and tactile aids when teaching abstract concepts of faith.

- Send "good news" notes home affirming not only the students' performance but their qualities and behaviors that are consistent with our faith.

- Review important material with the students before introducing new information.

- Relate the content of the lesson to the students' life experiences.

For additional ideas, activities, and opportunities, visit Sadlier's

www.WeBelieveweb.com

Catechist Corner

With thanks to:
Trace Woodson
St. Katharine School
Baltimore, Maryland

Trace incorporates cooperative group activities as a means of assisting those of her students with special needs. Trace has found that cooperative group activities that engage each child provide opportunities for children with special needs to receive support from their peers, practice the skills of teamwork, and build self-confidence. In her favorite activity (called "Surprise!), the class is divided into smaller groups. Every group is given a brown paper bag to decorate. Each child writes an affirmation for each member of his or her group. (For example, *John is a good listener.*) The affirmations are then placed in the individual group's bag. The "Surprise!" bags are placed on a table near the prayer corner. Then all the children come together in prayer to share the "surprises" in each group's bag, to give praise to Jesus, and to give thanks for the special gifts of each person.

Notes

Developing a Liturgical Sense in Children

by Sister Linda L. Gaupin, CDP, Ph.D.

Sister Linda L. Gaupin, CDP, is Diocesan Director for Religious Education for the Diocese of Orlando. She is the project director for the text, The Spirit Sets Us Free and is the former Associate Director for the Secretariat for the Liturgy at the USCCB. She has a Ph.D. from the Catholic University of America.

O ne of the most enjoyable tasks of catechetical ministry is forming children into the liturgical life of the Church.

Liturgical prayer has such tremendous power to form us in the faith. It is no wonder that it is one of the primary sources for catechesis. However, this rich source of formation is sometimes overlooked in catechesis. In fact, the *General Directory for Catechesis* identifies a weak link between catechesis and liturgy as one of the problems affecting the vitality of catechesis in recent years [*GDC* 30].

As catechists, we can develop a liturgical sense in children by celebrating the rich treasury of liturgical prayer, directing catechesis on liturgical symbols, keeping the liturgical year, and respecting repetition.

Liturgical prayer includes Mass and the sacraments, morning and evening prayer, liturgies of the word, blessings, and many other ritual celebrations. Encourage children to become familiar with all types of liturgical prayer throughout their catechetical formation.

By directing catechesis on liturgical symbols, children become aware of the symbols' beauty and placement within the liturgy. The assembly, water, oil, cross, laying on of hands, light, white garment, and bread and wine are the dominant symbols in our liturgical rites that mark and shape us as a people. Catechesis on the symbols and gestures, which go along with these symbols, opens up their many levels of meaning, and using the symbols and gestures in prayer forms us in the faith.

By keeping the liturgical year, the children learn the major truths of the faith that are unfolded throughout the liturgical year. Celebrating various liturgical prayers appropriate to a season, catechesis on the season, and respecting the integrity of the season form children in the major teachings of the Church.

Good liturgical prayer is repetitious. Repetition allows us to make the liturgy our own, to participate fully.

Resources

Huck, Gabe. *Preparing Liturgy for Children and Children for Liturgy.* Chicago: Liturgy Training Publications, 1989.

Mazar, Peter. *School Year, Church Year: Activities and Decorations for the Classroom.* Chicago: Liturgy Training Publications, 2001.

Ways to Implement Developing a Liturgical Sense in Children

- Incorporate a liturgical calendar within the program calendar. Schedule Masses on significant days. Include blessings from the *Book of Blessings* that address special seasons and/or events in the life of children. Plan special seasonal celebrations (such as in Advent and Lent). Celebrate the sacrament of Reconciliation on appropriate days in the calendar as well as during significant seasons.

- Attend to the environment. Ensure that the dominant symbols pervade (cross, light, water, etc.) and are not overshadowed by secondary symbols. Use the colors of the various liturgical seasons throughout the environment. Set aside a special area in each room for prayer. Include the word of God and dominant liturgical and seasonal symbols of the season.

- Form a liturgy committee. Good liturgy does not just happen! Form a committee of adults and older children in the school or parish to prepare the various liturgical celebrations.

- Get Scripture in the picture. Prominence should be given to enthronement of the word of God. A decorative Bible or lectionary should always be prominently displayed. Set aside time for proclamation and catechesis of the Scripture readings for the coming Sunday. Empower children to learn how to reflect on the readings and share their reflections.

- Make a liturgy and life connection. Our liturgical prayer, symbols, and seasons give meaning to all areas of our life. It is important to make a connection between liturgy and the other subjects that we teach.

For additional ideas, activities, and opportunities, visit Sadlier's

www.WeBelieveweb.com

Catechist Corner

With thanks to:

Mary Birmingham
Director of Liturgy/Music
Our Savior Parish
Cocoa Beach, Florida

Under Mary's direction, the children in Our Savior's Catholic parish community begin their liturgical formation very early. The children come together to prepare the liturgy in accord with the liturgical seasons. They prepare the environment and plan processions. The children are readers and cantors. They select the music. They prepare a reflection on the readings from their religion class. They give an explanation of the saints or feasts appointed for a given day. Everyone is involved in the process. By January, the third grade classes are ready to join the other children in the preparation of the weekly program. Mary has found that the children in the parish are as at home in the celebration of liturgy "as fish are to water." It is an integral part of their spiritual formation.

Notes

Appreciating Diverse Cultures

by Allan Figueroa Deck, SJ, Ph.D., S.T. D.

Father Allan is a Jesuit who has worked for more than 25 years in the Hispanic community as parish priest, teacher, and writer. He is currently director of the Loyola Institute for Spirituality in Orange, CA and adjunct professor of theology at Loyola Marymount University in Los Angeles, CA.

Pope Paul VI's *On Evangelization in the Modern World* says, "Evangelization loses much of its force and effectiveness if it does not take into consideration the actual people to whom it is addressed, if it does not use their language, their signs and symbols, if it does not answer the questions they ask, and if it does not have an impact on their concrete life."

Since the Second Vatican Council the Church has stressed the basic role that cultural awareness plays in its mission. The target of all the Church's teaching activity is specifically *culture*. Catechesis cannot occur when teachers are unfamiliar with culture—their own and that of their students.

Culture refers to the underlying values, ways of thinking and feeling of a people. Understanding culture does not rely on merely recognizing the *externals* such as customs, dress, food, or music, etc. as much as it does on appreciating and understanding the *internals*, a people's *core of meaning*: *What is life all about? Where are we going? What is right and wrong?* When viewed this way, culture is close to religion. Culture and religion both deal with matters that are of great, even ultimate, importance.

The process by which the gospel message engages cultures is called *inculturation*. The questionable ideal of the "melting pot" in the United States has led some to even think that one can legitimately ignore culture in communicating the faith. The Church teaches differently. Not incidentally, the teaching style of Jesus Christ in the parables demonstrated a keen sense of cultural awareness.

As catechists, we must engage the unspoken values that underlie one's own way of life, pursuits, and passions. At the heart of all cultures are narratives or stories, powerful symbols, and rituals. If you want to know your core culture, do a little self-analysis. What stories move you? What symbols elicit a response? Which rituals are most meaningful?

The same analysis must be made of the cultures represented in the classroom or parish setting. Saint Augustine in his treatise on Christian

(continued on next page)

Resources

Arbuckle, Gerald A. *Earthing the Gospel: An Inculturation Handbook for the Pastoral Worker.* Maryknoll, NY: Orbis Books, 1990.

Gallagher, Michael Paul. *Clashing Symbols: An Introduction to Faith and Culture.* Mahwah, NJ: Paulist Press, 1997.

education insists that one must *love* his or her students. If you know nothing about their culture or, even worse, find nothing lovable in it, your effectiveness as a teacher is limited.

The basic challenge of catechesis is "getting beneath the skin" and loving those we teach. Of course, the final and most important task of the catechist is communicating the gospel message. To do that effectively one must know the *difference* between one's culture and the Christian faith. The gospel and Church teaching are rooted in cultures but always go beyond them.

Ways to Implement Appreciating Diverse Cultures

• Identify the various cultural backgrounds in the class or group. Stress the *catholicity* (universalism) of the Church by sharing examples of how Catholics come in all cultural varieties. Encourage the children to learn that God is the creator of difference.

• Point out the stories, symbols, and rituals of Jesus' own Jewish culture, which was more rural than urban. Use this as springboard for discussion for students to give examples of anything similar in their culture.

• Plan a celebration of diversity by asking your class or group to play music or sing songs in languages from other countries, dress in ethnic clothing, make and share an ethnic food dish, retell a folktale or story that is from another culture, etc.

• If possible, ask your students to explain how they celebrate special days like *quinceañeras*, or Baptisms. Have them research special feasts or days celebrated in other cultures.

• Ask your students whether all the customs or ways of doing things in their culture are consistent with the gospel requirement that we love God, neighbor, and ourselves.

For additional ideas, activities, and opportunities, visit Sadlier's

www.WeBelieveweb.com

Catechist Corner

With thanks to:
Deborah Quirke
St. Philip and James School
Bronx, New York

Deborah helps her students appreciate diversity by using magazine pictures of people from around the world. Under Deborah's direction, the children talk about the ways the people are different, and the ways they are alike. This activity helps everyone to remember that we are all God's children. Deborah uses a camera to take a photograph of each child in her group. Then using these photographs and the magazine pictures, the children help to make a class bulletin board that helps them to celebrate the diversity of all God's children.

Notes

Religious Education Assessment

by Sr. Marie Pappas, CR

Sister Marie Pappas, CR, a Sister of the Resurrection, is currently associate superintendent for religious education for the office of the Superintendent of Schools for the Archdiocese of New York. She is also an adjunct professor of Catechetics at Dunwoodie Seminary.

The catechist asks, "Have I effectively imparted what I intended?" The student asks, "Do I know and understand?" Assessment in religious education measures both catechist and student: "Have we, together, achieved the goal for this lesson?"

The *General Directory for Catechesis* reminds us of the fundamental tasks of catechesis: knowledge of the faith, liturgical education, moral formation, prayer and missionary initiation. (73) Religious education is a formation in all of these dimensions of discipleship. It is an awesome responsibility to evaluate our catechizing and the students' progress. Yet, we cannot improve our catechizing nor facilitate the students' growth if we do not measure results and plan accordingly.

The content of religious education necessitates progressive development of higher order thinking skills, opportunities for practical application, and regular assessment by which the religious educator can determine whether or not, and to what degree, progress is happening. Assessment not only measures multi-faceted student faith knowledge and skills, but also redirects the efforts and effectiveness of the religious educator.

Religious education assessment should measure recognition of content, comprehension, capacity for reflection, critical thinking, problem-solving, and application. Religious education assessment should also include a capacity for creative meaningful construction that provides feedback for the catechist. These measure the students' assimilation, appropriation, and

application of the doctrinal, spiritual, liturgical, and relational content of Catholic belief. Assessment can be done through quizzes and tests; discussions; projects; research; portfolios; charitable service and social action; liturgical planning and participation; retreats for personal reflection.

Only through assessment can we know if the students and we are working effectively together. Only if we work effectively can we, with the Holy Spirit, continue to fully form disciples who can share the good news.

Resources

Convey, John J. *Assessment of Catholic Religious Education.* Washington, D.C.: NCEA, 1999.

Wiggins, Grant P. *Assessing Student Performance: Exploring the Purpose and Limits of Testing.* San Francisco: Jossey–Bass, 1999.

Ways to Implement Religious Education Assessment

- Compile a computer bank of objective questions, true and false, multiple choice, matching, definitions, or completions that reflect each key topic. These items can be used to create quizzes and tests.

- Have students design their own assessment to test one another.

- Use life situations for discussion and problem-solving activities. This enables students to practice applying faith to life.

- Have students conduct surveys or interviews related to key topics. Their ability to prepare appropriate questions will demonstrate what they have mastered. Interviewing people will foster the relational aspects of faith.

- Design a checklist related to the curriculum as a student self-inventory. Use these checklists to assess concepts that have been mastered. These checklists can also help you to assess what needs further work, and what students want to learn more about.

Catechist Corner

With thanks to:
Donna Grosso
Curé of Ars Parish
Merrick, New York

Donna assesses her fourth grade group in a fun format called "The Game." At the beginning of the year, teams of four children are randomly assigned. "The Game" is played in three phases. *Phase 1:* The team is read an answer and responds in the form of a question after huddling for one minute. *Phase 2:* The team is asked a question and responds with the answer after huddling for one minute. *Phase 3:* The team chooses either the question or answer format and responds accordingly. Points for each correct response are assigned. Donna has found that by using "The Game" on a weekly basis, she can assess her group and note their individual strengths and weaknesses regarding content. Donna also gives her students take-home sets of "The Game" to share with their families and to use as study guides during the year.

Notes

For additional ideas, activities, and opportunities, visit Sadlier's

www.WE BELIEVE.web.com

Using Children's Art

by Renée McAlister

Renée McAlister is an author and national creative consultant for William H. Sadlier, Inc. She received her B.S. and M.S. in early childhood development and education from Louisiana State University in Baton Rouge, LA.

In his 1999 *Letter to Artists*, Pope John Paul II wrote, "With loving regard, the divine Artist passes on to the human artist a spark of his own surpassing wisdom, calling him to share in his creative power." (No. 1) The catechist is in a unique position to foster artistic expression and to call forth this "spark of the divine" in children.

All children are naturally attracted to art. Given the chance, children will effortlessly produce artistic works. Children use art as a basic tool of expression. They paint, draw, color, and create with self-confidence, ease, and pleasure. Art activities are more than just fun for children. Art plays a major role in their development.

Cognitive Development Knowledge becomes permanent when the information is processed in an artistic way. Abstract faith concepts can be imagined and concretized through art. Using graphs, drawings, paintings, collage, coloring, and other art media strengthens the creative part of the brain. Through art, children explore the real world and invent their own meaningful sets of symbolic marks and colors. Their conceptual understanding of the world around them is depicted in their art.

Motor Development Creating art improves motor skills and eye-hand coordination. Spatial awareness is also developed through art experiences.

Emotional Development Art provides a unique avenue of expression for children of all ages. Their artistic creations represent not only their interpretation of experiences, but also of emotions relevant to these experiences. Art gives a voice to their feelings and to their beliefs.

Social Development Art provides expression for children who are deficient in social skills. Children will often verbalize as they create expressions of art. Sharing faith through art helps develop self-confidence by offering children a safe environment for socialization.

Resources

Costello, Gwen. *School Year Activities for Religion Classes.* Mystic, CT: Twenty-Third Publications, 2000.

Hurwitz, Albert *Children and Their Art.* New York: Harcourt Brace College Publishing, 1994.

Ways to Implement Using Children's Art

- Provide a special area for art activities. In this area, provide a table, easel, or covered floor space for independent art exploration.

- Collect a variety of art supplies and materials, such as crayons, markers, scissors, glue, different sizes and types of paper, clay, paints, brushes, and various other craft items. The greater the variety of supplies, the more creative the art projects. Have paper towels and/or rags available for clean up.

- Encourage the use of liturgical colors and symbols in artwork to express the Church seasons. Display children's art where parishioners can appreciate it.

- Send ideas for family art projects home to begin a liturgical season or to celebrate a feast.

- Respect children's expression of emotions, ideas, and thoughts. Refrain from changing the children's work into a more "perfect picture." Allow the children to direct the progress of their artistic projects. Ask, "Tell me about your artwork," rather than "What is that?" Encourage the children to share their artwork with the group.

- Call the children's attention to the variety of art in *We Believe*. Have them discuss what they see and how it makes them feel. You can also ask them how they would draw the same scene.

For additional ideas, activities, and opportunities, visit Sadlier's

www.WeBelieveweb.com

Catechist Corner

With thanks to:

Bobette Robideaux
Our Lady of Fatima School
Lafayette, Louisiana

By blending art, religion, and technology, children in Bobette's class use the Internet to find instant visuals and Web sites devoted to famous artists. These visuals then become a springboard to discuss the artist's life, artistic style, and subject matter. Later, one-of-a-kind "masterpieces" begin to emerge from the group. A student uses Matisse's cut-paper technique to display something special from God's universe. Other students paint Van Gogh-stylized self portraits with cotton swab brushes. Adventuresome students may even attach art paper to the bottom of their desks and crawl under to paint in the style of Michelangelo and his Sistine Chapel ceiling. Using art helps Bobette become closer to her students. "Watching youngsters accept their unique artistic gifts from God is a constantly inspiring experience."

Notes

T45

Sharing Catholic Social Teaching

by Joan Rosenhauer

Joan Rosenhauer is Special Projects Coordinator for the U.S. Conference of Catholic Bishops' Department of Social Development and World Peace. She has been a lead staff person for the bishops' program on Catholic Social Teaching and Catholic Education.

"The sharing of our social tradition is a defining measure of Catholic education," the U.S. bishops wrote in their statement, *Sharing Catholic Social Teaching*, page 3.

The Church's social teaching includes thought *and* action—both of which are essential elements of Catholic education. The Church has applied the lessons of the Scriptures to the world around us through a series of documents. This body of thought is known as Catholic Social Teaching. There are seven key themes of Catholic Social Teaching. These are:

Life and Dignity of the Human Person Every human is a precious gift from God and must be protected. People must be treated with respect. Public policies must be measured by whether they enhance human life and dignity.

Call to Family, Community, and Participation Human beings are social beings. Our relationships must reflect the values of our faith. This begins with supporting and sustaining the family. In society, all people have both a right and a responsibility to participate in economic, social, and political life.

Rights and Responsibilities of the Human Person A healthy society can be achieved only if basic human rights are protected and responsibilities are met.

Option for the Poor and Vulnerable We care especially for those who are in greatest need. A moral test of our society is how our most vulnerable members are doing.

Dignity of Work and the Rights of Workers Work is one way we participate in God's cre-

ation. If the dignity of work is to be protected, the rights of workers must be respected.

Solidarity of the Human Family We are our brothers' and sisters' keepers no matter where they live throughout the world.

Care for God's Creation We respect the gift of creation by protecting God's people and the environment in which we live.

(continued on next page)

Resources

Himes, Kenneth R. *Responses to 101 Questions on Catholic Social Teaching.* Mahwah: Paulist Press, 2001.

Sharing Catholic Social Teaching: Challenges and Directions. Washington, D.C.: United States Catholic Conference, 1998.

As catechists, our teaching about the Catholic social tradition must include practicing charity *and* working for justice and peace. Through our words and actions, we can encourage our students to build a more just world and to promote the good of all people, especially those who are in greatest need.

Ways to Implement Sharing Catholic Social Teaching

- When teaching about the Eucharist, remind your students that we are called to recognize Christ in the consecrated host and in the "least" of his brothers and sisters.

- When teaching about the Blessed Trinity, discuss the Church's understanding of human beings as social beings (created in the image of God) with important responsibilities to our families and the obligation to participate in society.

- Involve students in service projects such as collecting food or clothing for people in need. For each project, identify one of the seven themes of Catholic Social Teaching to teach in connection with the effort.

- Read about saints, heroes, public leaders, etc. who practiced charity and pursued justice and peace. Also read articles about people who do this today. Discuss how their lives reflect themes from Catholic Social Teaching.

- Work with your diocesan social action office to conduct an "Offering of Letters." Families can be invited to write a letter to a public official about an issue of justice and peace. Students can bring them to a parish or school Mass and include them in the offering. Those who choose not to prepare a letter can write a prayer intention on an index card and include it in the offering.

- If members of your parish belong to a legislative network or participate in a pro-life march or "lobby day" in the state capital, invite them to speak to your students about what they do and why it's important in light of Catholic Social Teaching.

For additional ideas, activities, and opportunities, visit Sadlier's

www.WeBelieve.web.com

Catechist Corner

With thanks to:

Eileen Scheibner
St. Thomas More Parish
Convent Station, New Jersey

Under Eileen's direction, the children in her parish are mindful of Catholic Social Teaching. One important activity is participating in making a yearly "Giving Tree." Eileen and the children compile a list of supplies for people in need throughout the parish community and surrounding areas. These are then illustrated as ornaments and placed on the "Giving Tree" by the children. Each family in the parish is encouraged to fulfill a request on the "Giving Tree." The children actively participate in the process of sorting food, clothes, etc. With the assistance of a social worker and other members of the parish community, Eileen and the children help to deliver the supplies to people in need. The children are eager to share their experiences which naturally leads to discussions on the broader themes of Catholic Social Teaching.

Notes

Catechist Development

Using Scripture

by Rev. Donald Senior, CP, Ph.D., S.T.D.

Donald Senior entered the Passionist Religious Congregation in 1960 and was ordained a Catholic priest in 1967. He has been president of Catholic Theological Union, Chicago, Illinois, since 1987 where he has also served as Professor of New Testament. He lectures and conducts workshops throughout the United States and abroad.

The use of Scripture in the Church's catechesis has been a new and exciting emphasis since the Second Vatican Council. There are several ways that Scripture plays a role in effective catechesis.

First of all, the Bible traces the overarching story of God's love for his people Israel (Old Testament) and the continuing story in the life of Jesus and the founding and spread of the early Church (New Testament). Even though we are separated in time and culture from the biblical peoples, they are our ancestors in the faith. Their experience of God sets the pattern for our own faith.

From God's creation of the world and the human person in God's own image, to the remarkable stories of Jesus and his disciples as the fulfillment of Israel's dreams, and culminating with the explosive power of God's Spirit bringing the gospel into the world, your students' knowledge of the biblical story gives them a share in this great heritage of faith.

The Scriptures also provide us with a rich set of symbols that, like great poetry, help put our experience of God into words. Crossing the Red Sea, climbing the mountain of Sinai, looking for a promised land, being tempted in the desert, following in the footsteps of Jesus, being a doubting Thomas or a confused Peter, saying "yes" like Mary, standing at the foot of the cross, the Church as the body of Christ—all these and a thousand other biblical metaphors and symbols capture the experience of faith. Communicating these images to young

Christians gives them a common language of faith with other Christians across the world.

Finally, the biblical stories also transmit the moral and spiritual wisdom of our faith. This is particularly true of Jesus' parables but also extends to many other stories. The parable of the prodigal son teaches us about the unlimited forgiveness of God, just as the parable of the Good Samaritan reminds

(continued on next page)

Resources

Catoir, John T. *Joyfulling Living the Gospels Day by Day: Minute Meditations for Every Day.* Catholic Book Publishing Company, 2001.

Cavalletti, Sofia, et al. *The Religious Potential of the Child: Experiencing Scripture and Liturgy with Young Children.* Chicago, IL: Liturgy Training Publications, 1993.

us that authentic charity is determined by what we do and not by our status. The stories of the Bible can help inform the imagination and the conscience of all students while affording them values to live by.

Ways to Implement Using Scripture

- Put a Scripture quote in a prominent place before beginning each lesson. It could be from your *We Believe* chapter, or the coming Sunday's liturgy. Invite students to reflect on the quote and to share what it means for their lives.

- Engage students in Scripture drama. Have them "try on" the characters and sense what it felt like to be one of the prophets or the first disciples called by Jesus, a leper, or Mary or Joseph on the journey to Bethlehem. To become the characters helps your students to remember them and their stories of faith.

- Emphasize the connections between what Jesus did in the Scriptures and the work of the Church today: healing, forgiving sin, standing for justice and against oppression.

- Encourage students to explore the Holy Land on appropriate Web sites. This stirs their imagination to "see" where the stories of our heritage happened as they study them.

- Compare today's news headlines to events that happened in Scripture. Do people today worship false idols as some people in the Old Testament did? Are there people today who are looked down on as the Samaritans were in the New Testament?

For additional ideas, activities, and opportunities, visit Sadlier's

www.WE BELIEVE web.com

Catechist Corner

With thanks to:
Sue Juliano, DRE
St. Therese of Lisieux Parish
Shelby Township, Michigan

One catechist reviews the Scripture Cake recipe (see below) with her students before asking them to bring in an ingredient in order to make the cake at the next class. They are asked to find the ingredients in each Scripture passage. The catechist then uses the kitchen in the parish hall to prepare the cake with her students. She has discovered that they enjoy finding the "ingredients" in the Bible as much as they enjoy eating the Scripture Cake!

Scripture Cake
$1/2$ cup **Judges 5:25** (curds-use butter)
$1^1/2$ tbsp. **1 Samuel 14:25** (honey)
2 cups **1 Kings 4:22** (flour)
$1/2$ tsp. **Leviticus 2:13** (salt)
1 tsp. **1 Corinthians 5:6** (yeast-use baking powder)
1 tsp. **2 Chronicles 9:9** (spices-use 1 tsp. each of cinnamon, ginger, and cloves)
$1/2$ cup **Judges 4:19** (milk)
1 cup **1 Samuel 30:12** (raisins)
1 cup **Nahum 3:12** (figs, dried and chopped)
1 cup **Genesis 43:11** (almonds)
4 **Isaiah 10:14** (eggs, beaten well)

Cream first two ingredients together in a mixing bowl. In separate bowl, sift flour, salt, baking powder, and spices together. Add dry ingredients alternately with milk to mixing bowl. Add raisins, figs, and almonds mixing well. Fold in beaten eggs. Bake in a 9 x 13 pan at 350° F for 45 to 60 minutes. Let cool, cut and enjoy!

Notes

Developing an Appreciation of Mary

by M. Jean Frisk, ISSM, M.A., S.T.L.

M. Jean, a Schoenstatt Sister of Mary, teaches Marian catechesis at The Marian Library/International Marian Research Institute in Dayton, Ohio. Sr. Jean also authors Marian works and co-develops the Mary Page at the Institute. She received her STL from the International Marian Research Institute affiliated with the Marianum in Rome.

"Today as ever, all laborers of catechesis, trusting in her intercession, turn to the Blessed Virgin Mary, who saw her Son grow '[in] wisdom, age and grace' (Luke 2:52). They find in her the spiritual model for carrying out and strengthening the renewal of contemporary catechesis, in faith, hope and love." [*GDC* 291]

As catechists, we can help our students develop an appreciation for Mary by considering the following in our lessons:

Mary's relation to the Blessed Trinity Mary said yes to the Father, accepted her mission for the Son, and was formed and overshadowed by the Holy Spirit.

Mary's relation to Jesus Christ Mary's story is irrevocably linked with Jesus. When we learn about Mary, we learn more about God the Son who became man. Mary was Jesus' most faithful follower and remains with him now to help show us the hope and fulfillment of our baptism into Christ.

Mary as model and mother of the Church Mary is "the Church's model of faith and charity. Thus she is a 'preeminent and . . . wholly unique member of the Church'" (CCC 967), "the symbol and the most perfect realization of the Church" (CCC 507), "a mother to us in the order of grace" (CCC 968).

The story of Mary based on Scripture All the gospels include Mary. She is part of the early Church after the Resurrection.

The Church's Marian feasts Liturgy honors Mary's role in salvation and her role as our spiritual mother who teaches us the faith. The Church teaches us how to ask Mary for her assistance in prayer.

Mary's humanness Mary listens. She helps her family and others. She works gladly and sees the needs of others. She prays. She praises God by

(continued on next page)

Resources

"Mother of the Christ, Mother of the Church." *Papal Documents on the Blessed Virgin Mary* edited by Marianne Lorraine Trouvé. Boston: Pauline Books, 2001.

http://www.udayton.edu/mary *The Mary Page* is an extensive resource for videos, art on loan, activities, book lists, devotions, prayers, etc. produced by the University of Dayton's Marian Library/International Marian Research Institute.

singing hymns. Mary questions things respectfully. Mary does what Jesus tells us to do. Mary shows us the integrity of a human person filled with divine life.

Mary and the hope for Christian Unity There are ecumenical dimensions to devotion to Mary. Her life, words, and example teach us how to love Jesus and what Christians can do to remain faithful to him. (See *Marialis Cultis*, 32.)

Ways to Implement Developing an Appreciation of Mary

- Include a picture or statue of Mary in the prayer space. Teach and pray Marian prayers: Hail Mary, Magnificat, Memorare, the Litany of the Blessed Virgin Mary.

- Honor Mary. Celebrate the Church's Marian devotions with a May crowning. Honor her in October, the month of the rosary, by teaching and praying the rosary. Various cultures have specific devotions. Invite students to share their unique ways of honoring Mary.

- Have a "Mary Day" once a month. Invite your students to learn Mary hymns. In preparation for Mary Day, let students select a project to help people who are poor, sick, or lonely in your area (food basket, brownies for workers, cards for shut-ins, pennies for the missions). Bring the fruits of that project to the liturgy, and find ways to distribute these afterwards.

- In Advent, have a Mary Festival between the Immaculate Conception (8th), Patroness of the United States, and Our Lady of Guadalupe (12th), Patroness of the Americas. Encourage the children to find ways to be like Mary and bring Christ's light to others. Plan liturgies and charities. Discuss ways to create a peaceful pre-Christmas atmosphere at school, in the parish, and at home.

For additional ideas, activities, and opportunities, visit Sadlier's

www.WeBelieve.web.com

Catechist Corner

With thanks to:
Karen Mackley
St. John the Baptist School
New Brighton, Minnesota

Under Karen's direction, her students develop an appreciation for Mary by participating in an activity called, "Following in Mary's Footsteps." As an ongoing idea throughout the year, Karen reads Scripture passages about Mary, and the group discusses the sacrifices and great things that Mary has done. The students brainstorm ways they can try to be more like Mary in their daily lives. Each time that Karen observes a student "following in Mary's footsteps," she gives the student a sticker on a chart or an inexpensive charm for a bracelet. (Paper bracelets work as well.) At the end of the year, all the students participate in a special way in a celebration of Mary.

Notes

Fishing in a Sea of Multimedia

by Caroline Cerveny, SSJ, D. Min.

Sister Caroline, director of educational technology for William H. Sadlier, Inc., is a nationally recognized speaker and leader in interactive media ministry for faith formation. She holds a D. Min. in Parish Revitalization from McCormick Seminary (Chicago), MA in religious studies from St. Mary's College (Winona) and an MA in educational technology from Governor's State University (Chicago).

Catechists today are challenged to proclaim the gospel in a world where tools, communication, children, and learning are different. Today, technology stands at the center of this very different world. Using the integration of sound, video, text, and graphics in a digital environment, multimedia is set to become the medium of choice for the 21st century.

Alert to the shifting patterns in all areas of life and culture, the Church recognizes the importance of her own incorporation of technology into all arenas of teaching and ministry. Pope John Paul II, in his May, 2002 Communications Day letter reminds us that online multimedia technology offers "magnificent opportunities" for evangelization, especially among young people who increasingly use the Web as a "window on the world."

While we can sometimes feel like we are drowning in the endless possibilities software companies offer, the following suggestions present "user-friendly" paths for incorporating multimedia into the learning experience of young Catholics of all ages.

Identify available technology. You will need at least one computer. Presentation software (e.g., Microsoft PowerPoint) or authoring tools like Hyperstudio can be used for creating multimedia projects for your lesson. These programs allow you or your students to turn an outline into a work of art using display type, graphics, animation, and even video clips. You can present this technology-driven creation on screen using a computer that is connected to

a television converter and large TV monitor [usually affordable and thus available in schools] or connected to a LCD panel and overhead projector. Or you may print color transparencies that may be used with an overhead projector.

Choose multimedia resources. Sources of religious information may be located in books, CD-ROMs, and on the Internet. What is important to remember is that finding quality and theologically correct

(continued on next page)

Resources

Druin Allison (editor). *The Design of Children's Technology.* Morgan Kaufmann Publishers, 1998.

Foley, Kim. *Using and Creating Virtual Field Trips.* Persistent Vision, 2001. If you'd like to order the book, please send email to info@ field-trips.org.

material may be a challenge using Internet resources. In today's interactive environment, it is possible for anyone to publish his or her thoughts and beliefs. A search engine does not discern if the material you find represents true Catholic theology. It simply finds information for you. Often you will need to take time to find material that reflects Catholic Tradition. If you are in doubt, check with your parish DRE, pastor, or someone whose theology and ministry you respect to verify that the material you are using from the Internet represents what the Catholic Church teaches.

Ways to Implement Fishing in a Sea of Multimedia

• Here are multimedia projects you or your students can create using a combination of media and format: prayer reflection; chapter summary of a lesson; interactive games ; pop quizzes; interpretations of words of the Our Father, Hail Mary, and other traditional prayers; weekly vocabulary words.

• Using *Printmaster Gold 4.0 and HP Restickables* Large Round Inkjet Stickers, invite students to create stickers to represent their favorite saints. They can share these stickers with their friends so that they can add them to their notebooks or bookbags.

• Multimedia projects lend themselves to team efforts. If you want to do a prayer reflection for your class that consist of five or more slides, assign one slide to a mini-team of two persons. They can work on the project and bring their diskette back to you as their completed assignment. You can then assign a student to merge these slides together to create one multimedia presentation.

For additional ideas, activities, and opportunities, visit Sadlier's

www.WE BELIEVE web.com

Catechist Corner

With thanks to:

Bill Beebe
St. Helena's Parish
Edison, New Jersey

Bill takes advantage of the fact that his older students know more about technology than many of the adults in the parish. Each year, Bill invites his students to mentor younger students in a "Safe Faith Day." During this time, the older students present ways to safely use the Internet to learn more about Jesus and the Catholic faith and tradition. A week before, Bill meets with his students to review Web sites and search engines that will be presented during the day. The theology presented as well as the links offered on each site are evaluated. On the actual "Safe Faith Day," Bill says, "I walk around and monitor the interaction between students. I am always amazed at what a positive, evangelizing experience it is!"

Notes

Forming Evangelizing Catechists

by Rev. John E. Hurley, CSP, D.Min.

Father John Hurley, a Paulist priest, is Executive Director of the Secretariat for Evangelization at the United States Conference of Catholic Bishops in Washington, D.C.

In the document *On Evangelization in the Modern World*, Pope Paul VI declared that "the task of evangelizing all people constitutes the essential mission of the Church." In fact, he went on to declare, "She exists in order to evangelize." (EN 14) One of the fundamental moments in evangelization is catechesis. After the initial proclamation of the gospel, catechesis deepens the understanding of the truths of faith and fosters the relationship of the believer to Jesus and to the Church.

It is not surprising then that the *General Directory for Catechesis* notes that among the six central tasks of catechesis is "missionary initiation." (*GDC* 86) Catechists are called to equip those whom they catechize to be evangelizers who are able and excited to share their faith. In *Go and Make Disciples, A National Plan and Strategy for Catholic Evangelization in the United States*, the U.S. bishops challenge us to be enthusiastic messengers of the gospel. Our enthusiasm can become contagious and invite others to know the Lord who is the source of our joy. This can be achieved when we:

- are enthusiastic about the message that we are inviting others to hear and accept,
- are contagious witnesses to the gospel so that others will invite us to tell the story,
- invite others to join us in public acts that help to transform society.

The vocation of the catechist is to be a formator of disciples. Therefore, our own discipleship to Jesus must be rooted in a profoundly religious catechesis that is nourished by the gospel. As catechists, we are first of all living witnesses of the good news of Jesus. To be such witnesses requires more than a cognitive grasp of theology and Scripture; it means we have experienced a conversion of heart, and that the deep joy of that turning to God then impels us to share the gospel message with others.

Resources

General Directory for Catechesis. Washington, D.C. United States Catholic Conference, 1997.

Go and Make Disciples: A National Plan and Strategy for Catholic Evangelization in the United States. Washington, D.C.: National Conference of Catholic Bishops, 1992.

Our Hearts Were Burning Within Us: A Pastoral Plan for Adult Faith Formation in the United States. Washington, D.C.: United States Catholic Conference, 1999.

Ways to Implement
Forming Evangelizing Catechists

- Sharing the good news means that we know our faith and are able to articulate what we believe. Encourage the development of the vocabulary of faith with games and activities which reinforce key terms.

- Help the students to understand the connection between assessments of their learning and their ability to help others learn the Catholic faith.

- Give students opportunities to share their knowledge of Jesus with younger children. They can dramatize a gospel story or help to teach a prayer. Let them choose something they are enthusiastic about.

- Have students identify ways they can be evangelizers at home, at school, on the playground, with teams or other specific areas of their lives. Help them to name behaviors, decisions, and attitudes as well as words that will witness to Jesus.

- Invite members of the parish evangelization team to share their work with the students.

- Ask students to name people they know who share the message of Jesus in their lives. Make a list and name those people during prayer. The children might make cards or certificates to affirm and encourage these evangelizers.

For additional ideas, activities, and opportunities, visit Sadlier's

www.WeBelieveweb.com

Catechist Corner

With thanks to:
Barbara Occhipinti
St. William the Abbot
Seaford, New York

Barbara invites her students to produce a sixty-second video message, "We can evangelize!" Students brainstorm the ways we can share the good news of Jesus Christ. The group enlists the help of the school art department, music teachers, and a few parents with video equipment and expertise. Students design background scenes, choose (and sometimes write!) music, and craft a script. Once the message is honed to fit the time restraint, the actual taping takes place. Usually, the video message is taped several times, with different students being on camera to give everyone a chance. The finished tapes are used at parish events, and open houses in school, in the religious education program, and even for the adult evangelization committee.

Notes

Developing an Understanding of Mission

by Most Rev. Gregory M. Aymond D.D.

Bishop Gregory M. Aymond, D.D. is the Chair of the U.S. Bishops' Committee on World Mission and the Bishop of the Diocese of Austin, Texas. He has been involved in the missionary work of the Church since 1976 and has visited numerous missionary countries.

At the end of his time on earth, Jesus commanded his apostles: "Go, therefore, and make disciples of all nations, baptizing them in the name of the Father, and of the Son, and of the holy Spirit" (Matthew 28:19). As Catholics, this, too, is our call. To be Catholic and to be a catechist is to be a missionary. To be a missionary is to take seriously Jesus' command to share our faith with others.

Through our Baptism, we become members of the Catholic Church. We receive the Light of Christ and are called to live our lives embracing Jesus and his message. Throughout the gospels, Jesus encourages us to share his message and his light with all people. Pope John Paul II reminds us, "Faith is not a private matter, it is to be shared with others." (*Redemptoris Missio*, December 7, 1990) It is through this sharing of our faith that we not only respond to Jesus' command, but also model him and continue his work on earth.

Catholic means "universal." Two thirds of the world's population do not know Jesus. Jesus' command to make disciples of all nations calls us to bring his message and open our hearts to not only our families and communities, but also to those

- who have never heard of Christ.
- who know Jesus and suffer persecution for their Christian beliefs.
- who live in developing countries where they hunger for food, justice, and a deeper faith in Christ and the Church.
- whom we will never meet but are nonetheless our sisters and brothers in the global Church.

As catechists we have a privileged ministry helping to expand the minds and hearts of our students in order for them to live fully the call of Baptism. It is our responsibility to teach our students the message of Jesus and to challenge them to embrace and live this message, not only in our homes and communities, but also throughout the whole world.

Resources

Written and video educational materials regarding one aspect of our mission as Catholics can be obtained from the Society for the Propagation of the Faith/Holy Childhood Association at 1-800-431-2222.

Redemptoris Missio (the Mission of the Redeemer) by Pope John Paul II

To the Ends of the Earth. Washington, D.C.: U.S. Catholic Conference.

Ways to Implement Developing an Understanding of Mission

- Invite your students to read passages from various books of the New Testament and to list any references to mission and evangelization.

- Take time to have your students, as a class, pray regularly for missionaries and for the people they serve.

- Teach students about other nations' cultures and religions. Take advantage of the cultural diversity that exists in your room. Explain that our mission is to *all* people.

- Provide the opportunity for your class or group to write to a missionary requesting information about his/her ministry in a developing country. This can be done by regular mail or on the Internet.

- Invite the students to communicate as "pen pals" with children in developing countries.

- Invite a missionary to visit your room and share his/her experiences of "making disciples of all nations." Possibly, this person could show photos or videos of his or her work to the people of God.

- Sponsor parish and school activities that encourage students to give of their time and talents to those in the mission world.

- Use education programs from the Holy Childhood Association and the Society for the Propagation of the Faith. Their address is 366 Fifth Avenue, New York, NY 10001.

For additional ideas, activities, and opportunities, visit Sadlier's

www.WEBELIEVEweb.com

Catechist Corner

With thanks to:
Thomas Doyle
All Souls Catholic School
Sanford, FL

Thomas joins other teachers and staff for a program called "IHS," or "In His Steps." Students and staff nominate students who have done a kind act for another. It might be a student who helps another student with learning computer skills. It might be a student who shares his or her book stickers with another. Or a student might help a teacher set up a class project. When a student does what Jesus would do in that situation, he or she receives a pin that is in the form of three footprints with the words "In His Steps." The students' names and kind acts are read out in the morning as everyone gathers for prayer.

Notes

Using Music

by Jack Miffleton

Jack Miffleton is a composer and teacher, known internationally for his work in children's religious education. His songs are sung in classrooms and churches around the world. Currently, he teaches music at St. Jarlath's School in Oakland, California.

"Among the many signs and symbols used by the Church to celebrate its faith, music is of preeminent importance." *(Music in Catholic Worship §23)*

It is difficult to imagine catechesis with primary and middle grade children without music, movement and song. It is a natural and spontaneous way that children express themselves. Punctuating a lesson with songs and acclamations is good pedagogy, good religion, and children like it!

Singing is good pedagogy. Young children have short attention spans. Movement and song are aids in helping them focus. Regular singing can help establish an easy rapport between catechist and child by allowing the catechist to enter the world of the child without being "childish." Singing the Scriptures adds a unique dimension to the process of hearing and learning about God's word. If students can sing it, they will remember it. Modern Catholic hymnals are filled with Scripture in song. Recorded songs or instrumental music can create an atmosphere of reverence during a quiet time or while your students are involved in individual or group projects.

Singing is good religion. "One who sings, prays twice," wrote Saint Augustine. Using music in a catechetical setting is not just a practical teaching device; it is also good religious education. The liturgies of the Church are sung prayers. From the beginning, children can benefit from an approach to prayer and catechesis that is modeled on liturgy. In liturgy, for example, a verbal proclamation is usually followed by a sung response. Acclamatory song can highlight a lesson or classroom activity. Beginning and ending a class with a seasonal psalm or song refrain can draw students into the liturgical year without preaching about it.

Singing is fun! An important aspect of catechesis is the socialization and friendships that take place among the children in your class or group. Singing with one voice strengthens this process of community building. Even when singing together just for fun, Christian children model what they are as one Body of Christ.

Resources

Rise Up and Sing. (Second Edition) Young People's Music Resource. Portland: Oregon Catholic Press.

Singing Our Faith. A New Hymnal for Children. Chicago: GIA Publications, Inc.

Ways to Implement
Using Music

- Select songs that express something to which the students can relate—nature, a joy, a sadness, a pet, a relative. Choose lyrics that contain something that parallels what the children are learning.

- For the primary grades, choose songs with movements and repetition. There are many catechetical songs that are developed to help children at the primary levels make connections between their everyday life and their faith.

- Middle grade children will enjoy and benefit from songs that pique their curiosity or require a challenge, for example, songs celebrating biblical personalities or a Bible story put to verse. Middle grade children will also relate more directly to the meaning of the words and can understand the place and flow of music in liturgy.

- Catechists can usually do more in song than they think. In planning a lesson first look at the music recommended by the *We Believe* program. The Scripture text or the topic of the lesson may suggest a song or refrain you already know. Get acquainted with some of the many musical resources developed for children.

- Teaching a song should not be tedious. When children like a song, they will take it over quickly. "Call and response" or "echo" style songs will have the children singing immediately. Songs that are more complicated or contain several verses can be learned a little at a time over several classes.

- The use of recorded music can be helpful in supporting the singing. Be sure to review the songs on the We Believe CD before class so that you can fully engage the children when leading the group in song.

- Remember—children will readily sing without accompaniment. Use movements and gestures to animate the song.

For additional ideas, activities, and opportunities, visit Sadlier's

www.WeBelieveweb.com

Catechist Corner

With thanks to:
Sister Maureen Viani, SNJM
Christ the King Church
Pleasant Hill, California

With the assistance of volunteer musicians singing is included within our faith sessions. The children gather bi-weekly in their respective grade levels for fifteen minutes of singing. The musicians involve the children in movement, gesture, and prayer using age-appropriate psalms, acclamations, and hymns, which support and enhance their sharing and reflecting around the Sunday readings. Besides allowing the children an opportunity to encounter God's presence through song, these sessions have helped build a repertoire of songs that continue to enhance and strengthen our prayer gatherings and Eucharistic celebrations.

Notes

Finding Value in Popular Culture

by Gloria Hutchinson

Gloria Hutchinson is an author of numerous books on religion and spirituality. She presents retreats and workshops across the country, often using popular videos and music in her presentations. Gloria has appeared in several Catholic Update videos.

While many dismiss "popular culture" as a wasteland, the wise catechist sees it as a field in which the wheat and the weeds grow side by side. Our task is to enable students to discern the difference and choose the good "grain" of spiritual nourishment.

The mass media, electronic, image-dominated culture of the twenty-first century exerts a compelling influence on youth. We cannot ignore the impact of MTV, the World Wide Web, cell phones and Walkmans, VCRs, DVDs and video games, super malls, fast-food chains, and logo-laden fashions. Religious education must take into account the expectations raised by popular culture. Our young people want to be entertained, stimulated, informed, and affected. And they want it all at a lively pace.

So how do we find value in a culture which has been described as "a competing religion"? We look with the eyes of faith rather than the glare of skepticism. We seek the good and enlist it in God's service. Pope John Paul II advises: "Contemporary reality demands a capacity to learn the language, nature and characteristics of mass media. Using the media correctly can lead to a genuine inculturation of the Gospel." (*Ecclesia in America*, 1999, #72)

The Holy Father's words apply to all aspects of popular culture. Whether we are evaluating a video game or a popular children's movie, we must "learn the language, nature and characteristics" of these products. What stories are they telling? Do they run counter to or parallel with the stories of Jesus?

Like Jesus himself, catechists need to immerse themselves in their own culture in order to communicate effectively with the people of God.

As Jesus employed the fisherman's net and the mustard seed, the music of the day and the coin of the realm, we, too, must learn to press into service all creative and technological works that may feed the spirit. If we fail to do so, we lose the wheat along with the weeds.

Resources

Cardinal Roger Mahony. "Film Makers, Film Viewers: Their Challenges and Opportunities" On the Internet at http://cardinal.la-archdiocese.org

Adriacco, Dan. *Screen Saved: Peril and Promise of Media in Ministry.* Cincinnati: St. Anthony Messenger Press, 2000.

Malone, Peter with Sr. Rose Pacatte. *Lights, Camera . . . Faith! A Movie Lectionary.* Boston: Pauline Books and Media, 2001.

Ways to Implement
Finding Value in Popular Culture

- Each week, take time to immerse yourself in one specific expression of popular culture such as: a youth-oriented radio station, family comic strips, video games, professional sports events, Web sites and chat rooms for the young.

- Teach children to analyze their favorite cultural works and products. Guide group dialogues on questions like these: How does this video game affect my feelings about violence? What is the key message of this song? How might this comic strip character help me to be a better disciple of Jesus?

- Involve groups of student film reviewers in choosing segments from popular videos for classroom use. Help them focus on characters who stand out as spiritual mentors or decision makers.

- Introduce age-appropriate role models from popular films. Have students decide how these role models show us gospel values in action.

- Design a popular culture bulletin board with a continuously updated display of symbols, photos, and articles on cultural works with spiritual values. Invite students to devise a ratings system for these works and to contribute to the display.

For additional ideas, activities, and opportunities, visit Sadlier's

www.We Believe web.com

Catechist Corner

With thanks to:

Kim Suttie
Immaculate Heart of Mary Parish
Fairfield, Maine

Kim likes to use popular music as a form of prayer. When she is listening to a current song, she asks herself "Do the lyrics answer one of these questions: Could it be me talking to God, God talking to me, or a conversation between the two of us?" She notes that more often than not the song puts her thoughts and feelings into better words than she could ever come up with! Kim invites her students to bring in CDs of their favorite music to ask them the same questions she asks herself. She always has her students write out the lyrics to their favorite songs before she decides to play them for the entire group. It usually surprises the group how many of these songs spark spirited discussion and even thoughtful prayer.

Notes

Developing an Understanding of Vocation

by Sr. Maureen Sullivan, OP, Ph.D.

Sr. Maureen, a Dominican Sister of Hope, is a national religion consultant for William H. Sadlier, Inc. She is currently assistant professor of theology at St. Anselm College in Manchester, New Hampshire. Sr. Maureen received her Ph. D. in theology from Fordham University in New York City.

One of the many topics addressed by the second Vatican Council (1962–65) was that of "vocation." The word itself comes from the Latin word *vocare*, which means "to call."

In Chapter 40 of *Lumen Gentium*, the Dogmatic Constitution on the Church, we read, "The Lord Jesus , the divine Teacher and Model of all perfection, preached holiness of life to each and every one of his disciples, regardless of their situation." (*LG* 40) By virtue of our Baptism, we are all called to holiness. We can be faithful disciples and holy people whatever our particular vocation.

There are those who are invited by God to become holy as lay persons. "By reason of their special vocation it belongs to the laity to seek the kingdom of God by engaging in temporal affairs and directing them according to God's will." (*LG* 31)

Lay people may be called to the married life. They witness to Jesus through their faithful love for each other and through their contributions to society. Married people may be gifted by God with children and become holy even as they form their children in holiness.

Lay people may be called to the single life. They grow in holiness through their loving relationships with family and friends and through their witness to gospel values in their work. God calls some men and women to become holy through living the vowed life in religious communities. "Religious life derives from the mystery of the Church. It is a gift she has received from her Lord, a gift she offers as a stable way

of life to the faithful called by God to profess the counsels." (*CCC* 926) Religious who vow a life of poverty, chastity and obedience serve the Church and the world in many ways. These sisters, brothers, and religious priests grow in holiness through a life lived in service and prayer.

God calls some men to the ordained priesthood. "Holy Orders is the sacrament through which the

(continued on next page

Resources

Lumen Gentium, Dogmatic Constitution on the Church, from the Vatican II Documents.

Lucy Kaylin, *For the Love of God: The Faith and Future of the American Nun.* New York: Harper Collins Publishers, 2000.

Kevin and Marilyn Ryan, ed., *Why I Am Still A Catholic.* New York: Riverhead Books, 1998.

mission entrusted by Christ to his apostles continues to be exercised in the Church until the end of time." (CCC, 1536) The priest represents Christ and teaches, governs, and sanctifies in his name. The priest grows in holiness as he cares for the Church, the Body of Christ, and is an example of service and compassion.

God may call us to become holy by any path he chooses. How can we know what God is calling us to be and to do? We can hear God in prayer, certainly through the celebration of the liturgy and the sacraments. We can hear God when we reflect on the gifts and talents he has given us which may point to a certain vocation. We can hear God in the wisdom of people of faith who advise and encourage us.

Whatever way we follow Jesus, we are called to holiness—and a life of love. "Love, in fact, is the vocation which includes all others; it's a universe of its own, comprising all time and space—it's eternal!" (Saint Thèrése of Lisieux, CCC 826)

Ways to Implement Developing An Understanding of Vocation

- Have the group read stories about Catholics in different vocations to demonstrate the universal call to holiness. We have many wonderful witnesses to draw from: lay missionaries, saints, etc.

- Invite the priests, sisters, brothers, and lay ecclesial ministers of the parish to share their stories with the group. Have the students prepare and submit questions ahead of time.

- Invite married couples, parents, and single people to share the ways their lives help them to grow in holiness.

- Talk to the students about your own experience of "vocation."

For additional ideas, activities, and opportunities, visit Sadlier's

www.WeBelieveweb.com

Catechist Corner

With thanks to:
Alice Caruso
Curé of Ars
Merrick, New York

Alice encourages her students to explore specific roles within life vocations. Working in groups, the students identify a vocation and role they want to research. (This might be a religious woman in the nursing profession, or a brother who does prison ministry, or a married couple in the Peace Corps.) Each group researches a "A Day in the Life of…" their chosen person, using the Internet, library, personal interviews, etc. The research culminates in a "Views on Vocations" panel. One member of each group is chosen to "become" the person researched and role plays that person's story on a "typical" day. Some students even use costumes and props to convey their message! Alice invites her group to follow up with a bulletin board about the many roles one might have within each life vocation.

Notes

Development Team

Rosemary K. Calicchio
Editorial Director

Lee Hlavacek
Product Developer

Blake Bergen
Grade Level Manager

Deborah Jones
Director of Publishing Operations

Vince Gallo
Creative Director

Francesca Moore
Associate Art Director

Jim Saylor
Photo Editor

Editorial Staff
Joanna Dailey, James P. Emswiler, Maureen Gallo, Susan Gleason Anderson, Kathy Hendricks, Gloria Hutchinson, Mary Ellen Kelly, James T. Morgan, Ed.D., Daniel Sherman, Mary Ann Trevaskiss, Joanne Winne

Design/Photo Staff
Andrea Brown, Kevin Butler, Ana Jouvin, Sasha Khorovsky, Susan Ligertwood, Maria Pia Marrella, Zaniah Renner, David Rosenberg, Bob Schatz, Debrah Wilson

Production Staff
Diane Ali, Monica Bernier, Barbara Brown, Suzan Daley, Tresse DeLorenzo, Arthur Erberber, Joyce Gaskin, Eileen Gewirtzman, Peter Herrmann, Maria Jimenez, Sommer Keller, Miriam Lippman, Vinny McDonough, John Mealy, Yolanda Miley, Maureen Morgan, Julie Murphree, Walter Norfleet, Monica Reece, Martin Smith, Sintora Vanderhorst

Sadlier Consulting Team Patricia Andrews, Director of Religious Education, Our Lady of Lourdes Church, Slidell, LA; Eleanor Ann Brownell, D.Min., Vice President, Religion; Michaela M. Burke, Director of Consultant Services; Judith A. Devine, National Sales Consultant; Sister Helen Hemmer, IHM, Religion Consultant for Spiritual Formation; William M. Ippolito, Executive Projects Director; Saundra Kennedy, Ed.D., Consultant Training Specialist; Marie Murphy, Ph.D., National Religion Consultant; Karen Ryan, Executive Researcher; John M. Stack, National Consultant

Photo Credits Cover Photography: Index Stock Imagery/Ken Wardius: *hand with seedling*, Ken Karp: *children*. Courtesy of Karin Anderson-Ponzer: 277 *bottom left*. Animals Animals/John Gerlach: 94–95 *dragonfly*. Art Resource, NY/Giraudon: 222; Scala: 55, 58 *top right*, 212 *top*, 218 *top right*, 247. Dave Bartuff: 121. Lori Berkowitz: 206 *bottom*. Jane Bernard: 68 *bottom*, 100 *top*, 106 *top left*, 142, 146 *top left*, 148, 149, 150, 154 *top right*, 158–159, 162 *top right*, 171, 173 *top*, 176 *top left*, 206 *top right*, 233 *top*, 242. Bridge Building Images/Fr. John Guiliani: 213. Bridgeman Art Library, London: 44, 50, 253. Karen Callaway: 59 *bottom*, 60 *bottom*, 64 *top left*, 65, 93 *top*, 102, 133, 143, 148 *top*, 173 *bottom*, 174 *sign*, 179 *top*, 190 *top*, 230, 232 *top left*. Corbis/Ariel Skelley: 59 *center*; AP: 86, 90 *top left*; David Lees: 86; Owen Franken: 92 *center right*; Sergio Gaudenti/KIPA: 92 *bottom right*, 243 *bottom left*; Joseph Sohm: 108 *center*; Tom Stewart: 108 *bottom*, 114 *top left*; Lawrence Manning: 109; Lindsay Hebberd: 196 *top right*, 202 *top left*; Peter Turnley: 196 *center*; Bowers Museum of Cultural Art: 212 *bottom*. Corbis Stock Market/Ed Bock: 29 *top*. Corbis Sygma/Caron Philippe: 198–199. Crosiers/Gene Plaisted, OSC: 68 *top*, 118, 120 *top right*, 122, 126 *top left*, 140–141, 146 *top left*, 179 *bottom*, 182 *top right*, 248. Bob Daemmrich: 174 *left*. Neal Farris: 27, 38 *bottom*, 39, 41, 42 *top right*, 49, 57, 64 *bottom*, 75, 78–79, 81, 91, 95 *children*, 101 *bottom right*, 105, 115, 116, 117, 120 *top left*, 123, 126 *top right*, 145, 147, 193, 227, 232 *bottom*, 241 *left*, 243 *center*. Getty: 66, 70, 84 *center*, 87 *bottom*, 94–95, 107 *background*, 131 *background*, 135 *rings*, 155 *clock*, 191 *top*, 195 *door*, 197, 206–207, 219 *background*, 236. Greene Uniform: 35 *sweatshirts*. The Image Works/Steve Warmowski: 37 *bottom right*; Bob Daemmrich: 87 *bottom*. Index Stock Imagery/James Frank: 139 *top*. Ken Karp: 17, 19, 20, 21, 25, 30 *bottom*, 33, 34, 35, 43, 51, 59 *top*, 73, 83, 89, 97, 98 *top center*, 99, 101 *children*, 107, 113, 129, 131, 137, 139 *center* & *bottom*, 153, 155, 161, 169, 172, 176 *top right*, 185, 187, 190 *bottom*, 194 *top left*, 195, 201, 209, 211, 215, 217, 218 *top right*, 219, 220, 226 *top left*, 234, 250, 252. Sr. Jane Keegan: 38 *top*, 251. Lonely Planet Images/Greg Lord: 134 *bottom*, 163, 165, 203, 214, 241 *right*. Courtesy of Maryknoll Father and Brothers/Breen: 110 *bottom*. Natural Selection Stock Photography/Isao Kimura: 166–167 *background*. Norton Simon Art Foundation, Gift of Mr. Norton Simon, 1976: 30 *center*. Operation Rice Bowl, Catholic Relief Services: 174 *logo*. PhotoEdit/James Shaffer: 166; Tony Carter: 167; Myrleen Ferguson Cate: 223 *center*, 226 *top right*. PictureQuest/Digital Vision: 83 *background*; Pictor Int'l: 204 *center*. Aaron Rosenberg: 132, 138 *top left*. Chris Sheridan: 78 *bottom*, 82 *top right*, 84 *bottom*, 84 *top*, 90 *top left*, 101 *top*, 204. Deacon Thomas Stadnik: 205. St. Joseph Abbey/Br. Emmanuel Morinelli: 110 *top*. Superstock: 29 *center*, 60 *top*, 64 *top right*. Lu Taskey: 207 *center*. Timepix/Ben Van Hook: 93 *bottom*; Robert Nickelsberg: 92 *top*; Jayanta Shaw/Reuters: 196 *bottom*; Jamil Bittar/Reuters: 238. W. P. Wittman Limited: 134 *top*, 151, 154 *top left*, 165 *top*, 170 *top right*, 177, 178, 180, 182 *top left*, 244.

Illustrator Credits Cover Design: Kevin Ghiglione. Bernard Adnet: 163, 190–191. Jo Lynn Alcorn: 211, 215–216. Teresa Berasi: 46–47. Lori Bilter: 43. Don Bishop: 102–103. Joe Boddy: 233, 235, 237. Ken Bowser: 27C, 64A, 83C, 99C, 176A, 203C. Carly Castillon: 139. Anne Cook: 82, 83, 99, 101, 106, 114. Laura DeSantis: 78–79. Nancy Doniger: 39. Patrick Faricy: 20, 22–23, 26, 28, 31, 34, 36–37, 42, 50, 52–53, 54, 58 *top left*, 66–67, 70, 76–77, 82, 156–157, 162 *top left*, 164, 170, 188–189, 194 *top left*, 228–229, 232. Mary Haverfield: 150–151. Donna Ingemanson: 75. W. B. Johnston: 138, 146, 154, 162, 164–165 *background*, 170, 195, 199, 219, 223. Ken Joudrey: 220–221, 226, 252. Rita Lascaro: 91C, 107C, 163C. Martin Lemelman: 75C, 120A, 155C, 219C. David Scott Meier: 187. Mark Radencich: 44–45. Mark Riedy: 35. Ursula Roma: 59, 60–61, 62–63, 64, 65, 66–67, 68–69, 70, 115, 116–117, 118–119, 120, 121, 122–123, 124–125, 126, 171, 172–173, 174–175, 176, 177, 178–179, 180–181, 182, 227, 228–229, 230–231, 232. Nigel Sandor: 110–111. Zina Saunders: 19C, 70A, 126A, 139C, 187C, 211C, 232A. Jane Shasky: 52–53 *border*. Victor Shatunov: 92–93. Susan Swan: 19. Kat Thacker: 148–149. Tom White: 108–109. Nicholas Wilton: 122–123.

Acknowledgments

Excerpts from the English translation of the *Catechism of the Catholic Church* for the United States of America, copyright ©1994, United States Catholic Conference, Inc.—Libreria Editrice Vaticana. English translation of the *Catechism of the Catholic Church: Modifications from the Editio Typica* copyright ©1997, United States Catholic Conference, Inc.—Libreria Editrice Vaticana. Used with permission.

Scripture excerpts are taken from the *New American Bible with Revised New Testament and Psalms*. Copyright ©1991, 1986, 1970 Confraternity of Christian Doctrine, Inc., Washington, D.C. Used with permission. All rights reserved. No part of the *New American Bible* may be reproduced by any means without permission in writing from the copyright owner.

Excerpts from the English translation of *Lectionary for Mass* ©1969, 1981, International Committee on English in the Liturgy, Inc. (ICEL); excerpts from the English translation of *Rite of Holy Week* ©1972, ICEL; excerpts from the English translation of *The Roman Missal* ©1973, ICEL; excerpts from the English translation of *Rite of Penance* ©1974, ICEL; excerpts from the English translation of *Eucharistic Prayers for Masses of Reconciliation* ©1975, ICEL; excerpts from the English translation of *Pastoral Care of the Sick: Rites of Anointing and Viaticum* ©1982, ICEL; excerpts from the English translation of *A Book of Prayers* ©1982, ICEL. All rights reserved.

Excerpts from *Catholic Household Blessings and Prayers*, copyright ©1988, United States Catholic Conference, Inc. Washington, D.C. Used with permission. All rights reserved.

English translation of the Lord's Prayer, Glory to the Father, and the Apostles' Creed by the International Consultation on English Texts. (ICET)

From *The Collected Works of St. Teresa of Avila, Volume Two* translated by Kieran Kavanaugh and Otilio Rodriguez. Copyright ©1980 by Washington Province of Discalced Carmelites, ICS Publications, 2131 Lincoln Road, N.E., Washington, D.C. 20002-1199 U.S.A. www.icspublications.org

From *The Diary of a Young Girl, The Definitive Edition* by Anne Frank. Otto H. Frank & Mirjam Pressler, Editors, translated by Susan Massotty, copyright ©1995 by Doubleday, a division of Random House, Inc. Used by permission of Doubleday, a division of Random House, Inc.

"We Believe, We Believe in God," ©1979, North American Liturgy Resources (NALR), 5536 NE Hassalo, Portland, OR 97213. All rights reserved. Used with permission. "Lift High the Cross," words: George W. Kitchin; rev. Michael R. Newbolt. ©1974 by Hope Publishing Co., Carol Stream, IL 60188. All rights reserved. Used with permission. "Whatsoever You Do," ©1966, 1982, Willard F. Jabusch. Administered by OCP Publications, 5536 NE Hassalo, Portland, OR 97213. All rights reserved. Used with permission. "Jesus Is with Us," ©1990, OCP Publications, 5536 NE Hassalo, Portland, OR 97213. All rights reserved. Used with permission. "We Sing Your Glory," ©1999, Bernadette Farrell. Published by OCP Publications, 5536 NE Hassalo, Portland, OR 97213. All rights reserved. Used with permission. "They'll Know We Are Christians," Peter Scholtes. ©1966, F.E.L. Publications. Assigned 1991 to the Lorenz Corporation. All rights reserved. International copyright secured. "Only a Shadow," ©1971, Carey Landry and North American Liturgy Resources (NALR), 5536 NE Hassalo, Portland, OR 97213. All rights reserved. Used with permission. "Prepare the Way," ©1991, Christopher Walker. Published by OCP Publications, 5536 NE Hassalo, Portland, OR 97213. All rights reserved. Used with permission. "Do Not Delay," ©1995, Anne Quigley. Published by OCP Publications, 5536 NE Hassalo, Portland, OR 97213. All rights reserved. Used with permission. "Jesus, We Believe in You," ©1990, Carey Landry and North American Liturgy Resources (NALR), 5536 NE Hassalo, Portland, OR 97213. All rights reserved. Used with permission. "Walking Up to Jesus," ©1993, Daughters of Charity and Christopher Walker. Published by OCP Publications, 5536 NE Hassalo, Portland, OR 97213. All rights reserved. Used with permission. Exclusive distribution by Hal Leonard Corporation. "Ashes," ©1978, New Dawn Music, 5536 NE Hassalo, Portland, OR 97213. All rights reserved. Used with permission. "We Are the Church," ©1991, Christopher Walker. Published by OCP Publications, 5536 NE Hassalo, Portland, OR 97213. All rights reserved. Used with permission. "We Are the Church" was originally from "Come, Follow Me" music program, Benziger Publishing Company. "Sing a Song to the Saints," ©1991, Jack Louden. Published by OCP Publications, 5536 NE Hassalo, Portland, OR 97213. All rights reserved. Used with permission. "Glory and Praise to Our God," ©1976, Daniel L. Schutte and New Dawn Music, 5536 NE Hassalo, Portland, OR 97213. All rights reserved. Used with permission.

Excerpts from *Sharing Catholic Social Teaching: Challenges and Directions*. ©1998, United States Conference of Catholic Bishops, Inc., Washington, D.C. (USCCB); excerpts from *Music in Catholic Worship* ©1983 USCCB; excerpts from *Catholic Household Blessings and Prayers* ©1988 USCCB; excerpts from the *General Directory for Catechesis*. ©1997, Libreria Editrice Vaticana—United States Conference of Catholic Bishops, Inc. Used with permission. All rights reserved.

Excerpts from the English translation of the "Norms for the Liturgical Year and the Calendar" from *Documents on the Liturgy, 1963–1979: Conciliar, Papal, and Curial Texts* ©1982, International Committee on English in the Liturgy, Inc. All rights reserved.

Excerpts from *Intelligence Reframed: Multiple Perspectives for the 21st Century* by Howard Gardner. Copyright ©1999 by Howard Gardner. Reprinted by permission of Basic Books, a member of Perseus Books, L.L.C.

Catechesi Tradendae, On Catechesis in Our Time, Apostolic Exhortation, Pope John Paul II, October 16, 1979.

Evangelii Nuntiandi, On Evangelization in the Modern World, Apostolic Exhortation, Pope Paul VI, December 8, 1975.

Letter of His Holiness Pope John Paul II to Artists, April 4, 1999.

Redemptoris Missio, On the Permanent Validity of the Church's Missionary Mandate, Encyclical Letter, Pope John Paul II, December 7, 1990.

Ecclesia in America, The Church in America, Post-Synodal Apostolic Exhortation, Pope John Paul II, January 22, 1999.

Lumen Gentium, Dogmatic Constitution on the Church, Pope Paul VI, November 21, 1964.

Constitution on the Sacred Liturgy, Sacrosanctum Concilium, Pope Paul VI, December 4, 1963.

Message of the Holy Father for the 36th World Communications Day, Theme: "Internet: A New Form for Proclaiming the Gospel," Pontificum Consilium de Communications Socialibus, Pope John Paul II, May 12, 2002.

Catholic Relief Services Message, Pope John Paul II, December 8, 1995.

Excerpt from the article "Liturgical Theology," by Kevin Erwin which appeared in *The New Dictionary of Catholic Spirituality*, p. 607, ed. Michael Downey, Liturgical Press, ©1993. Used with permission.